Gender Roles

Gender Roles
A Sociological Perspective

LINDA L. LINDSEY

Maryville College—St. Louis

With a chapter by Sandra Christie

Fact Finders, Inc.

Prentice Hall, Englewood Cliffs, New Jersey 07632

Library of Congress Cataloging-in-Publication Data
Lindsey, Linda L.
    Gender roles : a sociological perspective / by Linda L. Lindsey ;
  with a chapter by Sandra Christy.
        p.   cm.
    Includes bibliographical references.
    ISBN 0-13-347741-X
    1. Sex role.   2. Sex role—United States.   I. Christy, Sandra.
  II. Title.
HQ1075.L564   1990
305.3—dc20   89-37791
                                                                   CIP

Editorial/production supervision and
  interior design: *bookworks*
Cover design: **Suzanne Bennett Design**
Manufacturing buyer: **Carol Bystrom/Ed O'Dougherty**

Printed in the United States of America

10   9   8   7   6   5   4   3

ISBN 0-13-347741-X

Prentice-Hall International (UK) Limited, *London*
Prentice-Hall of Australia Pty. Limited, *Sydney*
Prentice-Hall Canada Inc., *Toronto*
Prentice-Hall Hispanoamericana, S.A., *Mexico*
Prentice-Hall of India Private Limited, *New Delhi*
Prentice-Hall of Japan, Inc., *Tokyo*
Simon & Schuster Asia Pte. Ltd., *Singapore*
Editora Prentice-Hall do Brasil, Ltda., *Rio de Janeiro*

To Ruth Margaret Lindsey

Contents

PART II
GENDER ROLES, MARRIAGE AND THE FAMILY

PART III
GENDER ROLES: FOCUS ON SOCIAL INSTITUTIONS

Chapter 9 – Women, Work and the Workplace
by Sandra Christie   **179**

Chapter 10 – The Impact of Education   **204**

Chapter 11 – Religion and Patriarchy   **219**

Chapter 12 – The Media   **232**

Preface

The only constant is change. Social change has been so rapid during this century that this statement remains true. For some it is agonizingly true. For others it has not been rapid enough. When social change impacts our attitudes and behaviors regarding gender and the roles which women and men are expected to play, we find ourselves confronted with challenges to our traditional ways of thinking and doing. We may eagerly pursue new directions in our gender roles or stubbornly resist them. In either scenario, our decisions will be wiser if we understand the myth and reality associated with gender issues, whether related to our relationships, homes, schools, or workplaces. Throughout this text you will be confronted with research and theory which will both reinforce as well as challenge your ideas about women and men; masculinity and femininity. A basic objective is to raise your level of consciousness or awareness about what you now take for granted concerning gender.

This text is mainly geared to students in courses on the sociology of gender or sex roles. It is also useful as a supplementary text for topics related to the family, psychology of women and women's or men's studies. For those students who have not taken any previous sociology courses, the opening chapter provides an overview of the major sociological theories (functionalism, conflict and symbolic interaction) and concepts and demonstrates how they are used in explaining the sometimes contradictory research on gender issues. The theories are cited at various points throughout the text and provide a logical framework for approaching a myriad of topics on gender roles. Both introductory and advanced students should find this approach useful in exploring the sociology of gender roles.

Since our gender roles are influenced by many factors, it is important to recognize the contributions of other disciplines in explaining them as well. Part I of the text overviews the impact of biology, psychology and history on our notions of the roles of women and men. We will also specifically view women's roles in selected countries to gain a better picture of how similar or different we are.

The sociological perspective dominates the rest of the book. Part II focuses on marriage and the family and highlights the research on love, relationships, mate selection and new family lifestyles. This section also shows how definitions of masculinity and the roles of men are being challenged. Finally, Part III looks at the continuities and changes in the social institutions, (the economy, education, religion, the media, and politics), and suggests future trends related to gender roles. Chapter 9, which focuses on women in the workplace, is written by Sandra Christy, who is president of a market research firm. As a sociologist and business executive Dr. Christy combines rigorous sociological analysis with insights from her work in business and the economy.

It is expected that at the outset material from this text will be disconcerting for many readers. For both women and men the area of gender roles is definitely a controversial one. However, once you have grappled with the research, explored the stereotypes, and latched onto the theory you consider most realistic in explaining the research, you will have not only gained a greater understanding of your own beliefs concerning your gender, but also have added insight about the other half of humanity.

The creation of a textbook from a manuscript is a process which relies on the time and talent of many people. I wish to thank a number of these people for helping see this project to fruition. Wayne Spohr of Prentice Hall has given me continued encouragement throughout the long process and I am indebted to him. Those who have read various chapters and provided critiques and suggestions for revisions have been extremely helpful, especially Phil Loughlin, Lynn Rees, Marshall King, Gary Reed, Renee Ridzon, Dennis Wachtel, and Norman Woldow. The administration and staff at Maryville College-St. Louis provided much needed support services and the flexibility in scheduling to allow me to finish this book. I thank Edgar Rasch, Dan Sparling, and particularly the library staff in this regard. The research assistance and manuscript preparation help of Lisa Jenkins, Staley Hitchcock, Kim Jones, Lorraine Fahey, Laura Balluff, Marsha Balluff, Sue Pearson, Sydney Bravi, Ann Spohr, and particularly Jennifer McGuire ensured that referencing was accurate, editing was precise, and deadlines were met. Jennifer's reliability and optimism helped cope with the stress that a project of this magnitude produces. Finally, I would like to thank my friend Cheryl Hazel who listened patiently on summer mornings as I dwelled on the various topics I was writing about and the stage in which the manuscript happened to be.

Linda L. Lindsey

Gender Roles

1

Theoretical
Perspectives

BASIC CONCEPTS

Every society places its members into a series of categories which determine how members will be defined and treated. These social categories or positions are known as **statuses**, and they become major organizing referents for how we relate to other people. We acquire our statuses by achievement, through our own efforts, or by ascription as we are born into them or assume them involuntarily at some other point in the life cycle. We each occupy a number of statuses simultaneously, such as mother, daughter, attorney, patient, and passenger. Acquired by ascription, the status of female or male is a **master status** in that it is one which will affect almost every aspect of our lives. A status is simply a position within a social system and should not be confused with rank or prestige. In this sense, then, there are high prestige statuses as well as low prestige statuses. For example, in American society, a physician occupies a status which is ranked higher in prestige than a secretary. All societies categorize members by status and then rank these statuses in some fashion, thereby creating a system of **social stratification**. To date, there has been no society where the status of female is consistently ranked higher than that of male.

The expected behavior associated with any given status is referred to as a **role**. As the dynamic aspect of status, roles are defined and structured around the privileges and responsibilities the status is seen to possess. Females and males, mothers and fathers, and daughters and sons are all statuses with different role requirements attached to them. Generally, the status of mother calls for roles involving love, nurturing, self-sacrifice, and availability. The status of father calls for expected roles of breadwinner, disciplinarian, and ultimate decision-maker in the household. Societies will allow for a degree of flexibility in acting out roles, but in times of rapid social change, the acceptable limits are in a state of flux and redefinition, producing uncertainty about what the appropriate role behavior should be. For instance, the largest increase in labor force participation involves mothers who have preschool children. In acting out the roles of mother and employee, women are expected to be available at given times. Unless new limits are set which provide for a greater range of acceptable role behavior, these roles inevitably compete with one another.

The concepts of status and role are key components of the social structure and are necessary in helping us organize our lives in a consistent, predictable manner. In combination with the **norms** or shared rules of behavior established by society, we have prescribed methods of acting and associating with others. Yet there is an insidious side to this kind of predictable world. When expected role behavior becomes rigidly defined, an individual's freedom of action is severely compromised. What follows is the development of **stereotypes** which involve the beliefs that people who belong to the same category share common traits (Brinkerhoff and White, 1988:253). Although stereotyping can be used positively, it is most often considered in the negative sense and used to justify discriminatory behavior against members of a given group. The categories of male and female are stereotyped such that members of the category are assumed to possess certain characteristics by virtue of their biological categories. This results in **sexism**, the belief that one category, female, is inferior to the other, male. As Robertson (1987:320) suggests, this belief in inferiority justifies and legitimizes the unequal treatment received by females.

DISTINGUISHING SEX AND GENDER

Today, the terms sex and gender now have much confusion associated with their usage. Overall, the term **sex** is considered in light of the biological aspects of a person, involving characteristics which differentiate females and males by chromosomal, anatomical, reproductive, hormonal, and other physiological characteristics. **Gender** involves those social, cultural and psychological aspects linked to males and females through particular social contexts. What a given society defines as masculine or feminine is a component of gender. Given this distinction, sex is viewed as an ascribed status and gender as an achieved one.

This relatively simple distinction is deceptive in that it implies either-or categories which are unambiguous. Certainly the status of sex is less likely to be altered than that of gender. Yet even here there are those who believe they have been born with the "wrong" body and will undergo sex change surgery to allow their gender identity to be consistent with their biological sex. From their perspective, only by becoming a transsexual can psychological harmony be manifest.

Sexual orientation or the manner in which people experience sexual pleasure or achieve sexual arousal also varies (Macionis, 1989:315). Males who have a sexual orientation for other males are also likely to consider themselves very masculine. These issues will be addressed more fully later but are mentioned here to highlight the problems of terminology. And as will be demonstrated throughout this book, gender itself is learned, is not immutable, has changed over time, and varies considerably in different societies. Therefore, it is reasonable to view gender, in particular, as a continuum of characteristics which an individual may demonstrate, regardless of biological sex.

When the word role is added to either sex or gender, the confusion of terminology may increase. Role is essentially a sociological or social psychological concept which, according to Sherif (1982), is misused when combined with the biological concept of sex. She would eliminate the use of the term "sex roles" altogether, since it may convey myths about males and females from both the biological and sociocultural components. On the other hand, the addition of the word role to sex or gender can also simplify discussion of the abundance of research which uses the terms sex and gender interchangeably anyway. Whereas there has been a marked increase and option in the literature for the use of the terms gender and gender roles, references to sex roles per se still abound. Journals like *Sex Roles* and *Gender & Society* deal with theoretical and research issues involving the interplay of many variables, including the biological and sociocultural.

I agree with Strong and DeVault's (1988:123) statement that **gender roles**, also known as sex roles, refer to the attitudes and behaviors the members of a society are expected to act out. Thus gender roles include the rights and obligations that are normative for the sexes in a given society (Brinkerhoff and White, 1988:278). To maintain a focus on the sociocultural component, this book will show a preference for the terms gender and gender role, rather than sex and sex role. However, research will be referred to which does not follow this convention and which is stated in the style of a specific author. The key term is that of role, which places the reference squarely on the sociocultural level.

SOCIOLOGICAL THEORY

In order to explain gender roles in any society, some type of organizing framework is necessary. A theoretical perspective guides the research process and then provides a means for interpreting the collected data. In essence, a **theory** is an explanation. More specifically, formal theories consist of sets of logically interrelated propositions which seek to explain a group of facts, phenomena or an entire class of empirical events. For instance, data indicate that women, compared to men, are more likely to be segregated in lower paying jobs which offer fewer opportunities for professional growth and advancement. As will become evident, such data can be explained differently according to a given theoretical perspective. The issue of gender crosses many disciplines, and certain models from biology, psychology, anthropology, and history are referred to throughout the text. However, since

sociological concepts provide the basic framework for addressing the topic, sociological theory will dominate. What follows is a view of how gender roles may be
explained from the three major theoretical models in sociology (summarized in
Table 1-1).

Functionalism

Functionalism, also known as structural-functional thought, begins with the
premise that society is made up of interdependent parts, each of which contributes
to the functioning of the whole. Functionalists seek to identify the basic elements
or parts of society, determine the functions these parts play, and then consider how
the entire society operates or functions. As Hess et al. (1988:15) state, the basic
question of functional analysis is "how does any specific element of social structure

TABLE 1-1.   The Three Major Theoretical Paradigms: A Summary

THEORETICAL PARADIGM	IMAGE OF SOCIETY	ILLUSTRATIVE QUESTIONS
Structural-functional	A system of interrelated parts that is relatively stable; each part has functional consequences for the operation of society as a whole	How is society integrated? What are the major parts of society? How are these parts interrelated? What are the consequences of each for the operation of society?
Social conflict	A system characterized by social inequality; any part of society benefits some categories of people more than others; conflict-based social inequality promotes social change	How is society divided? What are major patterns of social inequality? How do some categories of people attempt to protect their privileges? How do other categories of people attempt to improve their social position?
Symbolic interaction	An ongoing process of social interaction in specific settings based on symbolic communication; individual perceptions of reality are variable and changing	How is society experienced? How do human beings in interaction generate, sustain, and change social patterns? How do individuals attempt to shape the reality perceived by others? How does individual behavior change from one situation to another?

Source: Adapted from Macionis, 1989, p. 21.

contribute to the stability of the whole; that is, what is the social function of that structural element?" Functionalism, then, attempts to discover the consequences of any given pattern.

Dahrendorf (1959, cited in Smelser, 1981:14) summarizes the main assumptions of modern functionalism as follows:

1. A society is a system of integrated parts.
2. Social systems tend to be stable because they have built-in mechanisms of control.
3. Dysfunctions do exist, but they tend to resolve themselves or become institutionalized in the long run.
4. Change is usually gradual.
5. Social integration is produced by the agreement of most members of society on a certain set of values. The value system is the most stable element of the social system.

With its emphasis on harmony and stability, which is tied to strong value consensus, functionalism assumes that the system is always working toward equilibrium. Problems and conflict may arise, but they are temporary in nature and not indicative of an impaired social system.

In terms of gender roles, functionalists would argue that in preindustrial societies, such as those which depended on hunting and gathering, men and women fulfilled different roles and took on different tasks because it was most useful or functional for society to do so. As hunters, men were frequently away from home and, hence, centered their lives around the responsibility of bringing food or meat to the family. Since a woman's mobility is more limited by pregnancy, childbirth, and nursing, it was functional for her to spend more time near the home and take care of household and child-rearing tasks. Once established, this division of labor carried through to developing and developed societies. Even though women may also have been involved in agricultural production or were gatherers in their own right, they were still largely dependent on men for food and protection. The dominant role assumed by men, in turn, creates a pattern where male activities come to be more highly valued than female ones. Thus, the pattern becomes institutionalized and difficult to change; it rests on a belief that gender stratification is inevitable due to biological sex differences.

Functionalism dictates a similar set of principles when applied to gender roles in the modern family as well. Parsons and Bales (1955) argue that there is less disruption and competition, thus more harmony and stability, when spouses assume complimentary and specialized roles. When the husband–father takes on the **instrumental role**, he helps to maintain the basic social and physical integrity of the family, by providing food and shelter and linking the family to the world outside the home. When the wife-mother takes on the **expressive role**, she helps cement relationships, provides the emotional support and nurturing qualities which sustain the family unit, and ensures that the household runs smoothly. When deviation from these roles occurs or when they overlap to a great extent, the family system is propelled into a temporary state of disequilibrium. Functionalism maintains that the system will eventually return to a balanced state, but that disruption may have been avoided if traditional gender roles had been followed in the first place. A functionalist would argue, for instance, that gender role ambiguity is a major element in divorce.

It should be obvious from this that functionalism tends to be inherently conservative in its orientation and does not account for a variety of existing family systems which can be said to be functional for themselves as well as society. As detailed in Chapter 7, contemporary families and household units are immensely adaptable and exhibit a diversity of patterns and circumstances. Single parents, for example, are required to carry out numerous roles which are nontraditional from a functionalist perspective, and many successfully combine instrumental and expressive roles.

Ideally, social scientific theories are expected to be objective and value-neutral. Even if this ideal was achieved, theories can still be employed to support a specific position or viewpoint. Ideologically, functionalism has been used as a justification for the persistence of male dominance and overall gender stratification. Functional analyses of the family were developed and popularized in the 1950s when a nation, weary of war, latched onto traditional versions of family life and attempted to reestablish not just a prewar, but a pre-Depression existence. Functionalist views of gender and the family have not kept pace with the rapid social change which is altering them; hence its explanations of contemporary patterns suffer accordingly.

To its credit, functionalism does offer a reasonably sound explanation for the origin of gender role differentiation and demonstrates the functional utility of assigning tasks on the basis of gender in those societies where children are viewed as necessary to maintain the economic integrity of the family unit. Yet as Marwell (1975) points out, in contemporary industrialized societies, large families are actually dysfunctional and the family itself is no longer a unit of economic production. Families may be maintained without the previous rigid division of labor, which means that specialization of tasks within families, especially by gender, are now more dysfunctional than functional. For example, women who are relegated to family roles which they see as restrictive are unhappier in their marriages (Birnbaum, 1975). In this argument functionalist terminology is used to explain how a division of labor based on gender arose, but it has difficulty analyzing the current diversity of family patterns and marital roles.

Conflict Theory

Emanating from the nineteenth century writings of Karl Marx (1848; 1964, 1867-1895; 1967), conflict theory is based on the assumption that society is a stage where struggles for power and dominance are acted out. These struggles occur among social classes which compete for control over the means of production and the distribution of resources. It was Marx's cowriter, Frederich Engels (1884; 1942) who applied these assumptions to the family. He argued that primitive societies were essentially egalitarian because there was no surplus generated; hence no private property. Once private property emerged, capitalistic institutions developed and power came to be consolidated in the hands of a few men. As far as the family is concerned, the master-slave or exploiter-exploited relationships which occur in broader society between bourgeoisie (owners) and proletariat (workers) can be translated into the household. After the introduction of private property and the advent of capitalism, a woman's domestic labor "no longer counted beside the acquisition of the necessities of life by the man; the latter was everything, the former an unimportant extra." The household is an autocracy with the husband's supremacy unquestioned. "The emancipation of woman will only be possible when women can take part in production on a large, social scale, and domestic work no longer claims but an insignificant amount of her time" (Engels, 1942:41-43).

Modern conflict theorists such as Dahrendorf (1959) and Collins (1975; 1979) have refined original Marxian assertions to reflect contemporary patterns. Conflict is not simply based on class struggle and the tensions between owner and worker or employer and employee, but occurs among many other groups as well. These can include parents and children, husbands and wives, the young or middle aged and the elderly, the handicapped and nonhandicapped, physicians and patients, males and females, and any other groups that can be defined as a minority or majority—the list is infinite. Smelser (1981:14) states that modern conflict theory makes the following assumptions:

1. The main features of society are change, conflict and coercion.
2. Social structure is based on the dominance of some groups by others.
3. Each group in society has a set of common interests, whether its members are aware of it or not.
4. When people become aware of their common interests, they may become a social class.
5. The intensity of class conflict depends on the presence of certain political and social conditions (e.g., freedom to form coalitions), on the distribution of authority and rewards, and on the openness of the class system.

To apply the contemporary conflict framework to gender stratification, class can be redefined to mean groups who have access to and differential control over scarce resources such as authority and political power, in addition to economic power. In simple terms, men have an economic advantage over women, and this provides the basis for gender inequality. A man's superior economic position carries over from the society at large to the family. Unless domestic labor is given some kind of monetary value or, as Engels believed, unless women are not tied to domestic roles, male dominance over women will be perpetuated.

An extension of conflict theory has been developed by Hacker (1951) with her classic work on how women are viewed as a minority group. By using comparisons with racial minorities, Hacker demonstrates that women share similar characteristics. Besides discrimination, women are confined to sedentary, monotonous work when they are in the economic sphere, they occupy a marginal status in society and they are defined and stereotyped on the basis of ascribed attributes. What is interesting about her approach is that it was formulated over a decade before sociology as a discipline made any real attempt to address issues related to gender and society in other than a cursory fashion. And when a few such attempts were made, they were linked to functionalist analyses of the family. Since women outnumber men and generally share in the economic advantages or disadvantages of their husbands or fathers, the parallels to racial minorities are not completely congruent. However, her analysis has served to provide a useful framework where a conflict perspective can be readily applied to what are now referred to as nontraditional or "new" minorities, including women, the elderly, the handicapped, and homosexuals, among others.

Conflict theory, especially the Marxian variety, has been criticized for its overemphasis on the economic basis of inequality and its contention that conflict, competition and tension are inevitable between certain groups. It tends to dismiss the consensus families may show in how they structure family roles and allocate tasks on the basis of more traditional views. Also, there is a conspiratorial element which emerges when conflict theory becomes associated with the idea that men as a group are consciously organized to keep women "in their place." A number of social forces, many of them unorganized or unintended, come into play when explaining gender stratification. As with functionalism's inherent conservative bias, conflict theory must certainly be seen as exhibiting a bias toward change. This bias is perhaps less of a criticism for conflict theory, especially if stripped of some of its Marxian baggage, than functionalism, since most people are now uncomfortable with specific patterns of gender stratification and the sexism which results. Ideologically, it is easier today to justify change if that change is not viewed as individually and socially damaging. It is likely that toleration levels for overt sexism will lessen, as has occurred with overt racism.

Symbolic Interaction

Unlike functionalism and conflict theory which approach gender roles from a broad societal or institutional view, symbolic interaction, also called the interactionist perspective, takes a narrower, social psychological frame of reference. The interactionist model is based on the assumption that society is created and maintained through the interaction of its members and how its members define reality. In this sense, reality is what members agree to be reality. This process of negotiation is expressed in W. I. Thomas's (1931; 1966) classic statement, which is now referred to as the Thomas Theorem: A situation defined as real is real in its consequences. As developed by George Herbert Mead (1934), symbolic interaction is interested in those meanings people attach to their own behavior as well as the behavior of others. Interaction occurs in a patterned, structured way because people can agree on the meaning of shared symbols, such as words, written language, signs and gestures. Group members respond to each other on the basis of shared meanings and expectations for behavior. Thus people do not react automatically to one another. Instead they carefully choose among a number of options depending upon the specific situation. Once symbols are learned and internalized, it may appear that the interaction process is more or less spontaneous, but symbolic interactionists are quick to point out that a rational, individually determined series of actions is still occurring.

A variation of symbolic interaction theory, known as dramaturgical analysis, is especially meaningful when considering gender roles. The active role which individuals take in guiding their behavior is maximized if interaction is seen to occur on a kind of social stage. Associated with the writings of Erving Goffman (1959; 1963; 1971), dramaturgy maintains that when people attempt to create a certain impression, they actually assume various roles in a performance which others will evaluate. Each encounter with another person allows for a myriad of roles to be performed. Like a stage, settings can be constructed so as to convey the best possible impression with the hope of achieving a desired set of results.

Research on singles bars and dances demonstrates the utility of the dramaturgical model of symbolic interaction (Lever and Schwartz, 1971; Schwartz, 1973; Laws and Schwartz, 1977). Singles bars have fast become a specific kind of sexual marketplace where both men and women interact in identifiable patterns. Males usually initiate the encounter with those females whom they see as potentials for later pairing off. Both men and women are "stalking" for partners but they do so according to agreed-upon rules. For a man, who usually comes to the bar alone, a traditional masculine script operates which mandates that he must "make the first move" to the woman of his choice. The woman, who is likely to be with at least one other female friend, must first recognize and then either accept or reject his advances for conversation, a drink, or a dance. The selected woman must also disengage herself from her female companions in a manner that is not alienating to them, since they remain the "unselected or unwanted." In each encounter a process of often unspoken negotiation, interpretation, and choice is going on.

With some variation, these kinds of scripts are performed daily in a host of settings. What dramaturgical analysis exhibits in this regard is that gender roles are highly structured by one set of scripts designed for males and another designed for females. Although within each script a range of behavior options is permitted, the likely result is that the gender roles themselves promote competition, alienation, rejection, and a lack of self-disclosure. As Laws and Schwartz (1977:129) state, this pattern of quick meetings and hasty judgments does not make a very positive beginning for a serious relationship. As exemplified by symbolic interaction, the theme that traditional gender roles are stultifying and limit opportunities for meaningful encounters for both men and women will be a consistent one throughout the text.

A more sophisticated model of gender-related behaviors which combines concepts from symbolic interaction and broader social psychology is offered by Deaux and Major (1987) who propose that actions are influenced by the expectations of perceivers, self-systems of the target, and situational cues. This interaction-based approach allows for the prediction of both stable and variable sex differences in behavior and emphasizes what symbolic interactionists consider crucial in the explanation, the setting in which the behavior occurs. Gender thus becomes a "component of ongoing interactions in which perceivers emit expectancies, targets (selves) negotiate their own identities," and in which the context of the interaction shapes the resultant behavior (Deaux and Major, 1987:369). Their model points to the complexity of gender-linked expectations and provides a useful framework for analyzing data from a variety of situations.

FEMINIST THEORIES

Theory has been defined as an explanation for empirical events or data. Science assumes that theories are to be as unbiased or objective as possible, thereby contributing to the knowledge and understanding of the empirical world but without the entanglements of personal judgment or one's own values. In the late nineteenth century, German sociologist Max Weber argued that sociology as a science must be value-free, differing from earlier writers, such as Marx, who advocated that science and reform or revolution could, and *should*, be successfully combined (Weber, in Gerth and Mills, 1946). Today scientists are still grappling with the impact of values on theory building and data analysis but there is tacit agreement that the ideal of objectivity must at least be kept in mind during any scientific investigation. Although values are never eliminated in research, their potential impact on results needs to be considered. For this reason, the term value-freedom has been replaced by *value-specification*, the stating of one's values at the outset in order to recognize potential sources of bias. Even here there is a problem because of the assumption that we are aware of our own values and biases.

This issue of objectivity is involved in any theory, but more so in feminist theories because, by definition, **feminism** involves the opposition to the sexism and patriarchy inherent in most societies. Bolstered by feminist theory, the woman's movement has been organized to change the existing, and what is believed to be, unjustified social structure. Feminist theory provides the ideological framework for addressing women's inferior social position and the social, political and economic discrimination which perpetuates it. Some scientists may argue that to join the term feminist with theory is contradictory since the former is supposedly ideologically based and opposes the objectivity assumed in the latter. This argument, I believe, is too narrow and unrealistically views the canon of objectivity in science. The three sociological theories outlined above also contain ideological components but have not been completely rejected as a result. Although feminist theories may be more explicit in their value orientation, as we shall see, they can be viewed as modifications and extensions of the major sociological perspectives anyway, especially as related to conflict theory.

Liberal Feminism

Liberal feminism, also called "women's rights" feminism, is the most moderate branch of feminist theory, and is based on the simple proposition that all people are created equal and should not be denied equality of opportunity because of gender. Liberal feminism is based on the Enlightenment tenets of faith in rationality, a belief that women and men have the same rational faculties, a belief in education as the means to change and transform society, and a belief in the doctrine of natural rights (Donovan, 1985:8). Therefore, if men and women are ontologically similar, the rights of men should also be extended to include women.

The moderate approach of the liberal feminist model would allow for working with men, and an incorporation of men into the ranks of the feminist movement, since both sexes benefit by the elimination of sexism (Friedan, 1970). Women need to be integrated into a wider array of roles, including employment outside the home, and men need to assume greater responsibility for domestic tasks. Whereas assimilation is a key to this approach, it concentrates more on the assimilation and eventual acceptance of females in the world of males than males in the world of females. Critics would charge that it places a greater value on the activities of men, hence implicitly undervalues women's traditional roles.

By working within a system which is seen as pluralistic with no single group dominating, women can organize and compete with other groups. Demands will be met if mobilization is effective and pressure is efficiently wielded (Deckard, 1983:463). Liberal feminists believe it is not necessary to have a complete restructuring of society, but merely to alter it enough to incorporate women into other meaningful and equitable roles. This view tends to be adopted by professional, middle class women who place a high value on education and achievement. Because these women would be more likely to have a greater range of economic resources, they can better compete with men for desirable social positions and employment opportunities. Liberal feminism would thus appeal to "mainstream" women who have no disagreement with the overall structure of the present social system, only that it should be nonsexist.

Socialist Feminism

This feminist theory is indicative of the conventional Marx-Engels model described above which suggests that the inferior position of women is linked to a class-based capitalistic system and the family structure within such a system. Socialist feminism argues that sexism is functional for capitalism because it is supported by the unpaid labor of women who also function as a reserve labor force only when needed. If paid, women work for low wages which result in high corporate profits. Unpaid household labor is necessary for the reproduction and maintenance of the work force. The nuclear family, with the husband as sole supporter of the wife and children, also stabilizes a capitalist society. The wife is first economically dependent on her husband, but this soon turns into emotional dependence and passivity (Deckard, 1983:451). She is fearful of loss of economic security; so he retains complete power over her.

Unlike liberal feminism, the socialist view maintains that in order to free women, as well as the laborers who are exploited by the owners of the means of production, the capitalistic economic system needs to be changed. Sexism and economic oppression are mutually reinforcing; so to change both, a socialist revolution is needed. Marx provided a plan for a society where private property would be abolished and principles of collectivization in the workplace would be in effect. Engels called for the need to collectivize household labor and childrearing, thereby freeing women to pursue economic roles outside the home (Donovan, 1985). The family itself would not be destroyed, but the functions the family now performs would be socially altered.

Socialist feminism appeals to working class women and those who feel disenfranchised from the economic opportunities in capitalism. It has made a great deal of headway in Latin America and has served as a powerful rallying point for women in other developing nations. It is perhaps ironic, however, that its expression in the Soviet Union has been demonstrated more by Marx and less by Engels. As will be discussed in Chapter 5, women continue to carry the heavy burden of unpaid household labor while also functioning in the paid labor force. Many contemporary socialist feminists believe that unencumbered entry into the labor force must occur, but that housework must be socialized as well; otherwise women will find themselves with two jobs (Benston, 1971). Regardless of Marxian rhetoric, this is apparently what has happened in the Soviet Union.

Although socialist feminism is explicitly tied to Marxist theory, Mac-Kinnon (1982) argues that they still need to be analytically distinct. Whereas Marxist theory focuses on property and material conditions to build an ideology, feminism focuses on sexuality and gender. As MacKinnon states, "sexuality is to feminism what work is to Marxism." (1982:515). Despite the differences in terminology, both strains of thought would agree that fundamental changes are required in the institutions of the economy and the family if women's equality is to be achieved.

Radical Feminism

Radical feminist theory came to fruition during the late 1960s and early 1970s when a group of women who were working in the civil rights and antiwar movement "became aware of their own oppression through the treatment they received from their male cohorts" (Donovan, 1985:141). Donovan recounts that during an anti-inauguration rally in 1959, when women attempted to present their feminist position, not only were they booed, laughed at, and catcalled to by men in the audience, some men went as far as yelling out obscenities to the women on the stage. The radical feminist model thus originated as a reaction against the theories, organizational structures, and personal styles of the male "New Left" (Donovan, 1985:141).

Women's oppression stems from male domination; so if men are the problem, institutional change of the socialist variety will not overcome it. Therefore, women must create their own separate institutions and sever their relationships with men. Through the establishment of women-centered institutions, women will come to rely on other women and not on men. In order to fight sexism, the extreme version of radical feminism calls for the ending of heterosexual relationships and advocating that women become lesbians (Bunch, 1975; Sapiro, 1986). A society will emerge where the female virtues of nurturance, sharing, and intuition will dominate in a woman-identified world.

Certainly there is less agreement among the adherents of radical feminism than the other models. A blueprint for the total restructuring of society has yet to be worked out or agreed upon, especially concerning the future role for men in a woman-identified world. The conviction that male supremacy functions as the defining characteristic of a society which oppresses women unifies the disparate elements of radical feminism.

A NONGENDERED SOCIAL ORDER?

Each of these feminist theories begins with the notion that gender has provided an integral basis for social organization, and each offers a glimpse of society where this organization can be modified. None of these theories suggests that gender is to be eliminated entirely from a social order. Lorber (1986:567) contends that if gender is a social construction and that if the relations between men and women are essentially social relations, "what is socially constructed can be reconstructed, and social relations can be rearranged." Thus a social order without gender as an organizing principle is possible. The construct of gender rests on the physiological and biological dichotomy of the sexes which is then extended to other social realms, but Lorber demonstrates that this assertion is in fact debatable. And as this text will continually point out, evidence from biology, psychology, and sociology suggests that the division of humanity into two distinct, mutually exclusive categories is both unrealistic in the scientific sense and unproductive or inhibiting in the social sense.

The concept of **androgyny** refers to the integration of characteristics defined as feminine with those defined as masculine. A new model emerges which maintains that it is possible, and desirable, for people to express both masculine and feminine qualities since they exist in varying degrees within each of us anyway (Bem, 1974; 1975; Kaplan and Bean, 1976). Androgyny allows for flexibility in the statuses we possess and gives us greater adaptability to the variety of situations we must confront. Ideally, androgyny eliminates the restrictions imposed by gender roles and increases opportunities to develop to our fullest potential. Although the concept of androgyny has been criticized for its ambiguity and lack of definitional rigor (Trebilcot, 1977; Locksley and Colten, 1979; Morgan, 1982a), it at least provides an alternative to images of men and women based on traditional gender roles.

The theories and concepts presented here, and the visions of society which they suggest, are offered as tools to be used in approaching the following chapters and the diverse array of issues related to gender roles you will be confronting. Each has its own insight and explanation for any given issue. As these issues are addressed, consider which perspective you believe to be most realistic. It is hoped that at the conclusion of this book you will have developed a perspective on gender roles which is most meaningful to you.

2

Gender Role Development: The Impact of Biology and Psychology

Consider how often we have heard, engaged in, or refereed discussions that are more likely arguments concerning equality between the sexes. In such debates, the scenario follows a routine pattern where the "pro-equality" party will answer charges made by the other party by providing numerous facts documenting the benefits of equality. Since it is extremely difficult to deny the factual basis of these data, the "anti-equality" party cunningly waits to play the trump card. The inevitable statement that often stops but does not resolve the debate is: "you can't deny biology; it's only natural that women and men have different roles." The almost ruthless objectivity associated with what is seen as clearly "natural" dictates that the sexes are destined to inequality by virtue of biological differences which mandate different gender roles.

Certainly males and females are different. Patterns of differentiation between the sexes include not only the physiological component but the sociocultural, attitudinal and behavioral realms as well. Are these differences significant enough to exclude equality? Do the differences outweigh the similarities? What role does biology play in determining these differences? An examination of the theory and research generated by these questions will help shed light on the "it's only natural" argument. This argument is in fact an extension of the nature versus nurture or heredity versus environment debate.

Famed anthropologist Margaret Mead was interested in exploring such issues when she journeyed to New Guinea in the 1930s. Her original belief in the biological basis of gender roles was overridden by her work among three tribes which clearly supported the notion that cultural conditioning had a massive impact when comparing the sexes in terms of behavior (Mead, 1935). She found that among the gentle, peace-loving Arapesh, for example, both men and women exhibited the qualities of nurturance and compliance. A society which knew little about warfare, the Arapesh spent their time gardening, hunting, and child rearing. What American society would define as maternal behavior extended to both men and women. The joy of child rearing and simply being around children meant that child care responsibilities were eagerly assumed by men as well as women, a task from which the Arapesh derived immense satisfaction. Children grew up to mirror these patterns and learned to become as responsive and cooperative as their parents, with a willingness to subordinate themselves to the needs of those who are younger and weaker (Mead, 1935:124). Mead concluded that in this tribe, the personalities of females and males were not sharply distinguished by gender.

The fierce Mundugumor, on the other hand, exhibited characteristics which we would associate with males, such as competitiveness, strong independence, and even violence at times. Children were barely tolerated, left to their own devices as early in life as possible, and taught to be hostile and suspicious of others. Both mothers and fathers demonstrated little in the way of tenderness toward their children, with physical punishment being the common mode for assuring that children learned and adhered to family and tribal rules. Children quickly understood that success in this community was measured by aggression, with violence as the acceptable, expected solution to many problems. Since both males and females demonstrated these traits, the Mundugumor, like the Arapesh, did not differentiate personality in terms of gender. It may be argued that even by American standards of masculinity, the Mundugumor represented the extreme. As Mead points out, however, the traits described here as typical of both sexes would be viewed as definitive characteristics of males in American society.

Finally, the Tchumbuli demonstrated what we would call reverse gender roles. This tribe consisted of practical, efficient, and unadorned women and passive, vain, and catty men who took pleasure in decorating themselves and preparing the ceremonial rituals and festivities for the tribe. Through their fishing, weaving and trading activities, the women were the economic providers, while the men remained close to the village and practiced their dancing and art. Women enjoyed the company of other women, while the men strived to gain their attention and affection. While the women accepted this situation with tolerance and humor, they were apt to view men more as boys than as peers.

Mead concluded that what we define as masculine and feminine are culturally rather than biologically determined. If "it is natural" that women and men act in ways according to biology, then such cross-cultural differences should not be manifest. It is granted that the gender roles described here are aberrant compared to the majority of societies, that they are presented as generalizations, and that they have likely been modified a half century later. Yet if biology is considered the cause of certain behavior patterns associated with the sexes, it should have caused the men and women in these cultures to act similarly. After we examine the impact of biology on the sexes, we will return to this point.

THE HORMONE PUZZLE

Of the two types of sex chromosomes, X and Y, both sexes have at least one X chromosome. Females possess two X chromosomes while males have one X and one Y chromosome. It is the lack or presence of the Y chromosome which determines if the baby will be a male or female. That the X chromosome has a larger genetic background than the Y chromosome is advantageous to females with their XX chromosomes. The extra X chromosome is associated with a superior immunization system and lower female mortality at all stages of the life cycle. All of our other chromosomes are similar in form, differing only in our individual hereditary identities (Woldow, 1987).

Such comments concerning the chromosomal basis of the sexes are widely accepted and leave little room for controversy. When discussing the sex hormones, however, the roles they play in sexual development and behavior are less clear. This has generated heated debates about their impact on the sexes, especially in relation to the physiology of behavior and gender role socialization.

Hormones are internal secretions produced by the endocrine glands which are carried by the blood throughout the body, which affect target cells in other organs. Both sexes possess the same hormones, but they differ in the amount secreted. For example, the dominant female hormone, estrogen, is produced in large quantities by the ovaries, but in smaller quantities by the testes. The male hormone, testosterone, is produced in larger quantities by the testes and smaller quantities by the ovaries. The endocrine differences between males and females are not absolute but differ along a continuum of variation, with most males being significantly different than most females (Woldow, 1987).

We know that sex hormones have two key functions which must be considered together. They shape the development of the brain and sex organs and then determine how these organs will be activated. Because hormones provide an organization function for the body, their activational effects will be different for the sexes. A female given male hormones will not assume a male role in sexual activity since she does not have testes and cannot produce sperm. Her body is organized as a female and so the hormones are activated differently, with behavior shaped accordingly (Carlson, 1977:285).

The impact of hormones on sexual development has been studied on infants who are born with sexual anomalies due to the fact their mothers had excessive or impaired hormone production during the second or third months of their pregnancies (Money and Ehrhardt, 1972). The *androgen sensitivity syndrome* occurs when a genetic male, due to a metabolic error, is born with female genitalia; he develops female secondary sex characteristics in puberty and still has functioning testes which produce ineffective androgens. For genetic females, the *andrenogenital syndrome* occurs when abnormal amounts of androgens are secreted, thus masculinizing the female genitalia. This may result in the infant being born with a penis, empty scrotum, some degree of labial fusion, and/or an enlarged clitoris. Similarly, male external organs may develop on a genetic female if the mother is given progestin, a synthetic substitute for progesterone, to prevent miscarriage, and *progestin-induced hermaphroditism* occurs.

Research on the hormonal basis of such anomalies has helped to clarify the process of sexual development. From a sociological viewpoint, it allows a rare opportunity to study the physiological-behavioral link and to understand the important distinction between the biological aspect of sex and the sociocultural-psychological aspect of gender role. Children born with these conditions are referred to as **hermaphrodites**; they possess ambiguous genital structures, have external genitalia different from their genetic sex, or are inconsistent in terms of their sex hormones. The principle of **sexual dimorphism**, the separation of the sexes into two distinct morphologic and later psychologic forms, is violated. Assigned one sex at birth, the child's "true" sex is often discovered later. Depending on when in the child's development this discovery is made makes a crucial difference in psychological adjustment. Money and Erhardt (1972) suggest that sex reassignment has a greater likelihood of success if it occurs by age three, or four at the latest. Both language acquisition and gender identity are occurring, with the child beginning to develop the first sense of self. Once gender identity becomes stabilized, attempting to change it could be emotionally traumatic.

The power of cultural definitions related to gender is demonstrated by what is now a famous case described by Money and Erhardt (1972) involving sex reassignment of a 17 month-old genetic male, one of a pair of male identical twins. During a circumcision procedure at seven months, the electrical current used to remove the foreskin was set too high which resulted in the loss of the entire penis. Ten months later the agonized parents decided to raise him as a girl. Reconstructive surgery with the creation of a vagina began the process which would be followed by hormonal and estrogen therapy at puberty.

The determination of the parents in this endeavor coupled with a strong definition of appropriate roles for the sexes are responsible for this re-creation. By age five, the twins were demonstrating almost stereotypical gender roles. Preferences in terms of clothing, toys, and activities were differentiated by gender. She was being prepared for a life of domesticity while her brother was being introduced to the challenges of another world outside the home. Is this indicative of successful reassignment?

To some extent, the conversion was too successful. A follow-up of the girl shows she is confused about her gender identity (Diamond, 1982). Considering the uniqueness of the situation, there are at least two reasons for this. First, even with the hormonal therapy, the effects of her first biological sex could not be completely altered. Secondly, what I would consider to be the better explanation, the parents created an almost stereotypical girl who could never fulfill her ultimate role—that of biological mother. In this sense, then, she *should* be confused!

The debate on the influence of hormones versus socialization is further complicated when studies of aggression in females and males are considered. In most species, including primates, males are more aggressive than females. In an extensive research review by Maccoby and Jacklin (1974) on human sex differences in aggression, the evidence suggests that the higher aggression in males is apparent by about age two. Although girls and boys are about equal in learned aggressiveness, boys are more likely to carry out this learned behavior than are girls (Bandura, 1973). The biological explanation for this rests on the association between testosterone and aggression in males. Androgens, of which testosterone is one, are in part responsible for modifying the brain as it is being developed, making neural circuits more susceptive to testosterone. When newborn female mice are treated with testosterone, they react similarly to males, with aggression increasing (Edwards, 1968). When young female monkeys are given testosterone, aggression increases (Joslyn, 1973). In humans, correlations between testosterone levels and higher aggressiveness, such as committing violent crimes, have been noted in males (Kreutz and Rose, 1972).

Yet we cannot conclude that the male hormone testosterone is the crucial variable in explaining these findings. Testosterone may increase aggression, but aggression also increases testosterone. When male monkeys assume less dominant roles in a hierarchy, their testosterone levels drop (Rose et al., 1972). The social situation influences physiological response. As Williams (1987:169) points out, the differences between the sexes in aggression are real, but these differences cannot be accounted for by either socialization *or* biology. The apparent biological predisposition in males toward aggression is mediated by social influences.

On the female side, the hormonal argument has been used in postulating the existence of a maternal instinct. Animal behavior studies implicating the female hormones of estrogen, progesterone, and prolactin are used to support this contention (Weitz, 1977). Since only women bear and nurse children and men possess the androgens which are seen as inhibiting the formation of this instinct, it has been only recently that the concept has been challenged at all. The notion of human behavior as based on instincts has given way to the idea that most behavior is learned.

The idea of a maternal instinct is not supported. Many women suffer from postpartum depression and may even reject the child. The fact that most women more eagerly respond to their infants and readily take on the caretaking role is due to many factors, including the expectation that this will occur anyway because of a lifetime of socialization for these very roles. A woman's nurturing behavior will be heightened when she is in immediate contact with her newborn, even the first minutes after birth (Maccoby and Jacklin, 1974).

The birth experience will undoubtedly create a special bond of mother to child which cannot be experienced by even the father. This does not mean, however, that hormones will make one parent better or more nurturing than the other. Male sex-typing probably plays a larger role in the process than androgens. Consider Mead's (1935) study of the gentle Arapesh where both sexes enjoyed child care responsibilities. A study in Fiji by Basow (1984) also confirms that infant care can be a rewarding joint effort, especially if sex-typing is low. If these two cultures were studied in isolation, it might be concluded that there was a parenting instinct shared by both sexes.

The influence of hormones on human behavior is somewhat puzzling, and the research is equivocal at times. But it can be suggested that even if hormones predispose the sexes to different behavior, societal factors will ultimately activate this behavior. Overall, the relationship between hormones and distinctive social behavior exhibited by the two sexes is one of mutual interaction.

IN SICKNESS AND HEALTH

Biology and culture again come into play when viewing health related characteristics of the sexes. Sex differences in mortality and morbidity (death and sickness) are highly significant. Not only is life expectancy lower for males, but male deaths exceed female deaths for all diseases except diabetes (See Tables 2-1, 2-2, 2-3). Yet women as a group have higher rates of morbidity than men. After reviewing the research in these areas, we will consider the biological and sociocultural explanation of these differences.

The fact that females possess an additional X chromosome apparently contributes to their biological advantage. The weaker male physiology may be demonstrated using Table 2-3, which suggests that males have higher mortality rates

TABLE 2-1. Life Expectancy at Birth by Sex, Selected Years

SPECIFIED AGE AND YEAR	BOTH SEXES	MALE	FEMALE
At birth			
1900[1,2]	47.3	46.3	48.3
1950[2]	68.2	65.6	71.1
1960[2]	69.7	66.6	73.1
1970	70.9	67.1	74.8
1975	72.6	68.8	76.6
1980	73.7	70.0	77.4
1981	74.2	70.4	77.8
1982	74.5	70.9	78.1
1983	74.6	71.0	78.1
1984	74.7	71.2	78.2
1985	74.7	71.2	78.2
Provisional data:			
1984[2]	74.7	71.1	78.3
1985[2]	74.7	71.2	78.2
1986[2]	74.9	71.3	78.3

[1]Death registration area only. The death registration area increased from 10 states and the District of Columbia in 1900 to the coterminous United States in 1933.
[2]Included deaths of nonresidents of the United States.
Source: U.S. Department of Health and Human Services, 1987.

TABLE 2-2. Death Rates Per 100,000 Population by Selected Causes and Sex

YEAR AND CHARACTERISTIC	TOTAL [1]	DISEASES OF HEART	MALIGNANT NEO-PLASMS	ACCIDENTS AND ADVERSE EFFECTS	CEREBRO VAS-CULAR DISEASES	CHRONIC OBSTRUC-TIVE PULMON-ARY DISEASES [2]	PNEUMONIA FLU	SUICIDE	CHRONIC LIVER DISEASE, CIRRHO-SIS	DIABETES MELLITIS
Male: 1960, age-adjusted	949.3	375.5	143.0	73.9	85.4	(3)	35.0	16.6	14.5	12.0
1970, age-adjusted	931.6	348.5	157.4	80.7	73.2	(3)	28.8	17.3	20.2	13.5
1980, age-adjusted	777.2	280.4	165.5	64.0	44.9	26.1	17.4	18.0	17.1	10.2
1982, age-adjusted	733.1	264.4	164.8	55.2	39.2	25.5	15.2	18.3	14.9	9.8
1983, age-adjusted[4]	725.3	260.4	164.3	52.9	37.7	27.0	16.2	18.2	14.3	9.9
15-24 years old	140.4	3.2	6.6	74.8	.9	.5	.7	19.4	.1	.3
25-34 years old	174.6	11.6	12.8	62.8	2.4	.6	1.8	25.1	4.1	1.6
35-44 years old	265.8	60.6	41.1	49.9	7.4	1.6	3.7	21.9	14.3	4.3
45-54 years old	694.5	255.1	179.8	49.8	24.4	11.2	8.8	23.9	33.8	10.0
55-64 years old	1,725.6	690.6	524.2	54.9	65.9	59.9	23.7	25.8	50.7	26.7
65-74 years old	3,885.4	1,607.6	1,088.5	70.4	212.7	210.8	73.6	31.2	55.7	60.8
75-84 years old	8,539.1	3,618.0	1,823.3	145.4	720.3	479.6	291.1	49.1	45.9	126.2
85 years old and over	17,977.4	8,228.0	2,385.8	349.9	1,820.2	655.7	1,136.3	53.0	27.2	196.8
Female: 1960, age-adjusted	590.6	205.7	111.2	26.8	74.7	(3)	21.8	5.0	6.9	15.0
1970, age-adjusted	532.5	175.2	108.8	28.2	60.8	(3)	16.7	6.8	9.8	14.4
1980, age-adjusted	432.6	140.3	109.2	21.8	37.6	8.9	9.8	5.4	7.9	10.0
1982, age-adjusted	411.2	132.5	109.5	18.9	33.2	9.8	8.0	5.4	6.7	9.3
1983, age-adjusted[4]	411.5	132.3	109.9	18.7	31.8	10.9	8.8	5.2	6.6	9.8
15-24 years old	50.7	2.0	4.7	21.7	.8	.5	.6	4.3	.2	.4
25-34 years old	68.9	5.0	12.9	15.6	2.0	.6	1.1	6.5	1.9	1.3
35-44 years old	140.2	18.6	50.0	14.2	7.2	1.7	1.9	7.6	6.0	3.0
45-54 years old	386.0	79.6	165.0	16.4	21.3	8.7	4.7	9.0	15.4	8.6
55-64 years old	923.8	262.2	371.6	20.6	50.3	31.7	10.8	8.4	23.5	26.4
65-74 years old	2,092.3	777.0	628.7	35.1	158.6	84.8	33.7	7.3	25.1	62.4
75-84 years old	5,200.0	2,341.7	918.1	82.7	612.7	131.2	155.3	6.4	23.4	132.3
85 years old and over	14,010.6	6,967.8	1,252.8	219.4	1,950.6	166.5	746.0	5.1	14.9	212.0

[1] Includes other causes, not shown separately.   [2] Includes allied conditions.   [3] Data not available on a comparable basis with later years.   [4] Includes persons under 15 years old, not shown separately.

Source: U.S. Bureau of the Census, 1987:76.

TABLE 2-3. Number of Deaths Per 100,000 Population by Sex

SEX, YEAR, AND RACE	ALL AGES[1]	UNDER 1 YR. OLD	1-4 YR. OLD	5-14 YR. OLD	15-24 YR. OLD	25-34 YR. OLD	35-44 YR. OLD	45-54 YR. OLD	55-64 YR. OLD	65-74 YR. OLD	75-84 YR. OLD	85 YR. OLD AND OVER
MALE												
1960[2]	1,105	3,059	120	56	152	188	373	992	2,310	4,914	10,178	21,186
1970	1,090	2,410	93	51	189	215	403	959	2,283	4,874	10,010	17,822
1975	1,002	1,786	77	41	174	199	345	859	2,019	4,409	9,154	18,135
1980	977	1,429	73	37	172	196	299	767	1,815	4,105	8,817	18,801
1982	938	1,292	63	34	149	181	273	720	1,736	3,929	8,391	17,782
1983	943	1,224	63	33	140	175	266	695	1,726	3,885	8,539	17,977
1984, prel.[2][3]	946	1,176	57	31	144	180	270	691	1,703	3,859	8,473	18,034
FEMALE												
1960[2]	809	2,321	98	37	61	107	229	527	1,196	2,872	7,633	19,008
1970	808	1,864	75	32	68	102	231	517	1,099	2,580	6,678	15,518
1975	761	1,411	63	27	60	84	191	455	994	2,237	5,743	14,455
1980	785	1,142	55	24	58	76	159	413	934	2,145	5,440	14,747
1982	771	1,031	52	22	52	70	144	390	914	2,085	5,121	13,895
1983	787	985	48	21	51	69	140	386	924	2,092	5,200	14,011
1984, prel.[2][3]	792	975	43	19	52	67	144	381	924	2,092	5,197	13,614

[1] Includes unknown age.   [2] Includes deaths of nonresidents.   [3] Based on a 10-percent sample of deaths.

Source: U.S. Bureau of the Census, 1987:72.

during every stage of life. Even at the prenatal stage, spontaneous abortions of male fetuses are more likely to occur, with overall male fetal deaths approximately 12% greater than female. Males are also afflicted with a whole range of genetic disorders much less common in females such as myopia, night blindness, hemophilia, absence of central incisor teeth, icthyosis (scale-like skin), juvenile glaucoma, progressive deafness, and a white occipital lock of hair, to name a few (Montagu, 1974). The first year of life is the most vulnerable time for both sexes, but infant mortality rates are higher for males.

Mortality rates are calculated relatively easily since they are dependent upon generally objective criteria, with most nations having conventional rules for reporting and measuring the incidence of death. Morbidity, referring to the amount of illness in a population, involves more difficult measurement. By using available statistics, researchers are relying on cases of reported or treated disease, which may underestimate its incidence. Even household surveys are not always accurate because illness is in part a subjective experience. Many people do not recognize their own sickness, may recognize it but refuse to acknowledge it by altering their behavior by taking off work or seeing a physician, or prefer to treat themselves. This is particularly true of mental illness. These cautions are important in examining morbidity data related to the sexes.

One of the most striking features of these data is the trend of females to report more physical and mental disorders and use health services more than males. For example, morbidity differentials between the sexes are realized in types of diseases, with females more likely to suffer limitations due to acute conditions, while for males limitations are due to chronic conditions (Verbrugge, 1976).

There are interesting findings when morbidity rates are considered for women who work outside the home and housewives, both with and without children. Clerical women have the best overall health profile, with low rates of injury, fewer limitations due to chronic conditions, and average use of health services (Verbrugge, 1984). Clerical workers are not exempt from hazards, however, with negative health effects showing up perhaps twenty years later. With the word processing revolution, Love (1978) maintains that offices are increasingly feeling and even smelling like factories. Radiation exposure, chemical fumes from toners, stencil fluid, and liquid eraser, poor ventilation, and excessive noise are hazards which can lead to mental and physical fatigue, vomiting, visual problems, and confusion. Permanent damage may result.

More than half of women over the age of sixteen are now employed outside the home. Occupational health hazards for women are different than for men. Risk factors for men are more immediate and are associated with higher exposure to dangerous activities, such as crime and fire fighting, coal mining, bridge building, and other hazardous construction work. Women who are in seemingly less risky occupations must still be concerned about carcinogens which may affect pregnancy, the long exposure to display terminals, and the orthopedic effects of sedentary posts in front of word processors. Housewives are not exempt from the occupational menaces of heavy lifting, cleaning and often monotonous work. And as Sloan (1985) points out, housewives do not have the option of quitting work early.

Despite these observations, women who work outside the home in any occupational classification have better health than housewives (Sloan, 1985). And compared to working men, when health problems do occur, they are less severe and shorter in duration. Men experience more work-related and life-threatening injuries. Thus, according to Sloan, working in itself is no more stressful for women than men. Variables which influence this are powerlessness, which is unhealthy for both sexes, and the conflicting roles of the mother who works outside the home. A study of 2,300 working women by Wolfe and Haverman (1983) shows that the added burdens of child care and housework contribute to health problems. Higher rates of illness occur for working women with children when compared to working women without children. Their jobs did not influence the amount of time they devote to their children or homes. With time as a premium, this finding of poorer health status is understandable.

As mentioned above, males are more prone to certain illness and injury categories in which women tend to be exempt. Similarly, women are more prone to ailments men do not get, with most related to their reproductive systems. When women get sexually transmitted diseases, such as herpes or gonorrhea, the risks are greater than for men. Infertility and cancer can result. The alarming increase of AIDS among heterosexual women who become pregnant carries the potential of mortality for both the woman and the child who is born with the disease. Osteoporosis, toxic shock syndrome, and anorexia nervosa are women's diseases. The U.S. Public Health Service (1985) reports that 24% percent of the women between the ages of 20 and 74 are considered overweight and that 1 in 200 girls will develop symptoms of anorexia nervosa which will cause 10%-15% of them to die. The cultural importance attached to being thin, young and attractive affects women of all ages.

The fact of female menstruation has historically been viewed with suspicion, scorn, and fear. In some contemporary cultures the menstruating woman is forbidden to mingle with others and must undergo ritual purification at the conclusion of her cycle. The medical literature has viewed this normal physical process as a pathology which victimizes women. The myths associated with it have not been dispelled, even in the health care and scientific community.

The recent research on premenstrual tension syndrome (PMS) may be used to challenge some of these myths, but depending on the political overtones and how this research is interpreted, a backlash can occur. By virtue of the post-pubescent and pre-menopausal age, where most employed women fall, she could be passed over for promotion or admittance to certain jobs where emotional stability is deemed critical. Only now, a so-called scientific basis is used to justify the outcome. Few women experience PMS, and research findings should be interpreted optimistically for those who do. We need to be most diligent in monitoring how the PMS research is being conducted and how the results are ultimately used.

PMS has been associated with fluctuations in hormones, especially estrogen, which is seen to influence anxiety, depression, and other behavioral changes. However, a critical review of the PMS literature by Parlee (1973) contends that the research is correlational only and to infer that hormones cause mood changes is not justified. Also, it is virtually impossible to separate out the cultural components of what it means to be a menstruating woman. It is interesting, too, that research is now suggesting the possibility of even monthly hormonal cycles for men (Parlee, 1978). Would they be seen as emotionally vulnerable on their jobs if testosterone levels fluctuated in a patterned way?

The whole notion of PMS is still equivocal, but the acceptance of its legitimacy by some health care professionals has aided those women who experience great physical and psychological difficulty with their periods. These women have been turned away from a male dominated health care system with vague, paternalistic assurances that it is all in their heads. Another scenario is the prescribing of tranquilizers to cope with the resultant stress. Symptoms associated with menopause often have similar consequences. The severe distress accompanying menopause is experienced by only about 10% of women, with as many as half *not* reporting depression, irritability, headaches or the infamous hot flashes (Hyde, 1985:259). And as Hyde notes, when considering the psychological factors, menopause is probably not as bad as adolescence in a woman's life.

For both men and women the use of alcohol and other drugs, including caffeine and nicotine, is culturally acceptable, but sex differences in morbidity rates related to these usages are evident. More men than women use alcohol throughout their lives, but women suffer more from its acute as well as chronic effects. Fetal alcohol syndrome occurs in two of every one thousand births and is associated with low birth weight and mental retardation in the newborn (U.S. Public Health Service, 1985). Alcohol is a major factor in rape and spouse abuse, with homicide an all too frequent outcome.

A pattern of men being involved with illicit drugs and women with licit ones continues to hold true. Twice as many men use marijuana and other illicit drugs, but for women, the most common addiction is nicotine from cigarette smoking (U.S. Public Health Service, 1985). Today, more young women smoke than young men, and it looks as if this trend will not decrease in the near future. Rates of lung cancer for women have more than doubled, but men still exceed women in mortality for this disease.

As men turn to alcohol to cope with stressful situations, women turn to prescribed drugs, particularly psychoactive ones (Abelson et al., 1973). Current prevalence rates for those who take both over-the-counter and prescribed drugs are double for women, with sedatives and minor tranquilizers accounting for most of the differences (Parry et al., 1973). Alternative modes of treatment remain unexplored when a pill or capsule seems a legitimate solution to a physical or emotional problem. This has resulted in the frequent abuse and misuse of prescription drugs (Sutker, 1982).

The fact that women are the primary users of licit drugs, especially psychoactives, is a critical issue when examining morbidity rates related to mental illness and depression between the sexes and among different categories of women. Some of the data are inconsistent due to the difficulty in gathering such data at all, as well as the changing definitions of what constitutes the various groupings; mental health professionals may diagnose and label the same person differently. For example, whereas Chesler (1972) maintains that women are more likely than men to be labeled schizophrenic for similar behavior patterns, Bruce and Barbara Dohrenwend (1969) point out that sex is not a significant factor in schizophrenia. Chesler's data suggest that not only do women have higher rates of admission to mental hospitals than men, they also have significantly higher incidences of specific disorders, such as depression.

Review of data since the 1950s shows that this still seems to be the case. Women have more overall mental health problems, particularly depression and anxiety (Darnton, 1985). Darnton also notes that women have a three to four times higher suicide attempt rate than men. But in suicide, men are more likely to succeed than women (Lester, 1984). Rates of affective and anxiety disorders are higher for women, but rates of personality disorders are higher for men. These data should be viewed as consistent, but with the aforementioned cautions.

Marriage and employment are key variables in mental health. For men, it is much better to be married. Single men have the highest overall mortality and morbidity rates. Steil (1984) points out that for never-married, divorced, and single men, research shows higher rates of mental illness when compared to women. But married women suffer more mental health problems than married men (Bernard, 1972; Gove, 1973). A puzzling finding occurs when considering single women. Nemy (1980) reports that married women have higher depression rates than single, widowed, or divorced women. And since working outside the home contributes to better psychological and physical health (ISR, 1982; Sloan, 1985), single women would appear to be better off since, by necessity, they *must* have paid employment. Bernard (1972) also notes that single women show up as mentally healthier than both married women and unmarried men. However, these data also need to be viewed with the consideration that some single parents fall into the single category and some into the never-married. The female single parent is at higher risk for all areas of morbidity. This category of women constitutes the fastest growing poverty segment in the nation, with poverty the single most important variable in nutrition, housing, life chances and general physical and psychological well-being. Their problems are exacerbated by lack of education and job skills, with many dependent on welfare. Also, Bernard's data must be considered in view of the growing number of "single-by-choice" women who have achieved occupationally and are satisfied with their chosen life style. Thus, in explaining the mental health of the single woman, one needs to account for a range of socioeconomic variables.

These findings of sex differences in mortality and morbidity rates can be explained by biological and cultural dimensions. On the biological side, the immunological superiority of the second X chromosome is apparently at work. Women may have higher morbidity rates, but they are likely to recover from the same sicknesses that kill or disable men. In almost every society, women outlive men. Considering the oppression and extreme hardship of a life of physical labor which most women in developing societies must endure, this finding is all the more remarkable. There are also clear social and cultural determinants of these patterns, most often associated with gender role socialization. Females are taught as young girls to be sensitive to their bodies and be aware of changes in bodily states and physical processes. They openly express their concerns to the health care community. Thus, physician visits are higher. By the same token, they are more likely to take advantage of the new directions for preventive health and self- care. This is demonstrated by lowered mortality rates for breast and ovarian cancer.

When symptoms emerge, women are more likely than men to admit to them and seek help, especially for emotional distress. It is more culturally favorable for a woman to assume a sick role than for a man (Nathanson, 1975). The rigidity of the male gender role often prevents men from getting the help they need. This is certainly reflected in mortality rates for diseases which could have been arrested if treated sooner. Such lethal consequences of the male role will be discussed in more detail in Chapter 8. Women are less constrained in this regard. On the negative side for women, therapy can end with a prescription for a psychoactive drug which will not really address the problem for which they sought help in the first place.

Several possibilities for other gender role determinants for the psychological distress of women have been offered. Rendely et al. (1984) suggest that the traditional female role may be a mental health liability. Using the Bem Sex Role Inventory, they find that homemakers who are defined as more masculine or androgynous have fewer symptoms of depression and anxiety. Earlier studies by Gove (1972) and Gove and Tudor (1973) confirm that the frustrating position of the traditional woman, bound to housewifery and child care, is linked with poorer mental health in women and is a reflection of a secondary status that restricts them to passive and dependent roles. Depression results in women who feel pressured to conform to roles with which they are unhappy.

Are satisfying occupational roles for women mitigating these patterns? Again, the research is unclear. There is some controversy about whether carrying a dual role is harmful to a woman's or her family's mental health. Dr. Grace Baruch of the Wellesley Center for Research on Women finds that work is not a psychological jungle and that a rewarding career actually shields a woman against pressures encountered at home (Darnton, 1985). The homemaker role by itself or the homemaker, worker, and single parent roles in combination, appear to be the most stressful. Multiple roles which include a satisfying career are optimum when domestic responsibilities are shared by one's spouse.

Another explanation for such trends concerns how health care professionals differentially respond to their male and female patients. In advancing a feminist history of psychiatry in England between 1830 and 1980, Showalter (1986) states that mental illness is a protest against the subjugation and exploitation of women. From a symbolic interactionist perspective, women are mentally ill because male psychiatrists label them as so. As attitudes change, diagnoses, labels and treatments will also change. Also, males are not immune to these labels. By virtue of the definitions inherent to the traditional male role, male complaints may be overlooked or minimized when they should be seriously regarded. The discomfort males experience when assuming a passive role as patient is exacerbated by confronting a male physician. When they both inadvertently play a game based on gender role definitions, the consequences may be deadly.

Broverman et al. (1970) conducted the classic study which examined sex role stereotyping among mental health professionals, including psychologists, psychiatrists, and social workers. When asked to describe a mature, competent and socially healthy adult, their judgment was skewed in the direction of traditional gender role expectations. They were more likely to assign those traits characteristic of a healthy adult to a healthy man than a healthy woman. A double standard of health emerges. For a woman, health involves adjusting to her environment, even though this adjustment may not be socially desirable and healthy for a mature adult. Since this study, progress has been made. Phillips and Gilroy (1985) find no significant relationship between social desirability of traits and gender role stereotypes. Today, positive traits are chosen for healthy persons, regardless of sex. The negative evaluation of women which occurred almost twenty years ago is not as evident in studies with mental health professionals.

The devaluation of women as patients is slowly being eroded as women take more responsibility for themselves and as the male ideology in health care is challenged. Matria and Mullen (1978) argue that women must adopt new terminologies and reclaim in a positive way what has been denied or sanitized. This would hold true for everything from childbirth to menstruation to menopause.

The Women's Health Movement has emerged in response to the kinds of issues facing women who face a health care system dominated by attitudes which have not been in the best interests of a large segment of the population it is supposed to serve. Outdated and blatantly sexist attitudes regarding the sexual inferiority of women still run rampant in this system. Physicians trained in the fields of pediatrics, gynecology, and psychiatry adopt such attitudes from textbooks that suggest that women are passive, dependent, emotional, and accommodating (Scully and Bart, 1973; Howell, 1979).

In challenging such notions, the Women's Health Movement is helping to empower women with the belief that alternatives to traditional health care are not only possible, but beneficial to women as a group. The Boston Women's Health Book Collective (1984) has written the landmark work which has served as the foundation for this philosophy. Their book, *Our Bodies, Ourselves*, offers an awareness to women which challenges the male-dominated medical profession. The controversial issues of abortion, natural childbirth, rape, birth control, lesbianism, venereal disease, and others are discussed from various perspectives by a variety of women. Overall, the book encourages women to take a much more active role in their health care. Even with the objections of ultra-conservative groups led by people like Phyllis Schlafly who contend that the book is "laced with smut" and objectionable because of its frankness, the Collective continues to operate a clearinghouse for information on women's health (Eaton, 1979). The Collective operates on royalties received from its continued high volume sales.

The New York County Medical Society held a series of public meetings to discuss women patients' feelings about their male physicians. These women addressed the issues of receiving insufficient information about their conditions, hearing technical language they did not understand, being referred to as girls and called by their first names, and feeling rushed into certain procedures instead of discussing alternative modes of treatment. Mastectomies were specifically mentioned here.

More women are entering the health care field as physicians, especially as gynecologists, hospital administrators, clinical psychologists, and other mental health therapists. Nurses are assuming more responsibility in the decision-making processes involving patients. The concept of a health care team tied to a holistic health perspective has helped in this regard. All this provides impetus for change.

Finally, I end this section with a note on what many women patients dread most—the pelvic examination by the male gynecologist. Only women receive pelvics. For male physicians to at least understand the nature of this exam, they must listen closely and communicate well, since they can never share the experience fully. Concerning the female perspective on this, Magee (1975:29) offers the following example:

> I've heard of a very progressive medical school . . . where every male student is placed in stirrups and a strange female physician comes in, squeezes his balls and leaves without saying a word. If you think that would make you feel hostile and insecure, you might understand why women are so ready to complain.

THEORIES AND EVIDENCE

Explaining patterns of mortality and morbidity between the sexes must realistically take into account biology and society, physiology and culture. Several theories have been advanced which purport to explicate why these differences occur. These are more formal and integrated perspectives than those explanations which are suggested above. Based on the criticisms which have been leveled at these theories, they have achieved varying degrees of success.

Recognize, too, that each theory carries with it the baggage from the discipline with which it originates. This will necessarily limit its scope and applicability to certain cases. The following theoretical overviews summarize the contributions made to the area of gender roles related to biology. As we shall see, these contributions have added to our understanding of the connections between biology and society, but at the same time generated a great deal of controversy which to date has not been resolved.

Freud: Anatomy Is Destiny

This impact of Sigmund Freud (1856-1939) on medical science, psychology and the social sciences has been profound. As a discipline, there was no systematic psychology before Freud. He was the first to tie a specific theory of development to a therapeutic intervention strategy, that of psychoanalysis, which he founded. Although almost a century of empirical research on the foundations of Freud's work has produced more questions than answers and more inconsistencies than agreement, he remains a strong influence on the contemporary intellectual climate.

For Freud, the fact that a boy possesses a penis and a girl does not is the overriding element in his theory of sexual development. It is between the ages of three and six that children recognize the anatomical distinction separating the sexes. This is also the stage in life where gratification is focused on the genitals and when masturbation and sexual curiosity increase for both girls and boys. As identified by Freud, this is the phallic stage, where the clitoris is the area of greatest sexual pleasure for the girl as is the penis for the boy.

Sexual pleasure notwithstanding, the girl comes to believe that the male penis, unlike the barely noticeable clitoris, is a symbol of power denied to her. Penis envy results, which "reaches its highest point in the consequently important wish that she should also be a boy" (Freud, in Brill, 1962). Her mother is inferior in her eyes because she, too, does not have a penis and is rejected. The girl's libido, or sexual energy, is transferred to her father, and he becomes the love-object. This is called the Electra Complex by later writers. The resolution occurs when the girl's wish for a penis is replaced by her wish for a child. A male child is even more desirable since he brings the longed-for penis with him. In this way, the female child eventually learns to identify with her mother. In addition, clitoral stimulation is abandoned for vaginal penetration, which is proclaimed as a sign of adult maturity for women.

It is during the phallic stage when the boy's libido is transferred to his mother, with his father becoming the rival for his mother's affections. This is termed the Oedipus Complex. In his discovery that girls do not have a penis, he develops "castration anxiety," or the fear he will be deprived of the prized organ. This is the stage of the greatest turmoil and distress for the young boy as he works, unconsciously, to resolve the Oedipus Complex. With the underlying fear involved, he eventually identifies with the father and his masculinity, reduces his incestuous desires for the mother, and is later ushered into psychosexual maturity.

For boys the fear and distress experienced during this time is productive in that it leads to the development of a strong superego, which for Freud is the highest attainable mark of human mental evolution (Freud, in Brill, 1962). Conscience and morality, the very hallmarks of civilization, are produced with strong superegos. Girls, on the other hand, have weaker superegos, since resolution of the Electra Complex occurs through envy rather than fear. They experience less psychic conflict than boys which leaves its mark on later personality development. This explains why women are more envious, jealous, narcissistic, and passive than men. Indeed, biology *is* destiny for Freud. The anatomical distinction leaves ineradicable marks on both sexes, but particularly for the female.

It is understandable why Freud has come under serious attack by feminists, especially with his unabashed statements on female sexual inferiority. These were no doubt conditioned by the Victorian society in which he lived and worked; one which espoused strict differentiation of the sexes based on traditional roles of homemaker and breadwinner in a patriarchal world. The empirical work to support his theories has been inconclusive at best, with some of his ideas of sexuality disproven, such as the vagina being the "true" center of female sexuality.

It is impossible to dismiss the inherent sexism in Freudian theory, but Williams (1987:39) notes that Freud himself cautioned repeatedly that many of his statements were tentative and needed confirmation. Perhaps his own qualifications for his theories have been lost in the eager scramble to formulate rigorous scientific theories of personality. He wrote at a time when the fledgling discipline of psychology needed scientific bolstering to increase its credibility. Given a patriarchal scientific community where assumptions about men and women often go unquestioned, it is easy to see how Freud was severely criticized for his notions on infantile sexuality and the psychosexual stages but gained more quiet acceptance for his comments concerning the biologically inferior design of females.

Feminist scholars and therapists who are supportive of certain Freudian constructs and therapeutic techniques, particularly the successes of psychoanalysis for some patients, must come to grips with these criticisms. Mitchell (1974) implies that certain Freudian concepts are not incompatible with feminism and that to dismiss Freud completely because of his sexist statements would be counterproductive for those women who are helped by psychoanalysis.

As a feminist, Chodorow (1978) integrates psychoanalytic and sociological theory. She posits that since in most cultures it is women who do the child care, mothers produce daughters who then desire to mother. Mothering thus reproduces itself. Sons are produced who devalue women for these very roles. Penis envy occurs because women, even young girls, recognize the power of males; so it is natural to desire this kind of power. There is nothing inherently biologically superior about this. Women will continue to be devalued unless parenting responsibilities are shared more equitably.

Chodorow and Mitchell provide criticisms of Freud yet recognize his contributions to psychological theory. It remains to be seen if feminism is to be compromised as a result. Though it would require an inordinate amount of reinterpretation and empirical justification, it is possible that neo-Freudian scholars may be able to use his insights for the benefit, rather than the degradation of women.

Sociobiology

As Freud wrote on biological determinism a century ago, a new form has emerged in the writings of contemporary sociobiologists who use evolutionary theory as a foundation for their work. Within this framework, evolutionary theory can be applied to both animals and humans. More specifically, some sociobiologists believe that the principles of evolution will allow for a greater understanding of how our social behaviors developed. We can look to natural selection to find adaptive behaviors which can determine why males are aggressive, why females do child care, and why sex inequality where males are dominant occurs worldwide.

E. O. Wilson, the leading sociobiologist, maintains that it is such behaviors which allowed for species survival (1975; 1978). Aggressiveness, for example, allowed humans to successfully compete with the other wild animals who shared our primeval environment. Males are aggressive, too, in their competition between themselves for females who then decide with whom they will mate. Regardless of the immense variability of cultures, humans share certain traits in common. Human males and females are also differentiated by certain shared traits. The cultural universal of an incest taboo is used to provide the greatest support for sociobiology. Beyond this, most social scientists find no way to empirically link genes to specific behavior.

The sociobiological argument for women assuming the child care role maintains that a mother will always know her own child, whereas this is not always the case with the father. It is adaptive for the mother to care for the child to ensure the continuation of her own genes. Symons (1979) argues that the male and female human natures are extraordinarily different from one another. Each sex has evolved attributes which will increase its reproductive interests. Promiscuity in males is explained with the same reasoning. Hagen (1979) and Barash (1982), suggest that, whereas women are extremely selective in choice of their sexual partners, men will spread their sperm as widely as possible. Men can actually increase their reproductive success in this manner (Symons, 1979). This suggests that male sexuality is so different from female sexuality that sexual deviation by males from the norms is understandable. For both sexes, therefore, these behaviors are adaptive. Even the double standard is thus packaged and explained.

An earlier version of the sociobiological argument comes from Tiger (1969) and Tiger and Fox (1971) who state that humans still retain some of the primate heritage and behaviors which contributed to species survival. We share a common biological heritage, which gives rise to a kind of behavioral biogrammar. "That we speak grammatically and behave in regular and predictable ways are both outcomes of our common evolutionary history rooted in biology" (Tiger and Fox, 1971:5).

Bonding is one manifestation of our common history. Sociobiologists argue that the mother-infant bond is strong, invariable, necessary for the well-being of the child, and precedes all other types of bonds in time. Excessive separation of mother and child is devastating. "Nature is ruthless about this" (Tiger and Fox, 1971:64). Males bond, too, but to one another, originally for defense and hunting. Species survival was dependent upon these two bonds. That men and women eventually become segregated from each other and inhabit two different worlds is a natural consequence of these bonding patterns. Symons (1979) contends that it is biology which dictates that there are extraordinary differences between male and female human nature. Contemporary gender roles thus reflect this evolutionary heritage. Besides the lack of empirical support for its assertions, sociobiology has not had a great following among either social scientists or other sociobiologists who prefer to keep sociobiology, as it was originally developed, in the area of animal research. This is not to say that productive leads involving human social behavior are impossible, only that there is recognition that leaping into the human arena is tenuous at best. In a review of research on the biology of gender, developmental biologist Fausto-Sterling (1987) concludes that what we consider to be results of biology are really reflections of culture. And even here we cannot clearly mark their boundaries.

More importantly, biological determinism ushers in social and political conservatism. If something is defined as natural, then to tamper with it is to cause frightening, unforeseen consequences. Sociobiology provides a rationalization for a continuing patriarchal system which serves to subordinate women or even other men who do not meet the rigid evolutionary standards set forth. In essence, biological deterministic theories, like *any* deterministic theories, are overwhelmingly weak in the inability to account for the immense variation in human cultures as well as the rapid pace of social change.

HUMAN SEXUALITY

Major assaults on the biological determinism inherent in beliefs about sexuality and the sexes were led by the pioneering work of Kinsey and his associates (1948, 1953) and Masters and Johnson (1966, 1970). Until fairly recently, beliefs about human sexuality have been shrouded in myth and superstition, encumbering serious research. Just as Freud shocked the scientific and then the lay world with his assertions on sexuality, Kinsey had similar results upon revealing his data on sexual behavior.

Portions of his original data were at first dismissed as inaccurate and suffering from methodological flaws when it reported sexual activities vastly different from the supposed norms. It is interesting how even scientists question research on its methodology and scrutinize it more than usual when they are reluctant to accept findings which go against long held beliefs and practices. This shows how vulnerable science itself can be and may bring into question some of its tenets of objectivity. Yet in the long run the Kinsey studies have been integrated into the literature on human sexuality, especially as replications have shown the data to be essentially correct, though dated to some extent.

There are definite gender differences related to masturbation. Kinsey discovered that about 92% of males and 58% of females engage in masturbation to orgasm. Females also begin to masturbate to orgasm at later ages than males, often for the first time in their twenties and thirties. A more recent study by Hunt (1974) suggests that this has not increased significantly since Kinsey's original research. Both sexes may be starting earlier, but girls are still later than boys in this regard.

In orgasm achieved during intercourse, males and females also differ. Men are much more likely to have orgasm than are women. Kinsey found that over one-third of married women never had an orgasm *prior* to marriage and that one-third of married women *never* have orgasm. The later Hunt data show that this has decreased to approximately 10%-15% of women. It is likely that the new openness in expressing sexual concerns, gaining from the wealth of information on sex techniques now available, and a loosening of the double standard are responsible for these statistics.

Males continue to have fewer problems than females in achieving orgasm. The fact that females are less consistent with this may account for some of the male-female difference in desire for intercourse. Husbands generally would like more frequent intercourse than their wives, particularly early in the marriage. Later in life, this trend may be reversed. As women experience greater comfort and respond with less anxiety, the desire for intercourse may be heightened. In addition, orgasm should occur more often. A lifetime of socialization which suggests that women, who are later wives, are not sexual beings but are responding to their husbands because of duty rather than desire is difficult to alter. We know that sexual activities of a pleasurable nature are conditioned by prevalent attitudes. As attitudes regarding women as sexual beings change and become less restrictive, they should be reflected both in frequency of intercourse and achieved orgasm.

The above data demonstrate differences in marital sex. Published in 1953, Kinsey's data reported that only one-fourth of the women born before 1900 had experienced premarital coitus. In the one decade following that, the rate for women had doubled. When age is considered, one-third of young women reported they had premarital sex by age 25 in the Kinsey study. A dramatic increase is found in Hunt's study which shows that the figure had risen to 81%. For males it remained consistently high for both samples, with 95% of the males under the age of twenty-five reporting premarital coitus (Hunt, 1974).

It is obvious that almost universal premarital sex for both males and females is likely to become a new norm. But the double standard is still evident. A woman will have fewer sex partners than a man and will plan for her first intercourse. Women are more likely to assume a person-centered approach to sex with men whom they love or to whom they feel committed in some way. A man will probably still adopt a body-centered approach to intercourse, with their first experiences with women who are pick-ups or casual dates (Bowman and Spanier, 1978:92). It can also be argued that the fear of sexually transmitted diseases, especially AIDS, will a.fect the *number* of partners but have less of an impact on the rate of premarital sex per se. Males may come more in line with females in their choice of sexual partners.

These data would support the idea that a sexual revolution has occurred and continues to be manifest. However, if revolution implies an abrupt or sudden change from the past, the word is a misnomer. Scanzoni and Scanzoni (1988:103) contend that we are continuing with sexual *evolution*, which suggests a gradual change over a period of time. This evolution became apparent in the 1920s when a shift in attitudes toward sexuality was noticed (Reiss, 1972). By the 1980s the attitudes are more in line with the actual behavior.

Other challenges to ideas about sexuality, female sexuality in particular, continued with the work of Masters and Johnson on the physiology of sexual response and treatment approaches to sexual dysfunction. Whereas Freud attributed vaginal orgasm to the mature female, he discounted the clitoral orgasm as indicative of immaturity since it was practiced by children. Masters and Johnson show that physiologically, orgasms are the same, regardless of how they are reached. It is the clitoris which serves a purely sexual function and contributes the most to female sexual pleasure.

The clitoris is also responsible for allowing women to be multiorgasmic. Even the Kinsey (1953) data showed that 14% of the women in his sample had achieved multiple orgasms, but perhaps this was so against accepted notions about women, that the incredulous scientific community rejected the findings on methodological grounds. Males, on the other hand, have a single orgasm. After orgasm they experience a resolution and immediately go into a refractory period, during which they cannot sustain an erection (Masters, 1983). A myth related to male sexuality involves size of the penis. Organ size is unrelated to male capability or satisfaction of one's partner (Johnson, 1968).

For women, age and pregnancy are also related to sexuality and orgasm. Women tend to grow in their sexual activities and have satisfying sexual experiences later in life, peaking later and perhaps outdistancing men. Time is not a deterrent to female sexuality, although for both sexes there must be a regular pattern of activities to sustain sexual expression into old age. Pregnant women have an increased potential for orgasm and sexual responsiveness during their second trimester. Contrary to the myths that pregnancy reduces interest in sex in women or that it is somehow harmful to the developing fetus later in the pregnancy, the evidence does not support these beliefs. It is only in the two months following delivery that sexual responsiveness in a woman may be compromised and this, too, will vary depending on the extent of the recovery (Hyde, 1985:280). Regardless, we know now that pregnancy does not necessarily inhibit, and may actually enhance, a woman's sexual responsiveness.

By shattering beliefs about sexuality in general, Masters and Johnson opened new avenues in the treatment of sexual dysfunction. After first ruling out any physiological conditions inhibiting sexual response, work must be done at the social and psychological levels. Therapy sessions include both husband and wife, center on the complete reciprocal nature of the experience, and provide for a "sensate focus" which encourages touching one's partner for this alone rather than achieving the goal of orgasm. Coupled with an understanding of sexual physiology and the removal of cultural deterrents to sex, the Masters and Johnson approach to treating sexual dysfunction has had much success.

NATURE VERSUS NURTURE

Montagu (1974) uses the Kinsey and Masters and Johnson findings to present a view that women are not only sexually superior but are really more valuable than men because they protect and maintain the species during a child's crucial developmental stages. From a sociobiological standpoint, Montagu uses the idea of adaptive strategies to suggest that women are more necessary than men. In this way, he literally turns around earlier interpretations of women as passive beings who are sexually and biologically inferior. He presents the case that men suffer from a biological inferiority complex because they cannot conceive children. Their womb envy is compensated for by a drive to work and to produce in other areas. This is evident in their use of language. According to Montagu, when a man is proud of something, he says, "that's my baby." He conceives an idea and then gives birth to it (Dunn, 1986).

Though Montagu believes women are the superior sex biologically, he takes issue with the idea that natural superiority implies social inequality. We have seen that differences between the sexes, both perceived and real, have been used to subordinate women. This is one reason why any research which conveys the differences between males and females is regarded with suspicion by those who fear it may be used against women, as past patterns suggest. It is unreasonable to substitute the ancient myth of female inferiority for another equally untenable myth.

Let us return to our original question of nature versus nurture, of heredity versus environment, of biology versus society. All the evidence points to the impact of both in explaining the differences between the sexes. Deterministic theories which either dismiss or fail to account for biology and society are doomed as useful explanatory models in science. For example, feminist scholars like Alice Rossi (1984) are critical of social scientific explanations which deny or overlook the influence of a woman's biological makeup in explaining the bond between mother and child. Unfortunately, they still make their way into the public consciousness to affirm traditional stereotypes. They must continually be called into question and subjected to scientific scrutiny with results made available in a variety of scholarly and popular sources. In examining the relationship between women, feminism and biology, Birke (1986) demonstrates that biological arguments are consistently drawn upon to justify the continued oppression of women.

This book proceeds with the understanding that there are biologically conditioning elements which are demonstrated in differences between the sexes. However, the similarities outweigh the differences. As detailed in the next chapter, learning and socialization mitigate the differences which do exist. As a sociologist I am biased in favor of theories which are more indicative of sociocultural factors in explaining gender roles, which take into account a range of variables, and which imply that the potential for women and men to achieve in any direction they desire is virtually unlimited.

3

Gender Role Development: The Socialization Process

I'm Glad I'm a Boy

I don't like girls, I do not, I do not,
I know I didn't like them when I was a tot,
Girls hate lizards and rats, and snakes, bugs and mice,
And all the other things that I think are nice.
I sing a gay song and jump up for joy,
For I'm very happy that I'm a boy.

Poem appearing with an ad for boy's clothing
(Reproduced in Farrell, 1974:113)[1]

From the moment a girl infant is wrapped in a pink blanket and a boy infant in a blue one, gender role development begins. The colors of pink and blue are among the first indicators used by a society to distinguish female from male. As these infants grow, other cultural artifacts will assure that this distinction remains intact. Girls will be given dolls to diaper and tiny stoves on which to cook pretend meals. Boys will construct buildings with miniature tools and wage war with toy guns and tanks. In the teen and young adult years, although both may spend their money on records, girls buy more cosmetics and clothes while boys buy sports equipment and stereo components. The incredible power of gender role socialization is largely responsible for such behavior. Pink and blue begin this lifelong process.

[1]From THE LIBERATED MAN by Warren Farrell. Copyright © 1974 by Warren Farrell. Reprinted by permission of Random House, Inc.

CULTURE AND SOCIALIZATION

Socialization can be defined as the process through which individuals learn their culture and prepare to become functioning members of society. As a critical process in social life, socialization requires social interaction. As the ways of a particular society are learned, personality is also shaped. This simple definition does not do justice to the profound impact of socialization. Not only is an understanding of what is entailed in this process needed, but we must also recognize that it is our culture which molds our beliefs and behaviors about male and female, masculine and feminine.

A **culture** involves the total way of life of a given society. It includes both material and nonmaterial aspects such as buildings, books, and bridges, as well as institutions and modes of action which are considered appropriate. Indeed, culture encompasses all that we have developed and acquired as human beings, with each generation transmitting essential cultural elements to the next generation through socialization. As we are socialized into our culture, we begin to understand that males and females are expected to be different in many ways. Gender roles are differentiated in American culture according to workplace, leisure activities, dress, possessions, language, demeanor, reading material, college major, and even degree of sexual experience and pleasure. The list is seemingly endless.

In each of these areas, our culture dictates expectations and actions which differ according to gender. To choose another course of action, to deviate from the accepted norm, may mean risking social disapproval. Conformity becomes a matter of providing cultural mechanisms for **social control**. Every society has mechanisms to ensure that its members act in normative, generally approved ways. In many societies, when a woman asks a man for a date or a married couple decides to reverse occupational and household roles, they become vulnerable to a number of social control mechanisms which may include ridicule, loss of friends and family support, or exclusion from certain social circles.

Social control remains effective particularly when socialization processes encourage the perpetuation of stereotyped portrayals of the sexes. As already noted, a stereotype is a category which assumes that certain characteristics can be attributed to individuals simply on the basis of their group membership. Although they are general, often inaccurate, and usually unfavorable, stereotypes are extremely difficult to dislodge. Stereotypes are necessary since it would be impossible to enter every situation with a completely new perspective. As Mackie (1983:31) notes, "we place relevant stimuli into those categories designated as important from previous personal-cultural experience, and ignore the rest."

As classification devices, stereotypes in and of themselves are not necessarily negative. Stereotypical thinking becomes insidious when individuals are damaged because they are defined in terms of assumed group characteristics. If we stereotype women as passive, an individual woman may be passed over for a job requiring leadership ability. Her own individual ability in terms of job leadership is not even considered due to the stereotype given to her gender as a whole. A man may be denied custody of his child on the basis of stereotypes of both sexes which view women as inherently more qualified to raise children, and men as incompetent in this regard. As with other categories, gender role stereotypes emerge through socialization and are reinforced through social control.

From this discussion, it could appear that socialization is so powerful and all-encompassing that we are like little robots molded by our culture, who succumb to prescribed gender role behaviors uncritically. If this were so, gender role change would not be evident. To argue that the automatons of one generation produce their own carbon copies in the next ignores two important facts. First, socialization is an uneven process which takes place on many fronts, with different agents. We are socialized by parents, siblings, peers, teachers, the media, and a host of social institutions. We all know of women who are independent, achievement-oriented, and admired. There are men who are esteemed precisely because of their effectiveness with, and caring towards, young children.

Secondly, we live in a diverse, heterogeneous society made up of numerous **subcultures** which may exhibit gender role patterns at variance with the dominant culture's norms, attitudes, behavior, and life style. Numerous subcultures exist in contemporary industrialized societies, indicating their degree of heterogeneity. Subcultures may be based on many factors, including race, ethnicity, social class, or common interest. Research has been consistent in showing that gender roles are more flexible in middle and upper-class families than in working and lower-class families (Lambert, 1981; Weitzman, 1984). In reviewing Canadian research, Mackie (1983:142) suggests that rural areas exhibit more conservative gender patterns than urban areas, a pattern which would likely hold for American society as well. Socialization into gender roles can also vary according to ethnicity. Weitzman (1979:31) presents seemingly contradictory evidence from several studies which reveals that black women encourage independence and self-reliance in their daughters but also socialize them to accept traditional female roles. She believes that one way of resolving this discrepancy is to view the findings as representing aspects of the varied gender role of the black woman. "The findings are contradictory only if we assume that 'masculinity' and 'femininity' are unidimensional" (Weitzman, 1979:33). All of these examples demonstrate that gender role socialization can vary according to subculture.

The concepts reviewed here are important for understanding the process of gender role development. Socialization is a continual, lifelong process with various requirements designated as appropriate at certain age levels. **Primary socialization**, beginning in the family, allows the child to acquire what is necessary to fit into society, especially language and acceptable skills for social interaction. **Continuing socialization** provides the basis for the varied roles an individual will fill throughout life. Socialization is directional, with various paths and patterns appearing along the way. Two major theories have emerged which help explain this process as well as the development of our gender identities.

THEORIES OF SOCIALIZATION

As a modification of behaviorism or reinforcement theory, **social learning theory** considers socialization in terms of rewards and punishments. Specifically, social learning theory is concerned with the way children model behavior they view in others, such as aggression, cooperation, selfishness, and sharing. The child gains approval for appropriate behavior or is reprimanded for doing what is deemed inappropriate. Toilet training, table manners, and grooming habits are so determined. As with other behaviors, gender roles are learned directly through reprimands and rewards and indirectly through observation and imitation (Bandura and Walters, 1963; Mischel, 1966).

The logic is simple. Differential reinforcement occurs for doing either girl or boy things. In anticipating the consequences of girl or boy behavior, the child learns to get the label applied to herself or himself that is associated with rewards. This becomes the basis for gender identity. An awareness develops that the two sexes behave differently and that two gender roles are proper. As parents, teachers, and peers model gender role behavior during the critical primary socialization years, children imitate accordingly. Continued reinforcement of the valued gender identity results.

The social learning model has been extended by Lynn (1959, 1969) to account for the seeming difficulty that boys encounter in gender role socialization. Lynn asserts that during the first years of primary socialization, the father is not likely to be available as much as the mother. And when the father is home, the contact is qualitatively different from contact with the mother in terms of intimacy. In general, male role models in early childhood are scarce and boys must somehow manage to put together a definition of masculinity based on incomplete information. They are often told what they *should not* do rather than what they *should* do. The classic examples are "big boys don't cry" and "boys shouldn't act like sissies." Girls have an easier time in this regard because of the continuous contact with the mother and the relative ease of using her as a model.

Lynn (1969) further contends that it is the lack of exposure to males at an early age that leads boys to view masculinity in a stereotyped manner. This may explain why the male role is considered to be the more inflexible one and why males remain insecure about their gender identity. The consequences of this narrow view of masculinity are many. Male peer groups encourage the belief that aggression and toughness are virtues (Weitzman, 1979:14). Males are more hostile toward both females and homosexuals (Mackie, 1983:115). And at the extreme, it could be argued that machismo, an exaggerated notion of masculinity, is associated with the violent crime, including rape, that is essentially a male bastion. Although laden with uncertainty and inflexibility, the boy prefers the masculine role. He learns that his role is the more desirable one, bringing with it more self-esteem.

Yet it would also be a mistake to conclude that the socialization path for girls is easy simply because of the availability of her mother during early childhood. Weitzman (1979) suggests that even young children know that the two sexes are compared in terms of worth and that females are accorded the lower prestige. She hypothesizes that "a little girl becomes quite anxious about being encouraged to perform a series of behaviors that are held in low esteem" (Weitzman, 1979:15). In most households, for example, it is not considered fun to spend the evening over a sink of dirty dishes or with a load of laundry. But regardless of societal evaluation, like boys, girls soon learn to prefer their own role. It may be that this preference is augmented by the advantage of flexibility and less consistent reinforcement offered by the girl's role compared to that of the boy's.

In the most general sense, social learning theory has provided the foundation for a great deal of research on socialization, especially when it is combined with a symbolic interaction perspective emphasizing the importance of role-playing. Evidence for a broad social learning approach to socialization comes from research suggesting that both gender role stereotyping and behavior increase with age (Nadelman, 1974; Silvern, 1977), that role expectations in child rearing are different for men and women, which influence interaction with their children (Fagot, 1984), and that role models of mothers working outside the home influence their daughters' expectations to do so as well (Angrist and Almquist, 1975).

Certainly imitation and rewards are important, but social learning theory fails to account for the fact that even if socialization is not a random process, it is far from being a consistent one. A girl may be rewarded for a masculine activity, such as excelling in sports, but she retains other aspects of her feminine role. After reviewing the research in the area, Maccoby and Jacklin (1974) conclude that parents do not treat their children differently on the basis of sex.[2] During early childhood it is age rather than sex that is more likely to determine parental behavior. The only departure from this generalization is that boys are given less flexibility than girls, especially in terms of clothing and toys. This does support the notion that boys experience greater pressure to conform than girls.

Maccoby and Jacklin (1974) also maintain that modeling is more complex than social learning would propose. Children may not necessarily model the same-sex parents, or they may choose other opposite-sex models outside the family. The theory also needs to account for the variety of subcultural influences which children experience, as well as the increased number of single parent families where there may be many or few adults of either sex present, taking on a range of non-traditional roles. Additionally, social learning views children as passive, buffeted by rewards and punishments aimed at instilling in them a sense of who they are and what they should do. It ignores their active participation in the socialization experience as well as any differences in level of cognitive ability.

Cognitive development theory offers another view of the process of gender role socialization, which is based on Piaget's (1950, 1954) assertion that the child's reality is different from that of the adult. The child's level of understanding of the world varies with the stage of cognitive development. Simply stated, the mind

---

[2]Although Maccoby and Jacklin's (1974) review remains one of the most systematic and persuasive to date, there is some disagreement with their conclusions. Block (1979, 1984) maintains that there is a great deal of differential treatment in the preschool years and Weitzman (1984:162) suggests that research still has not measured the numerous subtle ways parents communicate their sex-typed expectations to children.

matures through interaction with the environment. Unlike social learning theory, the child takes an active role in structuring the world. Lawrence Kohlberg (1966), who formulated this model, claims that children learn their gender roles according to their level of cognitive development, and their degree of comprehension of the world.

In Kohlberg's view (1966), one of the earliest ways a child organizes reality is through the self, which becomes the highly valued component of the child's existence. That which is associated with the self becomes valued as well. By age three, children begin to identify themselves by sex and accurately apply the proper labels to themselves and often to others (Kessler and McKenna, 1978:96). Though they are too young to understand that all people can be so labeled and that sex does not change, this is the beginning of gender identity. By age six the girl knows she is a girl and will remain one, and only then, Kohlberg asserts, is a gender identity said to be developed (Kessler and McKenna, 1978:97). Since these developments occur at about the same point in time, gender identity becomes a central part of the self, complete with the "attached emotional investment associated with the self" (Laws, 1979:253).

Once gender identity is developed, much behavior is organized around it. It is at this point when children actively seek models which are labeled as boy or girl or female or male, and identification with the same-sex parent may occur. Now that the child understands his or her own sex, behavior will be consistent with the understanding of that label (Maccoby and Jacklin, 1974). As Kohlberg (1966:89) states, social learning theory contrasts with cognitive theory which sees the sequence as "I am a boy, therefore I want to do boy things, therefore the opportunity to do boy things (and to gain approval for doing them) is rewarding." And because of the active process on the part of the child, it is also a theory involving self-socialization.

As with social learning theory, the cognitive development model cannot account for the whole of gender role socialization. It has been criticized because of Kohlberg's exclusive use of male samples (Weitz, 1977), which makes generalizations to females tenuous at best. More damaging is its failure to explain the underlying mechanisms of cognitive development per se (Mackie, 1983:114). However, the model is supported empirically with data indicating that gender identity and cognitive development are closely associated in terms of timing (Brophy, 1977:250, cited in Mackie, 1983:113).

Other studies also offer some substantiation for the theory. Children, especially boys, value their sex highly, prefer same-sex individuals, and give gender role related reasons for their preferences (Geller, et al., 1979; Zuckerman and Sayre, 1982). Leahy and Shirk (1984:289) find that as age increases, there is an increasing agreement with adult stereotypes, which indicates that children "develop the ability to classify characteristics by gender." And in a test to measure cognitive maturity on children ages three to six, Coker (1984) observes that performance improves with age on gender concepts. Both boys and girls learn the gender concepts in the same sequence, and measures of cognitive maturity are "positively related to performance on the gender concept tasks" (Coker, 1984:19).

In general, then, both social learning and cognitive development offer productive avenues for explanations of gender role socialization. Table 3-1 summarizes the essential components of each model. Although these are the major theories, others have been advanced which attempt to refine and clarify concepts and developmental stages.[3] At this point a truly integrative theory which incorporates the basic elements of each model has yet to be delineated. Basow (1986:118) declares that

> such a coordinated explanation would include an active role for children in developing concepts of masculinity and femininity and in organizing their world consistent with their level of cognitive development. In this process, differential treatment by primary socializing agents and observation of different models all add to the information the child gathers about appropriate gender behaviors.

At a minimum, the models reviewed here will allow us to assess some of the research on gender role socialization. We now turn to those "primary socializing agents" which have a critical impact on our gender roles.

TABLE 3-1. Models of Gender Identity: Sequence of Events

Social Learning Theory

Exposure to ———→ Imitation of ———→ Sex-typed ———→ Gender
sex-typed   same-sex   behaviors   identity
behaviors   parent

Cognitive Developmental Theory

Awareness of ———→ Gender ————————→ Identification ———→ Sex-typed
sex categories   identity   with same-sex   behaviors
                                                                    parent

Source: Adapted from *Gender Stereotypes: Traditions and Alternatives*, Susan Basow, 1986, reprinted by permission of Brooks-Cole Publishing, Pacific Grove, Ca.

AGENTS OF SOCIALIZATION

Since socialization is a continuing process carried through to and including old age, it is understandable that there are many points in the life of any individual where it occurs. The agents of socialization are numerous and include a wide variety of structured situations and institutions. In each of these gender roles socialization is also evolving. The focus here will be on those agents which carry the most influence in determining our gender roles, especially as related to primary socialization.

[3]For example, Pleck (1975) outlines a model of gender identity but places more emphasis on the learning of gender roles through three developmental stages.

The Family

The family is by far the most significant agent of socialization. Even when social change adds other agents, the family maintains the major responsibility for socializing the child during those critical first years of life. Here the child gains a sense of self, learns language, and begins to understand norms of interaction with parents, siblings, and significant others in her or his life. Gender role socialization is pervasive in each of these.

The strength of gender role expectations is suggested in an important study by Rubin et al. (1974) which finds that sex typing of infants by parents begins on the day of the child's birth. Though both parents are likely to describe sons as strong, firm, and alert, and daughters as delicate, soft, and awkward, fathers are more stereotyped in their assessments. These findings are especially revealing in light of the fact that the infants did not differ in any health related aspects, such as weight or length. With gender role stereotyping evident on day one of life, it is easier to explain why parents hold such different expectations for their sons and daughters. Collard (1964) finds that mothers of four year olds believe boys can perform certain tasks without supervision earlier than girls. While Dick is allowed to cross the street, use scissors, or go to a friend's house by himself, Jane must wait until she is older.

If parents are defining their newborns within twenty-four hours of birth, it could be hypothesized that knowledge of the sex of the fetus could also engender sex-typed responses. Through medical advances such as ultrasound and amniocentesis, the sex of the fetus can be known months before birth. Would a woman carrying a male fetus behave differently than if she were carrying a female? If newborn males are described as hardy and strong, would the mother herself be more active or less cautious in her daily activities prior to the birth of her son? Would she exhibit more protective behavior if she believes that the female she will deliver is fragile and delicate?

Although these questions remain unanswered, we do know that preferences for one sex over the other are strong. Parents indicate that their first concern is for having a healthy baby. Beyond this, most couples prefer male over female children, especially if it is a first child (Markle and Nam, 1973; Williamson, 1976; Hoffman, 1977). This kind of favoritism is strongest where strong gender stratification is a dominant feature, such as in traditional or less developed cultures, and where it is bolstered by religious beliefs, inheritance norms, and naming customs. A family name may be "lost" if there is no son to carry it onward. A sad comment on these facts concerns contemporary China. In the struggle to curb a burgeoning population, couples are now restricted to having only one child, risking severe penalties if they do not comply. Given the heritage of patriarchy in China and regardless of governmental efforts to the contrary, reports of female infanticide are widespread.

Socialization, perhaps initiated before birth, continues once the proud parents leave the hospital with their daughter or son. The first artifacts acquired by the infant are toys and clothes. In anticipating the arrival of the newborn, friends and relatives choose gifts which are neutral to avoid embarrassing themselves or the expectant parents by colors or toys which suggest the "wrong" sex. Teddy bears and clothing in colors other than pink or blue are safe selections in this regard. Parents may have originally decorated the child's room to accommodate either sex. But within weeks after the arrival of the infant, such rooms are transformed and easily recognizable as belonging to a boy or a girl.

Along with this recognition factor, toys carry with them a formidable force for socialization. Toys for girls encourage domesticity while boys receive not only more categories of toys but ones which are more complex, more expensive, and suggest activities that are not homebound (Rheingold and Cook, 1975; Sutton-Smith, 1979). Little Jane uses her tea set to have a party for her dolls, most likely in her room, while same-age Dick is experimenting with baseball or racing trucks outside in the mud. Certainly these kinds of toys encourage higher levels of physical activity in boys. Parental expectations are tied to the kinds of toys they provide to their children. Although very active play emphasizing motor functions may produce anxiety in parents who fear for the child's safety, research indicates that they discourage girls from engaging in such play more than they discourage boys (Fagot, 1978).

Yet it might be argued that while boys are more vibrant physically, girls are more imaginative in their play. Both Jane and Dick are given prototypical toys at an early age. These are toys which "look like what they are supposed to represent," so that as the child gets older they can pretend *more* with toys which are *less* prototypical (Fein et al., 1975). By age two, there is a decrease in pretense of boys while girls' pretense increases. Pretend play is developed early in girls so that by the age of eighteen months, they are actually staging their manner of play, while boys are not (Sutton-Smith, 1979).

In examining these findings, Sutton-Smith (1979) is not as optimistic about the implications. Though girls are more imaginative than boys in the play of early childhood, after age seven the reverse holds true. Girls stage one type of activity, having to do with dolls and playing house, thereby assuming a caretaking, domestic role. Toys given girls bolster this pattern. If boys are restricted in any way, it is in the lack of encouragement in staging activities suggestive of later domestic roles.

Toy selection represents one of many instances of gender role socialization in early childhood. Suggestive of social learning theory, even infants receive reinforcement for behavior which is gender appropriate. In a study of firstborn infants and their mothers, Moss (1967) demonstrates that irritability is a signal for mothers to attend to their babies, and since boys are likely to be more irritable than girls, boys get more overall stimulation. Although the type of baby rather than the sex per se is the key variable, a process of differential treatment begins. Fox (1977) points out that the expectation is for girl babies to be "nicer" than boy babies and, therefore, more passive and controlled. When expectations are translated into rewards, girls soon learn the virtues of passivity.

Based on these early experiences, older children expect their parents to respond to them differentially. Children as young as age two have already developed a strong sense of sex roles (Kuhn et al., 1978). In an analysis using stories depicting children experiencing interpersonal conflict, eight to twelve year olds expect parents to respond according to traditional instrumental-expressive gender role stereotypes (Dino et al., 1984:709). This study would be consistent with cognitive development theory by indicating that the development of gender role identity is linked to children's perception of adult behavior.

Regardless of the awareness of parents, there are clear differences between men and women in role expectations concerning child rearing. Fathers have a higher amount of rough and tumble play with their three and four year old sons (Jacklin et al., 1984). Children of all ages are more frequently seen with women than men (Hoffman and Teyber, 1985). Mothers assume caretaking roles, talk to their children, and stay closer to them than fathers (Fagot, 1984). This research also demonstrates that children younger than age four do not elicit different types of play behavior from male and female adults and that both parents are responsive to their infants. The probability of gender role expectations increases with age. Maccoby and Jacklin's (1974) conclusion that the sex of the child is not a major determinant of parental behavior must be viewed in light of such findings.

The primary socialization experiences in the family provide the basis for gender role identity in later life. According to symbolic interactionists, even with the shift in gender role patterns we are now witnessing, our responses will be based on these early family influences. This does not mean change will not occur but that its degree of acceptance will be assessed by how we were first socialized. In reviewing the research, Weitzman (1979:3-4) states that

> sex role socialization begins before the child is even aware of a sexual identity: before he or she can have an internal motive for conforming to sex role standards. It also indicates that cultural assumptions about what is "natural" for a boy or for a girl are so deeply ingrained that parents may treat their children differentially without even being aware of it.

Peers and Preferences

As children get older, they are gradually introduced to the world outside of the family. We have seen that patterns established in the family are already gender role oriented, with children soon realizing that the same holds true for what awaits them outside with their peers. Parents initiate the first relationships for their children, with these often developing into later friendships chosen by the children themselves. Two and three year olds delight in playing with their same age companions and parents are not compelled to separate them by sex at this early age. As school age approaches, however, this situation radically changes.

Activities, games and play are strongly related to gender roles and become important aspects of socialization. These can be seen when a brother and sister play together. When Jane pressures Dick into playing house, she is inevitably the mommy and he is the daddy. Or she can convince him to be the pupil while she takes the role of teacher and relishes the prospect of scolding him for his disruptive classroom behavior. On the other hand, if brother Dick coerces Jane into a game of catch, he bemoans her awkwardness and ridicules her lack of skill. What would social learning theory say about the likelihood of Jane gaining expertise in catch?

Games such as these are usually short-lived, dissolve into conflict, and are dependent upon the availability of same-sex peers with whom siblings would rather play.

Peer play activities socialize children in other ways as well. The games of boys are more complex, competitive, rule-governed, and allow for more role differentiation and a larger number of participants than games played by girls. As such, they may be seen as preparatory for roles to be assumed later in life (Sutton-Smith, 1979:243). Girls play ordered games, like hopscotch or jump-rope, in groups of two or three, with a minimum of competitiveness. In an indictment of this, Harragan (1977:49-50 as cited in Sutton-Smith, 1979:253) almost bitterly concludes that

> girls games teach meaningless mumbo-jumbo—vague generalities or pre-game mutual agreements about "what we'll play"—while falsely implying that these blurry self-guides are typical of real world rules.

Beginning in the family with siblings, and then in other peer groups, games reserved for Dick and Jane continue into the school environment. We will view the consequences of this later.

Both cognitive development and social learning theory emphasize the importance of peer interaction in the socialization process. For example, Maccoby and Jacklin (1974) find that boys engage in more social interactions with peers than with adults. Waldrop and Halverson (1975) suggest that whereas preadolescent girls have *intensive* peer relationships, boys have more *extensive* ones. Intimacy would, therefore, be easier for girls to assume with their peers. Rotenberg (1984:956) hypothesizes that after children gain a pattern of same-sex relationships, these are reinforced through a same-sex pattern of trust. A lesser degree of trust could then inhibit later cross-sex friendships. The worlds of male and female are further divided.

Socialization into gender identity is nurtured through peers, with gender appropriate behaviors reinforced in a similar manner. As early as age three, boys have a strong preference for masculine behaviors which is maintained despite teachers' reinforcement for feminine behaviors in the preschool class (Fagot and Patterson, 1969). When these children interact, reinforcement for same-sex peers occurs more frequently than with opposite sex peers. Boys in particular are tenacious in their gender role attitudes and exhibit strong masculine preferences through preadolescence (Brinn, et al., 1984). Adulthood may soften the stereotypes but the preferences persist. Consistent with symbolic interactionist thinking, early peer and family influences can counter later attempts at resocialization.

Language

Primary socialization literally bombards children with mountains of information and learning they must effectively assimilate. This process includes mastering the rules and complexities of the society's language, both its verbal and nonverbal components. Language reflects culture and is shaped by it, therefore, it is fundamental to our understanding of gender roles. Once we learn language, we have a great deal of knowledge about how the culture defines the two sexes. The problem is that this knowledge must be discovered because language itself is taken for granted. As we shall see, it is for this reason that language is so powerful an element in determining our gender roles.

We begin with the idea that the English language constantly focuses attention on gender. Nowhere is this clearer than when the word man is used to exclude woman and then used generically to include her. This is the intended meaning when anthropologists speak of culture as man-made or the evolution of mankind. But more often the word is used to distinguish man from woman, such as in the phrases "it's a man's world" or "this is man's work." The word is definitely ambiguous and may be subject to interpretation even within one context. In both instances of usage, it is unclear where women belong, but it implies that they are somehow "part" of man. Sometimes no interpretation is necessary. At a wedding ceremony when a couple is pronounced "man and wife" she becomes defined as his. In learning language, children are also taught that the sexes are valued differently. Not only is language use ambiguous, it is discriminatory as well.

It is awkward to change language to make it more precise. If man is supposed to refer to woman, then he is also supposed to mean she. Because English does not have a neutral singular pronoun, he is seen as the generic norm, with she as the exception. A doctor is he and a nurse is she. More neutral designations are also he words. A consumer, writer, patient or parent are seen as he. In reality, many, if not most, of these people are women. But women are linguistically excluded. Now we see that language is ambiguous, discriminatory *and* inaccurate. To avoid sexism, many writers use he/she, she/he, or they to convey the fact that both sexes are being discussed. This is cumbersome but one way around the problem.

Titles and occupational terms are gender related. We write Dear Sir or Dear Mr. Jones even if we are unsure of the sex of the addressee, especially if it is a business letter. After all business*men* are seen as the likely occupants of these positions. The same can be said for chairmen, foremen, congressmen, newsmen and garbagemen. Physicians, attorneys, and astronauts are men. Nurses, school-teachers, and secretaries are women. If either sex deviates occupationally and chooses to enter a nontraditional field, we add linguistic markers to designate this remarkable fact. Children use these markers frequently in referring to females in traditionally male roles or males in traditionally female roles (Rosenthal and Chapman, 1982). What emerges is the idea of a female doctor, lady space man, or male stewardess.

Another linguistic marker involves adding appendages or suffixes to words to show where women "belong" occupationally. A poet becomes a poet*ess* and an usher an usher*ette*. Eakins and Eakins (1978:115) contend that such additions point out that women occupying these roles are exceptions to the rule. They are frivolous or mere imitators, and as exceptions, they are not taken seriously. This is what the acclaimed Broadway and movie performer Whoopi Goldberg means when she states: "I am an actor . . . and I do *not* mean actress. Actresses are sort of cute, you know? What I do is not cute" (Russo, 1986:9).

Women are a part of men. We address men as Mr. but have a major concern for the marital status of women. Miller and Swift (1976:99) argue that this simple distinction historically served a double purpose for men. Information was conveyed regarding a woman's sexual availability and pressure was on the single woman to think about marriage, since she was categorized with the young and inexperienced. Traditionally, Miss and Mrs. are considered the acceptable titles for women, who are defined according to their relationship with a man. Upon marriage a woman can lose her complete name and gain a new title. Jane Smith becomes Mrs. Richard Jones. A name and a title carry identity. Mrs. Jones is now linguistically encompassed by her husband.

To counter this titular sexism, Ms. has been offered as a substitute for a standard form of address for both married and unmarried women who want to be recognized as individuals. Although it is becoming more acceptable in business and academia, language change does not come easily, and the use of Ms. has also been accompanied by ridicule and contempt. Editors bemoan its style, while ignoring its precision. Miller and Swift (1976:101) believe it is not a question of style but of politics. Patriarchy is assaulted and another double standard is questioned.

English is hostile to women. It denigrates, debases and defines women in often derogatory sexual terms. Stanley (1972 as cited in Bernard, 1981:377), states that there are at least 220 terms for sexually promiscuous women with only twenty-two for promiscuous men. Consider the connotations of "mistress," and "madam" as opposed to the male counterparts of "master" and "lord." Females are sexual and males are superior. The word "girl" suggests both child and prostitute. It would be insulting for grown men to be called boys but we routinely refer to grown women as "the girls." As we raise our linguistic consciousness, such references will likely be abandoned. Until then, women must come to internalize a language that is belittling to them.

We are socialized into the language of our culture, but that language is used differently, according to our sex. Lakoff (1975) shows that women and men at times speak essentially different languages. First, women use more *tag questions* than men (Zimmerman and West, 1975). This means that after making a statement, there follows a question relating to that statement. "I enjoyed the concert, didn't you?" or "It's a beautiful day, isn't it?" As less assertive than declaratory statements, tag questions assume that women must ask permission for their feelings, likes, or dislikes. What is said then becomes equivocal.

Secondly, women tend to use more intensifiers, "empty" adjectives or adverbs and hedgers than do men (Lakoff, 1975). Some of these could be contained in a word list which is distinctively female. "This is a divine party," "Such a darling room," or "I think croissants are absolutely heavenly" serve as examples. The equivocation of a tag question shows up again through words which suggest uncertainty. "I guess this is correct" and "This sort of makes sense" are efforts at hedging or qualifying what is being proposed. A more blatant qualifier is when the sentence already begins with words which make it questionable. "This may be incorrect, but . . ." is an example. Pearson (1985:189) cautions, however, that even if such tentativeness occurs in female speech patterns, the context of the occurrence must be recognized. A manager in a boardroom adjusts her language to the situation at hand.

Speech style of the sexes differs also according to degree of politeness and use of profanity. Socialization into language forbids profanity in general, but more so for females. Men tell "dirty" jokes, and women are often the targets of them. Males believe profanity demonstrates social power and, ironically, can be used to make them socially acceptable (Selnow, 1985). Women are admonished to speak more politely and use different forms of requests than men. Men use imperative sentences. "Get the telephone" is a male request, while "Please get the telephone" is a female one. In studying verbal interaction between parents and children, Bellinger and Gleason (1982) show that fathers produce more directives phrased as imperatives, than mothers. Both men and women share the same stereotypes about what is considered "polite" speech (Kemper, 1984). Women should never speak like men.

Men interrupt women more than women interrupt men (Zimmerman and West, 1975). This is an indication of differential power but it also implies that men are more talkative than women. Is the stereotype that women talk more true? Swacker (1975) finds that when asked to describe paintings, males outtalked females four times over. In unstructured situations, Hoffman et al., (1984) demonstrate that women do not respond on the basis of a child's gender but that men speak more and used longer utterances with boys than with girls. In reviewing relevant literature, Doyle (1985:188) concludes that "when it comes to verbal output, males win the 'gabby' award hands down."

Whereas males talk more, females gossip more. Males gossip, but not to as great a degree as females. In a study of students, Levin and Arluke (1985) show that there are no significant differences in derogatory tones of gossip but that men gossip about distant acquaintances and celebrities while women gossip about close friends and family. Both sexes gossip about dating, sex, and personal appearance. In examining this research, a caution must be added about what constitutes talk and gossip. These definitional criteria are essential if the categories themselves are to be judged as objective from a gender viewpoint.

The language we verbalize expresses only one part of ourselves. Communication also occurs nonverbally, often conveying messages in a more forceful manner than if spoken. Besides bodily movement, posture, and general demeanor, sometimes referred to as **kinesics**, nonverbals include eye contact, use of personal space, and touching. Table 3-2 summarizes ways in which nonverbal behavior carries messages of power and domination. Besides the power implications involved, overall, women are better at expressing themselves nonverbally and are more accurate in understanding the nonverbal messages of others (Henley, 1977:13).

Research clearly shows that women engage in more eye contact than men, and retain longer eye contact with other women than men do with men (Eakins and Eakins, 1978; Exline et al., 1974; Russo, 1975). Eye contact can be an indication that the gazer is subordinate to the gazee. An employee is anxiously watchful of her or his employer in order to determine what follows next in their interactive

TABLE 3-2. Examples of Gestures of Power and Privilege

NONVERBAL BEHAVIORS	BEHAVIORS BETWEEN STATUS EQUALS		BEHAVIORS BETWEEN STATUS NONEQUALS		BEHAVIORS BETWEEN MEN AND WOMEN	
	INTIMATE	NONINTIMATE	USED BY SUPERIOR	USED BY SUBORDINATE	BY MEN	BY WOMEN
Address	Familiar	Polite	Familiar	Polite	Familiar?†	Polite?†
Demeanor	Informal	Circumspect	Informal	Circumspect	Informal	Circumspect
Posture	Relaxed	Tense (less relaxed)	Relaxed	Tense	Relaxed	Tense
Personal space	Closeness	Distance	Closeness (option)	Distance	Closeness	Distance
Time‡	Long	Short	Long (option)	Short	Long?†	Short?†
Touching	Touch	Don't touch	Touch (option)	Don't touch	Touch	Don't touch
Eye contact	Establish	Avoid	Stare, Ignore	Avert eyes, watch	Stare, Ignore	Avert eyes, watch
Facial expression	Smile?†	Don't smile?†	Don't smile	Smile	Don't smile	Smile
Emotional expression	Show	Hide	Hide	Show	Hide	Show
Self-disclosure	Disclose	Don't disclose	Don't disclose	Disclose	Don't disclose	Disclose

†Behavior not known.

‡Who waits for whom; who determines the length of the encounter; who ends the conversation, etc.

Nancy M. Henley, BODY POLITICS: POWER, SEX, AND NONVERBAL COMMUNICATION. © 1977, p. 181. Reprinted by permission of Prentice Hall, Inc., Englewood Cliffs, New Jersey.

situation. Superiors expect subordinates to be prepared in this regard. An alternative interpretation may view higher amounts of eye contact as assertive with the assumption that strength rather than meekness is being communicated. Women may capitalize on this nonverbal behavior and use it to gain a measure of prestige. Again, the context of the communication must be considered.

The dimensions of status and sexual intimacy are issues in touching. Men touch women more than women touch men (Henley, 1975). Subordinates are touched by superiors, such as a hand on the shoulder or pat on the back. These are not necessarily sexual in connotation. But when women flight attendants and bartenders are pinched and poked while on the job and when a man nudges and fondles a status equal in the office, sexual overtones cannot be dismissed. Recently cases of sexual harassment have called attention to the fact that women do not appreciate such acts and feel threatened by them, especially if the "toucher" is the employer.

Men, on the other hand, rarely touch one another, especially in what would be seen as an emotional display. Women hug each other after a long absence, while men are more likely to shake hands or give a quick squeeze on the shoulder. Men are more protective of their personal space and guard against territorial invasions by others. In American culture there is a sense of personal distance, reserved for friends and acquaintances, which extends from about one and a half to four feet, while intimate distance, for intimate personal contacts, extends to eighteen inches (Hall, 1966). Men invade intimate and personal space of women more than the reverse, and this invasion is more tolerated by the women. Males retreat when women come as close to them as they do to women and loudly protest if other men come as close to them as they do to women (Richardson, 1988:25).

It is evident that verbal and nonverbal elements of our language view the sexes unequally. When discussing language change, it is expected that one will encounter remarks like "so what?" Words are not seen as important in gender role change, even by those who fervently work on other issues involving women, such as equal pay or spouse abuse. What answers do we give? Several are suggested. Language pervades all areas of our lives. Once learned, language influences our perceptions of what is proper, accepted and expected. When we hear the word man or he, we conjure up parallel images. Alternative images of women in traditionally male occupations for example, are never expressed. Bem and Bem (1970) speak to the power of an ideology they define as nonconscious because alternative beliefs and attitudes about women remain unimagined. Language supports a nonconscious ideology concerning the sexes.

Another answer is that words assert position and power. Language reinforces female inferiority in a world of male superiority (Lakoff, 1975). As that world changes to accommodate newer, egalitarian roles, language needs to reflect these. Accuracy and precision are gained. Finally, language learning produces a double bind for women who are socialized into believing they must always speak politely and refrain from "man talk." But while using the language to which they are accustomed, they are made to feel inferior, lesser persons (Lakoff, 1975:61). Language learning in girls may be the counterpart for the difficulty boys may experience in gaining a sense of their identity from incomplete information they are offered. In either case, the socialization road is not easy.

Television

Television is a powerful source of socialization, especially in the child's early years. This observation is empirically justified considering that a child may spend up to one-third of the day watching TV. It sets standards of behavior, provides role models and communicates expectations in a host of areas, particularly the family. When television images are reinforced by the other mass media, like movies, magazines, and popular songs, the socialization impact is substantial. Chapter 13 will document how the mass media view the sexes, but here we will offer an overview of the influence of television programming directed at children.

Television teaches. Children in first grade say they copy what they see on TV (Lyle and Hoffman, 1972). Television encourages modeling. Miller and Reeves (1976) state that children, especially boys, identify with same-sex characters. Boys identify with characters possessing physical strength and girls with those who are physically attractive. Television is gender stereotyped. Gender role portrayals in shows which are deemed acceptable for children emphasize stereotyped female roles (Peevers, 1979). Cartoons which are high in gender role stereotyping influence girls in that the cartoons parallel similar attitudes girls hold about female roles (Davidson et al., 1979). Television influences self-image. Implicit in Saturday morning TV is the idea that boys are more significant persons than girls (Nolan, et al., 1977), if only by the sheer number of male characters compared to female.

The research is conclusive that children's television is generally sexist and gender stereotyped. Contrary to reality, children are presented with severely limited portrayals of women and men. In a major study of commercial children's TV programs, Barcus distinguishes several patterns. Children see more males in significant roles. Females constitute only 22% of all characters and are likely to be found in minor roles with little responsibility for the outcome of the story (Barcus, 1983:39). Few characters who work outside the home are female and these are in clerical or student positions. Men, on the other hand, are in a variety of occupations, notably professional ones, such as attorney, physician, and scientist.

Television themes can also be differentiated according to how the sexes are portrayed. Females pursue goals related to altruism, home, and family. Self-preservation is an important female goal, too, because female characters are likely to be the targets of threats and violence. Male goals are headed by self-indulgence, wealth, revenge and expressions of hatred (Barcus, 1983:49-50). Interestingly, women are more likely to achieve their goals when compared to men. This is not an inconsistent finding if we realize that the goals of women are traditional and socially acceptable. For those television women who step into a "man's world," the outcome is not as optimistic.

Children's television is supported by commercials aimed at products for children, mainly toys and sugared cereal. Younger children, heavy viewers, and boys from low income homes are most susceptible to commercials (Robertson and

Rossiter, 1977; Gorn and Goldberg, 1977). Advertisers orient children to the idea that products are waiting to be bought at local stores and that to do without them is an unfortunate hardship. This can be referred to as the be-the-first-kid-on-the-block syndrome. Commercials are blatant in creating desires for toys encouraging domesticity in girls and high activity in boys.

Parents who resist pressure from their children to buy these products or find that the products the children want are unavailable are made to feel guilty, by advertisers and children alike. Remember the frantic search several years in a row for Cabbage Patch® dolls by parents who feared a disappointed child at Christmas or on his or her birthday? Picture, too, the angry exchanges we have all witnessed or taken part in between parent and child in front of the toy, candy, or cereal displays. Parents searching for nonstereotyped toy alternatives may feel demoralized when the offer of a tea set to their son or a truck to their daughter is met with resistance. Tantalized by television, what the child desires is within reach. For toys, the desire is likely to be gender role oriented. The parent stands in between. Who is likely to give up the fight first?

School

Family life paves the way for the major agent of secondary and continuing socialization, the educational institution. The intimacy and spontaneity of the family is replaced by an environment valuing impersonal evaluation and rewards based on competition and scholastic success. For the next twelve to twenty years school will play a significant role in the lives of most people. We will view this institution's impact on the sexes fully in Chapter 11. It should be noted, however, that regardless of intent, schools are not immune to gender role stereotyping.

Teachers who honestly believe they are treating boys and girls similarly are unaware that they are perpetuating sexist notions. When Jane is ignored or not reprimanded for disruptive behavior, is encouraged in her verbal but not mathematical abilities or is given textbooks which show her that women are housewives at best, or literally invisible at worst, gender role socialization continues. Dick discovers his rowdiness will gain attention from his female elementary school teacher, he can aspire to any occupation except nurse or secretary, and he is rewarded for his athletic skills during competitive games at recess.

Educational institutions are given the responsibility for ensuring that children are trained in the ways of society so that they can eventually assume the positions necessary for the maintenance of society. Schools provide experiences which offer technical competence as well as the learning of values and norms appropriate to the culture. American culture believes that competition, initiative, independence, and individualism are values to be sought, and schools are expected to advance these values. From a functionalist viewpoint, schools are critical ways of bringing a diverse society together through the acceptance of a common value system.

Unfortunately, many schools unwittingly socialize children into acquiring one set of values, to the virtual exclusion of the other. The stereotype is that in filling breadwinning roles, boys will need to be taught the value of competitiveness. In filling domestic roles, girls will need to be taught the value of nurturance. Though both may be positive traits, they are limited to, or truly accepted by, only one gender. As schools begin the task of first discovering, and then working to eliminate sexist practices, differential gender role socialization can be effectively altered.

Toward Androgyny

We have seen that socialization is neither consistent nor uniform. Though its agents are diverse, patterns of gender roles still emerge. Children are taught that girls and boys should exhibit behavior that is either feminine or masculine. But major contradictions arise in this process. Girls climb trees, excel in mathematics, and aspire to become professors. These same girls are concerned about physical attractiveness, finding the right husband, and raising a family. Boys enjoy cooking, like to play with children, and are not ashamed to demonstrate their emotions. These same boys are concerned about finding the right wife, raising a family, and gaining a rewarding job. Yet they have all been socialized by similar routes.

It is apparent that our views of masculinity and femininity need to shift in the direction of reality. First of all, these terms need not be the opposite of one another. To reconsider an important concept from Chapter 1, Bem (1974) argues that many people exhibit androgyny, which combines or reconciles traits considered to be feminine or masculine. She has designed an attitude scale, the Bem Sex Role Inventory, which demonstrates that both men and women can score high or low on either set of traits or have a combination of them. Work with the inventory is revealing that large numbers of androgynous people do indeed exist. Biological sex is not an issue here. People know and accept their maleness or femaleness, but gender role rigidity is not as evident. Secondly, androgyny is by definition more flexible. As the situation demands, behavior can be adapted to it. By not being confined to rigid gender roles based on presumptuous assumptions of masculinity and femininity, people can respond according to their desires and abilities. Androgyny would certainly encourage this. Block (1984:159) contends that parents who manifest androgynous identification tend to be less stereotyped in notions of masculinity and femininity and offer a wider range of behavioral and attitudinal possibilities to their children.

Androgyny recognizes that socialization into two nonoverlapping gender roles is not a productive way of encouraging behavior that can be adapted readily to a changing society. Society as well as the individual is beginning to demand more. Agents of socialization must be altered to meet this demand. Androgyny is embodied in the last stanza of Marge Piercy's (1982:57) poem, "For Strong Women: What comforts her is others loving her equally for the strength and for the weakness from which it issues, lightning from a cloud. Lightning stuns. In rain, the clouds disperse. Only water of connection remains, flowing through us. Strong is what we make each other. Until we are all strong together, a strong woman is a woman strongly afraid."

4

History
and the Creation
of Gender Roles

It is impossible to understand the present without reference to the past. In order to explain the differential status of women and men in contemporary society, it is necessary to examine the impact of specific historical forces and recognize their power in creating attitudes about the sexes. Only recently has scholarly work started to scrutinize the past with the goal of uncovering the hidden elements of a woman's history. As this chapter will illustrate, throughout history women have assumed a myriad of critical domestic and extra-domestic roles, many of which have been ignored or relegated to inconsequential historical footnotes.

Rather than attempting a full historical reckoning of women's history, the intent here is to offer an overview of certain historical periods which have been important in influencing attitudes and subsequent behavior concerning the sexes. Although history is replete with numerous outstanding women and their accomplishments, I have chosen to focus on the general role and status of women in Western history. The exception to this is in reference to specific leaders of the women's movement. As Beddoe (1983:9) notes, "women's history is not the history of a few great names." It is a history of "most women," a massive group which has been largely ignored. In addition, history illustrates the impact of **misogyny** or the disdain, even hatred, of women. Hopefully this chapter will reveal another view.

This kind of approach has several objectives. First, the roots of patriarchy will be discovered in a format which is manageable. Secondly, misconceptions about the roles of women and attitudes toward these roles will become evident. A recognition of such misconceptions has implications for contemporary social change. Finally, this overview has a consciousness-raising objective because a discovery of history allows us to become aware of our culturally determined prejudices and stereotypes. Historians have traditionally provided us with *his*-story. We will now consider *her*-story.

CLASSICAL SOCIETIES

The foundations of Western culture are ultimately traced to the Greek and Roman societies of classical antiquity. The roots of Western civilization can be found in the literature, art, philosophy, politics, and religion of a time which extends from the Bronze Age (about 3000-1200 B.C.) through the reign of Justinian (565 A.D.). In particular the period between 800 B.C. and 600 A.D. witnessed spectacular achievements for humanity. With the achievements came ideological convictions which persist in modified form today. The dark side of classical societies was laced with war, slavery, deadly competitions, and a brutal existence for much of the population. Inhabiting another portion of this cordoned-off world was democracy, literacy, grace, and beauty. These opposites serve as a framework from which to view the role of women. Like the societies themselves, the evidence concerning women's roles is also contradictory.

The Glory that Was Greece

The Greek view of women varies according to the time and place involved. Greek literature is replete with references to the matriarchal society of Amazons. Though shrouded in mystery, Greek mythology saw the Amazons as female warriors, capable with a bow, who had little need of men except as sexual partners. Greek heroes were sent to the distant land on the border of the barbarian world to test their strength against the Amazons. The Amazons invariably lost (Pomeroy, 1975). The admiration for the skills of these warrior women is used as evidence for the belief that Greek women were held in higher esteem than women of later times.

According to Graves (1955:11), matriarchy existed in Europe prior to the invasion by patriarchal invaders from the north. Over time, a matrilineal system based on judging descent from the female line was replaced by a patrilineal system. The goddesses who dominated the ancient world lost their central position as gods were added to religious imagery. The earlier maternal religion lost its ascendance as patriarchal theology was grafted onto it (Peradotto and Sullivan, 1984). Patriarchy eventually prevailed. Whether matriarchal societies like the Amazons actually existed is to date unprovable. We do know, however, that patriarchy did not completely dislodge the revered goddess from Greek mythology. This points to the main realm where the women of ancient Greece maintained a degree of power and prestige. But except for religion, most of the Greek world saw women as inferior in political, social, and legal realms.

The Amazon legends and goddess images have helped to perpetuate the idea that Greece revered women. Plato called for girls to be educated in the same manner as boys with equal opportunities open to them to become rulers. As Wender (1984) notes, Plato believed that a superior woman was better than an inferior man. This supposed an enlightened image of women that does not take into account Plato's disdain, even dislike of the opposite sex. In championing the democratic state, Plato was a pragmatist as well as a misogynist. An inferior class of uneducated women might work against the principles of democracy. This is one reason why Plato championed the emancipation of women.

It is Aristotle rather than Plato who is more representative of the Greek view of women. In describing the patriarchal family of Athens, Aristotle assumed that the husband should rule over his wife and children and that the relationship between wife and husband was as a benefactor to a beneficiary (Pomeroy, 1975:74). The inferiority of women made this arrangement a natural one. The notion of inferiority goes as far as Aristotle's deliberations on women's souls, which he believed to be impotent and in need of supervision (Pomeroy, 1975:131).

The women of Athens can be realistically described as chattels. At one point in Greek history, even a wife's childbearing responsibilities could be acceptably taken over by concubines (Arthur, 1984), which lowered the wife's already subordinate status. As a group, women were classified as minors, along with children and slaves. Their husbands or male kin literally held the power of life and death over them. Some upper class women enjoyed privileges associated with wealth and were left to their own devices while their husbands were away at war or serving the state in some other way. Divorce was rare but possible and a woman could inherit property if she had no sons (Pomeroy, 1975). Considering the plight of most women of the time, these women achieved a measure of independence in their households if only because of the absence of their husbands. Yet Athenian society did not tolerate women in public places except at funerals and all female festivals; so for the most part, they remained secluded in their homes.

The few women who did become successful in this world of men were of two groups. One group consisted of those women who practiced political intrigue behind the scenes to help elevate their sons or husbands to positions of power. The second group were the hetairai, or high level courtesans whose wit, charm, and talent men admired. When pederasty was in vogue, men sought boys or other young men for their sexual and intellectual pleasure. By the fourth century B.C., Athenian men rediscovered women, but not their wives, because they had no desire to become "family men." The uneducated wives could not compete with the social skills and cultural knowledge exhibited by the hetairai, who were often thoroughly trained for their work when they were girls. Tannahill (1980:100-101) remarks that "as throughout most of history, courtesans had a better time than wives."

The subordinate position of Athenian women extended to most of the Greek world. However, when comparing Athens to Sparta, some differences can be ascertained. Sparta practiced male infanticide when newborns were deemed unfit enough to become warriors. Whether girls were killed is unclear. Pomeroy

(1975:36) reports that all girls were simply handed over to the care of women to be raised and later become mothers of Spartan warriors. But Tannahill (1980:97) suggests that all children were examined immediately after birth and that those seen as weak, feeble, or deformed, male or female, were left to die on the slopes of Mount Taygetus. Regardless, it cannot be said that male infanticide indicated a higher regard for females in Sparta. It is significant only to the extent that Sparta was organized and continually mobilized for war, a fact which did influence the role of Spartan women.

If Athenian men were separated from their wives by war, the situation was magnified in Sparta, in that this society was either always at war or preparing for it. The lives of citizen men revolved around all male groupings, with a resultant bonding which likely encouraged homosexuality (Pomeroy, 1975:39). Although age eighteen was the typical marriage age for males, army life effectively separated husband and wife until he reached the age of thirty. These years of separation, marked by infrequent visits by their husbands, essentially allowed the wives to develop some talent and capability of their own.

While the men were away, the women enjoyed a certain amount of freedom. Although the woman's responsibility was to bear male children who would become warriors, girls also were to be physically fit. Citizen women were expected to manage the household and associated properties and rear the children, but their lives were not completely relegated to domestic tasks. They also were skilled in gymnastics and music (Pomeroy, 1975:36). As Pomeroy (1975:38) points out, by the fourth century B.C. women owned two-fifths of the land and property in Sparta through their dowries and inheritances and were permitted to display their wealth in the form of jewelry, cosmetics, and dyed clothing. The earlier simplicity and rigors of Spartan life had formerly prohibited this. Perhaps looking for a scapegoat, Aristotle contended that the decline of Sparta itself was due in part to the moral degeneracy of its women (Pomeroy, 1975:39).

In comparison to Athens, the free women of Sparta had more privileges if only because they were left alone much of the time. But in the context of the period as a whole, the vast majority of women existed in a legal and social world which viewed them in terms of their fathers, brothers and husbands. Subordination rather than freedom was the rule.

The Grandeur that Was Rome

The founding of Rome by Romulus, traditionally dated at 753 B.C., led to an empire which lasted until it was finally overrun by invading German tribes in the fifth century A.D. The Roman Empire evolved and adapted to the political, social and cultural forces of the times and in turn influenced these very forces. Changes in gender roles mirrored the fortunes and woes of the empire. The prerogatives of women in later Rome contrasted sharply with the rights of women in the early days of the republic. It is true that women remained subservient to men and cannot be portrayed separately from the men who dominated and controlled them. But compared to the Greeks, Roman women achieved an astonishing amount of freedom.

Early Rome granted the eldest man in a family, the pater familias, absolute power over all family members, male and female alike. His authority could extend to death sentences for errant family members and selling his children into slavery to recoup the economic losses of a family. Daughters remained under the authority of some pater familias throughout their lives, but sons could be emancipated after his death. Even after marriage, the father or uncle or brother still had the status of pater familias for women, which meant the husbands could exercise only a limited amount of control over wives.

The absolute authority of the pater familias may have in the long run helped women. The right of guardianship brought with it a great deal of responsibility. A daughter's dowry, training, and education had to be considered early in life. If she married into a family with uncertain financial assets, the possibility existed that she and her new family could become a continued economic liability. The pater familias exercised extreme caution in assuring the appropriate match for the women under his guardianship.

Although the pater familias system was eroding anyway, Pomeroy (1975:151) suggests that the system became increasingly burdensome for men. By the first century A.D., Augustus passed legislation which allowed a freewoman to be emancipated from a male guardian if she bore three children. The roles of childbearer and mother were primary, but they allowed for a measure of independence later in life. Considering that at some level Rome was always involved in warfare, a declining birth rate was an alarming reality. The abandonment of the pater familias rule functioned to decrease the economic burden women caused for the family. Emancipation in exchange for babies was an additional latent function.

Unlike the Greeks, the Romans recognized a wider role for women. With their husbands, wives shared in the supervision of the religious cult of the household (Balsdon, 1962:45). Women had always held power in the religious life of the empire, with the highly revered Vestal Virgins symbolizing the economic and moral well-being of the society. Though open only to a select few, these women took on roles of great public importance. Roman women in general, however, knew that their lives would be carried out as wives and mothers. But wives also carried out the business of the family while their husbands were on military duty. These roles gradually extended so that it became common for women to buy and sell property as well as inherit it and participate in the broader economic life of the society.

Their expertise was both praised and criticized, especially as women amassed fortunes in their own names. The necessity for economic decision-making led to a much less secluded life style. The Greeks would have been astounded to see women in public roles and seated with men at dinner parties. Although most women remained illiterate, even the upper class women who had the most independence, other gains included greater opportunities for learning, especially in music and dancing. These women challenged a system where they were chained to their husbands or fathers, eventually gaining the right to divorce. The success they achieved can be determined by the criticism which was evoked at the time. Balsdon (1962:14) notes that in rebelling against the senseless austerity women had to endure, "history records the protests of the old men, the puritans and the prigs."

Freedom is relative. Roman society allowed a few women of higher social standing privileges unheard of in Greek society. Religion was the one area where women exercised much control, but with few exceptions religious dominance did not expand into other realms. The emancipated woman was a rarity even in Roman times. That a sexual double standard existed is unquestionable. As Hallett (1984) suggests, women were visibly independent but definitely not autonomous. When compared to almost any free male in Rome, the most assertive woman was still in bondage to the men in her life.

THE MIDDLE AGES

When the Roman emperor Constantine reigned, between A.D. 306 and 337, the empire was already in the throes of disintegration. Regardless of the religious overtones, Constantine's decision to wed the empire to Christianity was politically astute, since Christianity seemed to offer an integrative force in a period where the empire's decline was accelerating. Constantine's foresight on the impact of Christianity was remarkable. He did not envision, however, that the collapse of Rome itself would be instrumental in allowing Christianity to gain a firm grip on Europe that lasted throughout the Middle ages. And even the Renaissance era combined with feudalism did not radically diminish this powerful hold. Christianity profoundly influenced the role of women. Whatever improvements accrued to women during the classical era were lost when Christianity dominated Europe during the Middle Ages.

Christianity

To its credit, the Church, in the form of a few monasteries and abbeys, became the repository of Greek and Roman knowledge that surely would have been lost during the sacking, looting, and general chaos following the disintegration of the Empire. The decline of a literate population left reading, writing, and education as a whole in the hands of the Church. The power of literacy and the lack of literate critics permitted the Church to become the unreproachable source of knowledge and interpretation in all realms. Tannahill (1980:138) suggests that this unassailable voice prevailed to the extent that the Church's view of life and society took on an "aura of revealed truth" and was seen as absolute.

If certain sentiments of the early Church had persisted, Christianity might not have taken on such misogynous overtones. Extending from Jewish tradition, the belief in the spiritual equality of the sexes offered new visions of and to women. The ministry of Jesus included women in significant roles, thus demonstrating that spiritual equality could be actualized even in the steadfastly patriarchal society of the time. Also, the Church recognized that women provided valuable charitable, evangelistic and teaching services which were advantages to the fledgling institution. Some positions of leadership in the hierarchy were open to women, and served as models for women who might choose a religious life. The convent also served as a useful occupation for women, particularly of the upper classes, who were unsuited for marriage as well as providing a place of education for girls (Lucas, 1983).

But misogyny eventually dominated as the Church came to rely heavily on the writings of those who adopted a traditional view of women, such as Paul, Tertullian, and later, Aquinas (McLaughlin, 1974; Hyde, 1985). Biblical interpretations consistent with a cultural belief of the inferiority of women and placing the blame squarely on Eve for the fall of humanity became the unquestioned norm.

Christianity also changed the attitudes about marriage and divorce. Unlike in classical society, marriage could not be dissolved. Since divorce was unobtainable, women may have benefitted if only for the fact that they could not be easily abandoned for whatever transgressions, real or imagined, their husbands attributed to them. Whereas childlessness was grounds for marital dissolution throughout history, even this was no longer an acceptable cause. However undesirable the marriage, the marriage was inviolable in the eyes of the Church.

With the medieval Church as a backdrop, misogyny during the late Middle Ages created an outgrowth for one of the most brutal periods of history concerning women, that of the witch hunts. Accused of sexual impurity and in order to appease the wrath of God, thousands of women were burned as witches, confessing to anything their tormentors suggested. Although confession meant death at the stake, the horrible tortures used to extract confessions were impossible to endure, and it was common for women to publicly confess to such absurdities as eating the hearts of unbaptized babies and having intercourse with the devil (Tannahill, 1980). Daly's (1978:187-88) scathing comments on the witch craze, evidenced not only by her words but also her refusal to capitalize specific words, speaks to the attitude that slaughtering women meant doing God's will.

> Since the demonologies accused witches of lewd acts, their male persecutors were perfectly "justified" in destroying them. To this end, the good sons of the holy father projected their fantasies on the accused women. . . . Since their obscene "acts" were performed with the devil, god's enemy, their christian killer could feel totally religious and righteous.

Although Daly's view is caustic, it cannot be denied that the medieval Church's attitudes about women played a prominent role in sanctioning the witch craze.

Feudalism

In the feudal system where war was always a possibility, serfs and their families were protected by lords who in turn expected their serfs to fight when called upon. The serf owed his life to the lord of the manor and the wife of the serf owed her life to her husband. The lack of respect for serfs in general and their wives in particular is indicated by a custom which allowed the lord to have intercourse with the "bride of any of his serfs on her wedding night" (Duberman, 1975:8).

Women of noble standing fared somewhat better in that they were valued for their possibilities of extending the importance of the family lineage through arranged marriages, though here, too, the lord of the manor had to grant permission for any marriage. The young unmarried woman was a property worth guarding, with her virginity as a marketable commodity (Lucas, 1983:85). Her marriage would serve the purposes of uniting two houses and providing an heir.

At marriage, the bride would be given in exchange for a dowry of money or jewelry, and in some places, the custom required her to kneel in front of her husband-to-be to symbolize his power over her (Lucas, 1983:87). As her husband was controlled by the lord of the estate, she was to be controlled by her lord and husband. In this way, whether serf or noble, feudal wives had much in common.

The Renaissance

According to Casey (1976:224), the last three hundred years of medieval Europe, which included the Renaissance and Reformation, were years of ferment and change extending into realms which included women. She points out that many women did circumvent the hardships imposed on them by a harsh religious and literary atmosphere (Casey, 1976:225). In convents, not only were there women who wrote on religious subjects, but also poets and dramatists. Well-read lay women of aristocratic bearing were patrons of literature and art with some as authors themselves (Lucas, 1983). Lucas (1983: 179) also notes that these noble women set the standard for patrons of the arts for the centuries to follow. A few literate women of noble blood were accorded a certain amount of prestige for their accomplishments. But other forces were at work which kept traditional images of women from being seriously challenged.

With the Reformation came the startling notion that a church hierarchy may actually exclude people from worship. Preaching a theology of liberation from a Church charged with becoming too restrictive, Martin Luther advocated opening Christianity to everyone on the basis of faith alone. Critical of Aquinas' view that women are imperfect, or in essence "botched males," Luther argued that those who accuse her of this are in themselves monsters and should recognize that she, too, is a creature made by God (Maclean, 1980:9). The Reformation, so it appeared, offered an opportunity to present different interpretations of Christianity in regard to the sexes.

This was not to be the case. Luther himself believed women were inferior to men. Similar to the teachings in pre-Reformation Christianity, women were still seen as weak-willed temptresses who were designed for procreation, with a wife being the remedy for fornication. Though woman is a "beautiful handiwork of God," she does "not equal the dignity and glory of the male" (Luther, quoted in Maclean, 1980:10). Theological statements of the time abound with themes of superior man and inferior woman.

Maclean (1980:10) points out several of these: man is active, woman is passive, and active is the more honorable state; she is subordinate to him because of the curse put on her after the fall from Eden; she is "less robust" since she must feed her children; she is the image of man only in a restrictive sense since she was formed out of man. In all, a woman was positive, but never superior, only because of her maternal role and, inferior in all else. Thus, as the Reformation reverberated throughout the Western world, no dramatic changes relative to the Christian image of women occurred.

The Renaissance generated the rebirth of art, literature, and music in a world that was becoming transformed by commerce, communication, and the growth of cities. As a force in people's lives, Christianity now competed with others, especially education. More men and some women became literate, opening up intellectual life which had been closed to most except clergy and nobility. Women made some economic headway by working in shops or producing products in the home for later sale. As money replaced barter systems and manufacturing increased, a new class of citizens emerged who were not dependent on either agriculture or a feudal lord for protection.

Like other periods in history, the Renaissance presents contradictory evidence about women. In answering the question of whether women had a Renaissance, Kelly (1983) argues that the relative freedom enjoyed by at least noble women was actually eroded in this era. On the other hand, Rose (1986) mentions scholars who state that cultural traits like courtly love, which is dated in the twelfth century, long before the Renaissance, provides evidence for some female power and prestige. It is likely that both are correct in that the degree of freedom and authority offered to women was dependent upon their social class. Probably it is best to say that a dual attitude existed about women during the Renaissance, with admiration and respect coinciding with contempt and restrictiveness.

THE AMERICAN EXPERIENCE

The Colonial Era

The first settlers in America were searching for a kind of religious freedom which had been denied expression in the Old World. The Puritans sought to practice a brand of Christianity unencumbered by bureaucratic or doctrinal traditions which they believed hampered the expression of humanity's devotion to God. As with the Reformation, religious change was advocated, but the Puritans felt such change was impossible, given the political and theological climate of England and the Old World. Yet in challenges to the old order, the Puritans did not do so in terms of beliefs about women.

The Christian assumption of male superiority carried easily into the New World. Males were subordinate to God as females were subordinate to males. Puritan settlements such as the Massachusetts Bay Colony extracted a high degree of religious conformity which was considered necessary to the well-being and survival of the community. While organized on the precept that the community is made up of a priesthood of all believers, women were excluded from this priesthood (Katz and Rapone, 1980:17). Since religion extended to all areas of life and only men could be citizens, women were denied any public expression. The community was divided into public and domestic spheres. Though women had essential tasks in the domestic area, Puritan men still controlled both spheres.

The other side of the picture saw Puritan men being required to not only provide for the economic and physical needs of the family, but also to love their wives. The revolutionary idea that love and marriage must be connected was historically significant because until this time marriage was simply seen as an economic necessity. If the couple happened to love one another, so much the better. Much of the contemporary world would look at the Puritans with wonder in that love as a basis for marriage is rare for the majority of the globe.

Puritan women were also valued in part because they were so scarce. Most settlers were male and because many colonies were literally wiped out by disease or starvation, the colonists knew that it was vital to repopulate or see their religious visions doomed. Besides providing domestic services and children, women were deemed essential to build a foundation for a stable social order (Frey and Morton, 1986). Though wives were valuable, when it comes to starvation, patriarchy prevailed, as the following excerpt from a Jamestown, Virginia, historical record documents.

> And one amongst the rest did kill his wife, powdered (salted) her, and had eaten part of her before it was known, for which he was executed, as he well deserved. Now whether she was better roasted, boiled or cabonadoed (grilled), I know not, but of such a dish as powdered wife I never heard of. (Quoted in Frey and Morton, 1986:40)

In addition, women were important for their economic productivity within the family. Family survival, hence community survival, was tied to the efforts of both men and women. But planting gardens, weaving, canning, and candle and soap making, contributed to the family's economic fortunes, and these tasks were largely confined to women. Subsistence living was the rule, but surplus products could be bartered or sold. The family was the basic social unit for the colonists, and women were integral to its well-being.

Historians are at odds about the prestige of women during this era. Ryan (1975) suggests that the colonial period was a "golden age" for women. Although the colonists came to the New World with patriarchal ideas, adapting to the harshness of the environment required the modification of many beliefs. Women were economically productive and of necessity had to have expanded roles. Outside the home women could be found engaging in merchant, trading, and crafts functions.

The so-called golden age declined by the late eighteenth century when the family lost its centrality as the economic unit in society, to be replaced by a wider marketplace dominated by men. Women's work was once again confined to activities which were not income-producing. Attitudes about women in non-domestic activities were altered, so that resistance increased as women sought to work in enterprises not strictly defined as within the family realm (Katz and Rapone, 1980:4-5).

Whether women did achieve this colonial golden age is debatable. Katz and Rapone (1980:4) assert that the status decline thesis depends on the assumption that prestige is associated with value from labor, but that historical evidence, such as slaves, makes this questionable. This kind of conflict analysis also overlooks the crucial element that Puritan ideology was based on the assumption of female inferiority and subordination which was never really questioned throughout the colonial period. Finally, Frey and Morton (1986:6-7) note that regional differences in the colonies were striking, particularly regarding marriage and family life. To generalize about the prestige of women or the regard for their roles is difficult.

Katz and Rapone (1980:5) offer the best evidence against the idea of a status decline from a golden age by referring to specific social structures which prescribed social interaction, especially the family. Regardless of their economic functions, women's lives were rigidly circumscribed. Colonial society was based on a patriarchal family structure which placed women in dependent positions to men. Those women who had no male interceding for them, like widows, could approach the world outside of the home directly. Rather than gaining freedom of action, these women were seriously hampered, since they had no male looking out for their interests. They also were disadvantaged because their claims may have been seen as lacking legitimacy. In all, the colonial environment was a modified version of Old World notions about women.

The Victorians: The Cult of True Womanhood

The struggle for survival faced by the colonists gradually diminished as they prospered on farms and in shops. As judged by economic contributions to the family, a woman's productive role lessened and she became occupied with solely domestic tasks, like housekeeping and child rearing. By the nineteenth century her world had changed considerably. Victorian examples of womanhood made their way into magazines and novels directed toward women. Although many more women had achieved literacy, what they did read admonished them to be "True Women," and assume the cardinal virtues of piety, purity, submissiveness, and domesticity (Gordon and Buhle, 1976; Welter, 1980). These were the standards upon which society would judge them and which they would judge themselves.

Tied completely to her family, the middle class woman found herself with time on her hands, which was a luxury not shared by her colonial sisters. The reality of idleness was transformed into gentility, an ideal for which many families strived. This gentility was accompanied by attitudes which put women on pedestals that literally made them out of reach. Women were to be protected from the harshness of the world outside the home. Protectionism in reality meant repression. Victorian femininity meant that a woman was sexually, socially, and politically repressed. Gordon and Buhle (1976:285) mention that a woman during this time became a living object of art, of decorative value only, "existing for the pleasure and pride of her husband."

The strength of the Cult of True Womanhood was effective in silencing for many the voices of feminism which were being heard in Europe and America also during the Victorian Era. From pulpits throughout America, women were told that happiness and power could be found in their own homes, with society being disrupted if they chose to listen to voices calling them to other spheres (Welter, 1980:211). The True Woman was not to be swayed by so-called reformers speaking of other rights. The rights of the "True Woman" are summed up in the following poem (Little, 1848-49, quoted in Welter, 1980:210):

> The right to love whom others scorn
> The right to comfort and to mourn
> The right to shed new joy on earth
> The right to feel the soul's high worth . . .
> Such women's rights, and God will bless
> And crown their champions with success.

It is also interesting to consider these ideals for women over a century ago in light of contemporary arguments against extending greater rights to women. Perhaps history may be repeating itself in this regard.

Frontier Life

Idleness was impossible on the frontier. Victorian America extolled the gentility and supposed frailness of middle class women. Frontier society would have been disdainful of these very traits. As with the colonial era, women were valued for their work both inside and outside the home. And during the early frontier expansion, women were scarce. Yet colonial society never seriously questioned the notion of woman's inferiority; hence, her relative status remains unclear. Through the hardship and deprivation of frontier life combined with less adherence to religious proscriptions concerning the sexes, it is evident that the pioneer woman achieved a degree of freedom and respect unlike previous periods of America's brief history.

The frontier experience began with the grueling trip West which often took six months to complete. Surviving the trip meant that the normal division of labor according to sex was suspended. Faragher and Stansell (1980:295) state that the work of all adults was indispensable with the deprivation of the trail allowing, actually requiring, that women fill expanded roles. A partnership between men and women appeared to be the rule.

Yet rather than viewing the situation as an opportunity for male-female equality, diaries from these women suggest that they saw themselves as invaders of a male domain. Faragher and Stansell (1980:307) note that, although few women who emigrated West on the Oregon Trail came from the northeastern middle classes where the "Cult of True Womanhood" reached its zenith, they were not immune to it either. With their domestic role in a complete state of disarray on the trail, women apparently did not take advantage of the potential it offered for change, and fought to regain a role offering more definitive boundaries. This is understandable when considering that when entering the male sphere, they gave up a sense of independence from men which they held in their own world. As Faragher and Stansell (1980:308) astutely remark, there are more important advantages in a separate female province.

Frontier settlements saw the necessity of woman's labor not being confined to the home. Child rearing was often left to siblings as wives worked in the fields with their husbands. Subsistence farming required that as many goods as possible be produced and consumed within the home. Women took the major responsibility in these areas. Isolated farms, prairie loneliness, and the daily harshness of frontier living generated the understanding that men and women, wives and husbands, depended on one another for not only physical but emotional survival. This understanding served to elevate the status of women.

Stratton's (1981) accounts of women who emigrated to the Kansas frontier during the latter part of the nineteenth century provide testimony to their critical roles and how they withstood and accepted them. Using diaries, letters, and other autobiographical statements of these pioneer women, actual experiences and reminiscences are recorded. A daughter recalls the birth of her brother on a day when her father had made an all-day trip to town for wood. Her mother was alone with two babies, no neighbors, and no doctor, when the stork arrived.

> So my brave mother got the baby clothes together on a chair by the bed, water and scissors . . . drew a bucket of fresh water from a sixty-foot well; made some bread-and-butter sandwiches; set out some milk for the babies. . . . So at about noon the stork left a fine baby boy. . . . My mother, having fainted a number of times in her attempt to dress the baby, had succeeded at last; and when my father came in he found a very uncomfortable but brave and thankful mother, thankful that he had returned home with the precious wood, and that she and the baby were alright. (Quoted in Stratton, 1981:87)

Such accounts are characteristic rather than exceptional. They speak of women who, with their families, endured prairie fires, locusts, droughts, disease, and the ever present loneliness. Most did not return to their homes in the east, but accepted their new life with stoicism and a hope for making their own farm an economic success. Stratton's hundreds of excerpts provide a picture of matter-of-fact women who did not seem to begrudge their new lives on the frontier.

This is not meant to idealize the brutal existence many pioneer women confronted. It is only to point out that adversity was apparently an important ingredient in bringing men and women together as equals on the frontier, even if the participants themselves failed to recognize what was happening regarding alterations in gender roles. As with other times in history, frontier life undeniably demonstrates that a woman's contributions are as important as a man's. In this case, however, her contributions added to her status and have been recognized earlier by historians.

Industrialization

From the founding of America, women have always participated in the world of paid labor and could not be completely circumscribed by their domestic roles. When teachers or shopkeepers or planters or traders were needed and men were unavailable, women were encouraged to fill these roles. Industrial expansion during the nineteenth century required an entirely new class of workers. Faced with a shortage of males who continued to farm, industrialists convinced women that even if they were too weak for agriculture, work in the mills could suit their temperaments (Wertheimer, 1984:337). Thousands of women and many children answered the call.

By the latter part of the century, the shift from an agricultural to an urban industrialized economy for much of the nation was accelerating. New definitions of work recognized that the family was no longer a critical unit of production and that work was to be performed for wages at other locations outside home and farm (Mandle, 1979). The ranks of the new labor force were filled by men, single women and wives and daughters of working class families whose income was necessary to keep the family out of poverty. Mandle (1979:23) states that married women and children were eventually excluded from these ranks.

More specifically, it was the middle class married woman who again was expected to devote her time and talents to the emotional well-being of the family. This was happening at the very time when labor-saving products and appliances began to be introduced to the home. By the turn of the century an anomaly developed concerning this issue. The realization that housework and child care were no longer a full-time occupation led to more leisure, boredom, and restlessness for women who were discouraged from seeking paid employment outside the home (Gordon et al., 1973:41-42). This led to two important results. First, many middle class women became involved in social reform work, including the growing feminist movement. Second, the already existing schism between working class and middle class women widened. As we shall see, to date this schism has not been completely mended.

The working class woman was confronted with different issues, the basic one being subsistence. Industrial growth increasingly demanded an abundance of cheap labor and looked to poorer women and immigrants to take on this load. The urbanizing Eastern states accommodated the flood of immigrants who settled in areas close to the factories, mines, and mills in which they worked, often creating a ghetto-like atmosphere cutting them off from wider society. By the beginning of the twentieth century, 25% of unmarried immigrant women worked outside the home in comparison to 15% of native-born women, with the immigrant women overrepresented in unskilled labor activities (Banner, 1984:61). Black women worked on farms and as domestics because factory labor was, for the most part, closed to them.

The working conditions faced by women, and many men, were appalling, even by the standards of the day. Banner (1984:67-69) and Wertheimer (1984:339) point out that unsanitary conditions, no rest breaks, not being allowed to sit down, ten hour work days with a half-day on Saturday, and grueling, rote tasks were characteristic. In combination with an unsafe environment where machines had no safety guards and buildings were poorly ventilated and lacked fire escapes, it is understandable why job-related injuries and deaths skyrocketed. In 1911, the Triangle Shirtwaist Company in New York caught on fire, killing 146 workers, many of them woman. Doors were kept locked so that workers could be inspected before they left for possible possession of company merchandise, and what fire escapes were available were in need of repair and buckled under the pressure of those fleeing the fire (Wertheimer, 1984:345).

The garment industry was notorious in its treatment of lower level workers. A system of subcontracting finishing work to people, primarily women, became common. Women would work in what came to be called "sweatshops" in basements and workrooms of low-rent tenement apartments, thereby saving the company much in the way of production costs (Banner, 1984:67). What made an already dismal situation worse was that it was necessary for workers to purchase their own equipment which would then require years of arduous labor to pay off.

When men and women were employed in the same factories, women took less prestigious jobs and were paid less. The fact that the sexes were segregated by type of activity led to a stratification system which justified the lower wages paid to women. This has carried over to today and has generated much debate over the issue of comparable worth.

The scandalous conditions under which people worked generated much sympathy nationally and created a ripe atmosphere for unions to flourish, with major growth occurring from the 1870s through World War I. In 1881 the Knights of Labor was opened for women and blacks, calling for equal pay for equal work (Wertheimer, 1984:342). In 1885, 2,500 women members of the Knights of Labor endured a six month strike marked by violence in Yonkers, New York, at a mill where they worked as carpet weavers (Werthiemer, 1984:343). The International Ladies' Garment Workers Union (ILGWU) gained recognition in many shops as a result of a strike which lasted through the winter of 1909 and involved twenty thousand shirtwaist workers throughout the city, most of whom were women. With the support of the Women's Trade Union League and a public aroused after the Triangle Shirtwaist Company fire, legislation was passed requiring more stringent safety and inspection codes for factories (Wertheimer, 1984:345).

But compared to the union movement involving men, women's attempts to unionize were not nearly as successful. For both men and women, the courts, employers, police, and often the public were not supportive of union efforts. Many unions still refused to admit women, and even with an official policy urging the equal pay to women, the most powerful union, the American Federation of Labor (AFL), was unwilling to exert the pressure necessary for its affiliates to conform to the rule (Wertheimer, 1984:344). The AFL was also becoming a union of skilled crafts workers made up exclusively of men, and there was fear that the success of the union would be diluted if it took on the numerous women still in the ranks of the unskilled. Originally welcoming women as members, a period of economic recession saw members of the Knights of Labor competing with one another for scarce jobs. Women were no longer welcomed with open arms. In 1895, only 5% of all union members were female, and by 1900 only 3% of all women who worked in factories were unionized (Wertheimer, 1984:344; Banner, 1984:72).

The ILGWU had become the third largest affiliate of the AFL by 1913 (Banner, 1984:71), and it did capitalize on the power that was being wielded by the AFL itself. But because men and women were segregated by job, the unions representing women had less success. By 1900, women represented half the membership of unions in five industries (women's clothing, gloves, hats, shirt-waist and laundry, and tobacco), and they earned about half of what men earned; black women earned half of what was made by white women (Wertheimer, 1984:344).

The characteristics of the female labor force also made unionization efforts difficult. Work for women was unstable, temporary, and subject to economic ups and downs. In jobs performed by both sexes, men were given preference in slack periods, and women were laid off. Banner (1984:72) notes that young women worked until marriage. Marriage was the door which allowed women to get out of the factories and aspire to a middle class life style. Overall, unions were most helpful to women when they were allowed to join with men. Unions of women workers tended to be small, more isolated, and financially weak, although they did provide opportunities for women to develop both leadership skills and agendas representing their own interests (Wertheimer, 1984:346).

Women have tended to advance more in the labor force during periods of growth as well as in periods of war. During the Civil War women served as nurses, clerks, copyists, and produced the uniforms and munitions needed (Wertheimer, 1984:339). World War I also saw an expansion of job opportunities for women. Public sentiment for the war effort made the transition to the labor force easier for women who, if they had a choice, had not previously considered working outside the home. In both instances, however, women were summarily dismissed after the men returned.

The rule that scarce jobs go to men first continued through the Depression. Job segregation and the belief that there was "women's work" and "men's work" ironically protected the jobs of women who worked as waitresses, domestics, or clerks. Rather than accepting the loss of prestige that would be associated with doing a "woman's" job, some men abandoned their families because they were no longer breadwinners. In those instances where a job was not defined completely in gender terms, such as teacher, it was rare to see a woman either obtain it or keep it if a man could be employed instead.

In general, industrialization saw women make steady headway in the world of paid employment. Older attitudes about women's functions in the family continued to compete with the needs of an expanding economy. But the precedent for women working outside the home gained strength and was nurtured by gradual public acceptance for newer roles. Once the industrial era established this trend, it was the Second World War which provided the most important catalyst for expanding employment options for women.

World War II

It is perhaps ironic that historically war has been an impetus for positive social change that otherwise might not have occurred or would have occurred at a much slower pace. War suspends notions of what is considered typical or conventional and throws people into novel situations which, in turn, sensitize them to an awareness of potential never dreamed possible. This happens on and off the actual battlefield.

Women have consistently taken on expanded roles in wartime, by choice as well as necessity. As shown in this chapter, throughout history we see women managing the affairs of home, farm, and business while their husbands, sons, or brothers were away for extended periods. Considering, too, that the history of the world has been marked by frequent and prolonged periods of war, the roles women assumed were essential for social equilibrium. Usually these newer roles have been short-lived, with the prewar social order swiftly reestablished when the men returned home. Although this was indeed the case with World War II, it can also be stated that this particular war profoundly influenced American women involved in the war effort to the extent that its liberating effects not only endured but were consequential for the next generation of women. The impact was seen most in the areas of employment and family.

When America officially entered the war in 1941, government leaders quickly recognized that victory depended upon the total commitment of the nation. One task of the Office of War Information was to constantly monitor public opinion to determine the degree of commitment and willingness to sacrifice for the war. Used to men taking the lead in both politics and war, women were less enthusiastic about the war and less receptive to military themes and national and international events regarding the war than were men (Campbell, 1984:6-7). Socialized into values related to domesticity, the war was simply more remote for women. Within a few months of Pearl Harbor, when patriotism was at its height, a concerted national policy to fully mobilize the civilian population in the war effort was initiated. Much of this policy was focused on women.

The powerful War Production Board (WPC) and War Manpower Commission (WMC) were set up to convert the economy to wartime, coordinate labor for the various sectors of the economy and allocate workers for both war and civilian production. The booming wartime economy literally ended the Depression almost overnight. It soon became apparent to these agencies that the war machine required uninterrupted production schedules through an increased labor supply. Women were essential in filling the roles in the war production industry as the men were called into military service. An efficient propaganda program was put into effect which prompted women to respond to the employment needs of a nation at war.

The battle abroad could only be won if women would recognize their patriotic duty to become employed on the home front. After the Depression years, the higher pay and better working conditions offered in the war industry found many women eagerly seeking work in all areas. When jobs became available again, women were first hired in positions where women had previously worked, as clerks or semi-skilled laborers in factories producing uniforms or foodstuffs. The higher pay for work in defense plants enticed many women to apply for jobs, but they found themselves rebuffed.

At first, defense employers were reluctant to hire women, even if it meant paying men overtime or creating shortages in production. And when plants were converted from civilian to war production, thousands of women lost their jobs and were replaced by men. As Hartmann (1982:54-55) notes, women were also likely to be excluded from government training programs though there was official acknowledgment that women could be efficient and versatile employees. If implemented over a long period, such a policy would have had disastrous consequences for the war effort.

As labor shortages reached crisis proportions, job training for women and opportunities in almost all phases of defense work dramatically increased. Within six months after Pearl Harbor, employers indicated a willingness to hire women in 70% of anticipated semiskilled positions and 63% of professional or managerial openings (Hartmann, 1982:55). The employment of women reached its wartime peak in July of 1944, when 19 million women were employed, an increase of 47% over the level of March, 1940 (Anderson, 1981:4).

Propaganda campaigns created images of defense work as exciting, even glamorous, and offering much in the way of economic incentive. Appeals to both patriotism and guilt for being "slackers" in the war effort kept the civilian labor force at levels sufficient to carry out production needs with women constituting half of this labor force (Hartmann, 1982:56). "Rosie the Riveter," popularized through a wartime song, became the new home front heroine. She represented the millions of women who worked at munitions plants, foundries, and quarries as lumberjacks, shipbuilders, and plumbers.

Once the gender barrier eroded, women's opportunities in the war industry advanced, with less regard also paid to age, marital status, and race. However, preferences were given to women who were white, single, and younger. The war allowed black women to eventually gain access to employment in manufacturing plants and other offices and industries which had been previously closed to them, thus making them less reliant on domestic and farm work (Hartmann, 1982:60). Married women were actively recruited by 1943 because the reserve of single women had been exhausted (Anderson, 1981:4). Between 1940 and 1944, married women who were employed increased by two million, and for the first time, married women outnumbered single women in the United States labor force (Anderson, 1981:4).

The new encouragement for married women to enter the labor force challenged a society which firmly believed that a mother's place was at home with her children. By the close of the war, 32% of women who worked in the major defense centers had children under the age of fourteen (Campbell, 1984:82). Day care centers, foster home programs, and other variations of child care were developed throughout the country. By suggesting that defense production was tied to provisions for child care, day care services increased dramatically. The Federal Works Agency administered a program which, at its height, enrolled 130,000 children in over 3,000 centers (Hartmann, 1982:59).

Rather than viewing such options as a menace to children and an indictment for their mothers, such provisions were praised for allowing mothers of younger children to enter the work force where they were sorely needed. Campbell (1984:82) suggests that the lure the government used was to assure mothers that their children would be well looked after. Overall, day care centers were not that abundant and were used by relatively few employed mothers, with most relying on friends and relatives for child care. Some women remained suspicious of organized day care and preferred to remain unemployed rather than believe the media campaigns. The key issue here is that when women were needed for industry, innovative strategies were developed to help them in their quest for adequate day care. Also, the suspension of traditional beliefs combined with an effective media and government propaganda program allowed a nation to view day care, at least for a time, as a virtuous and acceptable choice. Although mothers were working in defense plants, for the most part their children were not regarded as being socially, physically or psychologically at risk as a result.

The earlier reluctance to employ women at all, especially married women, for the heavy industry of war, was replaced by an understanding that women could, and actually should, shoulder more of the responsibility for the war effort. But a paradox remained. The men were doing battle overseas to protect the cherished values of home and family, and yet these very values were potentially being threatened by the kinds of roles in which women found themselves. To get around this problem, another propaganda campaign suggested that women were in it only "for the duration," and they would reassume their domestic duties after the war, gladly giving up their jobs to the returning men. This would supposedly alleviate any problems of joblessness for the men. Of course, female unemployment was never an issue. Devotion to country meant the sacrifice of temporarily becoming employed for pay, with the home held up as where women would and should want to be. And to a great extent, this belief was accepted by both sexes after the war.

The ideal for which the war was fought, country and family, remained unshaken. Romantic visions of resumed, post-war lives as wives and mothers abounded during the war, alongside the images of capable women working in defense plants. Hovering in the wings during the war years, the cult of the home made a triumphant comeback to entice even the most reluctant women out of the labor force. The conversion to a peacetime economy was accelerated with soaring marriage and birth rates. Labor-saving devices and technological innovations were introduced which revolutionized housekeeping but did not allow for a lessening of a woman's domestic responsibilities. Whereas the wartime media appealed to a woman's efficiency in the home, peacetime standards advocated not only an expansion of her roles as childbearer, nutritionist, consumer, and decorator but also extracted higher standards of success in these realms (Hartmann, 1982:168).

In addition, wives were made responsible for the psychological adjustment their husbands had to undergo with the return to civilian life. This meant that her needs were to be subverted to his. Women were cautioned to be sensitive, responsive, and above all, feminine, since this is what civilian life meant for men. Hartmann (1982:169) points out that the authorities of the time did not necessarily ignore the responsibility of the veterans themselves in helping with their own readjustment, but that norms appeared which made women the focus of accountability for marital success after the war.

It is apparent from this that the new roles for women created during the war existed alongside traditional beliefs concerning their primary domestic duties. The view that World War II represented a watershed in the experience of American women is shared by several historians, while others argue that continuity and persistence of gender roles was the reality (Chafe, 1972; Rupp, 1978; Hartmann, 1982; Campbell, 1984). The women themselves were divided in their post-war plans. Some worked only for the duration for patriotic reasons. Although they enjoyed their work, they never intended to make a career of paid employment. Anderson (1981:162-63) mentions the tenacity of other women who gained such a sense of independence from their wartime jobs that they were resentful and bitter when returning veterans and postwar cutbacks forced them out of work. Single women, war widows, and those who had to support themselves anyway had no choice but to continue to work. The loss of pay and respect during the postwar years weighed heavily on many women.

Regardless of which side of the debate one is on, it is impossible to ignore the liberating effects of World War II on women because the war itself contributed to broad social changes in American society. The seeds of social change were planted during the war and took root in an atmosphere of economic growth. Campbell (1984:237) points out that recovery from the Depression, greater equality in the distribution of income, and urban expansion affected both women and men. Home and family remained integral to women's aspirations. But a doctrine of the spheres which had effectively separated women from any other outside existence was doomed after the war. In all, the roots of the sociocultural trends of the fifties and sixties can be traced to the war years. As Hartmann (1982:215) points out,

> While recognizing the overall continuities in women's lives between 1940 and 1950, it is also possible to identify in that decade seeds of change which worked a deeper transformation in women's consciousness, aspirations, and opportunities a generation or so later.

Attitudes do not change as quickly as behavior. Efforts which sought to restrict the nondomestic roles and activities of women in the postwar years relied on beliefs about biological determinism which were difficult to reject. Throughout history we have seen scores of women who have successfully broadened narrow role definitions. But World War II provided models for gender role change on such a grand scale that women's accomplishments could not be conveniently relegated to a forgotten footnote in history.

Contemporary women and men alike must contend with theories of biological destiny and other beliefs which seek to bolster the older gender role system. Yet such attitudes must inevitably erode in the face of massive evidence which contradicts these assumptions. The progress made by women during the war coupled with rapid postwar social and economic changes provided the framework for the reemergence of the women's movement in the United States.

THE WOMEN'S MOVEMENT

> In the new code of laws . . . I desire you would remember the ladies and be more generous and favorable to them than your ancestors. Abigail Adams, March 31, 1776.

Abigail Adams wrote to her husband John when he was attending the Second Continental Congress and cautioned him that if the ladies were ignored and denied the rights for which the Revolutionary War was being fought, they would eventually create a revolution of their own. She believed that women could not be bound by laws which they had no hand in creating. Abigail Adams persisted in her quest with additional letters to her husband and her friends. To her husband she also wrote

> That your sex is naturally tyrannical is a truth so thoroughly established as to admit of no dispute; but such of you as wish to be happy, willingly give up the harsh title of master for the more tender and endearing one of friend. Then put it out of the power of the vicious and the lawless to use us with cruelty and indignity and impunity . . . so whilst you are proclaiming peace and good will to men, emancipation for all nations, you insist on retaining an absolute power over wives. But you must remember that arbitrary power is like most other things which are hard, very liable to be broken. (Douglas, 1966:50-51)

John Adams, who would become the nation's second president, dismissed these warnings while helping to draft humanistic documents which proclaimed that all men are created equal. For the Founding *Fathers*, the business at hand was to build the infrastructure for an enduring democracy. That this democracy denied basic rights to females, as well as to blacks, was overlooked by most. The challenges which did emerge from a few individuals, even from such influential women as Abigail Adams, did not provide the momentum for any kind of organized protest. While Abigail Adams did accurately predict that women would themselves ferment another revolution, it took another half century before it would be actualized at all in America.

Two other events served as important ingredients for the rise of feminism and the beginnings of a woman's movement in the United States. The French Revolution ideals of liberty and equality inspired the "Declaration of the Rights of Man" in 1789. A reply by Olympe de Gouges came two years later with the "Declaration of the Rights of Woman," where she declared that "woman is born free and her rights are the same as those of man" and that "the law be an expression of the general will" and "all citizens, men and women alike . . . participate in making it" (cited in Deckard, 1983:207). For the first time, humanistic standards were applied explicitly to both sexes. More importantly, the democratic fervor which was sweeping France and influencing other parts of Europe and England created an atmosphere where such radical writings were at least considered. It is likely that had such a work appeared first in America, it would have been rejected, dismissed, and buried.

Second, in 1792, English writer and activist Mary Wollstonecraft wrote what was to become the bible of the feminist movement, *The Vindication of the Rights of Woman*. In this remarkable work, Wollstonecraft argues that ideals of equality should be applied to both sexes, and that it is only in bodily strength where a man has a natural superiority over a woman. She states that

> not only the virtue but the *knowledge* of the two sexes should be the same in nature, if not in degree, and that women, considered not only as moral, but rational creatures, ought to endeavor to acquire human virtues (or perfections) by the *same* means as men, instead of being educated like a fanciful kind of *half* being. (Wollstonecraft, 1967:75)

She maintained that women must strengthen their minds, become friends to their husbands and not be dependent on them. When women are kept ignorant and passive, not only do their children suffer but society as a whole will be weakened. In advocating full partnership with men, Wollstonecraft explicitly called for a "revolution in female manners" to make women part of the human species by reforming themselves and then the world.

> Let women share the rights and she will emulate the virtues of man; for she must grow more perfect when emancipated. (Wollstonecraft, 1967:287)

The Early Movement: 1830 to 1890

As mentioned earlier, the Industrial Revolution altered society through a drastic reorganization of the process of production. By the 1830s, women found themselves working for low wages in factories under dismal conditions. Middle class women saw factories taking over work which had been their primary domestic responsibility, such as baking bread, making soap, and producing clothing, thus robbing them of their economic usefulness (Klein, 1984:524). Whereas factory women used unions as vehicles for organized protest, middle class women realized that their aims could best be met through greater opportunities for higher educations and political rights. In both instances, these women had different class-based ambitions and used divergent strategies to meet their needs. But unique to American history, they organized into their respective groups as women meeting the needs of women.

The issue of economics generated the stimulus for working class and middle class women to first organize. But the major catalyst for the woman's movement was ostensibly humanistic in orientation and provided an outlet for mostly middle class women who had the time and money to participate in a social cause. It was only during the latter suffrage movement that more women of both classes joined together for a common goal. Before suffrage became the rallying point for women, slavery was the issue. When Wollstonecraft was calling for the emancipation of women, many women were already playing a critical role in the abolitionist movement to emancipate the blacks from slavery.

It soon became apparent to the women who worked in the antislavery movement that they were not on the same political level as the male abolitionists. Women abolitionists were often not allowed to make public speeches, and with the formation of the American Anti-Slavery Society in 1833, they were denied the right to sign its Declaration of Purposes. When the World Anti-Slavery Convention met in London in 1840, women members of the American delegation, including Lucretia Mott and Elizabeth Cady Stanton, had to sit in the galleries and could not participate in any of the proceedings. They were made painfully aware that slavery had to do with gender as well as race.

Women abolitionists began to speak more openly about women's rights to the extent that their male comrades feared the antislavery issue would be weakened. As progressive as the abolitionist movement was, the inherent sexism of the day served to divide and alienate its members.   While continuing their work for antislavery, women were also now more vocal about legislative reforms related to woman's property and family rights (Hole and Levine, 1984:535). Recognizing that the inferior status of women needed to be urgently addressed, the first Woman's Rights Convention was held in Seneca Falls, New York, in 1848, an event hailed as the birth of the women's movement in the United States.

The Seneca Falls Convention approved a Declaration of Sentiments modeled after the Declaration of Independence, which listed the forms of discrimination women had to endure, and which they vowed to eliminate. The following examples (cited in Hole and Levine, 1984:536) from this declaration demonstrate not only what the women of the time were up against, but they also convey messages to contemporary women.

1.   We hold these truths to be self-evident: that all men and women are created equal; that they are endowed by their Creator with certain inalienable rights; that among these are life, liberty and the pursuit of happiness.
2.   The history of mankind is a history of repeated injuries and usurpations on the part of man toward woman, having in direct object the establishment of an absolute tyranny over her.
3.   He has compelled her to submit to laws, in the formation of which she has no voice.
4.   He had made her, if married, in the eye of the law, civilly dead.
5.   He has monopolized nearly all the profitable employments, and from those she is permitted to follow, she receives but a scanty remuneration. He closes against her all the avenues to wealth and distinction which he considers most honorable to himself. As a teacher of theology, medicine or law, she is not known.
6.   He has endeavored, in every way he could, to destroy her confidence in her own powers, to lessen her self-respect, and to make her willing to lead a dependent and abject life.

This listing of the discriminatory practices against women was accepted by the convention as well as eleven of the twelve resolutions aimed at ending such practices. Whereas it was agreed that women had to submit to laws they did not help create, there was not unanimous agreement about whether they should seek the vote. History has given the Seneca Falls meeting the distinction of originating the suffrage movement, but the suffrage resolution was passed only by a small majority. Although the early women's movement has become synonymous with suffrage, this was the very issue which initially split its supporters. Perhaps difficult to understand by today's standards, many women believed equality could be approached without the vote.

The following years saw conventions for woman's rights being held throughout the North and West. Since abolition was part of its platform, the movement itself never spread to the South before the Civil War. During the war, activities on the behalf of women per se were dormant, but they emerged in earnest soon after. Even with no national agenda, disagreements as to strategy, and run by a few women who had the strength and spare time to work for its causes, the movement grew in strength. Deckard (1983:253) credits three outstanding women and their unique talents for this growth: Lucy Stone, the movement's most gifted orator; Elizabeth

Cady Stanton, philosopher and program writer; and, the organizing genius, Susan B. Anthony. They spoke on social, economic, and legal issues affecting women and pressed for reforms in such areas as education, wages, organized labor, child welfare, and inheritance.

As the movement grew, so did its opponents. First as abolitionists, then as feminists, and always as women, the movement was despised and ridiculed by many. Klein (1984:531) traces this to the use of militant methods of agitation and to the emphasis on enfranchisement. The ever present verbal abuse at women's rallies along with the threat of mob violence caused some supporters to advocate less militant tactics overall or to downgrade the importance of the vote. Again the ranks of the movement were divided so that by the end of the Civil war it was split into two factions.

Although both factions agreed on the need to get the vote, they were split on questions related to ideology and strategy. In 1869 two organizations were formed. Susan B. Anthony and Elizabeth Cady Stanton founded the National Woman Suffrage Association (NWSA). NWSA did not admit men, was considered militant in tactics, focused on issues which were controversial like husband-wife relations, and worked for the vote in order to achieve other rights for women. Enfranchisement, then, was seen as a means to a greater end.

The second organization, the American Woman Suffrage Association (AWSA), led by Lucy Stone and Julia Howe, was more moderate in character, attracting many middle and upper class women. concentrating on making the suffrage question more mainstream, the AWSA refrained from addressing issues thought to be controversial, such as marriage and church (Hole and Levine, 1984:539). The primary goal of AWSA was to work within each state to achieve the vote. Wyoming was the first state to grant the vote to women, doing so in 1869, for a pragmatic rather than strictly democratic reason. Women were scarce in the territory and it was felt that the right to vote would encourage more migrants to the area. Wyoming was almost not granted statehood because Southern congressmen argued that the states did not have the right to grant suffrage. But as Deckard (1983:262) explains, since the legislature was elected in part by the vote of women, they stated that Wyoming "will remain out of the Union for a hundred years rather than come in without the women." By a small margin Wyoming was admitted to the Union in 1890.

AWSA strategies eventually brought in many proponents to the movement, with suffrage gaining the respectability it needed to attract a broader base of support. In the meantime, NWSA increasingly turned its attention to suffrage, and campaigned for political and legal rights. In 1890, the two groups merged to form the National American Woman Suffrage Association (NAWSA). One unfortunate consequence of the merging and the gain in "respectability" was that the organization became isolated from the plight of black women, immigrant women, and working class women in general. It can be argued that the schism which excluded these potential allies at the turn of the century exists today in that the movement is largely made up of middle class and professional women.

The Nineteenth Amendment

The next thirty years saw renewed energies for passage of a suffrage amendment, though NAWSA actually accomplished very little. Strategies deemed as too radical were disavowed, militant members were expelled, conservatism set in and a crisis in leadership occurred. Some of the expelled faction joined a group founded by militant suffragist Alice Paul in 1913. Later known as the Woman's Party, this organization worked for a federal suffrage amendment using whatever tactics deemed necessary, however unorthodox, to meet their goal (Hole and Levine, 1984:540). In the meantime, Carrie Chapman Catt became president of NAWSA and in 1915 began a rigorous suffrage campaign.

NAWSA continued distributing leaflets, lobbying, and speaking to numerous influential organizations. Woman's Party members held rallies, mass demonstrations, and went on hunger strikes. Some were arrested and jailed for their activities (Hole and Levine, 1984:541). Although the tactics varied, the common goal was passage of a suffrage amendment that had been introduced and defeated in every session of Congress since 1878.

By the end of the First World War, the idea of giving the vote to women had widespread public support. In 1919 the Nineteenth Amendment was passed by votes of 304 to 90 in the House and 56 to 25 in the Senate (Duberman, 1975:13). But the struggle would not be over until two-thirds of the states ratified it. On August 26, 1920, by only two votes, the amendment was ratified in Tennessee making the Nineteenth Amendment part of the Constitution.

The Contemporary Movement

Once the right to vote was gained, feminism literally died in the United States for the next forty years. The end of the arduous campaign resulting in ratification of the Nineteenth Amendment found some feminists insisting that broader social reforms, rather than narrower feminist goals, were now necessary, since political equality had been achieved. Others, including Alice Paul, called for passage of the Equal Rights Amendment (ERA) which would prohibit all forms of discrimination against women. The ERA was first introduced in Congress in 1923, but even by this time the unity of support for a specific cause had been dissolved. Coupled with the Depression and a conservative national mood, most activism for women's issues was abandoned. It was not until after World War II that the women's movement emerged again on a national scale.

The reawakening of feminism was encouraged by three major events. First, President John Kennedy established the Commission on the Status of Women in 1961. The Commission issued a report documenting the inferior position of women in the United States and set up a citizen's advisory council and state commissions to deal with the problems addressed in the report. Second, in 1963 Betty Friedan published her landmark work, *The Feminine Mystique*. In this book, Friedan argues that women are given no road to fulfillment other than wife and mother. They have no identity apart from their families, find themselves unhappy, and cannot even name their problem. By restrictive roles and a society which condones and applauds such restrictions, women are beginning to voice their unhappiness. "It is no longer possible to ignore that voice, to dismiss the desperation of so many American women" (Friedan, 1963:21). The second-class status of women which was pointed to in the Kennedy report was bolstered by Freidan's assertions and research.

The third event heralding the return of feminism was the founding of the National Organization for Women (NOW) in 1966, with Betty Freidan serving as its first president. These events are not in isolation from one another. Many of the women first met when they worked on state commissions set up after the Kennedy report. They were also unhappy with the progress being made on their recommendations and felt that a separate effort to deal with issues related to women was important (Freeman, 1984:544). The creation of NOW can be viewed as an indirect result of the Commission on the Status of Women.

It is important to remember that NOW was formed during the turbulent 1960s during an era of heightened political activism and social consciousness. The drive to organize women occurred during a time when blacks, Native Americans, Hispanics, poor people, students, and anti-Viet Nam war activists were also competing for public attention through mass demonstrations for their respective causes. In comparison to many of the organizations which were spawned as a result of these causes, including other women's groups, NOW was, and is, much more moderate in its approach. Perhaps NOW's ability to survive into the 1990's as a viable organization can be tied to its mainstream emphasis.

NOW has been made up primarily of middle class, college-educated and professional women who have worked for economic and legal equality through political means. In the decades since its founding, however, NOW's membership has expanded considerably, bringing in more nonprofessional and younger women (Mandle, 1979:171). NOW is hierarchically structured with elected officers, a formal constitution, a national body, and semiautonomous local chapters. Richardson (1988:232) states that in 1967 the first NOW national conference adopted a Bill of Rights calling for

1. The adoption of an Equal Rights Amendment to the Constitution.
2. The enforcement of laws which were designed to eliminate discrimination by sex in employment.
3. Maternity leave rights in employment and in social security benefits.
4. Income tax deductions for child care expenses for working parents.
5. The establishment of day care centers.
6. Equal and nonsegregated education.
7. Equal opportunities for job training and allowances for women in poverty.
8. The right of women to control their reproductive lives.

As suggested by these goals, NOW has a wide orientation in terms of areas of interest affecting women, but with a focus on political tactics to achieve these goals. Using a traditional organizational format, other groups were also founded during the 1960s and 1970s which have more specialized interest area but with a similar focus on tactics. Thus, in addition to NOW, the moderate branch of the movement generated the Women's Equity Action League (WEAL), which seeks to enact legislation which is not as gender-specific, and the National Women's Political Caucus (NWPC), which promotes women as candidates for public office.

The second branch of the movement consisted of a more diverse array of women and was more radical in orientation. Many shunned the structure of organizations like NOW, believing that such a formal hierarchy could inhibit individual expression. This branch was made up of younger women and women who had been involved with the other social movements of the time, especially the civil rights movement. Unlike NOW, some groups excluded men from their ranks, others worked solely for reproductive rights, and many came together simply under the banner of sisterhood for the purpose of consciousness-raising. Freeman (1984:545) notes that the younger branch experimented with the "rap group" as a vehicle to bring women together for structured interaction in such a manner that they begin to recognize how their own attitudes as well as various social structures have limited their opportunities as women. Attitude change at one level can help serve broader social change later. Whatever the issue which spawned such groups, solidarity with other women was a critical by-product.

The two branches of the movement which developed in the 1960s are still evident today, although there is some overlap in membership. The belief in passage of the Equal Rights Amendment (ERA) is what all factions can agree on, and they have worked for this effort to varying degrees with a variety of approaches. The political impact of ERA will be discussed in the last chapter. ERA's importance in this context has to do with keeping the movement alive and its serving as a unifying force. As judged by the failure to gain the necessary two-thirds of the states for ratification before the legal deadline expired, the movement has not been successful. But considering that NOW was able to lobby to extend the 1979 deadline by three years, an unprecedented move by Congress, it was obvious that the movement was still a viable force in the 1980s. Until its ratification, ERA will continue to be a focus of activity for the movement. After ratification, concern will likely shift to issues relating to its enforcement.

Other activities remain on the agenda for the woman's movement, many which are international in scope. On both the national and global levels, this particular social movement has impacted on millions of women and men worldwide. The United Nations (UN) declared 1975 as International Women's Year and 1976-1985 as the "UN Decade for Women" with member nations working on resolutions for equalizing the status of women. Official conferences were held in Mexico City in 1975, Copenhagen, Denmark, in 1980 and Nairobi, Kenya, in 1985 to assess the progress of the resolutions. Alongside each official conference ran a parallel one made up of hundreds of nongovernmental organizations which brought women from all over the world and all walks of life together.

Both sets of conferences at all these sites were marked by political, religious, and economic factionalism which, unfortunately, became media highlights. As with national conferences, a concerted effort by conservative groups to discredit and disrupt the international conferences also occurred. This was to be expected more at the official level, but many women who attended the nongovernmental sessions in Copenhagen were discouraged by the amount of friction which appeared to separate rather than unify them as women. By Nairobi, however, much of this had been overcome and women left the conference with a sense of sisterhood and a better understanding of the unique problems faced by women around the globe, specifically in developing countries.

Even with the inevitable backlash with which any movement for social change must contend, the woman's movement has at the very least been successful in sending its message throughout the world. This message suggests that issues related to woman's inferior status will be ignored no longer and will be addressed through campaigns at all levels to end this inequity.

5

Cross-Cultural Perspectives

In its Charter of 1945, the United Nations announced its commitment to the equality of women and men. The year 1975 was declared as International Women's Year and as mentioned in the last chapter, the years 1976 to 1985 were recognized by the United Nations General Assembly as the United Nations Decade for Women. An international effort was put forward to focus on half of the world's population who "perform two thirds of the world's work, receive one-tenth of its income and own less than one one-hundredth of its property" (United Nations, 1985:3). The World Conference on Women held in Nairobi in July, 1985, provided much data from both governmental and private sources concerning the state of the world's women.

Given the inequality that exists in the world concerning the position of women relative to that of men, the findings are remarkable. These include the following (United Nations, 1985:3).

1. Women do almost all the domestic work. This means that when combined with additional work outside the home, they work a double day.
2. Women grow half the food of the world but own hardly any land.
3. Women make up one-third of the world's official labor force but are concentrated in the lowest-paid occupations. They are also more vulnerable to unemployment.
4. Women earn less than three-quarters of the wage that men earn for doing similar work.
5. The average number of children women want has dropped from six to four in just one generation.

6. Ninety percent of all countries have organizations which promote the advancement of women but women are still dramatically underrepresented in the decision-making bodies of their countries.

Overall, the underlying cause of the inequality of women is that their primary roles are domestic in nature, those of mother and wife, and although these roles are vital to the well-being of the society, they are undervalued and unpaid. Yet such roles consume half of the time and energy of women (United Nations, 1985:3).

This chapter will overview certain aspects of the position of women in selected countries, primarily in the developing world. Even with such a limited focus, the task is almost insurmountable. It is written with the understanding that generalizations are necessary and a myriad of exceptions exist. However, one objective is to demonstrate that as a whole, women find themselves in similar positions the world over, regardless of their unique cultures and historical backgrounds. Yet how they confront, acknowledge or deal with issues relating to inequality is culturally defined.

SOVIET UNION

"Women and men have equal rights," states the Soviet constitution. One of the first mandates of the Lenin regime in 1917-1918 was to upgrade women's position in the new society by abolishing all forms of discrimination against women which were inherent in tsarist Russia. This meant that women were to have full equality in educational and employment opportunities, family and property rights, and in competition for administrative offices (Moses, 1986:388). Women make up almost half of the deputies in state legislatures, approximately 25% of delegates to national party congresses and are well represented in the trade unions (Moses, 1986:389).

As impressive as these numbers are, women are at the lower levels of government, with the most influential political positions still almost exclusively male. The powerful Politburo has no women, nor does the secretariat of the Communist Party. Browning (1985:207) notes that the Central Committee of the party has less than 4% women and that this number has not increased since the founding of the USSR. These critical governing bodies are essentially devoid of women. The old adage of "the higher the position, the fewer the women" readily applies to the equality-conscious Soviet Union.

Soviet socialism has maintained a patriarchal attitude for a number of reasons. According to surveys, women are not as interested in politics (White, 1979) and must also bear the consequences of more time lost in accumulating political experience due to domestic responsibilities (Mandel, 1975). But a more important reason is suggested by Browning (1985:209), who states that many Soviet women assume that women do not need to be in positions of power to achieve equality and are not overtly bothered by their lack of representation. If men support equality anyway, then why is it necessary for women to hold such positions? Ironically, paternalism is viewed as a mode for the achievement of equality between the sexes. Soviet women who argue from this perspective have failed to recognize that the male leadership appears to be in no hurry to "surrender their political monopoly, either as elites or as males" (Browning, 1985:233).

In terms of paid labor, the USSR has the largest percentage of women in the labor force than any other industrial society. When compared with Western samples, Soviet women have much higher representation in law, medicine and engineering as well as in the skilled trades, such as metalworking and construction (Mamonova, 1984:3). Yet women are overrepresented in low-paying and menial jobs and underrepresented in managerial jobs in spite of negligible differences between the sexes in educational level (Peers, 1985:121). Though women have achieved a great deal of financial independence through the rigidly adhered to doctrine of equal pay for equal work, they make less money than men, even in the professions, and even if more highly qualified than men (Mamonova, 1984:3; Peers, 1985:122).

A unique combination of ideological factors explains this. Family barriers which impose a double burden on women, hindering career advancement, remain formidable. As in the West, men have not taken on an equal share of domestic duties when their wives, sisters, and mothers are also in the paid labor force. Women who manage to resolve the family issues, find they are denied access to certain jobs. The Soviet Union has put much effort into the expansion of its heavy industry. In the West, white collar jobs generally command greater salaries than manual work. In the Soviet Union, however, white collar jobs, despite a greater amount of training and expertise, are regarded as less productive for industrial growth (Peers, 1985:122). For example, although women make up most of the physicians in the USSR, their average salary is two-thirds of what male welders make (Moses, 1986:399). Also, although women may be found in such professional jobs, they are more likely than men to be employed in lower paying clerical, service, or menial jobs rather than in higher paying heavy industry.

Certain jobs seen as too heavy or too dangerous, such as underground mining, legally exclude women. In addition, there are restrictions put on women in terms of maximum loads to be lifted or carried, number of hours to be worked, and night time jobs. It is believed that women need to be protected from the burdens which a job may impose. Yet the fact that women cannot exercise their own choices related to these jobs is ignored. Contrary to constitutional wording, women and men do not have equal rights in this regard.

In addition, new protective legislation has been introduced to further curtail not only the kinds of jobs in which women may engage but also how long they must stay away from their jobs during pregnancy and after the birth of a child. Mamonova (1984) states that concern over women's reproductive role made legislation so stringent that women are now prohibited from working as carpenters, bus and truck drivers, and subway train operators. By denying all women access to certain job categories, gender stratification and segregation is perpetuated and economic equality between men and women is further diminished.

The dilemma faced by the Soviet Union is that there is alarm over a falling birth rate and the increased preference for smaller families. Yet women are vitally needed as workers and the economy could not withstand a mass exodus of them from the ranks of the paid labor force. Thus, measures are implemented which ostensibly are designed to encourage the health and well-being of the mother and her child while at the same time maintaining a high level of national productivity.

This is a mixed blessing for women. The supportive measures to encourage women to have children include an extensive network of day care facilities (though still in short supply), preferential opportunities for housing, inclusive prenatal and pediatric health care, liberal pregnancy leaves, and extra paid vacation time. The problem is that career goals inevitably suffer when women are absent from the work force for an extended time and take on full time domestic and child-rearing roles. Shirazi (1985:399), too, states that the Soviet Union has done little to alter the idea that housework and child care are women's work and that "the state's commitment to social equality has not altered women's status in many Soviet households."

Despite the fact that women will take on all the domestic responsibilities, the prospect of marriage and children is a high priority and may even be increasing, especially among rural women. Allott (1985) mentions that rural women are more preoccupied with romance and appear to accept the far from egalitarian arrangement that will likely emerge after marriage. Shirazi's (1985) interviews with Azerbaijanian women of Iranian descent suggest the same trend. They may be professionals or clerks, but their main concern is to be married and raise a family. The high divorce rate in urban areas of the USSR may attest to the role of romance in mate selection. This pattern will probably be evident in rural areas as well.

The picture of Soviet women which emerges is similar to what we have already seen for Western women in general, including American women. The major difference is that the Western political climate allows for more strident opposition to what exists and for organizations to be formed which are specifically aimed at change. This does not mean that feminism in the Soviet Union has died or discontent is buried. There has been a cautious opening of official channels to deal with women's issues. The last two decades have witnessed an expansion of opportunities for journalists, trade unions, and state organizations to debate areas of concern for women and from a woman's viewpoint (Holt, 1985:239). Unofficial channels also exist. The government has been unsuccessful in campaigns to halt the underground publications of dissident feminist writers who seek to expose the problems faced by women in the Soviet Union.

In an atmosphere of greater openness, the USSR is beginning to publicly acknowledge that there are specific issues which women face which keep them at a subordinate level when compared to men. With worldwide expressions of feminist concerns and the attention of the United Nations Decade for Women, there has been more evidence of Soviet women organizing *as women* to deal with these issues. Moses (1986:401) contends that as a group, Soviet women have had the ability to at least influence the direction of public policy discussions to the extent that political leaders, at a minimum, are anticipating how women will respond to their decisions. The USSR is also aware that without the involvement of female party leaders, policies have been both unrealistic and ineffective (Moses,

1986:408). This involvement may be indirect and influence may be severely curtailed in an authoritarian Communist regime, but indications are that women will increasingly have their voices heard.

CHINA

Even before the revolution which elevated Mao Tse Tung as head of the new People's Republic of China, the Chinese Communist Party (CCP) had recognized that women were valuable allies in building socialism. In order for the peasant revolution to maintain its momentum or hold ground during the construction of a new regime, it was believed that women's issues must be given a priority. Since women were inextricably bound to an ancient, oppressive, and seemingly immutable family structure, this was the area that was given the most priority. However, as Johnson (1986:440) points out, the CCP's promotion of women's rights and family reform continues to be tied to other more immediate priorities, such as economic development.

Official government policies aimed at increasing the labor force participation have proceeded with the argument that if women gain in the economic sphere, they will also gain in the family. As outlined in Chapter 1, whereas Karl Marx articulated the structure of classical social conflict theory, it was Frederich Engels who carried this approach specifically to the family. For Engels, the family is the basic source of women's oppression. As wives, mothers, and daughters, women take on the proletariat role, as compared to the bourgeoisie role assumed by men. The patriarchal family is a microcosm of a larger, oppressive capitalistic society. By this reasoning, therefore, once women expand their roles outside the family to become an economically productive part of the new socialist system, their servility to men will cease. This became popularized as a "liberation through labor" ideal (Johnson, 1986). Family reform would inevitably follow. Let us review the record of Chinese family reform since the revolution.

The traditional Chinese family was based on Confucian principles which gave complete authority to males, and then to the oldest males. The family was patriarchal, patrilineal and patrilocal (Baker, 1979). A woman's marriage was arranged, she could not normally inherit property, would move into her husband's household at marriage, and had to survive under the unquestioned authority of her husband, his father, and his grandfather, as well as other assorted male relatives. Her mother-in-law also exercised control. The bride would assume the lowliest position within her new family. She could be beaten for disobedience or sold if she tried to run away (Baker, 1979).

Running at all was impossible for those women who endured the technique of footbinding, which could reduce a foot to as small as three inches. Dating to the early part of the twelfth century, this crippling procedure was more likely to be practiced on women from the upper classes who did not have to work in heavy manual labor or in the fields. Besides becoming a status symbol and eventually being elevated to a prerequisite for marriage among the upper classes, footbinding ensured that women remained passive and under the control of men (Dworkin, 1974; Drucker, 1984). Indeed, for the family, and hence Confucian society, to function smoothly, the subordination of women was required and practices like footbinding helped ensure this.

The only real option for women to gain any semblance of prestige was to produce sons. Not only was inheritance and the family name jeopardized if there were no male heirs, the ancient practice of ancestor worship could not continue. People could exist only by virtue of ancestors, and would then continue to live on in the spirit world at their own deaths. Ancestors were powerful and could bless or curse a family; so offerings and prayers had to be bestowed frequently. A woman could gain ancestral status only through her husband and sons. Without male descendents she could have no afterlife to speak of (Baker, 1979). Dismal indeed were the prospects of a wife who conceived no male children or who remained unmarried or a childless widow. With so many obstacles to confront and overcome, it is understandable why suicide was seen as an acceptable solution to many peasant and gentry women (Wolf, 1975). It was better to die with honor than to bring disgrace to a husband's family for not bearing sons.

The Marriage Law of 1950 abolished many of the practices which had oppressed women in the traditional Chinese family. The fundamental principle on which the new law was based was free-choice marriage. It was expected that this would become the foundation for a new family structure which would release women from their abysmal existence in the feudal marriage (Croll, 1983:75). Not only did both sexes gain equal rights to divorce, but marriages had to be monogamous; bigamy and other forms of plural marriage, as well as concubinage, were abolished. Also eliminated were child betrothal, bride prices, and any restrictions placed on the remarriage of widows.

In 1980 another Marriage Law was passed which did not make substantial changes but merely updated some of the details of the older law. For example, Croll (1983:76) states that the modern version makes no reference to concubines or child brides since they were no longer viewed as problems in contemporary China. The 1980 law specifically mentions the rights of both sexes, some important ones being summarized by Charlton (1984:1899).

> Article 3. Marriage upon arbitrary decision by any third party . . . [is] prohibited.
> Article 9. Husband and wife enjoy equal status at home.
> Article 11. Both husband and wife have the freedom to engage in production, to work, to study, and to participate in social activities; neither party is allowed to restrain or interfere with the other.

By abolishing many of the blatant abuses existing in the feudal Chinese family, the two marriage laws have been beneficial to women, especially for urban women. But these successes must be tempered with the reality faced by rural women as well as other official policies which have undermined equality for women in China.

China is still a rural country with the vast majority of its population existing in villages oriented to a life based on farming and strong family ties. Despite the massive campaigns to create marriages and families based on egalitarian principles, this ideal is far from the reality. Kin customs pervade and parents of potential partners still wield much authority in arranging marriages. A patrilocal extended family structure continues to put the new bride at a disadvantage. Since daughters will marry and move to the home of their husbands, often in another village, the preference for sons continues. Parents know that daughters are only temporary commodities.

Women are valued for their domestic work and are not as likely as men to work outside the home for pay. Household money is collectively maintained; so even if women are bringing in other sources of income, it goes to the household which is under the power of the men. The male head of household usually collects all monies from family members. In all, the strength of the traditional family has continued to make women into a dependent class (Parish and Whyte, 1978; Croll, 1981). This is reinforced by evidence suggesting that when women, especially rural women, do work outside the home, they are in gender differentiated jobs and are paid less than men (Galston, 1975).

The extent of ancient traditions which put a premium on sons and devalue daughters has recently taken a more ominous turn. Official government policy has focused on upgrading the status of women. Simultaneously, they have introduced a stringent campaign to reduce population growth in a country of over a billion people already. These two goals have disastrously collided with one another. In 1978, a new family program was initiated which demanded that families should have no more than one child. Whereas China has had other programs to curb its rate of population growth, the one-child policy is unique in that enforcement has been much more uniform and even severe for noncompliance. Massive public campaigns have been conducted to make prospective parents aware of the incentives or penalties related to the policy. Croll (1983:89) explains that the program of incentives has become standardized throughout most of China so that the one-child couple can receive annually a cash health or welfare subsidy. Other benefits include free medical care for the child and priority admission to schools. For subsequent children, an "excess child levy" is imposed on the income of couples as compensation for the extra burden placed on the state in caring for them. According to Croll (1983:90), what makes these sanctions more punitive is that rewards for the single child must be returned with the birth of the second.

The policy has had more of an effect on urban than rural families. Although there has been a decline in the birth rate in rural areas, rural families are units of production as well as consumption and there is the continual necessity for agricultural laborers. Peasant communities recognize that they have power in this regard and continue to welcome two or three children per couple. Their attitude is expressed in the idea that "we have taken responsibility for the land [and so] there is no need for you [the state] to bother about our childbirth (quoted in Croll, 1983:97). In addition, enforcement of the new one-child law is much weaker in rural areas. And since the farm family has the ability to produce food, if sanctions are applied, they are not nearly as detrimental when compared to the smaller urban family which exists as a less powerful unit of production.

Most important, the one-child policy has reinforced the preference for sons in all areas. Strong vestiges of ancestor worship remain with many still believing that there can be no descendents without a son (Duley, 1986:269). With one child as the option, that child had better be a male. Female infanticide has been practiced in China for centuries, but it diminished considerably in the decades after the Chinese revolution in 1949. Charlton (1984:119) reports that despite the egalitarian ideology and the improvement in health care, incidents of female infanticide began to increase again in the 1980s. The 1980 Marriage Law explicitly condemns infanticide and the Central Committee of the Communist party has maintained that they will vigorously prosecute the "criminal acts of killing infant girls and mistreating mothers" (Charlton, 1984:119). This policy notwithstanding, female infanticide appears to be on the rise.

As Charlton (1984:119) maintains, female infanticide is a "particularly painful policy" because of the ingrained cultural preference for sons and "it is also a case of unintended effects of public policy, contradictory policies and the limits of government coercion." In a culture which prides itself on large families, the one-child program is likely to be the most unpopular policy in contemporary China. According to Croll (1983:91), the government faces the difficult task of seeking the cooperation of a reluctant populace in implementing the policy. At this point, it appears that implementation suggests dire consequences for families in general and females in particular.

INDIA

As with other developing nations, India is confronting challenges which threaten its economic, hence its political stability. By the turn of the century India's population is expected to reach the one billion mark. After China, it is the world's second largest nation. Considering the staggering problems related to population growth, land and food shortage, unemployment, and a growing disparity between poverty and wealth, India must look to all segments of its very heterogeneous society for solutions. Opportunities for women are perhaps the major factor in the solution of many of these problems. Yet, as noted by Duley (1986:128), economic planners have barely acknowledged this reality.

India is similar to Western nations in that its history reflects apparent inconsistencies when considering the role of women. Basham (1959) and Sharma (1983) indicate that goddess images, important female religious occupations, and critical economic roles for women in the pre-Vedic and Vedic eras (2500-300 B.C.) demonstrate that they had some degree of prestige and were not completely reduced to chattels. With the ascendance of Hinduism and the beginnings of technology, it appears that this kind of prestige was lost. As discussed in Chapter 11, Indian women share a parallel religious history with women of the West. Women's freedom and status becomes severely compromised when religion gains an institutional foothold. Patriarchy and religion have continued to go hand in hand.

By A.D. 200, India had gone through a period of decentralization of the authority of the various Indian states. High caste Brahmin scholars were powerful enough to interpret the ancient *Smitris* (laws). Duley (1986:136) suggests that by this time the "Laws of Manu" enveloped India and demonstrated the extent to which the position of women had deteriorated. Manu made a woman completely dependent on a man (husband, father, or son) and decreed women were naturally seducers of men. Manu may have been responsible for the practice of *purdah*, or the seclusion of women (Sharma, 1980). (Purdah, incidentally, operates in India under both Islam and Hinduism. Its form may vary, but under both systems it functions to physically and socially separate the sexes, thus confining them to nonoverlapping realms.) Manu also forbade widow remarriage and, in fact, reduced a widow's status to such a lowly extreme that *suttee*, or widow burning, gradually took hold. Faced with a life of derision, and abandonment, who can say if these widows voluntarily chose the fate of becoming a *suttee*?

By the nineteenth century, ideas concerning the status of women began to emerge in India and the roots of a reform movement took shape. The more blatant aspects of the inhumane treatment of women were attacked, such as child marriage, lack of property rights, purdah and the dismal condition of widows who were forbidden to remarry. D'Souza and Natarajan (1986:361) indicate that reformers believed that such customs were responsible for the condition of women and that through education, women would make better wives and mothers. Though raising the status of some women, reformers still accepted the notion that a woman's life was within her family. And the vast majority of rural and lower caste women remain untouched by the reforms.

The first serious questioning of women's roles came with Mahatma Gandhi, who felt that women were not only essential to India's quest for independence, but also that social justice demanded their equality. Given the nationalist sentiment and the charisma of Gandhi, women of all castes and regions flocked to the independence movement, assuming leadership roles and participating in all manners of political dissent. Gandhi's vision was shared by Jawaharlal Nehru, who wanted men and women to have equal places in society. As the first prime minister of India, and against much opposition, he pushed legislation which gave women the rights of inheritance and divorce, as well as the right to vote (D'Souza and Natarajan, 1986:363).

The Nehru factor in Indian politics has been played out politically since independence. Nehru's daughter, Indira Gandhi, succeeded to the post of prime minister in 1966 because she was a member of the Nehru dynasty and because her party believed they could control her. Her skill and strength proved them wrong. She was politically astute, using her gender as an asset rather than a liability. She identified herself as a member of the oppressed, but also appealed to those looking for a mother-goddess figure, so imbued in the Hindu tradition (Omvedt, 1980 cited in D'Souza and Natarajan, 1986:373). Until her assassination, Indira Gandhi ruled with an authoritarian hand for 16 years.

Though Indira Gandhi certainly served as a symbol for women who aspired to other than traditional roles, it must be said that her own commitment to elevating the position of women in India is far from realized. A very few educated women exist among millions who are illiterate. And when compared to the masses of unskilled female laborers in India, most of whom work in agriculture, professional women comprise only a tiny minority. Though there has been an expansion of female employment in general, this has not offset the decrease in the employment of unskilled women. Duley (1986:211) states that throughout this century there has been a steady decline in the overall employment of women. Today the bulk of women workers are found in the "unorganized sector," most as landless agricultural laborers, street vendors, day workers and those who are employed in village and cottage industries (Duley, 1986:211).

In principle it would seem that as a nation begins to modernize and development extends into rural areas, the population as a whole would benefit. In the case of India, however, the position of women has actually deteriorated. This is clearly the case when considering the rate of male to female population growth. In assessing the overall impact of development and the legal, social and economic programs designed to promote women's equality, the 1974 report of the Committee on the Status of Women in India (CSWI), presented some jolting data. The CWSI showed that despite modernization, higher mortality and lower life expectancy rates for women in many areas of the country not only persist but have widened in the last century (Charlton, 1984; D'Souza and Natarajan, 1986). As documented in Chapter 3, these data are highly unusual when considering that in almost every country in the world, the sex ratio indicates a marginally higher proportion of women.

Charlton (1984:34-35) summarizes possible explanations given by Indian demographers for the declining sex ratio.

1. Females are under-enumerated in the census.
2. Mortality rates are higher for females than males.
3. Sons are preferred, and female infants are neglected.
4. Frequent and excessive childbearing which severely compromises the health of women.
5. A higher incidence of certain diseases for women.

Though the data do not indicate specifically which factors are the most important, taken together Charlton (1984:35) believes that there is at least an inequitable involvement of women in Indian society coupled with the fact that females do not have access to the same facilities enjoyed by males. D'Souza and Natarajan (1986:365) argue that "the preference for sons is linked to the often fatal neglect of daughters." When a daughter is ill, medical attention is more likely to be delayed. And since males are seen as a reservoir of economic support for the family, they tend to receive more nurturing and attention by the parents, as well as preferential treatment.

Perhaps even more startling is that neglect of daughters is not connected to lower caste families. Miller (1981) documents the extensive nature of female child neglect in northwest India and demonstrates that it occurs more in upper than lower castes. The less attention girls receive is tied to the marginal economic position of women in the rural upper castes, and the burdens even relatively well-off families must face with providing dowries for their daughters at marriage. Dowry traditions exist throughout India, but in the southern regions what works against the male preference somewhat is the higher demand for female agricultural labor. In contrast to other parts of rural India in particular, the sex ratio is more equitable in the south (Charlton, 1984:36).

The inescapable conclusion is that the inferior status of females in India is intimately tied to the preference for males. Most disheartening is the fact that development has been as much a burden as a boon for women. Charlton (1984:36) presents a pessimistic view about the development by suggesting that when public services are available and provided in the course of development efforts, "they may either reinforce the traditional male biases or diminish the status that women enjoyed in traditional society." This assumes, of course, that the rigidity of traditional society offered at least a modicum of prestige for women.

There are some signs that the situation of women in India will be given more serious attention and that the government is willing to make greater strides in putting democratic principles into practice. In the area of health, programs are underway which are designed to combine traditional and modern medicine in a way that is acceptable to the rural population. Village midwives are being trained in techniques of delivery suitable for rural conditions and are also providing prenatal care. Rural women who have relied almost exclusively on midwives should benefit in this regard. Since women are responsible for the health care of the children, any program which can offer them more acceptable solutions in dealing with the diseases which rampage a family will be embraced. Although suspicious of intrusions into their traditional ways of thinking about health, village women are no longer summarily rejecting allopathic, or "modern" medicine (Lindsey, 1982, 1983). When programs take into account traditional beliefs and cultural practices, women in particular will benefit. The long term results should show up in reduced infant and maternal mortality rates.

The Indian Council of Social Science Research has suggested that when compared to the total female population, only a small number of urban, middle class women have actually realized the advantages of development. To extend these efforts to the rural and poor population of women, priorities in employment, health and education are essential. A five year plan which specifically addressed the issues of excessive female mortality and low literacy rates of women was recently adopted. Through their efforts on social and welfare measures, women's organizations are increasingly being drawn into the political process, with political parties beginning to recognize the importance of the woman's vote (D'Souza and Natarajan, 1986:376-77). A concerted government effort is necessary to even begin to approach Mahatma Gandhi's vision of an egalitarian society.

JAPAN

During the Second World War, Japanese and American women had much in common in that both groups assumed major responsibility for the functioning of the domestic economy, yet were denied leadership positions in the government and industries who relied upon their services. After Japan's surrender in 1945, occupation forces were determined to set down a policy which would ensure that a democratic system would emerge which would be compatible with a Japanese cultural climate. As Pharr (1977) suggests, the Occupation introduced an experiment in guided social change which had lasting effects. It can be argued that the single largest beneficiary of this experiment was the Japanese woman.

Occupation policy was also dictated by the provisions of the Potsdam Declaration, July 26, 1945, which mandated that democratic tendencies among the Japanese people be strengthened and that "freedom of speech, of religion, and of thought as well as respect for the fundamental human rights be ensured" (Pharr, 1977:231). With the enactment of the new Showa Constitution on May 3, 1947, five articles provided for rights of women. Included here are the assurances of equality under the law with no discrimination because of race, creed, sex, social status, or family origin; universal adult suffrage; equal education based on ability (which meant that women would be admitted to national universities); permitting women to run for public office; and marriage based on the mutual consent of both sexes (Sugisaki, 1986:110).

Although legal guarantees are only valid through stringent enforcement, Japanese women in 1947, in essence, had greater rights than American women, since their new constitution explicitly provided for equality of the sexes. A similar statement of equality is embodied in the Equal Rights Amendment to the United States Constitution, but this has yet to be passed.

The legal assurances of equality had their greatest impact on two crucial areas, work outside the home and marriage and family life. The courts have ruled, for example, that companies cannot discharge women for reasons not applying to men, such as marriage, childbirth, or a set age at retirement (Pharr, 1977:233). Japanese women are entering the work force in increasing numbers, especially married women and women returning to jobs after an absence during childbearing and child rearing. The Japanese economy is prosperous enough to show a decrease of women in the labor force who are in their 20s (Pharr, 1977:234). They are financially secure enough to exercise the choice of remaining at home while they have preschoolers.

This is not to suggest that discrimination against women in the labor force has been eliminated. Though women make up almost half of the Japanese work force, they are concentrated in lower level jobs and earn much less than the average male. Sugisaki (1986:122) considers it a paradox that Japanese working women continue to suffer both overt and hidden discrimination when their contributions make possible Japan's visibility as a world economic power. In explaining this she suggests that an ancient, rigid system of male supremacy cannot be rapidly changed and that men themselves remain unaware of their privileged position or its attendant discrimination. Women themselves may not recognize the true extent of discrimination and even if they do, they often subscribe to cultural principles dictating quiet, unassuming behavior for women.

Another paradox presents itself when considering the role of women in the Japanese family. Other postwar changes concerning women saw laws which no longer regarded women as incompetent, parental consent was no longer needed for marriage beyond a certain age, divorce could be obtained by mutual consent and in a divorce, property would now be divided between husband and wife (Sugisaki, 1986: 116). It would appear, therefore, that such laws were to augment a lowly status in the family. Herein lies the paradox. On the one hand Japanese women are depicted as relegated to domestic drudgery, stripped of power, and expected to be "demurely submissive, coquettishly feminine and hopelessly removed from the attainment of self-fulfillment" (Lebra, 1984:ix). But this stands in opposition to a strong tradition of decision making in the family to the extent that the Japanese housewife is viewed as being in full control of domestic life with almost unlimited autonomy (Lebra, 1984; Sugisaki, 1986).

Lebra's (1984) extensive study of Japanese women living in a prosperous city sheds light on this paradox. Her literature review finds that women are role-specialized in the domestic area, are socially and symbolically (among various forms) segregated by gender, and are inferior in terms of most measures, such as esteem, power, honor, privilege, and authority. Thus, women as a group are defined by the principles of domesticity, seclusion, and inferiority, although individual women can be placed at some point along a continuum for each element (Lebra, 1984:2). If inferiority is assigned to women in certain spheres, it is balanced somewhat by the powers of their domestic role.

Not only are mothers revered, almost idealized by their children, but husbands assume a child-like dependence on their wives. Lebra (1984:133-34) states that this may be characteristic of patriarchy but the wife then receives leverage to make her services indispensable. Lebra uses symbolic interaction language to describe how power is wielded by the wife. The husband who uses "onstage dominance" may be bought by the wife's "offstage manipulation." In fact, it is the husband who is domestically astute, does household chores and is indifferent to onstage dominance and who is *less* able to be manipulated in that "his domesticity deprives her of domestic matriarchy" (Lebra, 1984:134). Lebra contends that patriarchy and matriarchy are not mutually exclusive but can be reciprocal.

Nowhere is domestic matriarchy more in evidence than in how the household expenses are divided. While it is expected that the husband is the provider, in most instances, the wife maintains full control over the financial management of the household. Paradoxically, his authority is demonstrated when he hands over his paycheck to her. Consider the following scenario as described by Lebra (1984:134).

> He places his salary upon the kamidana (household god shelf) instead of dropping it into profane wifely hands; after a time the wife solemnly takes it. The wife, in turn gives the husband a portion of the salary ... as an allowance.... The husband who needs more allowance has either to beg his wife or to depend upon a secret saving of extra income.

A definite, culturally accepted financial division is upheld. Earning the money is his responsibility. Managing the money is hers.

When a married woman is also employed outside the home, she is expected to fully maintain her domestic functions. The principle of sphere segregation puts a greater burden on her when compared even to her American counterpart. There is no overlap between domestic and occupational roles. Lebra (1984:247) states that women must fulfill occupational demands regardless of losses in the domestic sphere, but that "the reverse is strictly forbidden." To make up for this, professional women, especially, employ substitute housewives or rely on their mothers who either live with or near them. Such an arrangement does not provide assurances of equality nor does it eradicate role overload. But it does allow some measure of professional or occupational success for women who refuse to give up the domestic sphere of wife and mother.

Who is the "average" Japanese woman? According to a survey by the prime minister's office, the portrait is of a person who values family life and will sacrifice for them; who is unwilling to divorce even in an unsatisfactory marriage; who believes she is discriminated against in both society as well as in the family; but who is also proud of her decision-making family role, especially in financial matters (Sugisaki, 1986:122). It is likely that as women achieve higher levels of education and social change continues, the principle of seclusion into separate domestic and occupational sphere will also be weakened. It is unlikely, however, that these women will disavow what they perceive as their basic domestic responsibilities.

Women in Japan have been vital in bringing their country to economic prominence in the world, in achieving a high standard of living and in amassing perhaps the best overall health record of any nation, particularly in terms of low infant mortality and high life expectancy rates. Legal reform has paved the way for challenges to the ancient patriarchal model in Japan. Rising expectations and the wish to improve one's lot in life will provide the basis for future reforms aimed at equalizing the positions of women and men.

LATIN AMERICA

The socialization of women and men in Latin America hinges on the concepts of *marianismo* and *machismo*, which are viewed as mutually exclusive beliefs which separate the sexes. Stevens (1973:91) defines machismo as a cult of virility which embraces an "exaggerated aggressiveness and intransigence in male-to-male inter-personal relationships and arrogance and sexual aggression in male-to-female relationships." For women, there is the ideology stemming from Catholicism with the view that the Virgin Mary is the perfect model which women must emulate. Marianismo is "the cult of feminine spiritual superiority which teaches that women are semidivine, morally superior and spiritually stronger than men" (Stevens, 1973:91). There is some indication that the men and women exhibited complementary roles and that women had important economic positions prior to the Spanish conquest, especially in Peru and Mexico (Burkett, 1978; Silverblatt, 1980). The conquistadores brought views of women stemming from Old World religious and feudal attitudes. Marianismo and machismo soon became entrenched in the New World.

In addition to religion and the survival of feudal attitudes, economic factors are also important in explaining the inferior position of women in Latin American cultures. Except for certain regions, most notably in Brazil and Argentina, Latin America remains underdeveloped after almost 500 years of European colonization and the establishment of independent republics in the nineteenth century. Nazzari (1986:376) mentions that underdevelopment can be approached through dependency theory which looks at the unequal relationships between Latin America and world markets. Dependency theory can be used to explain how processes of change have specifically affected women in Latin America. Unequal opportunities due to fluctuations in world markets negatively influence the country anyway, but the effects on women are disastrous.

This is especially true when the transformation from subsistence agriculture and household production to commercial agriculture occurs. Both psychologically and monetarily, women lose ground as a result. When women take nonagricultural jobs, their economic returns are very low. In expanding industrial centers, work is segmented by gender. Nash (1986:4) states that women work in low-paying, nonunion, dead-end jobs. Those women who produce items in their homes, such as handicrafts, have an economic advantage if they can cultivate their own markets for distribution of their goods. However, home production is always hampered by the continuous demands from domestic responsibilities. Although autonomy and the freedom to schedule the workday as she sees fit is an incentive for home production, a woman may face a typical workday of 15 hours.

The plight of the majority of Latin American women who are in poverty is contrasted sharply with upper and upper-middle class women who may be professionals or who are part of the elite leisure class. Career women are supported by their husbands, parents, and other bolsters which allow them to combine professional and family roles. Studies of women in Argentina and Columbia indicate that role flexibility is the key to their professional success (Cohen, 1973; Kinzer, 1973; Kinzer, 1977).

The irony here is that professional success is to a large extent dependent upon the hiring of domestic help. Domestics provide services which help to blunt the impact of a career on the family. Domestic servants in Latin America represent the majority of female wage-earners. There is considerable disagreement about whether working as a servant provides a channel for upward mobility or whether it allows for a more rigid stratification system based on class (Smith, 1973; Arizpe, 1977; Jelin, 1977; Rubbo and Taussig, 1977). It is thus difficult to determine the relative influence of class or gender in explaining the role and status of some Latin American women.

It would appear that the ideology of marianismo combined with jobs offering limited economic rewards reinforce norms suggesting that Latin American women are passive and dependent. Marianismo assumes that since women are relegated to the home, any influence they achieve is from this source. When venturing into other uncertain arenas, they risk loss of respect. But other studies are questioning such logic. Chaney (1979) and Jacquette (1980) argue that Latin American women have considerable political weight and that political participation must be measured in other than simply levels of voting. Political influence is exercised within informal settings and within accepted cultural norms which do not seriously challenge gender role differentiation. And when issues which are salient to women emerge, even voting levels indicate that there is a "gender gap" in Latin American politics (Jacquette, 1986:253). It is also likely that as women continue to make informal strides politically, the formal channels will eventually open more.

Women have been instrumental in human rights movements and, as in other parts of the world, have been mobilized effectively in revolutionary movements. However, an issue which has clouded women's political participation involves the increasing militarization of those societies where women have had a great deal of influence, such as Cuba, Nicaragua, and El Salvador. As Jacquette (1986:262) astutely points out, there are doubts raised "among feminist observers elsewhere in Latin America who associate feminist politics with resistance to military rule and to militarization itself."

Feminist scholars and political activists in Latin America also have yet to resolve the issue of whether class conflict is the critical issue which serves to perpetuate the lowly status of women. The question becomes whether feminist theory needs to focus attention on class or gender as the key factor. Jacquette states that Latin American feminists are now declaring both categories as valid and "that efforts to liberate women are consistent with and reinforce the class struggle." In sociological terms, this is congruent with a strong conflict theory orientation which suggests that patriarchy influences women to continue to uphold a system which perpetuates their inferior position. "And the fact that women are not seen (and do not see themselves) as 'productive' means they cannot be organized as workers" (Jacquette, 1986:246).

ISRAEL

Issues of equality between the sexes have been salient in Israel since its new beginnings as an independent nation. We are aware of impressive experiments which are designed to minimize traditional forms of gender stratification, such as in the military and on the kibbutz. The rise of Golda Meier to the highest political position in the fledgling state is another often-cited instance in how far women can progress. Legislatively, women in Israel have achieved what women in the United States continue to fight for, like maternity leave and equal opportunities with men in education and employment.

Yet despite impressive gains and the internalization of an egalitarian gender role ideology, feminists contend that gender equality in Israel is illusory (Brozan, 1986). Myths of gender equality abound and function to put the responsibility for the lesser achievement of women in Israel on the women themselves (Boneparth, 1986:125-126). In this manner, the system which informally serves to limit the choices of women remains intact. As Boneparth suggests, alongside the egalitarian ideal and all the improvements which favor increasing the status of women, "the overwhelming thrust of Israeli public policy is toward reinforcing women's traditional roles." Part of this stems from the fact that Israeli society is organized around the principle of the family as the dominant institution and the family as the cradle of Jewish heritage. As such, the Jewish family is tied to ancient religious traditions which are unquestionably patriarchal in nature. The family is what defines the woman's role. She may contribute to the social and economic life of the community, but it is her family life which takes precedence.

It may seem contradictory that a patriarchal family structure reinforced by seemingly immutable religious beliefs could give rise to an experiment in collectivization, the kibbutz, which literally calls for a radical departure from the traditional gender division of labor in the family. On the surface at least, the kibbutz represents an effort at eliminating distinctions between the work of men and the work of women, with men sharing in child care and women working in agriculture and construction. It also redefines the structure of the family. The kibbutz "family" is no longer extended or even nuclear, but collective in organization.

The kibbutz is oriented to children, with child rearing seen as a serious task which must not be left to haphazard arrangements. From infancy on, the child spends most time with his or her peers and lives in the children's house. On the Sabbath the children usually spend the day with their parents. Teachers and nurses do most of the socialization of the children. Although children do not live with, or for the most part are not raised by, their biological parents, the parents are still critical to their development. Children know who their parents are, identify with them as such and derive security, love and affection from them. Ideally, such an arrangement would free both parents from child care responsibilities which would in turn allow them to work for the betterment of the community as a whole, performing a variety of other critical functions. Again, based on the principle of gender equality, it is assumed that there is no substantial differentiation between the roles performed by women and men. These principles, however, have not been transformed into reality.

Even from the origins, the kibbutzim population has represented only a small group of Israeli society. But this group has been extremely influential. Stern (1979:100) notes that less than three and a half percent of the population lives on kibbutzim, but that their representation in the political, military, economic agricultural, and artistic life is ten times greater than their actual segment. From pioneering origins where economic survival was not assured, most kibbutzim have become middle class. The early kibbutzim were characterized by role-sharing and a minimization of gender differentiation. Women and men did each other's work, at least by the standards of other parts of the society. Today, however, this has changed considerably. Although the kibbutz "family" structure is still collectivized, women function almost exclusively as child care workers, nurses, teachers and kitchen workers. It is only when the child reaches high school that they will probably see male teachers. It is at this point when they begin to work directly in the economy of the kibbutz. The early ideal of equal sharing of work has been steadily assaulted, and is on the verge of elimination in many kibbutzim.

With the retreat from equality, sociobiologists claim that this is another instance where biology resists cultural definitions. From this perspective, women are almost destined to maternal or domestic roles, even if the structure of the family has changed (Tiger and Shepher, 1975). This is countered by other research which suggests that women of the kibbutz are dissatisfied with performing personal services to people who are not members of their family (cited in Stern, 1979:116). This may indicate that a restructuring of the collective principles may be in order rather than suggesting that a maternal "instinct" is involved. Also, once economic survival of the kibbutz is assured, women may be pressured to reassume child care roles in accordance with the norms, traditions, and religious precepts of the broader society.

While it is clear that the contemporary kibbutz is marked by gender division in work roles, especially related to child care, there are many who find such divisions unacceptable. It is not a call to return to the "pioneer" days, but rather a recognition that they must find ways to augment principles of equal opportunity and the development of full human potential on the kibbutz.

Beyond the kibbutz, when considering the position of women in Israeli society as a whole, Boneparth is not very encouraging. She states that family roles are still primary but they are changing and holding less significance, especially in relation to smaller family size and increased female labor force participation. But public policy has not significantly helped with the dual burdens women must face in carrying out domestic and paid employment roles. The policy-making process must be used to translate the needs of women into effective, enforced, accepted and acceptable legislation. Without this, Boneparth (1986:145-148) contends that traditionalism will prevail.

THE MUSLIM WORLD: FOCUS ON IRAN

To the Westerner, the Muslim world represents conflicting images and attitudes. On the one hand, the oil rich nations have created better living standards, and educational and job opportunities for their inhabitants. On the other hand, as Islamic nations, efforts at development occur within a unique socioreligious framework which Westerners view with both curiosity and suspicion. Nowhere do these conflicting images emerge more forcefully than when viewing women in Arab cultures.

Given the stereotypical attitudes surrounding Islam, it is surprising for many to find out that Islam first developed as both a new religion and as a movement toward social reform which was specifically aimed at challenging and ultimately changing the lowly status of women.[1] Minces comments that in pre-Islamic Arabia men had the right of unlimited polygamy, and a husband could end any one of his marriages as he saw fit. Women could be bought, sold or inherited. Their lowly position contributed to the common practice of female infanticide. With Islam

---

[1]When viewing the status of women during pre-Islamic times, caution must be exercised. The issue of how much freedom they had, especially related to sexual self-determination, has been hotly debated by historians. See Mernissi's (1987:66-85) account of sex and marriage before Islam.

came a specific legal status for women. A woman's dowry became her sole property, she could inherit and own property, she could become a guardian of minors, and could even enter into a business or trade. Polygamy was now restricted to four wives which, according to the Koran, had to be treated equally. Women were not prevented from participation in public life (Minces, 1982:15-16).

But the letter and the spirit of the law are different matters. Reforms are possible only in the context of a culture's willingness to undergo change and endure stressful transitions. This has simply not been the case in the Arab world. Pre-Islamic influences eventually prevailed in many Arab cultures and interpretations of the Koran have since become even more restrictive concerning women. Religious fundamentalists have provided Koranic interpretations which have sanctioned the inferior status of women.

Islamic legal reform has many advocates and interpretations can be provided which would provide Koranic evidence for upgrading the position of women (White, 1978; Pastner, 1980; Eposito, 1982). But reformist counterattacks are losing ground in the current era which is becoming known as the "Islamization" movement. What this means is that Islamic societies are pulling back to the "old ways" when modernization and development are seen as threatening to a more traditional way of life. The most extreme version of this movement is seen in Iran, but elements can be found in most Arab cultures as well as other Islamic societies, such as Pakistan (Lindsey, 1988a). Although Iran is not an Arab culture, it shares a strong Islamic orientation with its Arab neighbors. Indeed, it can be said that Islamic fundamentalism has reached its height in this non-Arab society. Countermodernization is selective, with certain ideas and technologies being accepted while others are rejected (J indsey, 1984). When a countermodernization movement occurs, women are likely to be its victims rather than its beneficiaries.

The case of Iran provides the best example of how countermodernization can serve to restrict women. What is startling about the overthrow of the Shah of Iran in 1979 and the establishment of the Islamic regime under the Ayatollah Khomeini is that women were a major force in propelling the Ayatollah to power. As sentiment against the oppression and exploitation of the Shah grew, women also became more politically active. Women took to the streets in anti-Shah demonstrations in mass numbers. At a time when the veil was becoming a remnant of the past, women actually embraced it as a symbol of solidarity against the Shah. The images of veiled women protesting in mass demonstrations shocked many. It seemed to contradict the liberal view of women which was supposedly a hallmark of the Shah's regime.

Actually, the veil served several purposes. It prevented the easy identification of the protesters which could make them targets of the secret police (the dreaded Savak) and it was a gesture against what many felt to be the excessive Westernization of Iran (Sanasarian, 1982:116). It may be that the veil was seen by women as a symbol of solidarity which was to be discarded or worn at will after the fall of the Shah. Tabari (1982:6) suggests that many women believed that under the new leadership, the sacrifices and militancy they showed would be rewarded and that the religious leaders would concede that rights for women should be extended. These would include greater opportunities for education and employment, as well as concessions granting them more self-determination in their domestic roles.

Khomeini's own position during the anti-Shah movement increased women's support of him. Though remaining rather indefinite about the role of women, the following excerpts from a 1978 interview appearing in *Le Monde* show his shrewdness in rallying the support of women to his cause.

> As for women, Islam has never been against their freedom. It is, to the contrary, opposed to the idea of women-as-object and it gives her back her dignity. *A woman is a man's equal*: she and he are free to choose their lives and their occupations. . . . But the Shah's regime . . . has destroyed the freedom of women as well as men.
>
> (Cited in Sanasarian, 1982:117, italics mine)

The new republic would not oppress women, according to Khomeini, and with such words, women flocked to his movement. Less than a month after the ousting of the Shah, illusions of equality were shattered. Since then, the new regime has systematically undermined the freedom of women. No longer was the veil a symbol of militant solidarity. In the eyes of many, it has become a symbol of oppression.

The Khomeini regime has been intent on "restoring" women to their primary role, that of domestic responsibility (Nashat, 1983). Both women and men were compelled by religious righteousness to work in overthrowing the Shah. Once this succeeded, her religious duty demanded that she concentrate on domestic roles, and as a result, women have been literally pushed out of public life and into the home (Nashat, 1983). It is likely that many women would have embraced domestic roles anyway, but with the new regime, options in other realms became severely circumscribed. The last decade has witnessed a continual eroding of women's freedoms. Women are now separated from most public life. The walls that surround them are many, the walls of their homes, the walls of illiteracy, and the walls of the veil.

This is not to say that attempts at reform have been silenced completely. But even reformists must work within definitions of an "Islamic identity" accepted by the regime. Sanasarian suggests that both reformist and fundamentalist Islamic women appear to accept the following ideological components of this identity:

1. Women are equal to but dissimilar from men.
2. Western values are a corruptive menace and to be avoided by women.

Reformists also add the idea that complementarity does not mean superiority or inferiority, but it does imply separate but equal (Sanasarian, 1986:214-215). Working from such interpretations, reform has not made great strides. As Sanasarian (1986:220) predicts, there is no chance for any genuine pro-women's movement under the present regime. However, there are signs that feminism is active among the Iranian exiles and that they may ultimately help influence at least a modicum of rebirth of feminist ideology within the country.

Iran is at one end of a continuum as far as women in the Muslim world. Other Muslim countries must be considered in light of their own unique traditions, beliefs, and interpretations of Islam regarding women. Mernissi (1987) contends that there are no real effective models for women's liberation which can appeal to Muslim women. They are either too Western or too pre-Islamic. Islamic societies are based on fairly rigid definitions of family which serve as the focus for societal organization. Tampering with these definitions brings fear that social chaos will result. This means that the traditional male-female and master-slave relationship existing in Islamic families which exclude love as a male weakness are accepted (Mernissi, 1987:174).

On the other hand, Mernissi further tells us, the Muslim view is also of "the female as a potent, aggressive individual whose power can, if not tamed and curbed, corrode the social order." It is this view which may serve to empower women and enable them to work for goals which go beyond equality with men. Some Muslim women are already rejecting what men have, in that they believe it is simply not worth getting. Mernissi (1987:175-176) is optimistic in her view that Muslim, especially Arab, countries are "condemned to promote change" no matter how much they claim to uphold the past in their quest for modernitization. She speculates that when women's liberation in Arab countries occurs, it will be quicker and more radical than in the West.

The extent of women's liberation in the Muslim world is debatable and must be approached according to the political and social structure within each society. However, these societies are linked in their views of women by certain cultural practices. While the veil may be a symbol of oppression from a feminist viewpoint, other customs suggest an even more frightening reality. It is the practice of female sexual mutilation which has stirred so much criticism among feminists the world over. Though predating Islam, this practice is still found in parts of the Middle East, though it is most pervasive in North Africa and sub-Saharan Africa. It is estimated that over 74 million mutilated women exist in these countries, and that these numbers would be increased if areas where it is known to be practiced made documentation available (Hosken, 1980:20).

According to Hosken (1980: p. 14) female circumcision is the popular but medically incorrect term for a variety of mutilating genital operations to which girls are subjected in certain countries. They are not done as a counterpart to male circumcision so to call them "female circumcision" is a misnomer. There are three types of operations which young girls can undergo and which vary according to region and country. There is the partial cliteridectomy, sometimes referred to as the Sunna circumcision, where excision of the clitoral hood is done. Practiced mainly in Egypt, a full clitoridectomy occurs when the entire clitoris is removed, usually along with labia minora (small lips) and sometimes the lips themselves. Infibulation is the third type, and is notably practiced in the Sudan, Somalia, and parts of Ethiopia. After the clitoris is removed, and excision of both the labia minora and the inner walls of the labia majora occurs, the two sides of the vulva are partially sliced off or scraped raw and then sewn together with catgut. A small opening is left for the release of urine and menstrual blood (Hosken, 1980; Sanderson, 1981; Minces, 1982). These operations are extensively performed without anesthetics and in unsanitary conditions.

The effects of these mutilations are many, ranging from psychological trauma, to hemorrhage, septicemia (blood poisoning), pain during intercourse, lack of sexual pleasure, and death from infections or complications during childbirth. The practice continues because it ensures female monogamy, practically by making intercourse impossible or extremely painful until the vaginal opening is slit immediately prior to marriage. Fidelity after marriage is also protected by eliminating any sexual pleasure. It also is rationalized as a method for controlling the aggressive sexuality women are seen to possess (Duley, 1986:424). Regardless of how it is justified, it is a grim reminder of the subjugation of women.

Consider the case of an Egyptian woman who recalled her own "circumcision" at the age of six when she was roughly taken from her bed and found a hand clapped over her mouth to prevent her from screaming.

> It looked as though some thieves had broken into my room and kidnapped me from my bed. They were getting ready to cut my throat. . . . I strained my ears trying to catch the rasp of the metallic sound . . . somehow it was not approaching my neck as I had expected, but another part of my body . . . I realized that my thighs had been pulled wide apart . . . gripped by steel fingers. . . . Then suddenly a sharp metallic edge seemed to drop between my thighs and there cut off a piece of flesh from my body. I screamed with pain despite the tight hand held over my mouth . . . it was like a searing pain that went through my whole body . . . I saw a red pool of blood around my hips.
>
> I did not know what they had cut off from my body . . . I just wept, and called out to my mother for help. But the worst shock of all was when I looked around and found her standing by my side . . . right in the midst of these strangers, talking to them and smiling at them, as though they had not participated in slaughtering her daughter just a few moments ago. They carried me to my bed. I saw them catch hold of my sister, who was two years younger. . . . (el Saadawi, 1980:7-8, cited in Minces, 1982:52-53).

WOMEN AS REFUGEES

This chapter concludes with a note on a population of women who number in the millions but who are virtually ignored in the literature on gender roles. In 1987, the United Nations High Commissioner for Refugees (UNHCR) estimated that there are approximately 12 million refugees around the world. This number is likely underestimated since many remain uncounted if they do not make it into the official camps organized under the auspices of their nations. They are forced from their homes by civil and international war, famine, disease, and politics not of their own making. There are almost three million Afghans in Pakistan and another two million in Iran. There are close to one million Ethiopians in the Sudan who cannot return to their homes because of the civil war and continuing famine. There are hundreds of Sudanese in Kenya who have been forced to flee because of civil war. Thailand has refugee camps with over 150,000 people forced from Viet Nam and

Cambodia (UNHCR, 1987:24-25). Almost every country in the world is touched in some way by the refugees.

The vast majority of refugees are women and children. On a personal note, I have visited a number of refugee camps mostly in Asia and Africa and have been struck by the sheer perseverance of women who manage to keep their families together through incredible hardships. The camps are almost devoid of men. Their husbands, brothers and fathers have been killed or returned to their homeland to fight as soldiers or optimistically to prepare the soil if they hear that rain has come. The reality is that many, perhaps most, never return. Women find themselves abandoned with their children and facing an uncertain future. With patriarchal tribal customs as they are, and now no adult male to provide the necessary interventions to the world outside the family, even in the best of circumstances a return to their villages will mean a dismal existence.

The plight of the Afghan refugees in Pakistan provides an example. Beyond physical survival, a refugee camp offers little psychological comfort to women. In reporting from several of the camps, Kamm (1988) suggests that Islamic fundamentalists are dominant to the extent that women are more restricted than when at home. They are suffering from boredom and melancholia, cry frequently, and see their domestic roles eroding. They must get permission from the men to go outside or visit a clinic. Ironically, when the men do give them permission to seek medical attention for themselves or their children, the women are eager to go. It is one of the few places outside their tents or huts where they can meet other women.

Camp life is harsher for urban women who have been educated. For such women the seclusion of purdah is a new experience. With the relaxed standards of the city and the ability to work outside the home, women from urban areas like Kabul find refugee life intolerable. A middle class urban life style allows for much more freedom of movement and a greater respect for education. With Islamic fundamentalism gaining a stronger foothold, women are discouraged from seeking opportunities beyond traditional domestic roles. For women who have already experienced the benefits of education, the psychological impact of decreased expectations for new roles for themselves and their daughters can be devastating. This helps explain why tranquilizers are becoming common prescriptions in the camps (Lindsey, 1988b:6).

In recognizing the situation of refugees and existing cultural patterns regarding gender distinctions, many nongovernmental organizations have begun to develop programs geared specifically at women. Some camps are also working to help female literacy and upgrade their own and their childrens' health status. The irony here is that a refugee camp may provide the only opportunity a woman may have for education and training for later employment. These organizations must also overcome the resistance from not only those remaining men who work to keep their wives and daughters from gaining valuable skills, but also from the women themselves.

Unfortunately, the few programs offered to women are far too low for the numbers of women who could benefit from them. When money becomes available for development projects aimed at economic independence, womens' programs have the lowest priority. Sons may be taught how to weave carpets while daughters stay back to help care for younger children and to cook and clean. If educational programs are available, a daughter cannot attend school if she is needed at home. So the cycle of poverty and ignorance is unbroken.

For the most part, the plight of refugee women remains bleak, especially as the months in a refugee camp stretch into years and the hope of returning home dims. A camp may be a bastion for physical survival, but psychological comfort is minimal. A refugee camp is a microcosm of a society in exile, including its gender rules and roles. Only in this case, alone and literally on her own, the position of the woman is even lower than in her home culture.

6

Love and Marriage
in Modern Society

Desire for a feminine destiny—husband, home and children—and the enchantment of love are not always easy to reconcile with the will to succeed. (Simone DeBeauvoir, 1953:622)

"Love and marriage," so the song says, go together like "a horse and carriage." We are so accustomed to the notion that love and marriage are inseparable and that romantic love is the primary determinant for marriage that it is rather startling to realize these concepts have been paired only since the nineteenth century in United States. The ideal of passionate love existed prior to this, but until recently in history, love was not seen as a basis, especially not *the* basis, for marriage.

LOVE

The poets and philosophers who sang the praises of courtly love during the feudal era elevated love to something unattainable in marriage. The ladies of the court would bestow gifts, blessings, and an occasional kiss on suitors who would do battle or endure hardships for such prizes. Love which would eventuate in sexual passion was unseemly, even discouraged. Courtly love was reserved for the highborn, almost a game to be played, and thereby excluded the vast majority of the population who did not have the luxury of games.

107

Marriage, on the other hand, was an obligation. A fairly rigid stratification system could be threatened if passionate love served as a realistic alternative for choosing a mate. Marriage was a practical and economic arrangement which influenced kinship ties, lineage, and inheritance. Since power, property and privilege are affected, marriage could not be taken lightly. The decision was a rational rather than a romantic one.

The Puritan era ushered in the idea that love and marriage should be tied. This was a radical departure from early Church teachings which warned men that even to look on their wives with lust made them adulterers (Goode, 1982:14). Now good Christian husbands and wives were admonished to love one another. If love was not the reason for marriage, it was expected to flourish later. Parental control leading to their approval of marriage partners remained the norm, but the fact that love should play a part in the process became etched into the fledgling American consciousness.

Marriage as a purely rational event was eroded by dramatic social changes. A political climate receptive to egalitarian attitudes was bolstered by the industrial revolution which almost mandated a further leveling of stratification and less separation between the sexes. As women moved into the world of paid employment, their economic power increased. Social change coupled with economic assets enhanced choices for both sexes, but particularly for women.

Murstein (1986:21) states that the improved status of women in combination with opportunities for youth to interact, privacy for such interaction and sufficient leisure time were the conditions that needed to be met before romantic love could truly blossom. By the beginning of the twentieth century, these conditions had been met. Love and marriage, with the assumption of freedom of choice, have since become inextricably bound.

Friends and Lovers

I fell in love with him at first sight.
Then why didn't you marry him?
Oh, I saw him again afterwards.
(Anonymous. Quoted in Mullan, 1984:226)

Since love is so complex an emotion and so difficult to define to everyone's satisfaction, it is easy to understand why it is encumbered with folklore, superstition, and myth. Love is extolled for its virtue and damned for its jealousy. Euphoria, joy, depression, restlessness, anger, and fear are all words used to describe love. The opposite of love is not hate, but indifference, suggests psychologist Elaine Hatfield (cited in Rubenstein, 1986:75).

The love for a friend, sibling, parent, or child is certainly different from the feelings accompanying romantic love and the strong emotional attachments we have for the opposite sex, but distinguishing among the different kinds of love is exceedingly complicated. In comparing love and friendship, for example, Davis (1985) develops three broad clusters of characteristics. The profile of friendship, especially "best" friends, includes enjoyment, acceptance, trust, respect, mutual assistance, confiding, understanding, and spontaneity. For love, we must add passion (fascination and preoccupation with the lover, exclusiveness and sexual desire) and caring (giving the utmost and being a champion or advocate for the lover).

Overall, the clusters differentiate the spouse-lover from the best-close friend, particularly for the passion cluster, but there are exceptions. Spouse-lovers would more likely give the utmost but best-close friends are likely to be advocates or champions of each other to the same degree. And the hypothesis that there are few differences between best-close friends and spouse-lovers in terms of enjoyment of each other's company is not supported. Davis (1985:25) suspects this may be an indication that a greater range of human needs can be met by a love relationship.

When men and women are compared in terms of the sex of their best friends with the explicit indication that it is not a romantic relationship, Davis finds that 27% of subjects listed a member of the opposite sex. When extended to close friends, 56% of the men and 44% of the women nominated at least one member of the opposite sex (Davis, 1985:26). Perhaps because the passion dimension lurks behind opposite-sex friendships and liking may turn into loving, as would be expected, Davis demonstrates that same-sex friends share more, give more and have more stable relationships.

Feelings of security, comfort and companionship are associated with being in love. To tap these and other dimensions, Rubin (1973) has developed a love scale which measures degrees of needing, caring, toleration, and trust, essential love components. Add to these the notion of sexual desire, passion, or erotic attraction and we begin to see how friendship and romantic love can again be distinguished.

Love Myths

Regardless of its definition, romantic love is idealized in the United States. We are literally bombarded with romantic stimuli throughout our lives which serve to reinforce these idealizations. The most complicated of emotions has produced a range of myths which demonstrate how we romanticize love. To the extent that these myths carry over into our beliefs and behaviors related to gender roles, marriage and the family, romanticization can have dire consequences.

The myth that love conquers all is a pervasive one. The "all" that is supposedly conquered involves the problems and obstacles inherent in daily living. By idealizing the love-object, problems are even more difficult to solve. Total agreement with another person's views on problem-solving is impossible. Lamm (1980, cited in Mullan, 1984:227) notes that romantic love offers a paradox. Idealization requires remoteness to be maintained, but intimacy evaporates remoteness. One's partner cannot fulfill all needs and make all problems disappear. Love does not conquer all, even for a short time.

With the sexual revolution, it is now widely believed that sex without love, or the standard of permissiveness without affection (Eshleman, 1988:35) is acceptable. It is assumed here that the double standard is eroding and that women would increasingly engage in sex with partners to whom they are attracted but not committed. Rubenstein (1983:40) finds that in comparing a 1969 survey with one done in the 1980s, both men and women actually express a *higher degree* of sexual conservatism. The figures still suggest the double standard is operating with 29% of the men and 44% of the women believing sex without love is unenjoyable or unacceptable.

Love is blind. This myth asserts that true love will dissolve social boundaries and that anyone has the potential for becoming the romantic love-object. The belief that "it doesn't matter, as long as I love her/him" is operating here. As we shall see in mate selection, love is very structured. We are socialized to fall in love at certain times in our lives. Rubenstein's (1983:45) data show that everyone has faith in romance. An amazing 96% agreed with this. But love is conditioned by a number of social and demographic variables which exert a tremendous influence on us. Both sexes are susceptible to these influences, but to a different degree.

Women are viewed as the romantic sex. They are believed to be starry-eyed and to fall in love easily. This belief is associated with the stereotyped idea that, as the more emotional sex, women succumb faster to romance, hence love. A number of studies have shattered this myth, demonstrating that men not only express a higher level of romantic love than women (Fengler, 1974; Knox and Sporakowski, 1968; Lester, 1984) but also fall in love earlier in the relationship than women (Kanin, et al., 1970). Overall, men are found to be more idealistic and romantic in their attitudes toward love (Knox and Sporakowski, 1968; Dion and Dion, 1973).

In the potential for a love relationship, women are the pragmatic sex and exhibit much caution. Once the decision is made to fall in love, however, women exceed men in levels of emotion and euphoria (Kanin et al., 1970; Rubenstein, 1986). The rational behavior eventually leads to the romantic idealism characterizing love in America. It is at the passionate first stage of love at least, where men are the more romantic sex.

Androgynous Love

The openness and sharing that most would agree are important components of love serve to separate the sexes in the later stages of love and marriage. Gender role socialization commands that masculinity be associated with lack of vulnerability. One becomes vulnerable through self-disclosure; therefore to love fully is to self-disclose fully.

At the beginning of a romantic relationship, men are likely to have higher levels of self-disclosure than later. Indeed, Lester et al. (1984) report that men who have a romantic orientation to love disclose more to parents and male and female friends. Yet as the relationship continues, even into marriage, men become the silent partners where women are expecting more responsiveness. The female partners become resentful and irritated by the males' unwillingness to express thoughts and feelings (Rubenstein, 1983:49). This has led to the belief that males are incompetent at loving. The argument is that to truly express love is to deny the masculine self (Balswick and Peek, 1971).

Cancian (1986:692) maintains love is so identified with emotional expression and self-disclosure, in which women are more skilled, that we often disregard the instrumental and physical aspects which men prefer. Men are viewed as incompetent at loving because romantic love ideals overlook the instrumental, pragmatic, dimension, thereby giving more weight to the expressive. This has led to an incomplete and overly feminized perspective of love.

For relationships to become more loving for women and men is to reject "polarized gender roles and [to] integrate 'masculine' and 'feminine' styles of love" (Cancian, 1986:693). She proposes an alternative, androgynous view on love which assumes that both the instrumental and expressive dimensions are represented and combined in meaningful ways. Schwartz (1979:408) posits the idea of the "androgynous self" which is open to giving and getting and the ability to transcend cognitive categories. If love and loving are sex typed, androgyny should overcome the imposed limitations.

Coleman and Ganong (1985) provide an empirical test for the idea of androgynous love. They hypothesize that androgynous individuals would experience love differently than sex-typed individuals, both groups being currently involved in a love relationship. The findings indicate that neither masculine nor feminine gender roles are as conducive to experiencing and expressing love as an androgynous gender role orientation, that gender role orientation is a better predictor of love behavior than is biological sex and that sex-typed persons are less able to love (Colemen and Ganong, 1985:175). The idea of androgynous love provides an escape from traditional sex-typing where love and loving become compromised. We sustain the belief that we marry for love and that love can last a lifetime. Rubenstein (1983:45) concludes that romance does not flourish, love does not survive, and marriages do not work.

It is apparent that women and men differ on attitudes and behavior surrounding the notion of romantic love and that traditional gender roles jeopardize love and loving. Moving toward an androgynous love ideal may overcome some of the barriers existing between the sexes. Loving relationships which endure the harshness of the "unromantic" world may result.

MATE SELECTION

In the United States we encourage the ideology of romantic love and adhere to it as the basis for mate selection, the sentiment being shared by both sexes. Love may be viewed as a panacea, but prior to making a marriage commitment, prospective mates are carefully scrutinized on a number of characteristics deemed important. What is suggested here is that in pursuing the objective of a marriage partner, love itself becomes structured by an array of social and demographic factors.

The family literature fully documents the importance of **homogamy**, or the likelihood of marrying someone similar to yourself (Heer, 1974; Carter and Glick, 1976; Murstein, 1980; Buss, 1985; Buss and Barnes, 1986; Nock, 1987). Similarity in terms of age, race, religion, socioeconomic status, and a host of social and cultural variables strengthens the role of homogamy in mate selection. The result is **assortive mating**, where coupling occurs based on similarity rather than chance.

Though considered nonaffective in nature, that is, not tied to the emotional expressiveness and highly charged romanticism entailed in love, these variables are more likely to predict mate selection than the more prized notion of romantic love per se. It is these nonaffective elements which help to determine with whom we will likely fall in love. The fact remains that romantic love is tempered by a market approach to mate selection (Rao and Rao, 1980). This results in a process that appears to be radically different from the ideology surrounding it (Melton and Lindsey, 1987).

Gender Differences

Differences between the sexes in orientation to romantic love continue when a prospective spouse is considered. Since men score higher on romanticism scales than women and fall in love earlier than women, women are the pragmatists, at least at the beginning of the whole mate selection process (Dion and Dion, 1973). This caution is justified because marriage for women probably will become the major determinant of their future social status (Murstein, 1980). The tradition that women have been expected to achieve their greatest source of fulfillment in marriage and motherhood roles continues even as they succeed in careers and opportunities outside the home.

Thus homogamy is filtered by a trend known as **hypergamy**, where women tend to marry men of higher social and economic status. This provides the conventional channel through which women have gained upward mobility. Women prefer men who are well-educated and have the financial resources and earning capacity necessary for assuming responsibility for a family (Berscheid and Walster, 1974; Buss, 1985; Melton and Lindsey, 1987). This corresponds to Melton and Thomas' (1976) research on attitudes of college students showing that females differ from males in that they place a greater value on the instrumental qualities of a prospective mate, such as working, saving, paying bills, and maintaining the basic physical integrity of the family unit. Buss and Barnes (1986:569) argue that traditional socialization practices support structural differences of this type and are used to instill role-appropriate values of males and females.

Men, on the other hand, value physical attractiveness much more than women and consider it more important for a spouse, especially for ambitious, upwardly mobile men (Eshleman, 1988:270). Physical attractiveness in women increases their probability of being married and appears to be more important than masculine attractiveness for such traits as popularity, number of dates and perception of having a favorable set of personality characteristics (cited in Murstein, 1986:37-39).

As Murstein (1986:39) points out, men do not have to be as attractive as women because men possess greater status and power in our society. Added to this is the economically subservient role in which many women find themselves. Physical attractiveness can be a bargaining tool for economic security. With women excluded from power, they are viewed by themselves and men alike, as objects of exchange. In terms which take on a degrading connotation, physical beauty enhances the value of women as sex objects. Buss and Barnes (1986:569) state that attractiveness is an important means for designating relative value among exchange commodities.

It would seem that the impact of the feminist movement and the increased economic integrity of women could alter these patterns somewhat. It is evident that many women are choosing to remain single, in part because they have the economic capability and self-assurance to do so. But in a study where we compared college students' attitudes toward prospective mates in the 1980s with those in the 1970s, we find that value preferences are not radically different (Melton and Lindsey, 1987). Females continue to place a greater emphasis on instrumental behaviors whereas males place substantially more emphasis on sexual and physical attractiveness. And for both females and males, the mean instrumental index score is *higher* for the contemporary groups of college students.

Our study is particularly surprising since the sample is made up of a high proportion of women who are pursuing nontraditional academic curricula, such as engineering and pharmacy, where earnings potential and professional advancement are quite high relative to other career possibilities. The research is conclusive that college women indicate that they want to successfully combine a career with marriage and children (Epstein and Bronzaft, 1972; Bronzaft, 1974; Gallup, 1980; Lindsey, 1985). Perhaps it is at those points of interruption for childbearing and/or child rearing where they see themselves as even temporarily economically dependent on their husbands which mandates their emphasis on instrumental qualities. Also, both sexes may view the current job market as extremely competitive and recognize that their mates must reinforce the economic stability of the family (Melton and Lindsey, 1987). This would explain the higher instrumental index for the contemporary males as compared to the earlier male group.

Age and Race

Age is another variable which influences mate selection, with most people marrying others near to their own ages. As we would expect, when gender differences do occur, the combination of the somewhat older man with the somewhat younger woman is the pattern. In later or remarriages, age differences are likely to be greater, but usually favoring the same younger woman-older man pattern. The major reversal of this trend is that elderly women who remarry after widowhood are likely to marry men younger than themselves.

Age at first marriage is legally controlled, with some states still allowing earlier marriages for females than for males. There is no state which has a legal marriage age for females which is higher than for males. Table 6-1 looks at median age at first marriage from the turn of the century. Except for the period between 1950 and 1970, the median age has remained relatively stable for both sexes. What is revealing is the fact that the median age is now the highest for women than at any time since 1900.

TABLE 6-1.   Median Ages at First Marriage

YEAR	MEN	WOMEN
1984	25.4	23.0
1983	25.4	22.8
1982	25.2	22.5
1980	24.7	22.0
1970	23.2	20.8
1960	22.8	20.3
1950	22.8	20.3
1940	24.3	21.5
1930	24.3	21.3
1920	24.6	21.2
1910	25.1	21.6
1900	25.9	21.9
1890	26.1	22.0

Source: U.S. Bureau of the Census, 1975; 1985.

Role differences and socialization factors between the sexes readily explain these trends. Men are discouraged from marrying too soon because they must gain the education and job skills necessary to support a family. Women, who are traditionally socialized into training for domestic roles, are not as bound. The contemporary trend where both sexes marry later is likely to continue, but it should be more pronounced for women. With over half of all college students now women and the increasing numbers of women entering the labor force, age at first marriage for women may eventually approach that of men.

Educational institutions which are age stratified through high school and continue for the most part through college, will maintain age homogamy in mate selection. Hypergamy will also function to support the younger woman-older man trend. However, a minitrend has appeared which indicates that the younger man-older woman marriage is becoming more acceptable. Nock (1987:99) cites census data showing that 14% of all marriages demonstrate this pattern, most commonly among the elderly. However, new role models for women, success in economic spheres, divorce and remarriage, the marriage squeeze (discussed later), and less constraint from family and society will likely accelerate this pattern for middle aged and younger women.

Of all the major demographic variables, homogamy is strongest concerning race, with interracial marriages fairly infrequent. Although all legal blocks to interracial marriage had been removed by 1967 in the United States, sociocultural norms continue to strongly discourage it, especially marriages involving blacks and whites. Of the almost 700,000 interracial marriages in 1982 (1.39% of the total), 155,000 were between blacks and whites, a mere 0.3 of 1% of all marriages for that year (cited in Murstein, 1986:47).

Of significance here is that 70% of the black-white marriages involve a white wife and black husband. When comparing race and class in these marriages, the data are unclear. In a review of the literature, Aldridge (1978) reports on studies which show that partners come from different socioeconomic statuses (SES) as well as other data finding that most spouses in interracial marriages come from the same socioeconomic level. If hypergamy is evident in these marriages, the trend would be that the woman is of a lower SES than the man. The idea behind hypergamy in this instance is that the wife compensates for her lower SES and the husband compensates for his lower valued caste. Both parties marry "up" in this sense.

Though explanations for the white female-black male pattern in interracial marriage are contradictory, Murstein (1986) suggests that homogamy is the factor of overriding importance. When blacks and whites become attracted to one another, it is for reasons similar to white-white or black-black marriages. The main mitigating factor is that race is weighted to the advantage of whites so that blacks must possess some desirable characteristics seen as better than the whites who are available. According to Murstein

> marital choice in interracial marriage seems to strike a bargain between exchange and availability. Blacks have to offer more to whites because of existing social prejudices, but this effect tails off at high levels of assets when availability of partners pushes black-white marriages more toward a homogamous principle. (1986:55)

The Marriage Squeeze

We have seen that age homogamy is strong and that most people marry for the first time in their early to mid 20s. But age at first marriage by both sexes is inevitably affected by a number of circumstances, including the proportion of marriage-age men and women who are available. When there is an unbalanced ratio of marriage-age men to marriage-age women, a marriage squeeze is said to exist, with one or the other sex having a more limited pool of potential marriage partners. Changing birth rates, male and female mortality rates, war, marriage and divorce trends, attitudes to premarital sex, and economic patterns are some of the factors which influence the development of a marriage squeeze.

At present, the marriage squeeze is limiting the range of choices of mates for women. The trends of women marrying men two to three years older than themselves and hypergamy, combined with higher male mortality rates, and economic independence for women help explain this. Widows make up a large portion of the single-women-living-alone category, but the proportion of single women at the prime marrying age is steadily increasing.

Perhaps for the first time in modern societies, women are caught in a paradox which both restricts and enlarges their choices relative to marriage. They are restricted in the number of what they deem to be eligible partners precisely because of their own successes outside the confines of domestic life. Women, like men, want to eventually marry. But women are less likely than in the past to marry simply for financial security. They can afford to be more choosy in mate selection, and even postpone marriage until career opportunities are realized.

The result of this flexibility narrows the range of partners when these women are ready to seriously consider the permanency of marriage. It is at this point when singleness may be chosen as the preferred life style because they find that they cannot realistically settle for those single men who are "left," as it were. Hypergamy results in two groups of people who may be left out of the marriage market. These are the highly educated, economically successful women and the poorly educated, lower SES men. Bernard (1972:36) refers to this as the "cream of the crop, bottom of the barrel" distinction.

When considering black women as a separate subgroup, the marriage squeeze is even more prominent. As demonstrated in Chapter 2, life expectancy rates are lowest for black males, in comparison to white males and all females. According to the U.S. Census Bureau, for blacks, women outnumber men at about age 18; for whites it is at age 32 (cited in Spanier and Glick, 1980:408). This significantly restricts the field of eligibles for black women making homogamy on a number of variables less likely to occur. As a result, in comparison to white women, black women are more likely to marry men who are older by at least four years, of a lower educational level, and have been previously married (Spanier and Glick, 1980:723). Other patterns for blacks as a group show that age at first marriage is lower and rate of marital dissolution is higher than for whites.

We can assume that homogamy related to age, education, and previous marriage would be more predictive of marital stability than when there are major discrepancies in these variables for any couple. When lack of homogamy is tied to additional stresses such as coping with prejudice, and lower levels of economic attainment, we can see how black marriages are at higher risk in terms of divorce. A marriage squeeze which requires many black women to select mates who are significantly different than themselves may influence overall marital stability.

The marriage squeeze may be responsible for the hard choices which all women must make. For many, this can mean whether to marry at all or forego childbearing altogether. I would argue that women in their thirties do marry, and find it less satisfactory, because they are unwilling to give up motherhood. However, given the options of marrying later in life and the advantages and disadvantage of "settling," singleness is now being embraced by confident women who see it as a positive alternative to marriage. After examining traditional marriage in terms of the genders, we will return to this point.

GENDER ROLES IN MARRIAGE

Marriage in American society is both idealized and feared. Images of loving couples with contented children coexist with those of abandonment, violence, and the potential of divorce. Regardless of the perception or the reality, the vast majority of us eagerly seek marriage and will marry at some point in our lives. However, shifts in gender roles have altered our views of marriage and the family. Attitude change is being manifest not only in marriage per se, but also in the emergence of a variety of life styles which are now options for those seeking alternatives to what they define as traditional marriage.

Views of Marriage and the Family:
Functionalism and Conflict

Functionalism argues that marriage and eventual parenting is good for society and the individual couple. The family system allows for orderly procreation, regulation of sexual behavior, socialization of the children, economic cooperation, conferring status on its members, personality formation, protection and security, and the expression of affection, to name but a few benefits. Companionship and ego support of family members, especially husband and wife, are enhanced.

Functionalism assumes that the family system operates best when husband and wife do not overlap roles. When marital roles are specialized, the efficiency of the family unit is maximized. If each partner begins to take on the roles of the other, conflict, which is harmful to the system, results, A stable family unit will help create and maintain a stable society. This is the argument which we constantly hear when the subjects of divorce, unwed mothers and fathers, premarital sex, and unconventional life styles are raised. Society is threatened because the basic values inherent in the traditional family are being eroded.

On the other hand, conflict theories view marriage and the family as made up of individuals who possess differing amounts of resources and power, and who have individual interests to consider and defend. It is conflict and not order and harmony which family systems demonstrate. In the traditional family where patriarchy is unquestioned, women are dominated by men. Only when women gain greater economic power will the system be significantly altered. Thus, conflict theory assumes that women and wives should explore and experiment with newer roles which have been the prerogative of men and husbands in the past. By this view, traditional marriage must change.

In Defense of the Traditional Family

If a family is viewed as traditional, it is because it combines certain normative characteristics involving roles of family members and living arrangements. The idea of a nuclear family is usually considered in this traditional sense. **The nuclear family** consists of wife, husband and their dependent children who live together in their own residence. In the traditional nuclear family, tasks are divided so that the husband is the breadwinner with the wife maintaining the responsibility for domestic tasks, including child care. This is the functionalist ideal and the model which we assume is the most prevalent.

Many are surprised to learn that this model is far from the norm today. Table 6-2 provides a summary of how Americans are distributed according to household type and wage-earning roles. The traditional nuclear family where one earner is present (likely to be the husband) and children are still living at home consisted of only 13% of households as late as 1977. As more women with preschoolers enter the labor force, and as couples delay having children, this figure is likely to decline even further. The family model that many believe to be the norm simply does not fit the reality.

TABLE 6-2. Distribution of Adult Americans by Type of Household: 1977

Living in childfree or postchildrearing marriages	23%
Single, separated, divorced, widowed	21
Heading single-parent family	16
Nuclear family, dual earners, children present	16
Nuclear family, one earner, children present	13
Living in an extended family household	6
Cohabitating or experimental family household	4
No-wage-earner nuclear family, children present	1
Total	100%

Source: Adapted from Ramey, 1978:1

But arguments in defense of this kind of family continue to abound, especially in response to feminists calling for changes in the worlds of paid labor and marital roles. At one extreme we have people like Phyllis Schlafly (1981) who maintain that women who work outside the home take away jobs from males, sabotage family stability and undermine motherhood. She is obviously unaware or disregards the fact that, as Table 6-2 suggests, 37% of American households are made up of single parents and divorced, separated, single, and widowed people living alone. Most of these are women. They do not have the luxury to decide whether to work outside of the home or not. In order not to undermine their families, themselves, or ultimately broader society they *must* work.

Schlafly would be supported by another of her ilk, Marabel Morgan (1973:80), who argues that if marital conflict occurs, the wife should always give in to her husband, because, after all "God planned for woman to be under her husband's rule." Peppered with biblical quotes throughout, Morgan's own plan for marital bliss is clear in the chapter titles of her book on how to become the "Total Woman," which include sections on accepting him, admiring him, adapting to him, and appreciating him. She caters to his needs in sex, salads and sports, among others, thereby minimizing the possibilities of two egos in conflict.

With all this and in the "Total Woman" (TW) classes she teaches, she insists that a woman is not inferior to a man and should not be subservient to him but that a "wife should be under her own husband's leadership" (Morgan, 1973:81). If her plan is meticulously followed, communication between the couple is opened up and the wife eventually gets what she wants, whether it be a fur coat or a vacation in the Bahamas. What else could a wife possibly want? It does not seem important to Morgan that her needs are subverted to his and that if she gains anything through these tactics, it is through manipulation and deceit. And of course, the only women who are candidates for her TW training are those who do not work outside the home.

Sakol and Goldberg (1975) defend marriage on the grounds that there is no other relationship possible which gives a woman as much happiness, pleasure, fulfillment, or purpose. Their idea is that feminism has attacked marriage and that feminists are "those same people who would take our babies away from us and put them in state nurseries so that we could march off to work in the mines" (Sakol and Goldberg, 1975:31). For married women who want a career, they believe that, too, is possible, especially since they argue that men take on so many domestic tasks, including child care. But even then it's better to "be taken care of" in the home since jobs are boring and difficult. We shall evaluate later the validity of these last statements.

Like Morgan, who admonishes wives to refrain from criticizing their husbands, Sakol and Goldberg (1975:37) contend that wives have the mandate to make their marriage work "instead of dragging it down by complaining that the world (meaning the guy across the breakfast table) isn't perfect." They idealize marriage for its intimacy and permanence, enabling the couple to love totally. They conclude with the statement that "marriage remains the most wonderful institution devised by man (yes, we'll even let the men take credit for it)" (Sakol and Goldberg, 1975:38). Conflict theory would ironically agree with the last part of this statement. Men would devise a system which they would then control.

These views of marriage and the family are extreme because their proponents are defending an ideal which they perceive is being threatened by feminism. Theologian and counselor David Mace (1975) is optimistically supportive of the nuclear family but does so while recognizing that change has both negative and positive effects. He quotes Ernest Burgess who says that the family is undergoing a transition from institution to companionate. It is a painful transition because in its new form the nuclear family becomes based on depth in the relationship as well as individual autonomy (Mace, 1975:26).

Nuclear families can malfunction during this transitional period. Rather than recognizing the potential advantages of this change, defenders of the "old ways" surface and adamantly attack whom they see as the perpetrators of the change, namely the woman's movement. The nuclear model should not be abandoned as an ideal, but some of its traditional arrangements need to be seriously questioned. If spouses are viewed as coleaders or partners where, ideally at least, neither has clear domination over the other; then the nuclear family still functions, is stable, but has changed.

Mace (1975:25-27) believes the functioning nuclear family can provide the model for the kind of human society we are trying to build. He states:

> It is a microcosm of that large world in containing both sexes and a variety of ages. In a manageable setting it enables its members to give and get in *just* proportion. It trains them to be sensitive to the needs of others, to work together for common goals, and to find joy and gladness in shared delights. . . . We desperately need large numbers of just such people. (Mace, 1975:27, italics mine)

Granted that this ideal is far from reality, it does point out that change is possible and the nuclear family can sustain the change and grow from it.

I would also assert that the definition of nuclear family is too limited to encompass the many new kinds of households and living arrangements which are emerging. Eshleman's (1988:100) idea of the nuclear family which "may or may not include marriage partners but consists of any two or more persons related by blood, marriage, or adoption assuming they are of the same or adjoining generations" is more indicative of the reality. A household where a single parent lives with two children becomes a nuclear family.

The family form has been altered to meet conditions of social change. When major changes affecting the roles of its members also occur *within* the new, modified nuclear family, it becomes essentially nontraditional. This has not yet been the case.

The Case against Traditional Marriage

As there is support for traditional marriage and family arrangements, much opposition exists. Opposing views have been steadily growing as mounting evidence attests to the inequality of wives and husbands and how that inequality has dire consequences for the family unit as a whole as well as the individuals within it.

At one extreme is Kathrin Perutz (1972), whose book title says it all, *Marriage Is Hell*. The expectations of marriage, she asserts, transform it into a "ghetto of lunacy" with an attempt at an impossible union where indignation, individuality, egoism, and pride must be compromised. With marriage comes an end to self-development and an unnatural death of the spirit. Modern Western marriage is the perfection of hypocrisy; it is not a decision but a fate (Perutz, 1975:47, 49). Women in particular are pushed into this fate, with but the "philosophically hardy or the unasked" getting married.

Moving from the ideological to the empirical level, there is much evidence demonstrating that the husband's marriage is different than the wife's. When husbands and wives are asked identical questions about their marriages, the replies are quite different (Bernard, 1972). Perceptions would likely differ to some extent on items regarding general happiness or feelings of romance which are less quantifiable. But Bernard (1972: 198) reports that when even basic facts on frequency of sexual relations, household tasks, and decision making are viewed, the couple appears to be speaking about two different marriages. Contrary to what one would expect, differences increase with the length of the marriage.

Marriage is beneficial to men. When comparing married to unmarried men on psychological, physical and social well-being, the married come out far superior (Bernard, 1972:17). Married men may have the best mental health because their wives are the buffers against emotional distress (Fleming, 1986:32). Married women suffer more psychological disability, depression, and anxiety than married men (Bernard, 1972:29). Although there is cultural support for men complaining about their marriages as if they were "roped into it," the data suggest that marriage is the preferred life style for men. Bernard (1972:19) states that most divorced and widowed men remarry and that at every age the rate of marriage for these same categories of men is higher than the rate for single men.

Marriage may be beneficial to men, but it is not as good a status for women. In another work Bernard (1975:85) reports that women make more adjustments in marriage than men and evaluate their marriages lower than men. Bird (1975) backs up the case against marriage for women by suggesting that in areas such as credit, social life, and job opportunities, married women lose. Marriage will of course survive, but alternatives to traditional marriage may entice young women to reexamine what it means to be married.

If wives are deprived of the expectations in marriages that are less than satisfactory, it is primarily due to a broader social system which strongly influences what occurs in individual marriages and families. The subordination of wife to husband mimics that which exists outside the home. A study of conflicted and nonconflicted marriages by Alsbrook (1976) concludes that sexism in the total social scene affects the interaction of husband and wife. From a conflict perspective, the interaction is similar to discrimination patterns experienced by other minority groups. The power of gender role socialization has seduced the husband into the oppressor role just as surely as the wife has inherited the oppressed role (Komarovsky, 1973, cited in Alsbrook, 1976:522).

In traditional marriages as defined here, the castelike status of husband and wife serves to separate rather than cement the marital relationship. If the woman's movement raised the consciousness of young single women to reexamine their relationships with men, it would seem that their eventual marriages would demonstrate less traditionality. This is only true in a minority of marriages, as the discussion below will suggest. Fleming's (1986) study on American wives sheds light on why traditional marriage appears to triumph. She states that "it is clear in 1986 that the brides of the 70s may not have been deferential to men, but were deferential to marriage" (Fleming, 1986:32). Powerful socialization factors pull women and men into marital roles and expectations which are difficult to discard.

Finally, it must be mentioned that some contradictions appear in the data concerning marital satisfaction. A Gallup (1980) poll shows that the majority of Americans are happy in their marriages. In a critique of Bernard's interpretation of marriage, Glenn (1975) maintains she is biased and propagandistic and overlooks the benefits of marriage for women. He cites his own research attesting to a higher rate of happiness of wives than husbands. He admits that wives have higher stress than husbands in marriage, but the psychological benefits outweigh the costs.

Data may be interpreted in various ways with each viewpoint having a certain degree of validity. Research on marital satisfaction continues to account for more variables, going beyond simple correlations of happiness of husbands versus that of wives. The impact of careers and household task sharing are critical factors which must also be examined.

Housewives and Housework

The housewife image is bombarded with contradictions. On one hand it is seen as the height of a woman's aspirations, a deliberate choice which gives her the maximum amount of pride and satisfaction. In this view, Lopata (1971) finds that homemakers-mothers are happy in that they can be expressive, creative, and autonomous, and interestingly, women with higher education are more likely to express this. Oakley's (1974a) study of London housewives shows that even if women feel that housework itself is less gratifying, they are generally happy as housewives. On the other hand, housewifery is relegated to a low prestige status in the eyes of many, especially more educated women, another finding of the Oakley and Lopata studies. Women may express satisfaction in what they are doing as housewives and mothers, but they feel it is a devalued position overall.

There are several factors which contribute to this feeling that the role is devalued. First, women must continually be on call to the demands of her husband and children. Her needs are often given the lowest priority. Because she is exclusively attached to and sacrifices for her family, she becomes more securely bound to it, and unlike her husband and children, alternative sources of gratification are reduced (Coser and Coser, 1982:209).

Second, the demands and time spent on the homemaker role have not decreased to any great extent, even with those wonderful appliances to make household tasks less time consuming. Vanek's (1974) study on time spent in household work suggests that *since* 1920, the full-time housewife spends approximately 52 hours per week on housework alone. When housework time is then added to child care and rearing tasks, this figure would be much higher. Baking cupcakes for an elementary school party is part of the housework and cooking time, but added to this is the time spent at the party itself.

Most importantly, the housewife role is devalued because it is not a paid role. Women carry out vital services to their families and society but receive no definitive remuneration. When the husband is the sole wage earner, those wages are distributed in a variety of ways. Some wives receive their husband's paychecks and determine how the money will be apportioned; other wives receive "allowances" from their husbands which go toward household expenses. Regardless of the myriad of ways the money is spent, she has not "earned" it in the same way he does. This perspective supports the power or resource hypothesis which assumes that since housework is undesirable, it will be "performed disproportionately by those who lack resources to enforce sharing or purchase substitutes" (Spitze, 1986:691).

This contributes to the burden of dependency experienced by many housewives. Fleming (1986) cites the case of one wife who believes that when a man outearns his wife, he is in charge. If the woman is a full time housewife, he is likely to be more dominant. His dominance is conducive to her dependency. To a very large extent, his paycheck becomes the controlling factor in her life. Many women who do not work outside the home and find themselves in conflict ridden, psychologically debilitating marriages see no alternative but to remain where they are. Financial and psychological dependency go hand in hand.

Although housewifery suggests that housework and child care is the woman's primary responsibility, men are expected to take on some of these chores. Lawn care, house repairs, plumbing and electrical work, and automobile maintenance are the conventional household tasks that husbands assume. Tasks may be specialized by the marital partners, but men are doing their fair share, so the argument goes, especially since *he* is working all day. The implications here is that what *she* is doing all day falls into some other amorphous category. The reality is that the old adage where "men may work from sun to sun, but women's work is never done" holds true.

The full-time homemaker is caught in a struggle to positively affirm her housewife role at a time when women's labor force participation is mushrooming. Her well-being is conditioned by satisfaction within her domestic sphere and how her role is socially defined. Shehan et al. (1986:414) find that there was less depression among housewives who were most satisfied with their work role and family lives in the early 1970s. Even given the increase in labor force activity of women, these findings are applicable today among women who have the social and familial support necessary to counteract the boredom and loneliness many housewives experience (Rubenstein and Shaver, 1982; Shehan et al., 1986:415).

Since housewives have not been included in rankings of occupations used in many studies, sociology must take part of the blame for the devaluation or at least underemphasis of the work roles assumed by these women. Nilson (1978) makes up some of this deficit by using a methodology which assigns a prestige score for housewives consistent with National Opinion Research Center (NORC) rankings. The NORC score is determined to be in the middle prestige range, with men and older raters giving it a higher score, and women who work outside the home and younger raters giving it a lower score (Nilson, 1978:541).

The mid-level range is startling if we see the housewife role as devalued. The author suggests that prestige may be higher because it is regarded as a luxury by some. This is especially true for women who work outside the home for the purpose of supplementing the working class family income (Nilson, 1978:546). These women often find themselves in low-paying jobs rather than potentially rewarding careers. For more educated women, Nilson (1978) would support Lopata's (1971) idea that the role has creative, artistic aspects.

The housewife role is obviously an ambiguous one. Regardless of how it is valued, the primary role responsibilities of the housewife involve housework and child care. Some specialized task sharing occurs between husbands and wives, but her full-time housewife status minimizes his contributions overall. Beyond gender, the key variable in household work allocation and general marital satisfaction is whether the wife also has some kind of paid employment.

Marriage and Dual Earner Couples

The movement of women into the paid labor force has profoundly influenced not only their drive toward greater equality, but has also impacted the other social institutions, particularly the family. By the mid 1970s numerous studies had been conducted in order to empirically determine the extent of this impact. The focus of most of the research had to do with wives' employment and marital satisfaction and division of household labor. When comparing the research of a decade ago with that of today, some interesting patterns are revealed.

It is logical to assume that lack of time for household duties normally assigned to the wife would cause the husband to take on significantly more of these tasks. An older study conducted by Blood and Wolfe (1960:63) concludes that husbands feel obligated to take on an appreciably larger share of the housework when their wives are also working. A closer examination finds this to be logically true but empirically false. If the husband seems to do a larger proportion of household tasks it is because the absolute level of his wife's household work goes down, not because his actually increases (Pleck, 1979). It is exceedingly difficult for a woman who works 40 hours a week outside the home to add another 40 or 50 inside. This gives no respite from work. She, therefore, leaves certain tasks uncompleted, and the research shows that husbands do not complete them (Goode, 1982:134).

Later studies on time budgets and household task sharing indicate that the husband's contribution to domestic work remains very small (Walker and Gauger, 1973; Vanek, 1974; Walker and Woods, 1976; Berk and Berk, 1979). By the 1980s some research showed a slight increase in time spent on household tasks by husbands (Geerken and Gove, 1983; Maret and Finlay, 1984; Pleck, 1985), but overall it is the wives who assume the major responsibility for household tasks, including child care arrangements. She may now be referred to occupationally as an administrator or attorney and may have shed the label of housewife. But the role of homemaker is still a salient one and persists for employed wives.

Task sharing in two earner families is also mediated by several other variables, such as income contribution of each partner, the social class standing of the family, education, number and ages of children, and the couples' gender role ideology. Different subgroups of dual earner families distribute tasks differently and may show a greater involvement on the part of the husband. Middle-class wives may decrease their housework because they can afford to hire domestic help. Bird et al. (1984:345) see the research as suggesting a trend for more equitable sharing of the tasks when both spouses are employed. To restate an important point, the family does not exist independently from the other social institutions. As Pleck (1985:155) states, how a family allocates its work and arranges its role structure "is a complex response to its social and economic environment."

The impact of the working wife carrying the load for household and child care responsibilities has tremendous consequences for her career success. This section uses the term "dual earner" rather than "dual career" because it indicates that while many couples have paid employment, they do not necessarily have meaningful careers. Jobs interfere with family in a different way than careers. Rapoport and Rapoport (1971) associate a career with personal salience, a developmental sequence which is intrinsically rewarding, and a high level of commitment. Women who have careers but still take on the bulk of the household labor find it difficult to achieve beyond a certain level.

The success stories of women who apparently "have it all"— great marriages, wonderful children, rewarding careers—are replete. Nelton and Berney (1987) report that women in business are in a second wave of progress, moving up the corporate ladder or advancing through their own business enterprises. They have found ways to favorably reconcile problems between career and family. The woman who is concerned about being neglectful if she left her children in someone else's care to take a managerial position resolves the problem by hiring live-in help (Nelton and Berney, 1987:19). Such women can afford to purchase services to allow for career mobility. Some adjustments are made by the husband, but the wife has to grapple with the changes the family will undergo.

These women are the exception to the rule. The rule is that for American women, while "it is possible to combine *work* and marriage, there is no evidence they are in a position to combine a *career* with marital obligations" (Poloma and Garland, 1971:536). The pull toward the wife and mother role is so great that many women, possibly even most, will not abdicate what they see as their primary responsibility, even if it means giving up career opportunities. Any career commitment is severely compromised by the intrusion of the traditional role (Poloma et al., 1982). It is not that these women are shirking their professional duties. It simply means that their career mobility is likely to be attenuated, specifically in comparison to men who are not constrained by domestic encroachments in the workplace. And some women favor an overall balance between career and family life rather than having what they would define as excessively high levels of professional involvement (Stratham, et al., 1987:119).

We saw in Chapter 2 that employment appears to have beneficial effects for women in a number of realms, such as self-esteem and mental health. Marital satisfaction is another consequence. Research indicates that women employed full time outside the home report higher degrees of marital and work satisfaction than full time housewives, especially if they are more educated and hold higher paying, interesting jobs or careers (Weaver and Holmes, 1975; Goode, 1982). Indeed, some research indicates that currently employed wives as well as those *formerly* employed have higher life satisfaction as they get older, when compared to the never employed wives who do not find increased satisfaction with age (Freudiger, 1983:218).

The research is less clear for husbands of wives who work outside the home. Goode (1982:136) and Kessler and McRae (1982) suggest that these husbands express less marital satisfaction and have higher degrees of depression and lower levels of physical and mental well-being. This may be due to the adherence to more traditional gender role attitudes where men feel threatened by a wife who is also employed. Bowen and Orthner (1983:223) show that marriages with the lowest evaluation of marital satisfaction are those with a traditional husband but a modern wife. He may feel less control as she gains more independence outside the home. Another possibility is that if his wife is working solely out of economic necessity, his breadwinner role is assaulted and he sees his masculinity in jeopardy.

In analyzing Kessler and MacRae's (1982) data, however, Rubin (1983) is much more optimistic about the state of happiness in the dual earner family. The age of the husband is a critical factor in evaluating the marriage. Men in their 30s, 40s and 50s who had working wives had lower levels of self-esteem than men in their 20s. Rubin (1983:72) points out that these younger men have grown up with different expectations concerning work and family and are more likely to see the breadwinner role as only one of several which are important to them. These are the men willing to assume more of the child care and household tasks in their homes. This corresponds to the fascinating finding that "wives' employment is more highly associated with ill health and anxiety among husbands who *seldom* or *never* help to care for their children than among husbands who help more often" (Rubin, 1983:70, italics mine). Other studies of dual earner husbands support the notion that they are as happy in their marriages and may experience less stress than husbands of full time housewives (Booth, 1979; Locksley, 1980).

For the dual-career marriage, there is an increased tendency for more egalitarianism. Although women, to date, retain the greater burden for household management, some changes are becoming evident. The questions which will be more definitively answered by the turn of the century are how much career success will married women experience and what will be the level of marital satisfaction of both the husbands and wives in dual career/earner families.

NEW MARRIAGE FORMS

Open Marriage

Traditional marriage is by definition a closed marriage, where the couple exists as a fused entity, but where they lead separate existences. This kind of existence allows for some growth by the husband due to his exposure to the outside world, yet constricts the wife's own development, thereby creating an imbalance where resentment tends to build up. The closed marriage, according to the O'Neills (1972) is a stifling arrangement which is based on the faulty assumption that two people can be all things to one another, with each fulfilling all the emotional, psychological, intellectual and physical needs of the other. Closed marriage is a rigid and unrealistic form of bondage for both husband and wife (O'Neill and O'Neill, 1972:54).

In their popular but controversial book, *Open Marriage* (1972), Nena and George O'Neill advocate an alternative marriage form resting on the belief that each spouse can maintain a joint as well as separate existence within the marriage and that, although bonded in marriage, the bonds are nondemanding in their quality. Options remain open for the couple to grow as individuals. The open marriage contract "does not substitute new regulations for old ones, but rather suggests ways in which you can learn to communicate freely with one another, in order to arrive at a consensus for living, mutually and fully understood" (O'Neill and O'Neill, 1972:74). The following contrasts the open and closed marriage (O'Neill and O'Neill, 1972:74):

THE OLD CONTRACT DEMANDS	THE OPEN CONTRACT OFFERS
Ownership of the mate	Undependent living
Denial of self	Personal growth
Playing the couples game	Individual freedom
Rigid role behavior	Flexible roles
Absolute fidelity	Mutual trust
Total exclusivity	Expansion through openness

The open contract is built on a foundation of flexibility and "synergistic enhancement" with the belief that "what is good for you is not only good for me *but better for both of us*" (O'Neill and O'Neill, 1972:263).

Since the open marriage concept argues for enhancement in marriage through altering, almost condemning, traditional marital roles, it would seem the ideal alternative to couples seeking an escape from the confines of gender roles in particular. The problem is that by following the route set up by the O'Neills, the marriage itself may flounder. Mintz (1975:75) argues that for open marriage to work, a reasonably secure sense of self must be established beforehand, an issue not confronted by the O'Neills. Mintz (1975:77) also questions the belief that outside involvements can be successfully integrated into the relationship without creating a threat to one's spouse, especially if personal weakness rather than strength is present.

The threat is maximized by the assumption that if the spouse is not meeting the sexual needs of his or her partner, then the option to seek sexual gratification elsewhere is open. Although extramarital experiences are not necessarily suggested, they are not ruled out either. Is finding a companion to go to the opera because your wife/husband does not like opera, different from finding a companion who becomes a sexual partner because your wife/husband is not meeting your needs? Since few marriages, open or otherwise, are devoid of gender roles, it is likely to be the wives who find themselves most compromised in this regard.

In reviewing open marriage five years later, Nena O'Neill (1977) has reevaluated the original concept based on the feedback from numerous couples who find it difficult to achieve the flexibility entailed in the idea, particularly if sexual permissiveness is involved. Considering the strong values associated with marriage per se, it is undoubtedly better to view open marriage as an effort toward a more equalitarian alternative which provides a range of choices for couples and which questions the restraint of traditional gender roles. As long as sexual permissiveness is implied, however, open marriage is not likely to be accepted by most American couples.

Commuter Marriage

The dual location couple is not new. Women who are married to men serving in the armed forces, for example, often maintain a home thousands of miles from their husbands and see them only during leave intervals determined by the military. What is new is the dual-career couple which has evolved into the dual location couple for reasons of the wife's, rather than only the husband's career mobility. Historically, the common pattern is for the woman, literally, to follow her man from city to city as he advances up the career ladder. The rarely challenged expectation is for her own career, if she has one, to be secondary to his. Today, the greater unwillingness for wives to abdicate their careers in favor of their husbands', and a determination of both to maintain the marital relationship, has spawned the commuter marriage.

The gains in career may be offset by the stress of living in two locations with only periodic time together. Gross (1980) finds that wives lament the loss of emotional protection they receive from their husbands but recognize that this is the cost of enhancing their independence. On the other hand, when husbands sense this from their wives, they feel guilty. When the couple has been married longer, have children who are already launched, and where one partner is already established and successful in his/her career, there is less stress in following the regimen associated with a commuter marriage (Gross, 1980).

The most thorough research on this nontraditional alternative has been completed by Gerstel and Gross (1984) who point out that the commuter approach occurs in part because early in their marriages the commuter wives had abandoned their careers and later suffered for it. Career subordination on the part of the wife led to unhappiness and stress that the eventual commuter marriage helps overcome. The following comments by commuter wives sum up this orientation to work and career:

> I go to pieces when I don't work. I get bored when I am not working. We probably work too hard and occasionally feel guilty about it. But we're not the kind of people who can just relax.
> I want to feel I am accomplishing something. It's important to work. And I suppose I do because I want to do it. I think it is FUN! (Gerstel and Gross, 1984:32)

About 90% of the commuter husbands strongly support the professional activities of their wives, as indicated in these comments:

> I want her to do it only because she wants to, not because I want her to.
> I like her to work. I've always encouraged her to work. It makes her more interesting to me. I couldn't even imagine not being with a professional woman. There is just no way the woman who is my wife could be a housewife. (Gerstel and Gross, 1984:36-37)

The resultant stress from dealing with the logistics of a commuter marriage is difficult to resolve. But comments like these suggest that the marriage is not likely to sustain itself if career ascendency on the part of the husband stifles that of the wife. Gerstel and Gross imply that the guilt and regret commuter couples feel when they are not together is due to the fact they accept the standard of career success while at the same time accepting most assumptions regarding marriage and the family (1984:200).

Commuter wives praise feminism in helping them achieve on their own and becoming equal partners careerwise with their husbands. Perhaps unforeseen, however, is that in foregoing what they perceive as traditional gender roles, these couples may inadvertently be reinforcing others. As Gerstel and Gross (1984:201) suggest

> The version of feminism they praised is a movement which values work outside of the home but, as a result, finds itself underplaying the work and emotion that go on inside

of the home . . . commuters as feminists must continue to ask what factors restrict the employment of women. But, in doing so, they must avoid devaluing the work women do and avoid accepting the conventional male model of what it is to be fully human.

The Egalitarian Marriage

Egalitarianism in marriage is strongly associated with employment opportunities for women. When wives contribute financially to the maintenance of the family, they also gain a greater amount of decision-making power. It is the relative power of husband to wife which has bolstered the patriarchal nature of marriage and the broader society. A more equitable arrangement in society will eventually carry over to the family. We have seen that dual-career/earner marriages are not necessarily equal ones because wives retain most household and child care tasks. But these are the very marriages which are moving in the direction of egalitarianism.

As the term denotes, the egalitarian marriage is one which is no longer tied to traditional beliefs about gender roles. Household tasks are divided by skill and desire, rather than what is seen as a masculine or feminine duty. She may enjoy lawn maintenance and he may enjoy cooking. The undesirable chores, such as cleaning or laundry, are equitably distributed. It is the sharing of the domestic chores which creates the most difficulty for the egalitarian couple, because they, too, have been socialized into a world of traditional marriage and family patterns where gender roles continue to intrude (Pietropinto and Simenauer, 1979; Haas, 1980).

Haas (1980) argues that regardless of the problems which the egalitarian model might bring, the benefits are overriding. Marital satisfaction is increased in part because communication and sharing are also enhanced. This carries over to an improvement in parent-child relations since both spouses share the burden and the joy of child rearing. The benefits accrue to children who learn that both parents are nurturers who demonstrate their love and support.

It is evident from survey data that attitudes about the roles of husbands and wives in marriage are shifting towards a model emphasizing more equality. The majority of both sexes believe that women working outside the home is positive, and that husbands and wives should share household tasks (Yankelovich, 1981). Nock (1987:124) states that younger, more educated women are also more likely to reject the traditional marriage idea if it means the husband-dominated, housewife arrangement. This is the group of women steadily increasing in numbers which will assure that the drive toward egalitarianism will continue.

It has been shown that attitudes about equality in marriage have not yet been translated into actual behavior. It is in the vital area of gender roles in marriage that needs to be significantly altered if the egalitarian ideal is ever to be achieved. The desire for marriage continues to be exceedingly strong. If marriages are to endure to the satisfaction of both partners, the traditional model must eventually be eroded in favor of one more conducive to the newer roles of men and women.

EMERGING LIFESTYLES

Singleness

The marriage mandate for both sexes remains very strong. Data indicate that over 90% of people expect to be married, with that figure holding steady since 1960 (Thornton and Freedman, 1986). What is surprising, however, is that this same study reveals that marriage may be losing its sway on young people. They no longer view marriage as necessarily better than remaining single (Thornton and Freedman, 1986:30). The shift in opinion of singleness as a legitimate status is in marked contrast to earlier beliefs which viewed failure to marry as not only undesirable but indicative of personal or social faults (Kuhn, 1955). For the first time, the choice not to marry is being seen as appropriate for some, or at the very least, not as degrading.

Because men conventionally have been the initiators in marriage proposals, it has been assumed that only unattractive or undesirable women would not marry. She is the lonely spinster; he is the carefree bachelor who must be wary of single women who are interested in matrimony. Even as initiators, the image of a man snagged into marriage by a woman in hot pursuit has been a popular one. These are stereotypes which are simply untrue.

We have seen that it is better for men to be married than remain single. They are healthier, happier, and live longer if they marry. Gove (1973) shows that single men have higher overall death rates but particularly in areas related to stress, such as suicide, accidents, and alcoholism. Even George Gilder, the avowed champion of traditional marital and gender roles, laments the single status for men. "Unless he can marry, he is often destined to a Hobbesean life—solitary, poor, nasty, brutish and short" (Gilder, 1974:31).

Socialized for domesticity, singleness would be the less attractive option for women. Yet, almost two decades ago, when women began pursuing higher education and careers in greater numbers, Bird (1971) posited that marriage was not necessarily the best state to pursue, particularly for the educated young woman. She maintained that marriage is not the only way to fulfill one's needs. It is no longer required to be married for economic, physical, social and psychological reasons (Bird, 1971). Single people now have many of the benefits formerly reserved for the married. The caution is not to get married, but to consider the number of available life styles open to young people, mainly women.

The marriage squeeze lessens the options for the highly educated woman who is financially independent. By shopping for the high quality mate she desires, she is likely to discover that they are just not around. As mentioned earlier, they choose not to settle for less but rather remain single; perhaps they continue to search; perhaps they consider their chosen life style to be a positive one. Richardson (1981:273) refers to a subset of this group as *monads*, because they see singleness as desirable and may reject marriage and any permanent and/or exclusive sexual relationship.

Whereas both men and women can be monads, the advantages for women appear to be greater, since marriage places a larger psychological burden on the career-minded woman. If the feeling that they must have children persists, the monad status will dissolve. But as more young women pursue careers and advanced education, all the while gaining a sense of well-being, they may continue to postpone marriage to the extent that they never marry. Rather than seeing it as a devalued position, they embrace singleness confidently as a positive alternative lifestyle.

Cohabitation

A couple living together without marriage was cause for condemnation, even in the recent past. The whispers, innuendos, and raised eyebrows accompanying this living arrangement have tended to fall by the wayside as more and more middle class couples choose cohabitation as their preferred life style, whether they intend to marry later or not.

The rise in cohabitation has led to the creation of a formal term to categorize this group. These people are designated as POSSLQs, People of the Opposite Sex Sharing Living Quarters. In 1983 there were 1.9 million POSSLQ households, double the figure from just a decade ago (Mooney, 1985:7). This is undoubtedly an underestimation of the true number, since the U.S. Census Bureau arrives at the number merely by counting households where an unmarried male and female reside. Couples may not report their arrangement or cohabit while still retaining separate addresses (Nock, 1987:108).

POSSLQ arrangements have previously been most popular among college students attending large universities, with Henze and Hudson (1974) reporting that on one such campus 18% of the women and 29% of the men had at some point cohabited. On the other hand, the POSSLQ numbers are increasing in other populations as well. Glick and Norton (1977) indicate that as early as 1970, a full 75% of cohabiting couples under age 25 were not enrolled in college. Cole (1977:78) also speculates that as noncampus cohabitation becomes increasingly viewed as an alternative life style, marriage rates for first marriage will also decline. Clearly, POSSLQs are much more than passing phenomenon and involve a cross-section of the population.

In reviewing the literature on cohabitants compared to married couples, Newcomb (1982:146) finds that the emotional closeness and perception of roles do not differ and that as a screening device for later marriage, traditional courtship patterns work just as well. Bentler and Newcomb's data (1978) show that the divorce rate is just as high among previous cohabitants as among others. If cohabitants experience the realities of living together before marriage, this should make a difference in their subsequent marital adjustment. However, contrary to what is expected, Watson (1986) finds that noncohabitants have higher marital adjustment scores than cohabitants.

Differences between the sexes in POSSLQ households occur on a number of fronts. In general, cohabitants are no more egalitarian than the rest of society in that the female assumes the burden of household tasks (Stafford et al., 1977; Macklin, 1983) and the couple gives precedence to the man's career over the woman's (Kotkin, 1983). The exception to this is that cohabitants not planning to marry are essentially egalitarian, but the males in these relationships are also less successful in career attainment than other cohabiting males (Kotkin, 1983:975). And, if cohabiting is assumed to be a trial marriage, women are more committed to it than men. Women look to the arrangement as security which will come through later marriage, whereas men are more likely to view it as an alternative to marriage and as a means of sexual gratification (Lyness et al., 1972; Arafat and Yorburg, 1973).

Considering these findings, it is somewhat surprising to witness an ever increasing population of cohabitants. Perhaps they are drawn to the idealism that is inherent in an arrangement which, on the surface at least, offers more benefits than liabilities. But the benefits appear to erode as cohabiting time increases. Indeed, the recent California Supreme Court decision in the famous Marvin versus Marvin case where a "palimony" suit brought against actor Lee Marvin by his cohabiting partner of seven years demonstrates that their relationship was in essence a marriage anyway (Kay and Amyx, 1982). Rulings such as this would lead one to question why cohabiting would offer as positive an option as marriage, at least in the eyes of the law. Data from the next generation of POSSLQs are needed to determine the overall consequences, specifically related to gender role change, marital satisfaction and divorce.

Extramarital Relationships

Extramarital relationships, commonly referred to as "affairs," take on a myriad of forms. These arrangements are extremely varied, involve different degrees of openness and include married as well as single people. Estimates of secret extramarital relationships for married people range from 65-70% for men and 45-65% for women (Stayton, 1984:4). When considering only the sexual component the original Kinsey et al. (1953) data indicate that 50% of males and 26% of females engaged in extramarital coitus by age 40. By 1975, the figure for women had increased to 38% (Atwater, 1982:16).

These data are not inclusive for a number of reasons. First, many extramarital relationships are more open, with the spouse and other friends aware of the relationship. In this sense, the label of "affair" is an erroneous one with its implication of secrecy. Second, single women and men are involved with married women and men but figures usually only give the married estimates. Third, depending on how an extramarital relationship is defined, a sexual component may or may not be part of it, although the potential is certainly there. Finally, reporting on these kinds of relationships is threatening to many, which is why the Kinsey data were suspect for what was originally believed to be exceptionally high numbers during a period seen as less promiscuous than today. In all, it can be assumed that the reported figures for extramarital relationships are lower than the actual.

Extramarital relationships occur, according to Atwater (1982), because we are unrealistic about love and the ability of our spouse to satisfy all our sexual needs. And if the O'Neills (1972) are correct, we can add the emotional need category as well, although an emotional relationship becomes defined as an affair usually when the sexual component is involved. The myths that contribute to our untenable faith in sexual exclusivity include

1. One person will supply all of another's emotional, social and sexual needs. Not only is this impossible, but it raises our expectations for satisfaction in marriage to extremely high levels.
2. People grow to love each other more through the years. Divorce rates and research show otherwise.
3. Sexual exclusivity comes easily and naturally. There is no evidence that this is true for humans. Also, as seen above, the double standard gives males different "rights" than females in this regard.
4. Husbands and wives should be best friends. A best friend is an intimate confidant who can share all subjects openly. Yet in marriage the shared burdens and responsibilities, and the special kind of intimacy dictate the need for more emotional privacy.
5. Extramarital affairs will destroy a marriage. The need for growth, variety or as an antidote for boredom suggest otherwise. Extramarital sex may enhance some marriages, make no difference to others but can be destructive to many. I would also add that emotional rather than purely sexual liaisons have similar potentials for all these occurrences. (Atwater, 1982:18; Lazarus, 1987:75-76)

Atwater contends that "we have seduced ourselves with myths of monogamy . . . and retain romantic attachments to these myths despite the pain and disillusion these unexamined beliefs are bound to bring us (p.18)."

As we would expect, men and women differ as to their desires and expectations in extramarital relationships. The sexual excitement is likely to be a stronger rationale for men to pursue such relationships than it is for women. The best study on extramarital relationships among married women has been done by Atwater (1982) who finds that nearly all the women she interviewed identified the least satisfactory area of their marriage as the expressive area. Half of these women also say that their relationships with their husbands actually improved as a result of the extramarital situation (Atwater, 1982:74). As their needs are being met outside the marriage, their behavior changed in the marriage. As one woman reports

> Since I have this second relationship on-going, I have been able to draw my husband out more and get him to talk more . . . and to be more open in expressing my feelings with him . . . I am slowly but surely trying to bring our relationship up to a level that meets more of my needs. (Atwater, 1982:75)

Atwater's research may not be generalized to other women involved in extramarital relationships because she specifically chose feminist-oriented women to interview. The sample reflects an interest in exploring the impact of social change, thereby allowing an understanding of women open to personal and social change (Atwater, 1982:28). It is less surprising, then, that even if the expressiveness dimension is emphasized in the involvements with other men, Atwater finds no evidence of a traditional model of female sexuality. These women did not live vicariously through their extramarital partners and evolved their own script of female-centered sexuality (Atwater, 1982:140).

Atwater's research is significant because it offers a different view of the extramarital relationship. Certainly the women in her study are not immune to the deceit and guilt which accompany many of the relationships. The case of the single woman-married man suggests a different pattern. They are primarily secret relationships that appear to protect both parties. We can see the double standard at work when a woman's reputation is threatened by exposure of the affair, with fewer penalties for married or single men involved in extramarital relationships. We may have the "other woman" but where is the "other man?"

With the marriage squeeze at work, more single women are opting for relationships with married men. Many of these women have no desire to marry their extramarital partner or anyone else. In thorough interviews with numerous "Other Women," as Richardson refers to her interviewees, she finds that unlike women who became mistresses in the past, this group has a very different agenda. "Today's woman wants to finish her education, build a career, recover from a divorce, raise her children, explore her sexuality. Getting married is not necessarily her primary goal" (Richardson, 1986:24).

She can be vulnerable and express weakness, which her professional role does not allow. The support and listening the married man offers strengthens her emotional attachment to him, which increases the likelihood that a long-term affair will ensue (Richardson, 1986:26). His willingness to expose his own insecurities can create a meaningful bond between both parties. And if the relationship has evolved from an open-ended marriage on his part, the liaison is further bolstered. In another study Richardson (1988:368) also suggests that single women in liaisons with married men "experience greater control over their sexuality because they feel freer to repudiate their sexual repressions, to abstain, to have safe sex, and to explore their sexual preferences."

The picture presented here is a rosy one, but many cautions should be noted. The research on extramarital relationships is relatively recent, and as Richardson (1986) notes, little systematic work has been done on the single woman-married man from the woman's perspective. However, some patterns are evident. If a woman desires to eventually marry at all, her relationship with the married man will effectively keep her out of the marriage market. By having her needs met by him, she does not avail herself of opportunities to meet other men. This is especially true for younger single women with low-paying, uninteresting jobs who enjoy the material benefits a successful married man can bring to the relationship.

It is likely that there will be more "Other Women" in the future, some who are satisfied in their relationships but others who invest too much and end up with a great deal of pain that is not easily, if ever, overcome. From a feminist perspective, the "Other Woman" ultimately contributes to the perpetuation of male power and privilege and female distrust of other women (Richardson, 1986:27). In the long run, women have more to lose than to gain by extramarital relationships.

7

Gender
and Family Relations

THE PARENTHOOD TRANSITION

The transition from the marital dyad to the family triad is a significant one. The addition of the first child brings with it numerous changes which affect the marriage itself and profoundly alters the life style of the couple. To say that parenthood is filled with uncertainty is an understatement. Parenting is based on skills which need to be learned but cannot adequately be mastered, if at all, until after the child is born. Preparation for parenthood is based on one's own family experiences, dealing with the children of other friends and relatives, formal classes through hospitals and educational institutions, folklore, and reading a variety of child care and parenting manuals. Whatever the degree of advance planning, new parents are likely to discover that the anticipation of what it means to be a parent is far different from the reality. Parenthood has differential experiences and consequences for the woman in comparison to the man.

Because of the element of uncertainty, and even shock, which first time parents experience, the literature on the transition to parenthood has focused on parenthood as a crisis. Backett (1982:16) finds that new parents retrospectively tend to devalue the objective preparations they made for the parental role, seeing them "as at best irrelevant and occasionally a direct hindrance." It is only their flexibility and capacity in preparing for a child which allows them to succeed during this critical period.

The view of the couple as undergoing an extensive crisis accompanied by major role redefinition is echoed in earlier studies of the parenthood transition (LeMasters, 1957; Dyer, 1963, cited in Belsky and Miller, 1986:109). By the mid 1960s however, this crisis orientation began to be replaced in the family literature with the perspective that parenthood is a normal developmental stage to which new parents gradually become accustomed (Rossi, 1968; Russell, 1975). The major shifts in life style which may add tension and anticipated or undesirable role change must also be viewed in light of the gratification the child brings to the new parents (Leifer, 1977; Feldman and Nash, 1984).

Obviously parenthood will alter marital roles and create new family roles. Whether the parenthood transition will be seen as a crisis, a stage in normal development, or something in between will depend on how the family will structure itself to meet the parenting challenge. This structure will be largely dependent on beliefs regarding gender roles. The labels husband and wife suggest different realities, the same can be said for motherhood and fatherhood.

Motherhood

The belief that a woman's greatest fulfillment and ultimate achievement will be in her role as a mother is socialized into girls very early in life. Referred to as the "motherhood mandate," this view assumes that it is the woman's obligation to dedicate her life unselfishly to the raising of her children and to be constantly on call for her child's needs (Russo, 1979). Although this means foregoing any other activities that she may feel personally worthwhile, a woman willingly submits herself first to her child-rearing responsibilities. The power of this mandate instills guilt in women who work outside the home, especially if they associate their employment with psychological, social or personal gain. Employed women who must work purely for economic benefits are not immune and may also find a heightened sense of guilt.

Although our culture tends to idealize the motherhood role, the actual support new mothers may receive varies considerably. If women are socialized into believing that becoming a good mother is easily achieved, they are severely jolted by their first parenting roles. The tension and strain experienced by first time mothers can be perceived by themselves as personal failure, which in turn lessens their motivation to ask for help. We saw earlier that the notion of a maternal instinct is highly questionable at best, but the view that the mother's role "comes naturally" stubbornly persists.

From a functionalist viewpoint, the motherhood mandate is essential. The socialization of the children, primarily the mother's responsibility, is necessary for later societal productivity. If socialization is inadequate in the family, the goals of the broader society may later be compromised. As Goode (1982:6) maintains, the family is an instrument, albeit a vital one, for the continuation of the society. There is little argument that the family plays a, perhaps *the*, critical role in socialization. But because functionalism assumes that a traditional division of labor in the family is the most efficient, less conflictive arrangement, implicit in the view is that if something "goes wrong" with the children, it is the mother's fault. She takes the responsibility, and hence the blame and ultimately the guilt associated with child rearing.

Another distressing consequence of the view that only the mother should care for the child is that if these very children suffer from later psychological problems they also tend to blame their mothers. In this sense, it is a no-win situation for mothers. If she works outside the home using others as caretakers and her children manifest psychological problems, she is at fault as a neglectful parent. If she is the primary caretaker in a traditional housewife role and her children experience problems, she is still seen to be at fault. Only this time she is viewed as overprotective, dominating, and an instiller of guilt in her family because she is doing so much for them, perhaps taking on a martyr role (Wilbourn, 1978). In either instance she incurs the disapproval of society, her own family and in the most painful circumstance, herself.

The motherhood mandate leads to a mystique associated with a glorification of her role. An often overlooked fact about the motherhood mystique is that it only came about in the United States by the middle of the nineteenth century. A frontier economy based on subsistence farming required that women assume other than child-rearing roles, which were deemed as more important for the survival of the family. As Hoffnung (1984:125) states, productive work was placed before reproductive concerns. Even children were viewed for their productive qualities. It is only since the turn of the century that the notion of having children for purely psychological reasons has been firmly ingrained on the American consciousness.

According to McBride (1973) and Hoffnung (1984:128) the motherhood mystique is made up of certain qualities.

1. Ultimate fulfillment *as a woman* is achieved by becoming a mother.
2. The body of work assigned to mothers—caring for child, home, and husband—fits together in a noncontradictory manner.
3. To be a good mother, a woman must like being a mother as well as all the work that goes with motherhood.
4. A woman's intense, exclusive devotion to mothering is good for her children.

An acceptance of the motherhood mystique precludes other activities, accomplishments, and individual growth for women, especially within careers. By this definition, motherhood is the only worthwhile role. The obvious problems and contradictions emanating from the mystique are conveniently overlooked. Can women feel good about themselves as mothers if they also seek other roles?

One answer lies in the demographics of motherhood, which have changed significantly, especially since the 1950s. As women achieved career and educational goals, marriage and motherhood were delayed. This explains why so many women in their 30s are now having children for their first time. It also supports the idea of motherhood as a salient goal. Most women are unwilling to give up biological parenthood, although the families will be smaller than in their parents' generation. Since career oriented women are also unwilling to give up either motherhood *or* professional roles, they are adapting their beliefs about family and parenting accordingly.

Today's young women assume that motherhood, as the mystique suggests, gives them a sense of personal fulfillment. But unlike their own mothers and grandmothers, they see motherhood as a choice that some women may legitimately disavow (Hare-Mustin et al., 1983). The views that a woman or even a wife is incomplete without children and that children are a prerequisite to a woman's happiness are also being challenged (Knaub et al., 1983). This is especially true for younger professional women who are already demonstrating higher rates of childlessness than older professional women (Yogev and Vierra, 1983). This study finding is unusual since we have already seen that the majority of professional women expect to pursue motherhood as well as their careers. Yogev and Vierra (1983) suggest that the women in their study may not be as confident in the ability to combine conflicting motherhood and career roles. If this is indeed the case, it may indicate a further weakening of the motherhood mandate.

The acceptance of feminist values by a larger proportion of women would also likely affect notions about motherhood. Scott and Morgan (1983) show that women who have traditional gender role orientations desire families, especially larger families, when compared to nontraditional women. Gerson (1984) finds that college women who subjectively identify with feminism are less interested in having children, which reinforces other studies indicating that there is generally a negative relationship between feminism and motherhood (Gerson, 1980; Hare-Muston and Broderick, 1979 cited in Gerson 1984:289). But a unique point about these findings is that for feminists who desire motherhood and intend to have the same number of children as other women, they also believe that motherhood offers opportunities for active mastery and assertiveness (Gerson, 1984:395). Motherhood can be redefined in terms acceptable to feminists who want to creatively master a number of roles. The motherhood mandate is itself being redefined to fit the newer life styles of contemporary women.

A final note on the voluntarily childless couple is necessary. Even if the motherhood mandate is weakening, couples must still contend with a prochild orientation in society. The belief that couples should have children is so strong that those who choose not to do so, especially the women, are viewed by others as misguided and selfish (Silka and Kiesler, 1977). Another study finds that voluntary childless couples are viewed as deviant in a number of respects, statistically, socially and maybe even psychologically (Veevers, 1972).

But what majority opinion suggests about the childless couple appears to be different than what couples themselves suggest. A literature review by Peterson (1983a:322) concludes that the voluntarily childless spouse is "just as adjusted and happy as the spouse who is a parent or plans to be a parent," and that "evidence of a negative view of the childless spouse can be interpreted as a negative bias than a statement of reality." And, as for overall marital satisfaction, children apparently create a great amount of tension for the couple, particularly for the wife (Harriman, 1986). Married couples without children are more likely to be happier and actually have improvement in happiness over time than do married couples with children (Renne, 1976; Campbell et al., 1975).

Although couples in general and women in particular continue to view parenthood as desirable, the number of voluntarily childless couples is increasing. This suggests that, along with the weakening of the motherhood mandate, there is also less pressure to conform to traditional family norms regarding parenthood.

Fatherhood

When considering nurturing and child care functions, the American father is viewed as peripheral at best when compared to the mother. Unlike our colonial American ancestors who expected the father to provide for both the economic needs and spiritual education of his children with the less literate mother as his able assistant (Vinovskis, 1986:188), the contemporary father is cast mainly into the breadwinning role.

Public policy and federal and state legislation regarding custody of children, child support, welfare, definitions of desertion and child neglect, and so on have served to fortify the emphasis on the primary role of father as the economic provider for the family. Vinovskis (1986) notes that some efforts are now being made to involve fathers, specifically unwed adolescent fathers, in the care and upbringing of their children. Whether this is to go beyond financial support, which can be viewed somewhat as a punitive measure, to direct involvement with child rearing, remains to be seen.

The fact that most fathers take their breadwinning role very seriously does not diminish other interests they have in their families. Like women, men also see raising a family as a very important goal in their lives, although they still believe women should be primarily responsible for child care (Astin, 1985). As will be documented in the next chapter, fathers have been discouraged from involvement with their children by a masculine ethic which discourages them from assuming more nurturing behavior.

As first time parents, men appear to adapt more easily to the rigors of fatherhood than women do to motherhood, and husbands can predict with more success than their wives what kind of parents they are likely to be (Feldman and Nash, 1984; Harriman, 1986). Traditional fatherhood may not bring the same profound personal and marital changes that mothers experience, but research reveals that fathers can and do form strong immediate bonds with their newborn children and are able to successfully take on subsequent child care tasks (Greenberg and Morris, 1974; Parke and Tinsley, 1981; Mooney, 1985). From these data, we can presume that it is mainly the emphasis on the provider role and the de-emphasis on the childhood socialization role which keep men from assuming greater responsibility for nurturing their children. We have accepted a masculine imperative which denies men the opportunities for more meaningful parent-child relationships.

The prime directive for fathers is to provide for the economic support of their families. Yet in comparison to mothers, the effect of fathers on the development of their children is often overlooked. Chapter 3 demonstrated that parental influence on childhood socialization is critical. Mothers assume the major responsibility in this area. But fathers also send important messages regarding roles to their children that are probably accentuated by the reduced contact and differing quality of interaction.

While mothers take care of the children and respond more in terms of their physical needs than fathers, fathers engage in more play behavior with them (Parke and Tinsley, 1981). As children get older, fathers direct more attention to their sons than their daughters (Lamb, 1979). Though fathers exhibit much warmth for their daughters as infants, a dramatic withdrawal soon occurs on his part. Perhaps due to a feeling that sex-typical behavior must be generated, by age two fathers are less than half as active with their daughters as with their sons (Lynn, 1979:124). During the early school years fathers reward their daughters about half as much as their sons for good behavior (Lynn, 1979:125).

The concern for behavior that is gender appropriate carries through to father-child interactions during adolescence. Recent research indicates a strong positive relationship between fathers and adolescent sons' gender role beliefs and expectations (Emihovich et al., 1984). Fathers who are less traditional in their gender role beliefs, holding less stereotyped expectations, have sons who match their fathers in this regard. As the father is the critical figure in determining his adolescent son's willingness to accept changes in his own gender role, despite changes in broader society, we cannot expect sons to drastically modify their gender role behavior unless their fathers support them (Emihovich et al., 1984:867).

Traditional gender role expectations, though stronger for sons, carry through to daughters as well. The tendency is for fathers to use strong discipline on sons in order to enhance what they view as masculine behavior, while at the same time allowing their daughters to retain elements of dependence, thereby encouraging a continuation of childhood qualities. Konopka (1976) describes accounts of adolescent daughters who felt that their fathers were either virtually invisible in their lives or who discouraged them from growing up. The effects of this kind of behavior, Lynn (1979:126) suggests, is to leave little choice but for the girl to respond in a traditionally feminine way which heightens her desire to be pampered, as well as fosters her flirtatiousness.

The extreme scenario of undue discipline for boys treating girls as sex objects during adolescence revolves around violence, abuse and incest. Increased parent-child conflict at this stage of life is typical, but it is heightened as far as fathers are concerned. Fathers who are inconsistent in their discipline, or who are neglectful or cold are more likely to have adolescent sons who are delinquent or express irresponsible behavior (Martin, 1985:1983). When the father engages in incest with his adolescent daughter, he is not only relating to her as a sex object but "also expressing the extreme of the presumed right of the male to access the female" (Lynn, 1979:126). Herman's (1981) study of father-daughter incest indicates that it is the daughter and not the father who stops the sexual involvement, with most girls reporting that fathers would continue the contact if possible. A typical pattern of father-daughter incest is recounted by Fisher and Berdie (1978; cited in Martin, 1985:183).

My name is Alice. I'm 14. My Dad has sex with me. I'm sure my mom knows, but she's afraid to do anything about it. Maybe she doesn't care. . . . I love my Daddy, but I don't want to do it with him anymore. I'm scared.

It is evident that father-child relationships are enhanced when fathers are nurturant rather than aloof, visible rather than invisible, and consistent and fair when administering discipline to both their sons and daughters. Although Maccoby and Jacklin (1974) find few major differences in the way mothers and fathers treat their children, the differences that do occur are significant. Fathers who are successful in parenting provide the kind of caring and warmth which may be contradictory to the established patriarchal family role assumed by most past and many contemporary fathers. Lynn (1979) and Martin (1985) indicate that fathers who move in the direction of androgyny, with its inherent role flexibility, will meet the demands of contemporary society. Research suggests that they will also be better parents.

Children of Dual Earners

With the influx of women into the paid labor force the dual-earner family is becoming increasingly common. As shown in Chapter 6, there are now more dual-earning nuclear families with children present than one-earner nuclear families with children present. The largest overall increase is in families with preschoolers. Since women are traditionally responsible for child care, particularly in the preschool years, all eyes turn to them when questions arise as to how children are affected when both parents work outside the home. It is the wives rather than their husbands who reap society's disapproval if it is established that when both parents enter the world of paid labor their children suffer. Disregarding the claim that women should be solely responsible for primary socialization of their children anyway, how legitimate is the "suffering children" theme?

It has already been demonstrated that paid employment benefits women socially and psychologically, especially when they work in positions that they find challenging, rewarding, and personally meaningful. Their marriages appear to be enhanced and shared decision-making makes for a semblance of an egalitarian arrangement. The cost for women involves maintaining responsibilities at home and for the children when their husbands do not share on anywhere near an equal basis, household, and child care chores. These women can suffer from an overloaded role which may add strains which the employment per se cannot eradicate. In general, however, the evidence from dual earner families shows women who are enriched by their labor force activities.

If parents are happy and the family is enhanced by a dual-earning structure, this should logically carry over to the children. Not so, states writer Harry Stein (1987), who maintains that with infant day care as the answer to the needs of the dual-earning couple, the child is not provided with a sustained one-to-one relationship with a primary care-giver that is essential to her/his healthy emotional development. According to Stein (1987:162), surrogate care is more of a luxury when one parent is free not to work but both partners are intensely career oriented. He points his finger at women who *choose* to work outside the home *rather* than stay home with the children. He states (1987:162)

> Now, there's no reason to be coy here. Invariably the parent who is obliged . . . to grapple with the choice between home and office is the woman; no matter how unfettered by convention any of us purports to be, no matter how vividly we might wish it to be otherwise . . . men simply do not put their careers on hold in the interests of family.

Apparently both men and women are condemned by unalterable roles, "no matter how vividly we might wish it to be otherwise."

Stein's case for the mother staying home rests on the argument that the long-term consequences of day care results not just as "mere inconvenience or temporary dislocation but a wounding sense of loss" when the young child is removed from the primary care giver (Stein, 1987:164). He quotes psychologist Lee Salk, an anti-day-care advocate, who dismisses the argument that quality time with the children justifies time away from the children. Salk contends that quantity is even more vital and that people who cannot "provide sufficient time for their children would be better off if they didn't have any" (Stein, 1987:164).

If parents, especially mothers, are not filled with remorse and guilt by this stage Stein goes on to say that parents have an obligation to find some other way of coping than day care. Implicit in this is that most other options which do not involve mother staying home are either deemed unrealistic by working parents or dismissed as unacceptable by Stein. The final thrust of Stein's (1987:165) opposition comes from a quote by a literary agent, "herself a onetime day-care worker," who argues that "a lot of people plead poverty . . . when what they mean is that they just don't want to lower their standard of living."

The case Stein makes for staying home is based on his own conversations with dual-earning parents, former day-care workers who now oppose these kinds of arrangements, and psychologists and therapists who treat people who are unable to form current relationships due to their feelings of lack of love when they were children. The contention is that a generation of such children will soon be upon us unless something is drastically changed. The essential point and the tone in which it is made is that parents are abandoning their children to day care so they can selfishly pursue their own careers which in later years will damage children and by extension, society. Is the evidence sufficient to warrant such a conclusion?

Certainly we will not be able to answer this fully until the current day care generation is itself established in their own families and careers. But from the numerous studies which have been done on the effects of the dual earner family on children, the evidence does not support the "suffering children" theme. In fact, one major source of information is often overlooked by both sides in debating the issue. When women were desperately needed during World War II to work in defense plants, they were recruited by the thousands in campaigns designed to alleviate their anxiety and guilt about leaving their children with others. Creative approaches to day care became the norm of the day, with centers operating for many women who could not rely on relatives or whose options were limited. Given the tenor of the time, thoughts of potential negative consequences which may accrue in the long-run for these children were dismissed or conveniently ignored.

After the war, traditional attitudes prevailed and women were expected to return home and be full time housewives. They were not guilty of being neglectful mothers during the war, but if they chose to continue to work outside the home afterwards, the guilt returned. Weingarten (1978) maintains that the guilt mothers feel when they do hold paid positions is compensated for by the amount of time they assume in child care tasks, thereby relieving their husbands of the bulk of these responsibilities. Husbands willingly give up child care tasks because they have not been socialized into the nurturing role and because their wives accept the script that mothers who work outside the home are somehow "bad" mothers.

Research demonstrates that working mothers are not "bad" mothers and that children are not jeopardized by maternal employment. Berg (1987:68) cites evidence from an ongoing longitudinal study by psychologists Adele and Allen Gottfried indicating that there are no differences in the home environment or development of children with employed mothers than those who are not. In reviewing literature on studies of infants who had some day care experiences, the conclusion is that mothers are not replaced by child care workers as the primary or preferred source of a baby's affectional or emotional ties, though children can develop such ties for a variety of people (Berg, 1987:69).

Though myths and ideology about the effects of a working mother prevail, children of dual earning couples appear to express high degrees of confidence, resourcefulness and independence (St. John-Parsons, 1978). Studies are consistent in providing evidence that children are neither deprived nor neglected with maternal employment, and in fact may demonstrate more positive social, psychological, and interpersonal characteristics than do children of mothers who do not work outside the home (Propper, 1972; St. John-Parsons, 1978; Etaugh, 1980; Joy and Wise, 1983; Scarr, 1984; Margolis, 1984).

If maternal employment could be shown to have adverse effects on the child, many of these should logically show up during adolescence, since this is often a time filled with a great deal of stress and family turmoil. Again, research does not warrant this conclusion. Stephan and Corder (1985) find that adolescents from dual career families actually prefer this kind of family structure, and not surprising, have less traditional gender role attitudes than children from traditional single-earner homes. In general, adolescents in dual career families view their lifestyle positively and report high degrees of parental closeness, supportiveness and interest in their personal problems (Propper, 1972; Knaub, 1986). As would be expected, a problem area adolescents identify is that of time constraints faced by their parents related to a dual career family life style (Knaub, 1986).

The idea that children are adversely affected by maternal employment is simply not supported, especially with the dual-earner family. In dual-career families where both parents are employed in professional capacities it is likely that the children are actually enriched by this kind of family arrangement. For poor women or single mothers who must rely on less than adequate child care arrangements, this may not be the case. But for dual-earner couples, the following statement by Dr. Berry Brazelton (quoted in Berg, 1987:70) most likely holds true.

> It is no longer a question of whether or not mothers should work. A woman's identity is really tied up with a career and with nurturing. The task ahead of us is to give her the most support possible to do both, for only then will we be helping parents and children to reach their fullest potential.

THE BLACK AMERICAN FAMILY

Family patterns in the United States have been altered and become more diverse in response to a rapidly changing society. Since the family is our most conservative institution, when we can actually witness modifications in the family, we know that broader social change must be rampant. As American families in general have adapted to the refashioning of societal norms, black American families have also changed accordingly. However, given a minority status based on a different historical foundation, the resulting family patterns demonstrate a unique series of adaptations.

Economic oppression rooted in racial discrimination has been responsible for a blurring of gender roles and role sharing evident in many black American families. With the underemployment of black men, black women have often assumed provider roles for the family. As McCray (1980:74) points out, the ability of these women to take on such roles when necessary has been a positive factor for blacks, adding to the stability and even survival of many families. According to Malson (1983:101), "one of the fundamental differences in the lives of black and white females is the experience of black females as paid workers." Their paid work has been a necessary, but constructive adaptation to the reality of economic and social inequality in America.

McCray (1980) argues that unlike their counterparts in white families, black husbands who are unable to work for a variety of reasons may suffer less emotional turmoil when their wives do work. Staples (1973, cited in McCray, 1980) further believes that the role flexibility demonstrated by the wife increases the esteem and appreciation of her held by the husband, and may actually help cement their relationship. This is not to dismiss the tension which arises in periods of economic uncertainty, only to suggest that less rigid gender roles can be indicative of family strength in difficult situations.

Yet this very strength has been viewed as a weakness inherent in black families. In a report which gained widespread national attention, Moynihan (1965) intimated that in the numerous black families headed by women a "black matriarchy" exists in which decision-making and other family powers and responsibilities rest with women rather than men. By this way of thinking black men are emasculated, stripped of authority and driven from the family under an aura of self-defeat. The family is left with fewer defenses against poverty, delinquency, and illegitimacy. The notion of a black matriarchy continued to gain credibility by statistics indicating that a sizable proportion of black families are female-headed compared to white families (Eshleman, 1988:202). The idea of a black matriarchy has done untold damage by creating and reinforcing stereotypes of superhuman women and castrated men (Ladner, 1972) who are then blamed for the circumstances in which they find themselves.

The myth of the black matriarchy has been challenged on many fronts. Although the proportion of black families headed by women has increased since the 1970s, recent census data indicate that over half of all black families consist of a married couple, with or without children (Glick, 1981). The married couple exists in an egalitarian family structure whose roles are complementary yet flexible, with the husband engaged in stable employment. This kind of family pattern is not only the most common among blacks, but indicative of working class or middle class socioeconomic status (Cazenave, 1979; Eshleman, 1988). An egalitarian arrangement is supported by black women who work outside the home by choice rather than economic necessity. Using a Boston sample, Malson (1983:111) finds that most married mothers work in spite of having husbands earning over the median income for area families. Beckett (1976, cited in McCray, 1980:75) notes that black husbands are more willing than white husbands to accommodate themselves and the household to the needs of their working wives such as in the area of child care.

For poorer black families with fewer resources, where the stereotype of black matriarchy is assumed to be the most relevant, the majority stable black family tends to be ignored by social science. Billingsley (1970) asserts that the focus has been on the very poor, problem-ridden black families. Both Ladner (1972) and Billingsley (1970) find it unconscionable that where this kind of family exists in the black community, it is blamed for problems that blacks experience in other segments of society. Role sharing by the poorest black couples is a necessary adaptation which enhances their ability to remain together as a family unit (Blackwell, 1985). The dilemma is that the acceptance of rigid gender roles by such families would be potentially harmful; yet by altering them, the family is considered deviant or unstable.

In reporting the trends and statistics on black American families, it is important to keep the above facts in mind, especially the data showing the married norm. The 1980 census reveals that approximately one-half of black families with children are married couple families (31%) and one-half are single parent families (31%) (Glick, 1981:107), and as expected, the vast majority of these single parents are women. Over half of all black children live with their mothers or other female relatives, which puts them at higher risk for living in poverty (Williams, 1987:380). Black women who work outside the home have the lowest earnings of any group, when race and sex variables are considered (U.S. Department of Labor, 1982). Williams (1987:380) cites census data which indicate that fully one-half of children living in father absent homes are in poverty.

Black women must carry the double burden of their minority group status. Few would argue with Staples' (1970) conclusion that the black female is exploited by virtue of both race and sex. If she is a single parent, the prospects of decent wages to maintain her family above poverty level are severely reduced. This is in spite of a strong commitment to employment (McCray, 1980) and an image shared by both black women and men that the woman to be revered is one who is independent and achieving (Crovitz and Steinmann, 1980).

While black women are worse off economically and face the double minority burden, black men must contend with a double bind of their own. Men are socialized into instrumental family roles which tie masculinity with being a good provider. Cazenave (1981:178) maintains that black men accept this standard for masculinity but are denied access for opportunities to do so. Masculinity must then be found in other channels. As Cazenave (1981:180) states, "even before an underclass black male inherits the economic problems that have contributed to a low level of involvement for his father in family affairs, he is socialized to expect that men demonstrate their manhood in the streets, not the home." Family life inevitably suffers as a result. One indication of this is a divorce rate among blacks which is twice that of the overall population.

In addition, the black community is not immune from stereotypes concerning black male-black female relationships. Cazenave's (1983:341) recent research reports that a majority of a sample of middle class black men believe that black women have more opportunity than black men, with a large minority feeling that black women are in part responsible for the low status of black men. For these men, racial discrimination is less an issue. They prefer traditional gender roles for women and men (Cazenave, 1983:341). This pessimistic view supports the contention that a self-fulfilling prophecy may be operating. Although the black matriarchy argument has been successfully challenged, many black men may have internalized its assumptions, which in turn creates tension between the sexes. Cazenave's research is significant because it may herald a trend among the black middle class which could in the future embrace more traditional gender role ideology.

However, this discussion has still suggested that gender role flexibility has helped rather than deterred the black American family and contributed to a more equalitarian pattern, particularly among the middle and working class. It is in the black lower class family where role sharing is not as prevalent and where more restrictive masculine role definitions held by the wider society play a greater part in male socialization. It appears that the family which is economically stable is more at ease with altered gender roles, with this being more evident in black rather than white families. Considering that the socioeconomic attainment of blacks remains tied to institutional racism, the strength of the black family is even more remarkable. If SES is held constant, black families and white families are more alike than different.

DIVORCE

The choice to dissolve a marriage has been an alternative throughout most of the history of the United States. The fact that it is now a largely acceptable alternative has contributed to a staggering divorce rate which has steadily increased since as early as the mid-nineteenth century. Though subject to historical anomalies and economic fluctuations such as the Depression and World War II, the rate of divorce appears to have peaked in the 1970s and has been relatively stable since 1980 (Cherlin, 1981; Kemper, 1983). Masnick and Bane (1980) cautiously suggest that the increase in divorce may be leveling off, and that if the divorce trend does continue, it will do so at a slower rate. Whatever the future trend, we now have the highest divorce rate of our relatively short history.

Marital dissolution has profound social, psychological, and economic effects for the divorcing couple and their families. Research is accumulating which shows that divorce has differential consequences for women compared to men. Men and women who are defined as nontraditional in their gender role orientation adjust better to the divorce trauma. This indicates that those who are less conventional, such as the androgynous man and the assertive, independent woman are better at reconciling themselves to divorce than passive women and men with very traditional gender role perspectives (Chiriboga and Thurnher, 1980; Hansson et al., 1984). On measurements involving gender roles for women, masculinity is related to positive self-esteem, competence, and personal effectiveness, while femininity is negatively related or unrelated to them (Brown and Manela, 1978; Hoffman and Fidell, 1979; Sadd et al., 1979). Since these are the very characteristics which are essential for coping with the loss and bereavement often concurrent with divorce and its aftermath, the woman who rejects traditional feminine roles would be better off should she find herself facing dissolution of her marriage.

Younger women are also better at rebuilding their lives after a divorce. In a ten year followup of divorced families, Wallerstein (1984) finds that for both men and women, the ones who first sought the divorce have adjusted more readily. But for younger women, especially those under 40, divorce leads to a wider range of growth options and enhanced psychological changes when they are compared to men and older women. In a study of mothers with children who are between the ages of 7 and 13, after some early reservations, the women accepted the divorce and were not eager for a reconciliation, through the children remained committed to the parents as couple (Grossman, 1986).

When a divorce involves children, the mother usually gains custody. Although men and women have a statutory equal right to custody in almost all states, approximately 90% of the time custody is granted to the mother and is the preferred pattern for most mothers and fathers (Weitzman, 1985:49). Women must now assume the multiple roles which had previously been shared. Even if she is working outside the home, the divorce increases financial obligations, child care, and household responsibilities. Conflicts at work which were previously resolved with less effort can intensify and create a greater sense of insecurity. Older women, housewives, and those reentering the labor force after a long absence are in an extremely precarious position. They are at a distinct disadvantage in the job market at the exact time when they need an adequate income to support the family.

One of the most widespread misperceptions about divorce involves the belief that a divorce settlement "sets up" a woman and her children for life. The newspapers are replete with examples of women who are awarded huge sums of money from their famous and wealthy husbands. The truth is that the economic effects of divorce on women and children are dismal. Alimony is itself a myth, awarded to only a small percentage of women. Weitzman (1985:144-45) reports that only 14% of divorced wives in a census survey indicated that they were awarded alimony, and then in amounts so meager that they barely matched welfare or Social Security payments anyway. Such awards certainly do not free these women from "worldly cares or assure them a perpetual state of secured indolence" (Weitzman, 1985:145).

A related issue concerns not simply what is awarded by the courts but if what is awarded can be collected. Eckardt (1968) cites evidence indicating that for child support, in one year after the divorce, less than half of all the fathers contributed nothing, and after the passage of ten years, the figure rises to 87%. Almost 60% of fathers fail to support their children after a divorce and 49% have not even seen their children in the last year (Hewlett, 1987). These data must be viewed in light of a wage gap between men and women which indicates that in 1939 a woman earned 63 cents for every dollar a man earned and that by 1986, almost half a century later, she earned 64 cents to his dollar (Hewlett, 1986). These disheartening statistics are augmented with others which show that in the first year after a divorce, women with minor children suffer a 73% decline in standard of living while men experience a 42% rise in their living standard within the same period (Weitzman, 1985:36).

Alimony is rarely awarded, child support is insufficient, and both are not guaranteed to be collected. Making economic matters worse for women is the trend toward the no-fault divorce. The states are increasingly allowing couples to decide for themselves if they want to remain married without the expectation that one must prove that the other is guilty of some transgression, such as mental cruelty or adultery. The no-fault divorce can also allow one spouse to divorce the other without her/his consent. Most important, alimony and/or property settlements are supposedly designed to treat the man and woman on an equal basis in order to amend the gender biases of past laws. The no-fault divorce is seen by many as an amicable and just solution to a bad marriage.

Although such divorces may be amicable, they are assuredly not just. The idea of equity is a sham when it is assumed that a 40-year-old woman who may have been sporadically employed is on an equal footing with her husband at the time of a divorce. The trend in the no-fault divorce settlement is to divide current property equally, focusing on savings and the family home. Courts have been reluctant to consider assets such as future earnings, medical and life insurance, or pensions in no-fault settlements. This explains why housewives are penalized in later divorces. The prior agreement between a husband and wife which gives priority to his career and assumes career assets will be shared with her has little legal standing (Weitzman, 1985:371).

When the home is sold and the assets divided, it is unlikely that either partner can purchase another home right away. The loss of the family home makes an already difficult situation worse for children who must adapt to a new physical environment while simultaneously dealing with the emotional turmoil of the lessened contact with one parent. The financial hardship and lowered living standard of divorced women and their children has literally changed the picture of poverty in the United States. Jencks (1982) believes that many women are forced into the morally deplorable situation of marrying a man in order to escape poverty. We are aware of many secure, financially independent women who choose not to marry. Unfortunately, numerous women who were encouraged to choose other routes become so economically trapped that they succumb to dependent roles to allow a better life style for their children.

For some divorced mothers who recognize that they simply do not have the financial capability to adequately provide for their children, the decision may be to give up custody. No-fault divorce does not lead to a rise in either the number of fathers requesting custody or actually gaining it (Weitzman, 1985:225). Custody remains essentially a mother's domain. The belief that children should stay with their mothers is so strong and pervasive that women who voluntarily give up custody are viewed as unnatural and immoral, a pariah in society's view (Markey, 1986). She may relinquish custody out of love, knowing that her ex-husband is financially in a better position to offer them what she cannot. But the anguish and guilt can continue for years, reinforced by negative societal definitions telling her she has abandoned her children. As Markey (1986) states, noncustodial fathers are not made to feel like freaks. That is reserved for the noncustodial mother.

The new divorce laws assume that husbands and wives are being fairly treated while in reality it is wives and mothers who are penalized. According to Weitzman (1985:371), if the newer laws would have provisions which gave each spouse "credit" for the roles they had chosen in marriage, such as breadwinner or home-maker, they would more accurately reflect the complex variety of marital options couples are now assuming. As existing now, however, flexibility and individual choice are denied. Given the legal reality and its economic results, it is preposterous to believe equity is being served.

If women with dependent children are perceived as a financial liability, they are also at a disadvantage as far as remarriage. Many men who may want to marry are reluctant to take on a ready made family. Also, the time constraints and emotional stress accompanying increased multiple roles leave many women too exhausted to begin the dating process. These women may be caught in the old scripts which tell them that men are the initiators as far as dates. There is the anxiety and insecurity of entering new relationships for romantic purposes soon after a divorce or, for many, after maybe twenty years in the confines of a housewife role. Finally, they must contend with the marriage squeeze and the limited options that they feel are acceptable.

Although most divorced people remarry, the rate for women is lower than for men. After a divorce, five out of six men and three out of four women remarry (Nock, 1987:171). When compared to divorced women overall, there is a lower remarriage rate for highly educated women in the 35-44 age group (Glick 1975). These are the women who may view their first marriages more negatively if they felt that career mobility had been stifled and now have the economic means to support themselves, particularly if they do not have children. The marriage squeeze notwithstanding, they are likely to be the small but growing percentage of divorced women who find singleness an attractive option.

ALTERNATIVES TO TRADITIONAL FAMILIES

The massive social change occurring in other segments of society has impacted the family to a great extent. As a result of alterations involving such areas as expanded employment opportunities for women and men, divorce and remarriage, and definitions regarding acceptable parenting behavior, nontraditional families are emerging. These alternatives not only exhibit different organizational structures when compared to the so-called "traditional" family, but almost by necessity the structures have produced variations in gender roles. It is impossible for these families to exist as they do without rather profound deviations from traditional notions concerning female and male, wife and husband.

Househusbands

When out of choice or necessity a husband takes on the tasks traditionally assigned to a wife, there is little in the way of wider social support for these endeavors. The paths are virtually uncharted for men who give up their breadwinning roles to take on primary responsibilities for household tasks and child care. With few models and guidelines from which to draw, Lutwin and Siperstein (1985:272) say that the passage to the househusband role is an emergent one since it is created, discovered, and shaped as they proceed.

Their research focuses on men, ages 23-57, who made the transition to househusband. The majority of these men are white, middle class managers and professionals who had been at the mid or top level in their careers, most of whom left their jobs because of disability or being fired. Lutwin and Siperstein (1985:281) find that the degree of adjustment is related to a number of variables, such that the best adjusted househusband

1. Has entered the role voluntarily,
2. Is committed to an alternative life style,
3. Has definite plans for the future,
4. Receives support from extended family and friends,
5. Does not experience stress from boredom, alienation, and other related factors.

They conclude that the role reversal does not alter the perception of their marriage or how their wives and children view them. However, they become more appreciative of their family, their former job and the household work formerly assigned to their wives (Lutwin and Siperstein, 1985:278).

Beer's (1983) study of New York area househusbands is more inclusive but has some similarity of findings. Though disliking the routine, boredom and inevitability associated with household tasks, the relaxed pace, feeling of accomplishment, and "artistry" of the job appeals to many househusbands (Beer, 1983:68). While it cannot be said that these men have an androgynous orientation to work and family, the househusband role allows for insight into problems housewives face and for more egalitarian attitudes in their marriages.

Though we have seen that husbands in dual-earner families take on some additional household task responsibilities, child care continues to remain essentially the wife's domain. But the househusband role requires this traditional division of labor to change. Pruett's (1987) research on families with primary nurturing fathers demonstrates that these men resemble traditional mothers. Though having been raised in traditional families themselves and coming from all social classes, the fathers form deep reciprocal relationships with their children, are competent in their child care skills, and help to create thriving, robust children. Free from child care worries, mothers report a high degree of satisfaction with their careers (Pruett, 1987:205).

If women become consumed with guilt and men feel their masculine identity is threatened by this kind of role reversal, househusbands are not likely to increase in numbers. Pruett (1987:251) believes that joint ownership of the children can create a place where both fathers and mothers can "mother" in a way that does not induce competition for being the "first-place" parent. He thoughtfully suggests that it is not the sharing but the competition which can confuse children (Pruett, 1987:251).

For the househusband role to be accepted as a legitimate choice for men, there must be considerable change in the way both male and female gender roles are viewed. Household tasks and child care need to be valued as much as paid employment. But as Rosenwasser et al. (1985) show in investigating college students' attitudes toward male and female housespouses, there is still a devaluation of the housespouse role, particularly when it is taken on by men. Students who are androgynous and whose mothers worked outside the home evaluate housespouses more positively. The impressions are less positive in descriptions of male home-makers. Homemakers of either sex are seen more positively when they are success-fully pursuing activities which extend beyond housework and child care (Rosenwasser et al., 1985:258). This suggests that the housespouse role for men is yet to become a viable one.

Gay Families and Relationships

Marriage between homosexuals is not generally legally recognized, although many churches will conduct the religious rites for such unions. Family law works against sanctioning these arrangements not only by prohibiting marriage but also by denying custody to the homosexual parent. Yet a small but growing number of gay men and lesbian women have gained custody of their own children or have adopted children and live in permanent households with them and/or their homo-sexual partners.

These families face a great deal of hostility and suspicion by a society accepting myths about homosexuality in general and idealized notions of the family in particular. During the antigay campaigns in the 1970s spearheaded by Florida orange juice promoter Anita Bryant and supported by American Conservative Union leader Phyllis Schlafly, homosexuality was viewed as the ultimate enemy of the patriarchal family and the American way of life (Lewis, 1979:6). It is doubtful that the latter sentiment can be subjected to much evidence, but gay families do exhibit characteristics which are in opposition to the traditional structure and behavior patterns of the patriarchal family. This seems more to the credit of these families than to their detriment.

In a literature review Maccoby and Jacklin (1974) find that homosexual couples exhibit more equality in their arrangements than do heterosexual couples. The stereotyped image that gay relationships inevitably have one partner in the dominant, breadwinning, sexually active "male" role and one in the subservient, housekeeping, sexually passive "female" role is simply a myth, found only in a minority of cases (Bell and Weinberg, 1978; Wolf, 1979; Caldwell and Paplau, 1984; Harry, 1984). An overall egalitarian arrangement, or at least the advocating of it, is more prevalent in homosexual than heterosexual relationships. This pattern appears to hold true for both lesbians and gay men, although it is especially valued among lesbians. Basow (1986:218) suggests that lesbians may engage in less sex-typed behavior and less role playing than either heterosexual couples or gay men because the men, specifically the gay men, are less influenced by the feminist movement than the lesbians.

Although homosexual couples tend toward egalitarianism, one of the major differences which separates homosexual men and women mirrors gender roles in the wider society. Monogamy is valued among gay men, but it is difficult to achieve. Sexual prowess is admired by heterosexual and gay males and is often the most important part of a relationship, mainly in the beginning stages. As one would expect, for women, sex is less important than emotional commitment. Research confirms this to be the case for lesbian women who maintain that sex grows out of later feelings as the relationship progresses, and that sex and physical closeness are not as important as friendship (Bell and Weinberg, 1978; Fleener, 1977, cited in Lewis, 1979:144). As Lewis (1979:144) states, "the axiom of lesbian relationships is equality and it is carried into their sex lives."

Children growing up in households with lesbian mothers would be likely to experience more equitable family arrangements, if custody is indeed granted to the mother. We have already seen that in the vast majority of cases women gain custody of their children. With lesbian women, however, this is not often true. Some women hide their lesbian identity to win custody and then live in constant fear of being exposed by their husbands and having the courts reverse the decision. Others who are granted custody after bitter court battles may endure continual harassment from their ex-husbands and even their own relatives and friends. Some mothers fear their children will be traumatized by a publicized custody fight and voluntarily accede to their husbands demands.

Lesbian mothers themselves can internalize the stigma of their sexual prefer-ence to the extent that they fear their children will be harmed if they know their mothers are lesbians or will grow up with severe problems in a household with one or two lesbian parents. To the contrary, research is now reporting that children are more adaptable, understanding, and accepting than society, the courts, or even their lesbian mothers assume. Studies showing that children can develop normally and happily with lesbian parents are now being used as ammunition for custody and adoption cases (Bell and Weinberg, 1978; Greene, 1978 cited in Lewis, 1979:115). When problems arise with the children of these natural or adoptive parents, it is usually due to outside interference and the degree to which society accepts the negative stereotypes of lesbian mothers.

Just as lesbian mothers can lose the opportunity of raising their children, gay fathers are even more likely to be denied custody. It is estimated that 20 percent of gay men have been married at least once and that between 350,000 and 700,000 are natural fathers (Bozett, 1985:328). Gay fathers can find that visiting their children is so discouraged that they may be reluctant to subject themselves and their children to the turmoil and upset accompanying visits or attempted visits. If their children remain unaware of their father's gay identity, the gay fathers live compartmentalized existences and, like lesbian mothers, fear being exposed and traumatizing their children. Bozett (1985) suggests that when these men make the transition to the gay world after a divorce, they do so without the "fetter of marriage" but maintaining their identity as fathers.

Miller (1979:249) contends that gayness may not be compatible with traditional marriage, but it is compatible with fathering. After resolving the tensions of an undisclosed gay identity in marriage, divorce and movement into the gay world resolve some tension. For publicly gay fathers who do have custody of their children or who adopt through "marginally legitimate channels" and are living with a lover, Miller's (1979) exploratory study shows positive histories for these families. Problems in rearing children exist, but Miller (1979:249) cites several studies which demonstrate that gay fathers appear to have no more problems than single heterosexual fathers who have custody of their children.

Gay men have limited opportunities for raising children if they proclaim themselves to be gay despite the fact they may be natural fathers. Another possibility is to maintain a liaison with a heterosexual woman with whom he may have children. Women who desire children without the confines of marriage may choose to have a child with a gay man with whom she may or may not be emotionally attached, who then helps in later parenting and support. There is no legal obligation, they do not live together and the child is "hers." In this way, desires on both sides are met.

New kinds of relationships involving gay men and heterosexual women are evolving. Nahas and Turley (1980:11) report on the "new couple" which involves a primary love commitment between a man and woman but one in which the man is gay and the woman accepts and understands it. Sex may not be part of their relationship but the intimacy and time spent together makes for a unique relationship. By this definition, the new couple are lovers, but sex is not the qualifying factor. As Nahas and Turley (1980:12) state, other factors predominate "such as compatibility, mutual acceptance and need for companionship of a sort which the gay life of the male and the heterosexual experiences of the female have not

provided." Success with such an arrangement varies considerably, but its acceptance by a number of couples indicates that relationships and families may be even
more nontraditional in the future.

Affiliated Families

As originally described by Clavan and Vatter (1972:499), the affiliated family
consists of "any combination of husband-father, wife-mother, and their children,
plus one or more older persons recognized as part of the kin network and called by
a designated kin term." The "extra" older persons may or may not reside with the
family but the bond between them takes on a degree of commitment and responsibility which is similar to the expectations and obligations existing with actual kin.

Affiliated families are particularly convenient arrangements for single parents who work outside the home and have preschoolers. Parents feel more secure
in leaving their children with people they view as kin. If the residence is shared,
child care in one's own home is considered to be an even better solution. Although
the additional persons provide services, the family recognizes that obligations are
also involved. As would be expected with other kin, the affiliated family shares
decisions, tasks, and responsibilities in a reciprocal fashion. The flexibility offered
by this structure allows for its adaptability to a wide variety of family situations,
especially if the notion of the affiliated family is expanded somewhat.

Clavan and Vatter's (1972) definition is perhaps too narrow to describe all
the arrangements families have made in response to social change and alterations
in gender roles. Rather than creating a new concept, it seems more appropriate to
eliminate the qualifier that the additional persons in affiliated families must be
"older." Thus, older people may still be considered part of the affiliated family,
but others can be included as well, such as children. An example in point would
be the "Kate and Allie" variety of family, modeled after the television show by the
same name. In this situation, two single mothers with their children share a
residence and relate to one another on a kin basis. The children see one another as
brothers and sisters, with the mothers viewing each other almost as sisters.

Benefits relating to child care, finances, and emotional bonding are factors
which keep such families intact. However, potential problems involving parenting
styles, privacy, and budgeting must also be resolved for the affiliated family to
successfully operate. Social change will be persistent in its impact on the family.
The emergence of affiliated families and the diversity of life styles they offer may
help mitigate some of the difficulties associated with this change.

SINGLE PARENT FAMILIES

Both the high divorce rate and the greater tolerance and acceptance of illegitimate
children has led to a dramatic increase in the number of single parent families.
Since 1970 the number of single parent households has more than doubled, with
the number of children living in single parent families increasing by an incredible

60% (Schorr and Moen, 1982; Gelman et al., 1985). If these patterns continue, it is estimated that one half of all children will live in a single parent household at some point in their lives, many on a permanent basis (Bumpass and Rindfuss, 1979). Approximately 90% of these single parent homes will be headed by women (Hetherington, 1979).

Mothers and the Single Parent Household

Not only are female headed families the fastest growing type of family in the United States, over one-third of these families are below poverty level (Shortridge, 1984:497). Many factors contribute to this situation. We know that child support, alimony, and joint custody are not the financial salvation for these women. Neither are welfare payments in a restrictive system which may contribute to, rather than deter, the cycle of poverty. Since women are more likely than men to be undereducated and engaged in menial or low-paying jobs, if employed at all, the income is far from adequate to meet the needs of the family. The financial burdens of the single parent family headed by a woman has created a situation known as the "feminization of poverty." At this point in time, public policy has been unable to satisfactorily address the issue. The women and children in single parent homes continue to remain at high risk for a life of poverty.

Financial uncertainty is one of a number of problems faced by the single parent family, particularly for women. The exorbitant demands on the single parent leads to stresses perhaps more easily faced in two parent homes. Weiss (1979) has identified the factors of responsibility overload, where critical family decision-making is left to the single parent, such as in the areas of child-rearing and financial obligations; task overload where there is simply not enough time to do all that is necessary in the household, which means greater reliance on children and family to get tasks completed; and emotional overload, always being available for any crisis which comes up at home or in the workplace. These findings are corroborated by McLanahan's (1983) study which concludes that women who are single parents experience more stress than women in intact households. The single parents have fewer social and psychological supports, more chronic life strain involving lower income and education levels, and more disruptions in major life events, such as with employment, residence, and health.

On the positive side, through his interviews with separated and divorced parents, Weiss (1979) also establishes that certain rewards, such as autonomy in decision-making, come about with single parenting and that for many it is better to be divorced and a single parent than stay in a miserable marriage. Women who are financially more secure are better able to adjust to the situation and may find themselves much closer to their children after the divorce. In reviewing the research on the children in female headed households, Cashion (1982) finds that levels of emotional adjustment and self-esteem appear to be good. Problems which arise are more likely attributable to poverty situations and stigmatizing by the wider society rather than the fact the household is headed by a woman or by the divorce per se.

Fathers and the Single Parent Household

More fathers than in the past are gaining custody of their children or are sharing the responsibility with their ex-wives. Although single fathers account for only 35% of all male-only headed households, between 1970 and 1982 the number of children living with their single custodial fathers increased by 101% (Hanson, 1985:370). With different standards being adopted by the courts in terms of custody arrangements and adoptions, the rise in numbers of fathers heading single parent households is likely to continue.

When compared demographically with single parent mothers, single parent fathers present a far different picture. The fathers are usually better educated and occupy professional or higher level employment roles and continue their prior career patterns after becoming single parents, which means a financial situation which contributes to their being awarded custody in the first place (Hanson, 1985:372-373). However, she also notes that there is a trend where fathers of all socioeconomic categories are starting to gain custody as well.

As far as household tasks and child care, single fathers appear to adapt rather well, perceive themselves as capable as the primary parent, share most of the household responsibilities with their children, and do not rely on outside help to a great extent (Orthner et al., 1976; Chang and Deinard, 1982; Greif, 1985a). For the most part, the children are also resilient and seem to pull together after the divorce (Greif, 1985b:148). As children get older, they participate more in housework, but with gender role differences evident. Fathers who are raising teen-age girls receive more help from them than fathers raising teen-age boys (Greif, 1985a). These fathers, as Greif (1985a) points out, are in nontraditional roles as the custodial single parent but "fall into traditional patterns of handling home related tasks."

Research on single fathers has been infrequent, so that which exists is paving new territory in exploring the myths and realities associated with this newer family life style. One of the best studies completed to date is Geoffrey Greif's (1985b) examination of single fathers and the tasks they face in parenting. Like single mothers, they have difficulty in balancing the added demands, dealing with the legal system, and maintaining satisfactory relationships with their ex-spouses (Greif, 1985b). For fathers who adapt well, the following characteristics are present, according to Greif (1985b:151).

1. They have higher incomes.
2. They were involved in housework and child care during the marriage.
3. They attribute the marital breakup to shared reasons; they do not entirely blame themselves or their wives.
5. Their ex-wives are involved with the children on a regular basis.
6. They sought custody or said they wanted sole custody at the time of the breakup.

When these factors are not present, fathers are more likely to have a difficult time adjusting to the rigors of single parenthood. As Greif notes, "it is not the sex of the parent that makes parenting difficult or easy, but the task with which the parent is confronted." Considering the inordinate responsibilities associated with single parenting, he concludes that it is impossible to weigh whether single fathers or single mothers as a group have an easier time adapting (Greif, 1985b:153).

8

Men and Masculinity

So I put my hand over the flame—just to show how tough I was. (G. Gordon Liddy's autobiography, *Will*)

In a culture where men are viewed as the superior gender and imbued with power and privilege, it seems ironic to consider their roles as potentially lethal to themselves. Whereas women wage uphill battles for equity in economic, political and social spheres, men wield the power which will determine the outcome of the fight. By virtue of their gender alone, males gain and maintain positions allowing for greater rewards and satisfying life styles. The male role, so the story goes, is an enviable role.

Although any role is made up of both responsibilities and rights, the latter for men clearly outweigh the former. Men have careers, women have jobs. Men are breadwinners, women are bread makers. Men are sexually aggressive. A man's home is his castle. His family is a minikingdom to be ruled. Father knows best. Is this the true story? We shall see that the role which appears to offer so many rewards also has it's deadly side as well.

These negative aspects are highlighted by what Farrell (1975:224) refers to as the "Ten Commandments of Masculinity."

1. Thou shall not cry or in other ways display fear, weakness, sympathy, empathy, or involvement before thy neighbor.

2. Thou shall not be vulnerable but shall honor and respect the "logical," practical, or "intellectual"—as thou definest them.
3. Thou shall not listen for the sake of listening—it is a waste of time.
4. Thou shall not commit introspection.
5. Thou shalt be condescending to women in every way.
6. Thou shalt control thy wife's body and all its relations.
7. Thou shalt have no other breadwinners before thee.
8. Thou shalt not be responsible for housework or children.
9. Thou shalt honor and obey the straight and narrow path to success: job specialization.
10. Thou shalt have an answer to all problems at all times.

Taken together these "commandments" emphasize what is considered masculine by the standards of American culture. The trenchant tone of this list implies that the male mystique is based on a rigid set of expectations which few men can attain. The social and psychological consequences of striving for the impossible plus the impractical can be devastating.

HISTORICAL NOTES

Today the images of masculinity appear to be confusing and contradictory. The media heroes are Clint Eastwood, Eddie Murphy, and Stallone's Rambo side by side with Alan Alda, Phil Donahue, and Woody Allen. Women praise the sensitive man who can admit to his vulnerability yet admire the toughness of the man who refuses to bend in the face of overwhelming odds. Most men fall short when attempting to satisfy both standards. History provides some insights into how this situation arose.

Patriarchy is tied to male dominance, which is the current theme in Western, or for that matter, Eastern civilization. It is a theme that remains unquestioned, taken-for-granted and accepted. Using a Western civilization perspective, Doyle (1983) categorizes the male role in terms of five historical periods, ranging from the Graeco-Roman era to the eighteenth century. Table 8-1 suggests that the contemporary concept of masculinity which most men strive to meet continues to be based on ancient beliefs. When the basic features of a male ideal persist after two centuries, this attests to the stubborn rigidity of a definition which defies even global social change.

With patriarchy already firmly entrenched the peculiarities of American history tightened its hold. From the Puritans to the frontier era to the Civil War and World War I, the value of individualism had furiously taken hold of the nation. Americanism and individualism became inseparable and eventually took root in the consciousness of the new nation as masculine markers. Opportunities with few restraints other than initiative beckoned men into farming, politics, business or whatever the imagination sought.

Granted that some men (non-white) and most women were to be excluded from these opportunities. But as Dubbert (1979:15) states, "nothing was too big,

TABLE 8-1:   Five Historical Male Role-Ideals

IDEAL	SOURCE(S)	MAJOR FEATURES
Epic Male	Epic sagas of Greece and Rome (800-100 B.C.)	Action, physical strength, courage, loyalty, and beginning of patriarchy.
Spiritual Male	Teachings of Jesus Christ, early church fathers, and monastic tradition (400-1000 A.D.)	Self-renunciation, restrained sexual activity, antifeminine and antihomosexual attitudes, and strong patriarchal system.
Chivalric Male	Feudalism and chivalric code of honor (twelfth-century social system)	Self-sacrifice, courage, physical strength, honor and service to the lady, and primogeniture.
Renaissance Male	Sixteenth-century social system	Rationality, intellectual endeavors, and self-exploration.
Bourgeois Male	Eighteenth-century social system	Success in business, status, and worldly manners.

Source: Doyle, 1983:26.

too dangerous, too far or too powerful . . . to thwart dedicated American males from achieving their objectives." Most objectives related to financial rewards achieved by hard work tied to physical expenditure of energy, with a secondary emphasis put on intellectual cunning. Success based on material wealth and getting ahead were, and are, integral to American notions of masculinity.

With the closing of the frontier, manliness can no longer be validated with reference to the danger and deprivation basic to earlier Americans. America turned wholeheartedly to sports to fill this role. Theodore Roosevelt argued that the athletics in general aided society as a whole by focusing not just on a small number of players. The sporting impulse focuses on spectator aspects, sports to build character, the comradeship of teaming, new heroes to worship, and for men specifically, displays of prowess and virility to emulate (Dubbert, 1979:175).

It can be argued that even today the intellectual aspects of masculinity have not kept up with the physical aspects where sports are considered. Dubbert maintains that America went sports crazy in the 1890s. Athleticism today is no less significant. A billion dollar industry flourishes on contests where winning can literally call for the obliteration of the athlete. Boxing, race car driving, football, hockey, skiing, diving and even gymnastics often brutalize competitors. Sports violence occurs on and off the playing field. And scandals involving payoffs and kickbacks to athletes and college programs do not dampen the thirst for sports. The physical and mental stamina required of modern athletes allow men who are not themselves athletes to validate their own masculinity, if only in a vicarious manner.

War and soldiering provide another validation mechanism. War historically brings with it idealized rhetoric emphasizing its virtue and glory, while ignoring its destruction and sheer horror. Functionalism views war as integrative for society when disparate elements rally together to face a common enemy. In both World Wars, military training was seen as the way to build the manhood of the nation.

Women served men as nurses, clerical help, or during World War II, builders of war equipment. Women were considered helpmates to the men who fought the "real" battles. War and the preparation for war supposedly induced men to their highest levels of masculinity. A military uniform encourages a man's self-respect and a woman's admiration (Dubbert, 1979:193). Traditional gender roles are bolstered.

The Second World War helped bring the nation out of the Depression, a time which had serious consequences for the American version of masculinity. The loss of jobs and daily economic uncertainty for those fortunate enough to have jobs assaulted the self-esteem of men accustomed to their role of breadwinner. The fact that the entire nation faced similar circumstances offered little assurance to these men. Many blamed themselves for their inability to get or retain a steady job. When their wives were able to find work outside the home, their emasculation may have been complete.

The effects of this kind of male self-indictment reverberated throughout the nation. Beyond the economic results of a high jobless rate, the psychological toll was also sadly demonstrated. Many men became estranged from their families, others coped by deserting them. Alcoholism, mental illness, and attempted suicide increased. Contrary to the image of the American man as invincible and able to overcome any obstacle, men and women alike recognized how vulnerable they really were.

The Depression provided an opportunity to seriously question an impractical definition of masculinity. This was not to be the case. With war came a revitalization of the old image, and the harshness of the Depression added luster to it. Even considering that Korea and Viet Nam were not the victories Americans had learned to expect, beliefs about war as a proving ground for manhood continued. A "cult of toughness" emerged to sway public opinion in favor of escalating the war in Viet Nam (Fasteau, 1974). America, like its fighting men, was tough.

Although politicians cultivated this image of toughness, the carnage of Viet Nam which was seen on the nightly news, coupled with an untenable political situation abroad, served to fuel protest against the war. The first young men who burned draft cards or sought asylum in Canada or Sweden were viewed as cowards and sissies, afraid to face the test of war. As the protesters grew in number and the war became increasingly unpopular, more potential draftees joined in the anti-war movement. Comments about bravery and cowardice were not wiped out, merely driven underground for a time.

Here was another opportunity to challenge what it means to be a man. War, at least as embodied in Viet Nam, was not the answer. But the cult of toughness has reasserted itself in the 1980s. The Reagan era was predicated on a show of toughness and not backing down. During his presidential campaign, George Bush was able to successfully demonstrate that deriding labels such as "wimp" did not in any way characterize him. Like Reagan, he is a "man's man." Politicians believe that this image must be maintained at all costs. To do otherwise is "unmanly." Masculinity is almost synonymous with toughness. And behind this assumed toughness lurks aggression.

"The masculine imperative to be tough and self-reliant plays a decisive role in many men's lives" (Doyle, 1983:232). The Depression and Viet Nam did not effectively alter the image of masculinity. In fact, I would argue that after periods when assaults on traditional masculine ideals are at their heights, the old definitions reemerge with a greater tenacity. The sad comment to this is that when men and women alike assume that males must be invulnerable, they become more vulnerable as a result.

ON MASCULINITY

It is mentioned above that masculine images have a contradictory quality which may seem confusing to men. Such contradictions are explained with particular reference to the impact of the women's movement and the media. Men are presented with alternative images which challenge the traditional version of a male mystique. In accepting these revised images as legitimate and offering more benefit than liability, it has been assumed that men would soon rally behind a new definition of masculinity. This assumption has proven false for the vast majority of American men.

Definitions of masculinity have remained remarkably consistent over time. Contemporary images flow from the past and history has demonstrated their tenacity. Robert Brannon (1976) suggests the following characteristics as being ingrained in modern notions of masculinity and the male gender role.

1. No Sissy Stuff: The stigma of all stereotyped feminine characteristics and qualities, including openness and vulnerability.
2. The Big Wheel: Success, status, and the need to be looked up to.
3. The Sturdy Oak: A manly air of toughness, confidence, and self-reliance.
4. Give 'Em Hell: The aura of aggression, violence, and daring. To this list I would add a fifth.
5. Macho Man: An emphasis on sexual prowess and sexual conquests.

The first characteristic admonishes males to reject any behavior which has a feminine quality. To be masculine by this standard is also to be antifeminine. Research by Thompson et al. (1985) demonstrates that college males who endorse traditional male role norms are also likely to be homophobic; that is, they fear or are intolerant of homosexuals and are supportive of Type A behavior where rationality and tough-mindedness are revered despite the heightened medical risks of stress-related diseases. They also disapprove of equal decision-making power with their partner or spouse.

It is the endorsement of antifemininity or the "No Sissy Stuff" theme that is most significant here. The authors warn, however, that this does not necessarily mean misogyny is endorsed as well. It simply recognizes that the "antifeminine norm within the traditional male role is more pervasive and salient than other norms" (Thompson et al., 1985:425). One consequence of this is that by refusing to identify with anything that is viewed as feminine, males reduce their interpersonal skill level. If intimacy and self-disclosure are seen as feminine qualities which men must disavow, men learn to conceal their emotions. As documented in Chapter 2, the ultimate consequence of "no sissy stuff" can offer more liabilities than benefits.

The second theme of "The Big Wheel" suggests that men are driven to succeed at all costs. Their manliness is tied to career success and the ability to provide for their families in the breadwinner role. Prestige is gained from their work outside rather than inside the home. Competency as a parent is less important than competency in the world of paid labor. It is expected that the wives, children, colleagues, and peers of these men judge them accordingly. Self-esteem suffers with the loss of a job and the inability to quickly gain another one.

According to Peterson (1983) the breadwinner syndrome pressures men to perform and to identify their careers with their sense of self-worth. As a male who himself is working for gender role change, he is aware of his own biases in this regard. He reports his own feeling of being devalued when he becomes unemployed or underemployed. "Even after all my male liberation and feminist theory upbringing, I get sick when I don't have a career. Jobs are not enough" (Peterson, 1983b:7).

The success orientation is associated with the traditional norm of male intellectual superiority. The feminist movement ushered in the idea of intellectual companionship between the sexes, which conflicts with the older norm. In studying masculine strain among college students caught with contradictory expectations involving these two norms, Komarovsky (1973) finds that the men could be categorized into two groups. Interviews with the first group, "the troubled third," suggests that intellectual insecurity with dates was a past or current problem. Some of these men are able to avoid the strain by consciously seeking out women who they believed would pose no intellectual threat. The "adjusted majority" includes men who report that intellectual relationships with dates is not a problem because they either felt superior or equal to their dates in the first place or because other problems in the relationship are more salient. Komarovsky (1973:884) concludes that the absence of strain among the majority can be explained by a changed role definition where the norm of intellectual superiority is being challenged by the ideal of intellectual companionship between equals.

The major qualification of this trend is the fact that when viewing marriage roles, the traditional pattern, with only some modifications, is still strong. Women are admired for their careers but should take on full time responsibility for child care and household responsibilities. Careers should be interrupted to do so. More importantly, males expect that the husband should be the superior achiever and are threatened by equal achievement in occupational roles between husband and wife.

Pride and self-esteem are lowered in the eyes of these young men if they saw their future wives "winning" over them occupationally.

Komarovsky's (1973) research was carried out at the height of the women's movement. She expresses cautious optimism about the ideal of intellectual companionship between the sexes while recognizing the possibility that the men in her sample might have been giving liberal lip service to challenges facing their traditional roles. After a decade and a half, the ideal of intellectual companionship appears to have deteriorated with a retrenchment favoring the older norms of male superiority in terms of success and the "Big Wheel" theme.

In the occupational sphere, Astrachan (1986) contends that men are threatened by women's competence and their entry into traditional masculine occupations, thereby kindling controversy about what constitutes a "man's" job. Blue collar men express the most hostility, but the resistance comes from men in the professions as well. These feelings relate to both the antifeminine and success themes. They may believe that their jobs will take on the taint of something feminine, hence unmanly. And success at a job where women are doing essentially the same work can be demeaning for men who favor the conventional gender roles. In each instance, their sense of masculinity is assaulted. The proportion of men who are genuinely supportive of the demands of women for equality, especially in the workplace, is quite small, probably between 5% and 10% (Astrachan, 1986:402). Males remain bound by a concept of masculinity which assumes occupational dominance of women and a strong breadwinner role, with their self-esteem tied to both.

The "Sturdy Oak" perspective of masculinity tells men to be tough and independent. He must express confidence in his ability to carry out tasks that appear insurmountable. He must do so with a sense of stoicism which shows he is in command of the situation. Again, the antifeminine element intrudes here by implying that compliance and submissiveness are the negative qualities which the sturdy oak male disdains. The "henpecked" husband of the Dagwood Bumstead variety possesses such qualities.

We have seen that manliness as connected to aggression has been a central view throughout history, and the "Give 'Em Hell" theme endures today. Boys learn early that turning the other cheek is less respected than fighting one's way out of a difficult situation, especially if bullied. The media reinforce these images by directing stories at youngsters which show war comprised of guts and glory on the battlefield of honor.

As a nation we readily bestow the title of hero on those who come out on top through the use of physical means. Diplomats who quietly work behind the scenes hammering out vital peace agreements are less likely to command public admiration than front line soldiers battling to keep the peace. President Jimmy Carter, who pursued a diplomatic solution to the Iran hostage situation, was seen as soft for his refusal to use military channels. The aborted rescue attempt was a way to escape some of this pressure.

The argument has been raised that aggression, even war, has been necessary to solve past problems. By socializing boys into a masculinity with the aura of violence and aggression surrounding it, the soldier role, which they may eventually assume, will be easier to accept. Fasteau (1974) counters this by asserting that when heterosexual masculinity calls for aggression, war may be the maladaptive consequence. What was harmless or adequate at one period of history is certainly outmoded today (Herek, 1986:569).

The final theme is the "Macho Man" image which portrays manliness in terms of sexual ability. Sexual competence, according to Tiefer (1986), is basic to contemporary masculinity. The man who is seen as impotent is cast into a stigmatized, demeaned category since the term is used to describe more than just his penis. Sexual performance is used to confirm his masculinity with success in this endeavor carrying over into other parts of his life.

The performance aspect is particularly tied to working-class notions of masculinity. Boys develops a series of stories, jokes, and routines documenting their sexual escapades. Performances describing successful pick-ups are highlights for these youths. "It captures exactly the mixture of bravado, self-assertion, and collective recognition that characterizes a working-class adolescence" (Tolson, 1977:44). These boys know, however, that the machismo or super-sexual aggressive image, is merely a front, never a realization, of potential power. The suggestion of violence expresses a desperation and lack of self-confidence which condemns them to failure (Tolson, 1977:45). The kind of script which relies on sexual function to describe masculinity inevitably leaves males vulnerable.

Tiefer (1986:597) calls for a transformation of sexuality from a rigid standard defining masculine adequacy to one which does not impose control, but instead affirms relating and cooperation. She aptly points out that in pursuing the illusion of masculinity, one set of anxieties will be exchanged for another.

The cultural construction of masculinity encompasses a series of fairly inflexible elements. They stay as defining characteristics in spite of evidence attesting to their negative consequences for men as well as women. For a time it was thought that the older labels were on the decline and that sensitivity and openness could be added to the accepted male role. Perhaps as a backlash to the women's movement and a comment to the fledgling men's movement, traditional masculine norms have been reasserted.

A study by Lueptow (1985) comparing "typical" personality traits of college men and women between 1974 and 1983 confirms this trend. Considering the changes in roles for women, especially the increased acceptance of extrafamilial ones, it would be expected that perceptions of personality would change as well. Although female attitudes are less traditional than male attitudes, a pattern of increased stereotyping of sex-related personality traits holds. Demographic differences do not change the findings.

Both sexes adhere to rather rigid views of masculinity. Men in particular are threatened by changes in definitions of masculinity regardless of the virtual impossibility of meeting the traditional standards. Social change has influenced the male role, whether it is acknowledged or not. Changes in attitudes about masculinity, however, are likely to take a longer time. As far as masculinity is concerned, the more things change, the more they remain the same.

HOMOPHOBIA

Whereas women are slowly gaining entry into what were once male occupational bastions, males have lagged behind in entering those occupations that have been traditionally reserved for women. One practical reason for this is the income differential which would discourage men from going into the domain of women's work roles. But the decision to reject the "world of women," both inside and out of the home, is tied less to economic than to social and psychological factors.

To be a man in contemporary American society is to be homophobic. To be homophobic is to possess fear, loathing and/or intolerance of homosexuals and homosexuality. Homophobia functions to reinforce culturally stereotyped definitions of masculinity, particularly the antifeminine norm. The most devastating label a young boy can receive from his peers is that of sissy or queer. Homophobia is learned early. As an adult, he fears the labels of gay, faggot, or homosexual. He thereby distances himself from any behavior which would suggest these labels. Consider the implication in the cartoon in Figure 8-1.

The traditional male role constantly encourages homophobia for several reasons. First, women and anything perceived as feminine are less valued than men and anything perceived as masculine; so why would a man take on roles offering fewer rewards? Second, men generally accept pervasive myths about gays and homosexuality. As we shall see, these myths, although generally untrue, are uniformly negative and incredibly powerful. Men see little if any need to seek out the facts because, just by doing so, they may feel besmeared and threatened by a homosexual label.

Finally, early socialization offers few alternative models for boys other than the rigid standard of masculinity already described. Boys learn quickly that gestures of intimacy with other males are discouraged and that any expression of femininity, verbally or nonverbally, is not tolerated. Male role models such as fathers, teachers, and brothers provide the cues and sanctions to ensure compliance on the part of the young boy.

In elementary school, boys strictly segregate themselves from girls to bolster their formative masculinity. As an early instance of male bonding, segregation of the sexes extends into adulthood. Lionel Tiger, (1969) an anthropologist who is supportive of sociobiology, argues that the male bond was necessary during prehis-

Figure 8-1. Reprinted with special permission of NAS, Inc.

toric times to maximize efficiency of hunting and gathering bands. Today male camaraderie occurs in secret societies, fraternal organizations, the military, sports teams, or the neighborhood tavern. In such environments, according to Tiger, the gregarious propensities of men are acted out in safety from a broader society which would normally be suspicious of such close male interaction. Garfinkel (1985:106) contends that even though men are taught that intimacy among males is taboo, the desire to have at least some opportunity for informal interaction is so strong that men must form separate groups. But, even here, homophobia blocks the expression of the deepest feelings of affection between men.

Homophobia also takes its toll on gay men who inevitably undergo the same socialization processes as heterosexual men. Gay relationships, sexual and otherwise, demonstrate the impact of socialization into masculinity and its homophobic stance. For example, a machismo element is steadily growing in the gay subculture. Exaggerated masculinity taking the form of dress (leather, motorcycle regalia, military uniforms), rough language, and potentially violent sexual encounters may result. Gay machismo is popular, Humphries (1985) believes, because it allows gays to present an image of masculinity which they have been taught is the proper one. Sexual potency, power, and control are its integral characteristics. But the adoption of a standardized, stereotyped view distorts reality because it is merely an approximation. The man is still gay and is "open to being a scapegoat for the fears of others" (Humphries, 1985:79).

Beyond becoming a scapegoat for others, gay men must contend with their own feelings of self-worth in a society which labels them as deviant. The message gays receive from the heterosexual world is that "I am straight, correct, normal and good. You are abnormal, wrong, deviant and bad" (Garfinkel, 1985:167). By internalizing the negative labels of the dominant group, minorities such as gay men may learn to accept the stereotyped, pejorative view of themselves. Self-hatred is a common result.

The emergence of a gay rights movement in the 1970s has helped gay men deal with homophobia in themselves as well as the heterosexual world. Patterned after the women's movement to some extent, one faction of the movement is working to escape the bonds of a sexist culture where they recognize the common oppression they share with women. Abandoning restrictive role playing with women and casting aside the emotional straight jackets which keep men distant from one another are two avenues currently being pursued.

Unfortunately, gays with other views probably make up the majority. Astrachan (1986:377) relates the story of an advertising man who told him "we want to be the equals of straight men, and if that means screwing women—figuratively—we'll do it." This response can be explained from a conflict-minority perspective with reference to how the oppressed classes are stratified. In a society that sees women and gay men as subordinate, the men can use their male advantage to deal with their own oppression. Male remains higher in the stratification system than female.

This does not mean that gay men must be either feminists or misogynists. Moore and McDonald (1976, cited in Doyle, 1983:248) find, for example, that gay males are more likely to be oriented to egalitarian attitudes towards women than are heterosexual males. What is recognized is simply the power of socialization. Males are socialized into accepting standards of masculinity to which they continue to adhere, whether they are gay or not. Homophobia is a part of that standard.

HUSBANDS AND FATHERS

Can men have it all? We usually connect this phrase with women who want to combine a satisfying career with marriage and children. Ideas of femininity have been flexible enough to accommodate women with such aspirations. Masculinity norms are more inflexible. They dictate that men take on the responsibilities of parenthood primarily through their breadwinning roles.

Like women, most men want marriage and children. Men envision the American Dream as a successful career, contented children, and a beautiful and understanding wife who is good in bed (Hamill, 1986). Idealism notwithstanding, men willingly abdicate daily family living duties to their wives. They are stunned with the realization that fatherhood means more than a weekly paycheck and picnics with the family. Hamill believes that career priorities for men do not allow for the broader education they really need for other family roles. Males cannot segment their lives into convenient packages which deny them the opportunities to take on parenting chores. Images of success for men do not presently include diapers. Contrary to what many women and men believe, men do not "have it all." Men can be better fathers and husbands, but not if they continue to enter marriage as if they were accepting parts in a movie (Hamill, 1986:82).

Fatherhood means more than paternity. The word "fathering" is associated with sexual and biological connotations. The word "mothering" is associated with nurturance. The biological father who takes his economic responsibilities to his family seriously, has met the necessary criterion for masculinity in American culture. This narrow outlook disregards, even belittles, those men who want to expand their parenting and other household duties. These include diapers, dishes and dirty laundry as well as picnics, parades, and pizzas.

The demeaning stereotypes of bumbling men who do not know the proper way to hold a baby or turn on a washing machine persevere. The antifemininity norm of masculinity serves to bolster such images. Men who freely choose either to take care of their own children as househusbands or take care of other's children in careers like early childhood education are suspect. They must justify their existence to a skeptical society which questions their manhood. The late John Lennon was an exception to this rule. He wanted to project an image that included more than his talent for singing, songwriting, and making tremendous amounts of money. Pride in his parenting skills is shown with the following quotation shortly before his death: "I like it to be known that, yes, I looked after the baby and I made bread and I was a househusband and I am proud of it" (Gerzon, 1982:207). He apparently disdained the sex object, macho rock and roll image into which he had been cast.

Although fathers traditionally have had fewer expectations built into their roles as far as socialization of the children is concerned, the smaller roles they take have been important ones. We have already seen that fathers, especially in the working class, are stricter overall in sex-typed intentions for their children. In all classes, males are given less latitude than females in experimenting with different role definitions.

A replication study by Intons-Peterson (1985) comparing fathers today with those of 30 years ago in terms of what aspirations they hold for their children, shows how these socialization patterns continue. Sons and daughters are still sex-typed by their fathers but with the qualification that both should receive college degrees. The college degree, however, provides a different option for the son rather than the daughter. Fathers continue to pay close attention to the breadwinning role of their sons. In sum, gender stereotyping occurs in an atmosphere of more latitude in roles, but much less so in boys, and much less so in the working class.

For the middle and upper classes, socialization of sons in particular extends from the Victorian standard where fathers were so distant as to become estranged from their sons (Dubbert, 1979:141). Fathers were gone much of the time and sons were sent off to prep school, thus minimizing contact during the formative years. Fathers were mysterious beings who wielded power in the household but who distanced themselves from it. A hundred years later we can see the vestiges of Victorian standards in the father's role.

To make parenthood more of a partnership, fathers and children need to be brought closer together. One mechanism, often overlooked, is the father's inclusion in the delivery room itself. The expectant father is portrayed as nervously pacing in the waiting room chain-smoking until the doctor brings him news of the birth. Until the mid-1960s, fathers were kept out of the delivery room, and even now some hospitals discourage fathers from remaining with their wives throughout the whole birth process. The image of the father who would faint at the sight of blood or get too emotional or out of control in the delivery room are pervasive myths. The father is viewed as an irrelevant appendage who gets in the way when his wife needs to be calm. Gerzon (1982:203) argues that males are not destined biologically to be remote from their infants and that being present at childbirth offers a bond which will never be erased. After sharing in the birth of the child, the marriage itself is likely to be stronger, particularly if the father is involved in child care, including trips to the pediatrician's office (Mooney, 1985:100).

At childbirth, men are constrained by a double standard built into their role. They are encouraged today to actively participate, but at the same time they are seen as outsiders (Shapiro, 1987). Shapiro states that while we view pregnancy and motherhood as positive, there is no corresponding view for the expectant father. Except for his laughable nervousness, his fears are not addressed. Fear of his wife's death during childbirth and anxiety over new family responsibilities are two concerns most men have but rarely discuss. When natural fears experienced by expectant fathers are discussed openly and unashamedly with their spouses, relationships are deepened. The therapeutic and medical communities must be aware of their own stereotypes in working with expectant fathers. The evidence is clear that benefits will be realized for the marriage and for later parenting.

Divorced fathers must contend with restrictions on their parenting role when many would like to take on more responsibilities for their children. However, the statistics are bleak concerning child support payments by fathers. Even when women are awarded child support, less than half actually receive it regularly, if at all (cited in Richardson, 1988:105). When a joint custody arrangement is determined, child support payments increase, perhaps because it allows for more self-esteem on the part of the father. Much has been written about the disrupting effects of divorce on children, with less attention paid to fathers. Meredith (1985) states that many men exhibit an involuntary child-absence syndrome where they get depressed and anxious and feel cut-off from their children. Joint custody sanctions their remaining in the lives of their children.

When taking full responsibility for children, through gaining custody in a divorce or because of the death of his wife, the single father, once parenting skills are better learned, is almost indistinguishable from a woman in how he parents (Greif, 1985b). A recent study by Risman (1987) confirms this. Single fathers, unlike married fathers, adopt parenting behavior which is very similar to women who mother. Regardless of the image, men can and do parent successfully.

MEN AND THE MIDLIFE CRISIS

The idea that men between the ages of 35 and 50 experience a crisis of sorts has been debated by professionals seeking to explain a series of physical and emotional symptoms which appear unique to this group. Variously referred to as the male climeractic, male menopause, or midlife crisis, many men present symptoms of night fears, drenching sweats and chills, and depression which, upon investigation, have no specific cause.

Some researchers conclude that the climeractic is associated with a sharp decline in testosterone for approximately 15% of men with the other 85% experiencing slow but gradual change where there is considerable hormonal variation (Sheehy, 1976:314-18). Unlike women, where there is a more dramatic change heralding the cessation of menses, in normal aging for men, the changes are subtle. Feeling that the word menopause is inappropriate, Hallberg (1980) coined the word metapause (meta meaning change) to describe the male experience.

The hormonal changes must be considered in light of social and psychological factors. Men in their forties become acutely aware that time is finite. They sense their own mortality and review their accomplishments and their goals, many times focusing on what they have not done rather than what they have done. Nolen (1980) believes that a life's review which is disconcerting for males is responsible for the sudden drop in testosterone levels. Unless the man alters his environment to produce a more optimistic mindset, his health can be adversely affected.

Some men turn to family to sustain them when they realize that a career orientation cannot meet all their needs. They discover that their children have been launched and may regret the fact that contact with them has been limited due to career priorities. In an attempt to recapture the lost parenting experience, men may turn to grandchildren. Grandparenting for many men is a rewarding, emotional time, and the aloof, stern family patriarch is the stereotypical exception. Grandfathers are frequently the soft spot in man-to-man relationships. As Garfinkel (1985:45) notes, the grandfather "is quite possibly one of the very few men in a man's world with whom you were practically guaranteed to be free of power struggles, competitiveness and ego-class."

The significant personal transition men in their forties experience can have both negative and positive consequences. Depression, suicide, and alcohol problems often become manifest at this time. Understandably, families are at higher risk for divorce. Though changing the social environment is a practical coping device, the choices can have disastrous effects. Some men turn to younger women in the hope of regaining lost youth. One student reports that her ex-husband began to drink heavily and date women almost as young as their daughters. He eventually remarried but committed suicide less than a year later. She states it is an oversimplification to say that his behavior was due to his metapause, but she certainly recognized the parallels in researching the topic (Covalt, 1982).

On the positive side, a man's heightened sense of self during midlife can be useful for reintegration of the masculine and feminine traits which our culture mandates as being separate for most of a man's life. His masculine drive is tempered by a more well-rounded personality which takes into account his roles of husband and father as well as breadwinner (Tamir, 1982). He will make decisions reflecting how much his occupation or his family and friends will become a focus for his time and talent. Overall it is the socially active man who is the least stressed during this period.

It is at this stage where men become more nurturant and women more independent. Her capability of standing apart from him may help relieve him of the burden of responsibility he feels he has carried for the family. It is interesting that the woman who grows in assertiveness and independence provides the best source of support for a man in this phase of life. Each spouse may begin to loosen the bonds of restrictive gender roles as they enter middle age.

The idea of a midlife crisis for men which brings personal disorganization and increased psychological and health risks has been questioned. Ciernia (1985) presents research results suggesting that divorce, alcohol problems and suicide actually decrease during the 35-55 age span. Problems exist and maladaptive behavior occurs, but there is no quantitative basis for a focus on these particular problems.

The subject is complex and there is no consensus about what actually constitutes a midlife crisis. The time of life in question appears to be disruptive for men. But this age span needs to be considered in light of problems existing during other periods of life, such as adolescence, where crises are also likely to occur.

MEN WHO RAPE

Until recently, rape had been viewed as a crime committed by a few demented men of lower intelligence who have uncontrollable impulses. The reality is that less than 5% of rapists are judged to be psychotic at the time of the rape (Abel et al., 1980). While this and other myths about rape remain prevalent, rape and other forms of sexual aggression toward women continue to increase.

The following myths have been disproven by research but are accepted by a large segment of society.

MYTH	REALITY
1. Rape is first a sexual act.	Rape is an act of violence to show dominance of the rapist and achieve submission by the victim.
2. Most rapes are committed by strangers.	Rape is more likely to occur between acquaintances. Date rape is a common instance.
3. Most rapes are spontaneous, with the rapist taking advantage of an unforeseen situation.	Rape is likely to be preplanned. If spontaneity occurs it may be an added "bonus" to a robbery.
4. Women wear provocative clothing or flirt with men, thereby causing their own rape.	This is the classic blaming the victim myth. Since most rapes are preplanned, the rapist will strike regardless of appearance.
5. Women enjoy being raped.	The pain, violence, degradation, and psychological devastation experienced by the victim are overwhelming. Consider, too, that she may be killed in the rape.
6. Most rapists are psychologically or sexually abnormal.	It is difficult to distinguish the rapist from other men in terms of personality or ideas about sexuality.

Rape is behavior learned by men through interaction with others which is consistent in critical ways with socialization into masculinity. Violence and male sexuality are, in essence, blended (Fasteau, 1974). What separates the rapist from other men is the tendency to actually express the violence (Amir, 1971). In this argument, male socialization itself sets up the predisposing factor for rape. Russel and VandeVen (1976:261) state that "being aggressive is masculine; being sexually aggressive is masculine; rape is sexually aggressive behavior; therefore rape is masculine behavior."

Socialization into masculinity is reinforced by stereotypes concerning women. The rape myths mentioned above are imbued with such images. Another example is the belief that women want to be dominated by men. This rationalizes men's violent behavior in rape as an expression of that domination. Blaming the victim justifies the crime. Also, if women are viewed as passive, sex is something that is done "to them." Deckard (1983:431) asserts that the very words "fuck" and "screw" signify both sexual intercourse *and* doing someone in. Men not only dominate, but sexually conquer passive women. The rape fulfills the prophecy of the stereotypical image.

The profile of the rapist is difficult to determine since research indicates there is no specific personality pattern or character disorder which discriminates rapists from other groups of men (Scully and Marolla, 1985). Rape is a crime perpetrated by a wide spectrum of men. Although there are certain characteristics shared by some rapists, these must be viewed with caution since incarcerated men and convicted rapists usually make up the samples. Rape convictions are fewer in comparison to other crimes, it is the fastest-rising crime and it is significantly underreported. It is estimated that only one in ten cases of rape are reported to police (Deckard, 1983:433). Women who do call the police risk being demeaned as a result. It is only recently that some municipalities have incorporated counseling and more humane approaches in questioning victims of rape. Unfortunately, the victim herself is often treated like the criminal.

Given the problems of accurate statistics, the following profile of the rapist is at best a tentative one. He appears to have a high need for dominance and a low need for nurturance. He deals with his perceived inadequacies by aggression and the sexual control of women. Socially insecure and interpersonally isolated, his aggression is likely to be followed by expressions of remorse (Scott, 1982). He sees himself as compelled to rape. He justifies his behavior in terms of rape stereotypes that he has learned as a member of society. In doing so, his victim is made to seem culpable (Scully and Marolla, 1984). The rape act is presented in socially acceptable terms. Sexual violence is used as a means of revenge or punishment (Scully and Marolla, 1985). It is not difficult to understand why this profile is a sketchy one. It can fit many men who we would view as "normal" members of society.

Pornography and sexually explicit material as factors in sexual aggression have come under much scrutiny. Aggressive stimuli, like rape scenes and erotic films, stimulate sexual arousal (Briere et al., 1984; Silbert and Pines, 1984). Whether the arousal actually leads to later aggression has been questioned. Feshbach and Malamuth (1978) argue that it is the sadomasochistic pornography that is harmful because sex and violence are shown together.

The issue of what actually constitutes pornography and once determined, making it illegal, is being hotly debated. Much of this debate surrounds the victimization of women, which pornography is seen to fuel. The other side argues that banning sexually explicit material is an effort at censorship and is in violation of basic constitutional rights. Both sides use social scientific research to support their contentions. One side argues that violence against women is increasing and we are more desensitized to it due to exposure to pornography. The other side argues that pornography may actually reduce sex crimes because it provides for a nonharmful release of sexual tension. The battle lines are clearly drawn but to date neither side has been victorious.

BATTERED WIVES

Although wife beating has been commonplace throughout history, there is little precise research on the topic. We do know that wife beating spans all ages, classes, and racial groups. The law has generally supported a man's right to beat his wife, even for such infringements as talking back to him. The infamous "rule of thumb" can be traced back to feudal times. This allowed a husband to beat his wife with a stick no bigger than his thumb (Gingold, 1976). In the United States, it has only been since the end of the last century that the courts began to decide that wife beating was not a husband's right.

The available research indicates that battering wives is the most underreported of all crimes. The most comprehensive study done to date on family violence using a probability sample of over 2,000 families indicates that about 16% of couples report some type of violence, ranging from hitting and pushing to severe beating (Straus, 1980). According to Straus, in approximately 5% of all marriages, the wife experiences a beating at some point. Resick (1983) estimates that the incidence of wife beating is in the 4% to 40% range.

The privacy of the American family and the reluctance of police to get involved in family disputes exacerbates the problem of getting accurate statistics on family violence in general and wife battering in particular. Battered wives suffer from low self-esteem and often see themselves as responsible for their beating. A pattern of learned helplessness emerges for these women. The beatings are endured, they feel guilty about them, and they are unlikely to speak to others, even close friends and family, about the situation.

When the police are called, arrest of the husband is rare, and then only when obvious physical injury is indicated. The psychological consequences which are not as easily erased are ignored. In a Kansas City study, 96% of family homicides were preceded by a call to the police for domestic disturbance (cited in Deckard, 1983:438). If it is not guilt which keeps a woman from calling the police, the fear of her husband's retaliation will often keep her from doing so.

There are many battered women who seemingly accept their situation because they feel financially trapped, especially if they have small children. The advent of safe shelters for women and children, crisis hot lines and self-defense classes have helped somewhat. In St. Louis, an organization known as ALIVE (Alternatives to Living in Violent Environments) has been instrumental in providing shelter and counseling for abused women and their children. It is estimated that over 100,000 women in this metropolitan area alone will suffer physical abuse. It is a beginning, but the shelter-crisis-counseling concept needs to be supplemented with public education documenting the scope of the problem.

Public education on family violence has found its greatest strength in dealing with child abuse. Wife battering has not gained as much attention because it remains subtly condoned. A national sample shows that 32% of college graduates approved of husband-wife battles (cited in Martin, 1976:19), the very situation where violence is likely to occur. Another national sample reveals that one in four men and one in six women would approve of slapping a wife under certain conditions (Gelles and Straus, 1979). Slapping, hitting, and shoving are precursors to more violence but are generally approved of by American adults.

Like the rapist, the wife batterer fits no specific personality or demographic type. Alcohol is associated with spouse abuse with some men beating their wives only when drinking (Roy, 1977), perhaps using it as an excuse for the attack. They also tend to come from violent families, with the cycle of violence perpetuating itself from generation to generation. In a study of men arrested for assault, mainly against their wives, Faulk (1974) finds an incredible diversity. The personality types include those who are dependent, jealous, bullying, dominating, and passive. The first three types are more likely to experience violent episodes than the last two, although passive men may strike out at their wives after being poorly treated by them for a long period of time. The "henpecked" husband is not judged as severely by society for his behavior. The victim is again blamed for the attack.

In the stable and affectionate marriage where violence would seem least likely, the wife takes the brunt of psychological problems her husband is manifesting. His depression leads to her abuse. She becomes the scapegoat for his inability to deal with emotional problems any other way. The commercial admonishing the man with "sure you have a headache, but don't take it out on her" is an example of how scapegoating operates. The stable and affectionate marriage on the surface may really have a hidden volcano waiting to explode.

A husband's prerogative in using physical force to "control" his wife for the most part remains unchallenged. Eshleman (1988:574) sees violence against wives as a logical extension of a patriarchal system where the husband is viewed as the ruler and head of the family. Obedience is extracted from his family by whatever means he deems necessary. Society rarely questions this behavior.

MEN'S LIBERATION

Change cannot occur in a vacuum. As women have been taking on new roles, changes inevitably occur for men, some which they eagerly support, others which they find unpalatable. The movement for male liberation originated on college campuses as a reaction, albeit a positive one, to the feminist movement. These men recognized that their support of feminist causes and their involvement with feminists as husbands or significant others had influenced images of themselves as men.

The movement began with informal consciousness-raising groups on college campuses and the formation of men's centers throughout the nation, the first at Berkeley in 1970. The first National Conference on Men and Masculinity was held in Knoxville, Tennessee, in 1975. Since then men interested in altering conceptions of gender roles and taking on a decidedly feminist stance have met nationally about once a year.

The themes around which these conferences are organized vary, such as "Men Supporting Men," "Straight-White-Male: Wrestling with the Master Culture," and "Men and Sexism" (Doyle, 1983:286). Unlike the women's movement and the lead taken by the National Organization for Women, these conferences had first focused on personal and social rather than political change. Sessions on fathering, rape and violence against women, and sexuality demonstrate this emphasis.

A workshop on violence against women at a 1977 men and masculinity conference in St. Louis was instrumental in forming RAVEN (Rape And Violence End Now). This group is concerned about the tolerance in our culture, in men specifically, for the objectification of women and its violent manifestations. They contend that the support system for oppressive behavior towards women is so pervasive that an individual man's decision *not* to participate is a personal one which has little peer support. Masculine labels serve to undermine men who refuse to go along with the system. RAVEN has since established a counseling resource and support center for men seeking to change a system in which violence against women is institutionalized. Although individual men are aided through counseling services, the organization is expanding with the intention of educating the public on abuse of women. Broader social change is a longterm goal.

The men's movement is becoming more politically oriented with each conference more activistic in this regard than the previous one. But its lack of unity on basic goals has hampered resolutions. Most men who support a liberation movement to free men from culturally restrictive roles would also support the Berkeley Men's Center Manifesto, below. Beyond this, there is broad disagreement on the role of gays in the organization, the support for some feminist causes, such as abortion or male contraception, divorce and child custody laws, and the critical question of avoiding or accepting power in a changed system.

BERKELEY MEN'S CENTER MANIFESTO

We, as men, want to take back our full humanity. We no longer want to strain and compete to live up to an impossible oppressive masculine image—strong, silent, cool, handsome, unemotional, successful, master of women, leader of men, wealthy, brilliant, athletic, and "heavy." We no longer want to feel the need to perform sexually, socially, or in any way to live up to an imposed male role, from a traditional American society or a "counterculture."

We want to love ourselves. We want to feel good about and experience our sensuality, emotions, intellect, and daily lives in an integrated way. We want to express our feelings completely and not bottle them up or repress them in order to be "controlled" or "respected." We believe it requires strength to let go and be "weak." We want to enjoy masturbating without feeling guilty or that masturbation is a poor substitute for interpersonal sex. We want to make love with those who share our love, male or female, and feel it should not be a revolutionary demand to be either gay, heterosexual, or bisexual. We want to relate to our own personal changes, motivated not by a guilt reaction to women, but by growth as men.

We want to relate to both women and men in more human ways—with warmth, sensitivity, emotion, and honesty. We want to share our feelings with one another to break down the walls and grow closer. We want to be equal with women and end destructive competitive relationships between men. We don't want to engage in ego battles with anyone.

We are oppressed by conditioning which makes us only half-human. This conditioning serves to create a mutual dependence of male (abstract, aggressive, strong, unemotional) and female (nurturing, passive, weak, emotional) roles. We are oppressed by this dependence on women for support, nurturing, love, and warm feelings. We want to love, nurture, and support ourselves and other men, as well as women. We want to affirm our strengths as men and at the same time encourage the creation of new space for men in areas such as childcare, cooking, sewing, and other "feminine" aspects of life.

We believe that this half-humanization will only change when our competitive, male-dominated, individualistic society becomes cooperative, based on sharing of resources and skills. We are oppressed by working in alienating jobs, as "breadwinners." We want to use our creative energy to serve our common needs and not to make profits for our employers.

We believe that Human Liberation does not stem from individual or social needs alone, but that these needs are part of the same process. We feel that all liberation movements are equally important; there is no hierarchy of oppression. Every group must speak its own language, assume its own form, take its own action; and when each of these groups learns to express itself in harmony with the rest, this will create the basis for an all embracing social change.

As we put our ideas into practice, we will work to form a more concrete analysis of our oppression as men, and clarify what needs to be done in a socially and personally political way to free ourselves. We want men to share their lives and experiences with each other in order to understand who we are, how we got this way, and what we must do to be free.

Astrachan (1986) argues that many men in the movement avoid power because they see that it is the powerful men who have created oppressive systems. They assume that it is the power which lends itself to oppressiveness. It is as if they fear becoming corrupted by power. This is tragic by Astrachan's estimation. "We, especially we the powerless, we the weak, could take power—at least some power. We could change the way power is exercised. If we refuse to do this, we will only continue to be oppressed by others and therefore to oppress others" (Astrachan, 1986:301).

The men's movement with its efforts at male liberation has attracted a minority of men. The conferences consist mainly of men in the helping professions, social sciences, or academic realms. Other professional men, attorneys, corporate executives, physicians, and politicians, are rarely seen. Working class men and men of color, unless they are students, are almost nonexistent. This supports Astrachan's contention that few men really identify with a men's movement calling for liberation from male stereotypes. Unlike the women's movement which has touched the lives of millions of women, the same cannot be said for the impact of a men's movement on men.

On a more optimistic note, Gerzon (1982) believes that new masculinities are emerging which emphasize the development of a deeper awareness of the two sexes mutuality. Gender identity is being transformed, which allows us the opportunity to acknowledge and respect its diversity. The range of masculinities and femininities is so wide that they overlap (Gerzon, 1982:236). He calls for an examination of what works and does not work in gender roles, not for a codified set of rules which define men and women, masculine and feminine.

Men's roles have not kept pace with the changes in women's roles. The evidence is clear that the attitudes toward masculinity have served to hamper those men seeking to free themselves from restrictive male stereotypes. The majority of men, however, are on no such quest. They quietly adhere to images and roles which society tells them are proper but which may be disabling in their effects.

9

Women, Work, and the Workplace

By Sandra Christie

"A woman's place is in the home!" This neatly summarizes American society's stated preference for women's work roles and work location. However, this preference is not a norm in modern America, nor has it been the norm throughout most of history and in most societies. If most women do not confine their work sphere to the home, a series of salient questions arise.

Where do women work?
How many women work, especially if they have preschool age children?
Why do women work outside the home?
Who takes care of the home and children?
Do women have careers?
What are the economic effects of women working?
What are the effects of women working on the work setting?
What do men think about working with women?

These questions are only "the tip of the iceberg" of the controversy about women working. Some fundamentalist Christians and business leaders point out that the American family is in a crisis because women are not taking care of their children when they work outside the home. Some feminists, "liberals," and labor leaders point out that women are not treated fairly when it comes to wages and other forms of compensation.

Everyone is concerned about the effects of working women on our basic social institutions, especially the economy and the family. Everyone acknowledges that these effects are major, but there is no consensus on whether these changes are positive, negative, or some of both. In fact, the same statistics are frequently cited by both sides in the legal and policy debates which are currently raging. Women themselves take various positions about working outside the home, although the right to "equal pay for equal work" comes closest to generating consensus among women. Many men still believe that their ability to support their family is compromised by the movement of women into the labor force. "Equal pay for equal work" has been a linchpin of the most recent women's movement, but evidence suggests wage differentials between men and women have not altered significantly, for most female workers, in the last decade.

The sociological perspective will be used to specify women's work roles and behaviors, that is, the kinds of work women do, how many women work, in what occupations, and what careers they pursue. Then the factors that influence women's choice of work, occupation, or career will be discussed, topics like what causes women to do certain kinds of work and not others, why women are not evenly distributed throughout the work force, and why housework is not really work. Next the effects of social institutions on a woman's decision to work will be examined, how the marital status, presence, and age of children affect women's participation in the labor force. Finally, the effect flowing from women's decision to work outside the home rather than inside it will be discussed, the affect that working women have on our social institutions, and what difference it makes whether women work in the home or elsewhere. Each of these questions will be addressed in order to determine women's position in the labor force and their impact on the family and society.

SOCIOLOGICAL THEORY

Most of the theoretical treatment of women has focused on the mother-wife role which is embedded in the institution of the family. Talcott Parsons (1942, 1955, 1964) represents the functionalist orientation when he states that gender role specialization is functional for society and designates the woman as the *socioemotional specialist* within the family while the male is the instrumental figure. Parsons's pattern variables categorize the personality, cultural, and normative social systems in terms of a series of five dichotomies.

1. Affectivity (women) versus affective neutrality (men) deals with immediate self-gratification or deferment of self-gratification.
2. Diffuseness (men) versus specificity (women) deals with the scope of relationships, broad ranging or narrow.
3. Universalism (men) versus particularism (women) deals with the use of general standards or standards particular to the situation or setting.
4. Achievement (men) versus ascription (women) deals with characterization of people based on what they can do or based on who or what they are.

5. Self-oriented (women) versus collectivity-oriented (men) deals with primacy of personal interests or primacy of shared interests.

Building on this Parsonian legacy, Jessie Bernard (1971) argues that women and men inhabit different social worlds which can be dichotomized using Parsons's pattern variables (as noted in the parentheses above). Bernard specifically characterizes women's functions as reproductive, homemaking, child rearing, glamour, emotional support, and industrial production. All of the above conceptualizations closely link female gender role behavior and the family, except the last one. Bernard's inclusion of industrial production can be cited as an example of separating gender role definitions from the family sphere.

Theorists in the sex differences tradition (Erikson, 1964; Money and Ehrhardt, 1972; Horner, 1972) posit a biological cause for differentiation, but descriptively they, too, rely on the evidence of women's socioemotional performance within the family to support their theories. As discussed in the first chapter, even the radical theorists such as Marx (1964) and Engels (1942), Firestone (1970) and Mitchell (1971) recognize the close relationship between definitions of women's roles and the family, usually emphasizing the negative impact of the family on women and the need to radically alter or abolish families as a prerequisite for developing more egalitarian gender roles in general and work roles in particular.

Theoretically, the interactive affects of home and work are generally recognized. There is a tendency to treat these interrelations as a priori assumptions upon which theories can be built and supportive evidence then gathered, rather than treating them as variables for hypothesis testing. Consequently, the objective determination of causal factors in the development of women's work roles and the effects of women working on the families and other social institutions is often obscured. However, the questions researchers invariably comment on are the interactive effects of working and home.

To discuss women in the work force without commenting on theories of change would be impossible. Inherent in this topic is the notion of change, as suggested by the following diagram.

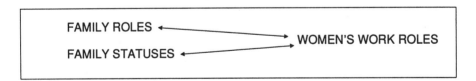

The popular literature, as well as that of sociology, is replete with notions that the institution of the modern family is in flux (for good or ill, depending on one's perspective). With the advent of the women's movement, the emphasis of changing roles for women is also in evidence. As the functionalists and others point out, change is usually accompanied by strain, conflict, or tension which in turn influences the amount, type and direction of change (Parsons, 1955, 1964; Goode, 1960; Komarovsky, 1946, 1976).

From the conflict perspective, two positions are evident. First, stratification theorists have struggled to explain the inequities that abound in the work place. Discrimination and prejudice are two salient concepts. Sex discrimination is differential treatment of men and women in the work place based solely on their sex. Prejudice is the attitudinal dimension which emphasizes negative attitudes toward women in the workplace based solely on their sex. There are various other explanations for workplace inequities which will be discussed at length later.

Second, conflict theory uses the concept of power for understanding the work setting. The struggle to explain wage differentials for the same work has resulted in use of this concept. Power is generally defined as the ability of one person or group to impose their will on another person or group, regardless of what the other wants. Reskin (1988:61) restates the position of the radicals when she says

> the basic cause of the income gap is not sexual segregation, but men's desire to preserve their advantaged position and their ability to do so by establishing rules to distribute valued resources in their favor.

In other words, men exercise their power in a manner which will maintain their power advantage. Female employment and the inequities which are empirical facts are leading to renewed attention to the power dimension in the labor force setting.

One of the major strategies used to maintain power has been the use of a "protégé system" which is a system of sponsorship wherein both entree and upward movement in a job setting requires selection by a powerful member who acts on the behalf of the protege because they have similar goals. In other words, "the old boy system" acts to keep males in power. Kanter (1976), Cook (1980), and others indirectly point out the need for an "old girl system" to increase the success of women, especially in certain professional occupations.

THE HISTORICAL PERSPECTIVE

Cott and Pleck (1979) summarize the need for a historical overview of women's work roles because it lets us "know where we have been, so that we will know where we are going." The myth of feminine fragility and nonworking women is easily dismissed when the activities of hunting and gathering bands are examined. Gathering activities tended to be female roles and usually accounted for more of the total food supply than the meat provided by the male hunters. Throughout both prehistory and history, women have made major economic contributions to their societies and families through their labor.

Blau (1978) points out that women have traditionally engaged in three types of productive work, producing goods or services at home for sale or exchange elsewhere (cottage industry), producing goods or services for consumption within the household itself, and working for wages outside the household. It was only with the advent of the Industrial Revolution that men, and later women, turned to gainful employment (work outside the home for wages) as their major type of work. Women's work roles have traditionally been closely tied to the home.

Farm work required all family resources, including women and children. Women produced cloth from raw material, soap, shoes, candles, and most other consumable items required in each household. Female domestic servants in the seventeenth and eighteenth centuries produced most necessary items for their employers' households as well. Chafe (1977) points out that 40% of Boston's taverns in 1690 were operated by women. Colonial women functioned as inn-keepers, shopkeepers, crafts workers, nurses, printers, teachers, and child-care providers. In more remote areas, women also acted as dentists, physicians, and pharmacists. Widows and single women were most likely to work outside the home.

With the advent of Samuel Slater's water powered textile factory in 1789, the Industrial Revolution was underway in the United States. However, women and female children continued to be the producers of cloth, but in a factory, not at home. Female employment in textile mills also reflected the lack of available surplus male labor which was needed on the farm. Many of the other products women traditionally produced at home gradually switched to factory manufac-turing. As the nineteenth century progressed, women were gradually defined as physically and mentally incapable of working in a factory setting.

The transition of America and western Europe from agrarian societies to urban industrial societies took about 150 years. During this time, farm women continued to engage in meaningful work. It was the single and widowed white women, immigrant women, and black women who were industrial employees. The current ideology was that women's place was at home; however, the above groups, through necessity, were working outside the home. During this same time, women were establishing their control in several occupational categories, nursing and elementary and secondary teaching.

The two world wars resulted in major changes in the deployment of women into new industrial areas because men were in short supply as laborers. It was during this period that women replaced men in both factories and offices. Greenwald (1980) points out that World War I mainly reshuffled existing female workers into new areas, rather than increasing the overall participation rates. It should also be noted that as women increasingly took over the male clerical positions, there was a marked decrease in the status and wages of these positions.

World War II produced a revolution in the number of women working in the industrial sector, as well as their occupational distribution. While women were essential to the wartime production effort, their pay was not the same as men received for the same jobs. Attempts by the War Labor Board to encourage "equal pay for equal work" were not successful (Fox and Hesse-Biber, 1984). In 1940, women constituted 25.5% (slightly less than 11 million) of the civilian labor force. By July, 1945, women's labor force participation peaked at 19.6 million.

After World War II, women were again told to go back home, but they did not return to hearth and home in the same proportions as after World War I. They did lose the more lucrative industrial jobs, but a new trend developed—married women began entering the labor force in greater numbers. This trend has

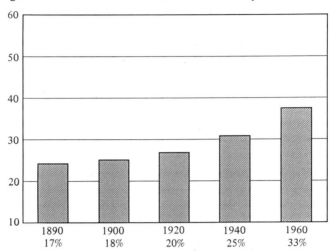

Figure 9-1. Historical Female Civilian Labor Force Participation: 1890-1960

Source: U.S. Department of Labor, 1969; 1975; 1986b; 1986c.

continued and is probably the major labor trend of the second half of the twentieth century. Figure 9-1 shows the historical changes in the civilian labor force participation between 1890 and 1960.

WOMEN'S WORK ROLES AND BEHAVIORS

The question of the appropriateness of women working is currently receiving scrutiny with pros and cons being weighed and considered. However, this broad question is not the crux of the matter because women have *always* worked, as discussed above. The real question is whether women *should* have occupations and/or careers and receive the same compensation for their work that men receive.

Part of this difficulty is rhetorical and can be cleared up by defining terms. Duberman's (1975b:83) simple definition of work will be used: "work [is] that activity in which man [woman] engages primarily for the purpose of supporting himself [herself]." An occupation (Pavalka, 1971:3) is an achieved social role wherein work is a central concern and also a major source of personal identity. Career is a concept that includes both work and occupation, but also adds commitment (defined as the willingness to work more than eight hours per day), hierarchical stages through which one must move vertically, and goal oriented behavior, which will be actualized in the future. As can be seen, all careers and occupations involve work behavior, but the converse is not necessarily true.

The major dichotomy in the work performed by women is whether one works outside the home and family sphere (gainful employment, occupations, and/or careers) or one works *only* within the home and family sphere (house-work).

HOUSEWORK AND THE STATUS OF THE HOUSEWIFE

Oakley (1974a:1) defines a housewife as "the person, other than domestic servant, who is responsible for most of the household duties." She further states that it is a "feminine role" with the following characteristic features.

1. its *exclusive allocation to women* . . .
2. its association with *economic dependence* . . .
3. its *status as non-work* . . .
4. its *primacy* to women, that is, its priority over other roles. (Oakley, 1974a:1)

Point number three is particularly interesting and is supported by data which show that housewives do not have any direct formal qualifications and training for the job is almost nonexistent, remuneration for the tasks performed is nonexistent, one cannot accrue social security or other retirement benefits based on this role, and its value as represented by measures of socioeconomic status is literally zero. Yet studies would also lead one to assert that according to the definition of work above, a substantial amount of work is being done.

    The notion that mechanization of housework has increased the leisure time of nonworking women by reducing work time is also questionable. In 1951, upper-lower class mothers spent 31 hours per week while middle class mothers spent 34 hours per week doing household chores. By 1965, wives averaged 40 hours per week, and if the chores done by husbands and children are included, the figures are even higher (Bernard, 1971:74). The lesson is that gadgets may save energy, but not time.

    Soo (1969) made an early attempt to determine the replacement value of women's housework. Galbraith (1983:125) reports that recent calculations indicate that an average homemaker is worth about $25,000 per year in terms of replacement value, as calculated by insurance companies for husbands who have to replace a wife due to injury or death. In 1966 the effect of defining housework as "work" would be to increase the GNP 38%.

    It should be noted that gainfully employed women still do housework. In fact, the total amount of time devoted to work activities is extremely high for women if paid employment is added into the second column of the chart below. More recent research has shown only minor shifts in these trends. Men are sharing household tasks somewhat more, but women are experiencing only slight decreases (one hour per week) in the time spent doing household tasks at the same time their time spent at work is increasing. Table 9-1 summarizes Blau and Ferber's (1985:29) review of the literature on the daily time spent doing house-keeping chores in 1975-1976.

WOMEN IN THE LABOR FORCE

Although nearly all women are housekeepers, it would be a mistake to say that this is their major work role (at least statistically) because by 1985, 54.5% of all women

**TABLE 9-1. Estimated Daily Housekeeping by Gender Role
and Woman's Work Status**

Gender Role	Not Employed	Employed
Wives	4.6-6.8	2.3-4.0
Husbands	.6-1.8	.6-1.9
Total	5.2-8.6	2.9-5.9

Source: Adapted from Blau and Ferber, 1985:29.

age 16 or over were in the labor force. As Figure 9-2 shows, the proportion of all noninstitutionalized women in the labor force has been growing rapidly. The U.S. Department of Labor projects that 60% of all women will be working in the civilian labor force by 1995. Nearly two-thirds of all labor force growth will be among women. As these trends continue, the proportion of women in the labor force will be approaching that of men, which is estimated to be 76.1% in 1995 (U.S. Department of Labor, 1985).

The most remarkable feature of this trend is found when these figures are broken down by marital status. It is married women who have been responsible for the largest proportion of this growth. During the 1950s the largest increase was "among married women beyond the usual childbearing ages" (age 35 and over) (U.S. Department of Labor, 1975:7). This trend has led authors to discuss the impact of mature women, who would not be expected to leave jobs for child-rearing purposes, on the labor force. However this trend was fairly shortlived; by the 1960s married women were still entering the job market in large numbers, but the emphasis shifted to younger women with children still in the household. Simmons, et al. (1975:44-45) summarize these trends as follows:

Figure 9-2. Total Percent of Women in the Labor Force: 1960-1985

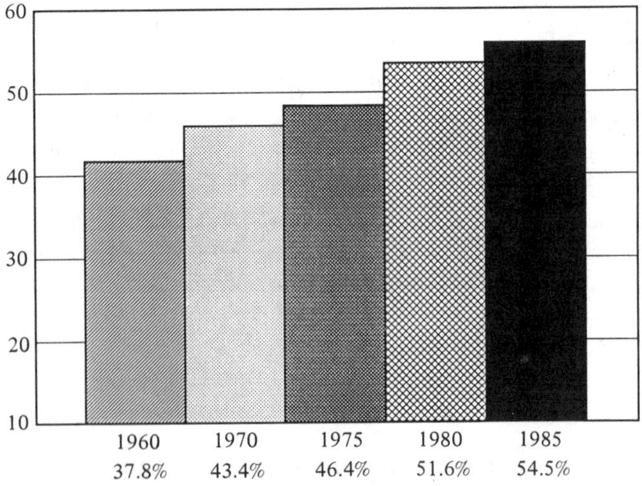

	1960	1970	1975	1980	1985
	37.8%	43.4%	46.4%	51.6%	54.5%

Source: U.S. Department of Labor, 1987a; 1987b.

in 1969, the median age "was" forty-two for the entire female population. Similarly, 21% of married working women and 28% of all married women had children under six, while 34% of married women workers and 28% of all married women had children between the ages of six and seventeen. Thus it is rapidly becoming more difficult to consider working women as an unrepresentative or atypical group.

For married women with children, the age of the youngest child greatly influences the probability of participating in the work force. In 1981, 43.7% of married women who lived with a spouse and had children under age three were employed. The percentage jumps to 54.8% for children aged 3 to 5 and 62.5% for children 6 to 17, while only 46.3% among those with no children living at home (Blau and Ferber, 1985:23). The proportion of single women in the labor force has declined from 48.5% in 1940 to 23.3% in 1974 (U.S. Department of Labor, 1975:16,18).

As alluded to above, most of the increase in working women is among younger women, especially those 25 to 44. A woman's status as head-of-household also differentiates rates of participation. In 1974, 54% of the 6.8 million female headed households were in the labor force and constituted 10% of all female workers. Having an employed husband present does not obviate labor force participation, because 51% of these women worked in 1981. Women whose husbands' earnings were low were more likely to work in the past. However, this inverse relationship has become less consistent in the last decade, probably because of increased opportunities for better educated women.

Women are more likely than men to be working part-time (under 35 hours per week) rather than full-time. In 1981, 23% of women and 8% of men worked on a part-time basis. It should be noted that 28% of these women were voluntarily working part-time; they chose this schedule. The reasons for women not working full-time, year-round is largely influenced by responsibilities related to home and family. The trends of higher absenteeism and turnover rates among women have also been changing to a more stable pattern.

Occupational Distribution of Women

As would be expected, women are not equally distributed throughout the occupational structure. They are highly represented in occupations defined as feminine. The process and fact of this maldistribution is called sex-typing of occupations. Generally, women are very underrepresented in high status occupations and largely overrepresented in the lowest status jobs which receive the lowest wages. Sex discrimination accounts for much of this trend.

Women work throughout all occupational categories, but are most underrepresented in blue-collar transportation, and nonfarm labor areas. Even within the white collar area where they are dominant, women tend to have jobs with less status, such as clerical and retail sales positions. Table 9-2 presents major categories of occupations and some representative occupational subcategories.

The trends in women's occupational distribution are also enlightening. In 1940, women constituted 45% of all professional and technical fields, but only 40%

TABLE 9-2.   Women as a Percent of Total Employed in 1972 and 1981

OCCUPATION	1981	1972
	%	%
White-Collar Workers	53.5	48.4
Professional & Technical	44.6	39.3
Lawyers	14.1	3.8
Social Scientists	33.8	21.3
Physicians	14.4	9.3
Managers & Administrators	27.5	17.6
Sales Workers	45.4	41.6
Stocks And Bonds	17.0	9.9
Sales clerks	46.6	44.2
Clerical Workers	80.5	75.6
Blue-Collar Workers	18.6	16.7
Crafts	6.3	3.6
Carpenters	1.9	.5
Plumbers & Pipe Fitters	.4	—
Operatives	39.8	38.6
Drill Press	26.3	21.3
Welders	4.7	3.6
Transport Operatives	8.9	4.2
Delivery	8.5	2.5
Truck Drivers	6.1	2.0
Non-Farm Laborers	2.2	.5
Service Workers	62.1	62.4
Private Household Workers	96.5	97.6
Fire Fighters	.9	.5
Police & Detectives	5.7	2.6

Source: U.S. Department of Labor, 1982.

in 1970. Furthermore, women constituted 10% of all upper level professionals in 1970, but 12% in 1900 (Theodore, 1971:3). Until the last decade women had actually lost ground in some higher status jobs and were being more concentrated in sex-typed occupations both for white-collar and blue-collar jobs. There are some minor effects of marital status on occupational distribution, but they are narrowing and will likely disappear in the near future.

Within professions where women are underrepresented, there is further sex-typing into subspecialities with less status and lower pay. In medicine, for example, women constitute large proportions of pediatricians, psychiatrists, and public health physicians. Female lawyers are more likely to be in domestic law or trust specialties than corporate law. Many women find positions in the semiprofessions which are female dominant, like nursing and teaching.

With the exception of nursing, feminine occupations also tend to find males in the highest positions. So even in jobs which are designated female, most women are subordinate to males who hold the most powerful, high status, and high paying positions. This phenomenon is called hierarchical segregation and is seen as a strategy which further prevents women from earning equal pay and/or exercising equal power with males.

Women have also not made inroads into the skilled trades in the numbers expected. Even though there has been an 80% increase in female skilled workers, the total percent of female workers in 1981 tended to be low: 4% of painters, 3% of machinists and 1% of auto mechanics. The lack of growth in these lucrative occupations over the past two decades only partly explains this situation.

One business trend of the 1980s has received popular press coverage. This is the rise of small female-owned businesses. Entrepreneurial women have found small business formation an alternative to management positions in large organizations which have seen few women enter the ranks of upper management. Between 1977 and 1980 female-owned sole proprietorships increased 33%, while analogous male enterprises increased by 11%. Most of this increase has come from traditional areas of female work, such as services and the retail trades.

The Wage Gap

The income or earnings of the working women tends to be substantially less than that of men even when education, work experience, ability, and drive are the same. This issue has generated the greatest amount of agreement in all segments of American society.

The wage gap has been a persistent economic fact in America since records have been available. Contrary to what many believe, the wage gap between men and women has not substantially decreased. Between 1967 and 1974, this gap actually widened from 62% to less than 61%. In 1973, the median income for males was $8,056 and $2,796 for females. If only full-time, year-round workers are

Figure 9-3   Ratio of Female Wages To Male Wages Based On Median Annual Income

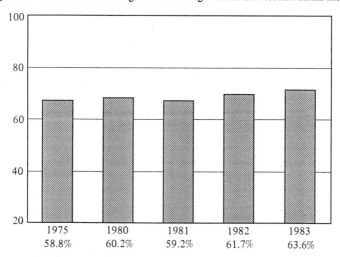

Source: U.S. Department of Labor, 1977; 1983.

TABLE 9-3. Median Weekly Earnings of Full-Time Wage and Salary Workers in 1984

OCCUPATION	MEN	WOMEN	RATIO FEMALE/ MALE	PERCENT FEMALE WORKERS
	$	$	N	%
Managerial & Professional	553	378	68.4	41.6
Executive/Admin/Manager	568	358	63.0	33.6
Professional Specialty	534	394	73.8	48.5
Technical/Sales/Admin Support	404	256	63.4	64.4
Technical & Support	451	312	69.2	48.1
Sales	403	212	52.6	47.9
Admin Support/Clerical	380	257	67.6	79.9
Service Occupations	259	180	69.5	60.8
Private Household	208	130	62.5	96.2
Protective Services	378	288	76.2	12.9
Other Services	224	182	81.3	64.8
Precision Production/Craft	401	254	63.3	8.5
Operators/Fabricators/Laborers	321	209	65.1	26.0
Machine Operators/Assemblers	331	208	62.8	41.1
Transportation/Moving	354	253	71.5	8.3
Handlers/Cleaners/Helpers/Laborer	258	207	80.2	16.6
Farming/Forestry/Fishing	205	177	86.3	15.6

Source: U.S. Department of Labor, 1986a.

considered, the median for males was $11,468 versus $6,488. In 1973, 21% of employed women earned less than $1,700, but this was true of only 8% of men (U.S. Department of Labor, 1975:126-131). In the past 15 years, the dollar figures have changed but the ratio of women's earnings to men's earnings remain virtually unchanged. Today, for every dollar a man earns, a woman earns about 64 cents.

Occupations which have been redefined as feminine have experienced relative wage losses. Knudsen (1969:192) finds that female sex-typed occupations, especially clerical and related jobs, were subject to the largest relative loss of income (12%) of all categories in the last 25 years. In the 1970s both the popular and academic literature reported that employers of college graduates intended to pay women less than men. Simmons et al. (1975) report that these plans were made prior to any hiring; so these differentials could not reflect differential job performance.

This wage gap exists for women, regardless of their ethnic or minority group status, educational achievement, and experience. The picture painted of employed women in terms of earning is not a very positive one. Women's patterns of employment are different from men's, but for equal work there is not equal pay. A plethora of studies have been conducted to account for this difference but after factoring in education, full-time and part-time status, and every other imaginable variable, the bottom line is that discrimination is "alive and well in the American labor force" (Cain, 1984; O'Neill, 1985). The estimates of what proportion of the inequality can be attributed to discrimination varies, but 25% to 50% is typical.

FACTORS INFLUENCING WOMEN'S CHOICE
OF WORK, OCCUPATION, OR CAREER

The task of this section is to elucidate the factors which influence a woman's decision to work outside the home, as well as the type of employment chosen. Generally, these factors can be divided into two categories. One set is influenced by the family, and the second set is influenced by broader sociocultural patterns.

Most women at some point actually have two families which can exert differential influences. For this discussion, Koltaks' (1974:314) definitions will be used.

Family of orientation is the nuclear family in which one grows up.
Family of procreation is the nuclear family established when one marries.

Effects on the Family of Orientation

The *family of orientation*'s effects can be broken into three areas: socialization, status and role correlations, and differentiation of opportunity structures. As discussed earlier, socialization may be broadly defined as the inculcation of skills and attitudes needed for carrying out social roles. Status and role correlations refer to attributes possessed by family members which correlate with the female's choice and/or decision to work. "Differentiation of opportunity structure" means those overt behaviors wherein parents allow children of one sex (usually male) to receive necessary and needed training rewards because the family has inadequate resources to provide these opportunities for all children.

As already discussed, a generally recognized function of the family of orientation is the socialization of children. However, families do not have sole responsibility for this task, especially after the child enters the educational system. By the time the child is ready to enter nursery school or kindergarten, basic gender role identities are formed. Much of this socialization directly affects later work force participation. Boys have learned to be more aggressive, competitive, and demanding, and to be more valued than girls. These traits are considered absolutely necessary for success in many occupations, especially in business and professions.

Differential gender role identities are also fostered by media presentations and books read to or by children, both in the home and at school. However, the lack of active female roles in general, and work roles in particular, make it difficult for girls to have *adequate* female role models, except as homemakers. Since school and home-based socialization can impact cognitive styles and creative interests, then the impact on career choice becomes obvious. Women tend to select occupations which match the creative areas and cognitive skills which they have or can acquire.

The major thrust of female socialization has been towards marriage and childbearing. To quote Epstein (1971:62), "All arrows direct the girl to marriage." The thirty-year old summation by Sears et al. (1957:122) is still an accurate reflection of the socialization effect on young girls.

In elementary school, although the curriculum is usually the same for girls and boys, the experience is often quite different. Most parents and teachers encourage boys, but not girls, to adopt the personality characteristics related to occupation success. While girls are encouraged to be sweet and passive, boys are told to be active and aggressive. Girls receive more affection and more protection. They are subject to more control and more restrictions. In contrast, higher standards are set for boys, more achievement is demanded of them, and they are punished more often if they do not succeed.

Other posited consequences are aspirational and motivational. While women are achievement oriented, their differential socialization results in different goals. Other elements of the achievement syndrome are present, such as striving and persistence. Girls perform better on feminine or gender-appropriate tasks, but competition with males inhibits performance levels (Stein and Bailey, 1973). Thus women often avoid being labeled as hard driving or ambitious which are pejorative descriptions of female behavior in general and maternal behavior in particular. A socialization process which emphasizes the wife role as most salient has many ramifications: Careers may be abandoned if conflict with the family needs arise, it may lead to underachievement in the work setting, work will probably not be encouraged as part of the female's identity, training received will be viewed as needed only if the marriage fails, or comprehensive future planning may be interfered with until after marriage.

The conclusions reached about the impact of a women's family orientation on her decision to work is fairly unequivocal: She is socialized to be passive, affectionate, supportive, marriage and family oriented, noncompetitive, and dependent. Women receive the message that home and family are of paramount importance and jobs are secondary to home and family obligations, regardless of occupational preparation. However, two trends may be reversing this. First, the American ideology regarding education and equality is also operating within the family and, if possible, all children will be equally educated. However, males tend to benefit from the situations when resources disallow education for all. Secondly, most college women now assume they can successfully combine career and family roles. Yet, the female is also presented with the dilemma of reconciling her marriage and family orientation with her job orientation.

It is difficult to specify which family statuses or roles correlate with choice of specific occupations. However, two factors do seem to have some impact: First, if a woman's mother has worked outside the home, the daughter is much more likely to do likewise; second, positive paternal desires and (perhaps) the father's status as a professional seem to be positively related with a woman choosing to enter a profession.

Effects on the Family of Procreation

This discussion will focus on resocialization, the acquisition of new role playing skills or attitudes necessitated by changes encountered in adulthood, and status and role correlations. When a woman marries, a new set of family contingencies has impact on her decision to work and her choice of occupational arenas.

The resocialization process begins at this point because the woman now has two new roles and statuses to consider, those of wife and eventually mother.

Even though American women tend to be well educated, their education parallels men's in that little formal preparation for adult roles, other than occupational, is provided. Women tend not to be formally prepared for their roles as wife and mother, the exception being women who take home economics in high school. They must learn to carry out these new roles, and this process appears to be one of trial and error. Many women are frustrated with their role of housewife because it results in feelings of incompetence, isolation, and lack of recognition.

There is agreement that husbands who feel women should work or can work (if they so desire) and who are supportive of their wives' employment are significantly more likely to have wives working outside the home. Since women with higher educational attainment are more likely to work outside the home, these same attitudes regarding support for improving the quality and quantity of work preparation through the educational process are crucial. On the other hand, the explanations for lack of husband support are extensive and include the following: Men will no longer have a wife as a refuge from the work world; wives are male success or status symbols, especially a leisured wife; wives need to be available to support the husband's career mobility; he may be threatened by her achievements, especially if she earns more money or requires supportive work from him; or, he may be less mobile if his wife has a career, too.

The role of mother probably has even greater effects on women's work choices than the ones already mentioned. Obligations of the maternal role spill over into other roles, and consume increasing amounts of time and energy. Women, even those with professional careers, retain responsibility for child care, as well as housework, in our "modern liberated world." The pressure to not work when a child is young, tends to be mitigated in communities where women working is normative.

If a mother decides to continue or start working after the birth of a child, a related factor influences her ability to carry out this decision; that is whether or not adequate child care arrangements can be made. Increased demands for child care comes at a time when the supply of domestic help is shrinking, grandmothers are returning to the labor force, and the necessary government support for increasing day care is not forthcoming. This problem is so large that some women terminate job training because it seems futile to make long term career plans when children will probably result in a five to ten year withdrawal from the labor force. As more women with young children are joining the labor force, out of both desire and need, this crisis must be addressed.

Other family related variables that are important include age at marriage, age at childbirth, and professional status when married. Women who marry after they have completed their education and begun their career bring more maturity to their marital relationship, thus reducing the likelihood of a spouse expecting the woman to give up her career. Smaller family size is also correlated with working. The percentage of employed mothers decreases rapidly for families with five children or more.

There have been few attempts to combine some or all of these effects into a theoretical model which predicts which occupations a woman will select. However, Epstein (1971:180-188) creates a model which combines four of these contingencies to explain possible female career patterns and their consequences for professional women. The four contingencies are (1) age at marriage, (2) age at childbearing, (3) age at professional preparation, and (4) age at assumption or resumption of professional practice. The following patterns are possible.

TYPE	CAREER PATTERN	LABEL
A	3 1 2 4	Early Interrupted pattern
B	3 4 1 2 4	Late Interrupted pattern
C	4 3 1 2 4	Late Interrupted Pattern
D	1 3 4 2 4	Late Interrupted Pattern
E	1 3 2 4	Late Interrupted Pattern
F	1 2 3 4	Uninterrupted Pattern
G	1 - 3 4	Uninterrupted Pattern
H	- - 3 4	Uninterrupted Pattern

The idea inherent in this model is that by controlling the timing of the four contingencies, as well as their temporal ordering, the professional woman can influence her career achievement. Specifically, the uninterrupted patterns seem to maximize career achievement because professional training is followed by professional practice without any interruptions. Likewise, the early interrupted pattern is least facilitating because the woman receives training, but never gets experience until after the children are raised; thus upon entering the job market her skills may be obsolete. As one moves down the categories, the likelihood of maximizing career achievement increases.

The conclusions reached about the impact of the family and procreation on women's decisions and choice of labor force participation are unequivocal, in that she must perform the household domestic duties, assume responsibility for child rearing is primarily hers, and accept her husband's training or career as taking precedence over hers. The women's age at marriage, age at childbearing, family financial condition, and marital status greatly influence whether or not she will work and the probable level of occupational advancement she will be able to attain. Finally, the availability of child care and family size also have a great deal of impact.

Social and Cultural Factors

The important social and cultural factors which influence work patterns are many, including education and training, economics, the political and legal situation, and cultural norms, values, and attitudes. Each of these will be briefly considered. However, effects can be interactive and may be related to family influences enumerated earlier.

There is general consensus that the more education a woman has received, the greater the likelihood that she will engage in paid employment. Since education is discussed in detail in Chapter 10, suffice it to say here that job specifications usually include requisite levels of training. There is a strong correlation between years of education and occupational distribution. The U.S. Department of Labor (1975) reports that 75% of all employed female college graduates were in professional or technical occupations, while approximately 80% of women with less than eight years of schooling were operatives or service workers. Education is "paving the way" to occupational and economic success. Given their level of training, one must ask why women are not more successful in the job arena. Some answers are that more gifted women stop training short of college, women get married and drop out of training, the dilemma of socialization tends to steer women away from some areas and into others, and lack of motivation. Finally, there is the ever-present possibility of discrimination based on gender.

Economic factors also act as an impetus and constraint upon women's aspiration to work outside the home. In times of need women are pressed to join the labor pool. The effects of industrialization and advanced machine technology, followed by information technology, have facilitated extra household employment for women, as well as men. However, there are counter pressures to stay home and consume. Veblen's (1899/1953) work on conspicuous consumption and conspicuous leisure first dealt with the phenomenon of middle class women as consumers. In fact women are the major consumers for their entire family. Friedan (1963:206-207) sums it up well.

> Why is it never said that the . . . really important role that women serve as housewives is to buy more things for the house? In all the talk of femininity and women's role, one forgets that real business of America is business. But the perpetuation of housewifery, the growth of the feminine mystique, makes sense (and dollars) when one realizes that women are the chief consumers of American business.

Thus the fact that America is a consumer society with the majority of consumption carried out by women does make the smaller time available for consumption by the working woman problematic. However, industry and the retailing sector, in particular, have responded to changes in female employment by modifying old patterns to facilitate the times available for consumption. For example, mail catalogs facilitate consumption without leaving the home.

The effects of our economic system are not limited to the general principles of facilitating or deterring women's decisions; they can also be specific. The majority of women cite economic need as the reason they originally sought employment outside the home. Working class women have cited economic pressures and the need for income as the motivation for working at "boring, repetitive, and unsatisfying" jobs which also offer limited wage payoffs. The phrase "I work to make ends meet" is heard frequently from women throughout the occupational structure, but especially on the lower end of this structure.

In 1980, the Virginia Slims Poll found that only 14% of women worked because they wanted something interesting to do. Another 43% were supplementing family income, 27% were working to support themselves, and 19% were supporting their families (Roper, 1980). Given the rise in female, single head-of-households, it should not be a surprise if such a poll were conducted today, the proportion of women supporting their family would be even higher. This is not to suggest that all women who work, do so out of gross economic need. In some cases it may be a desire to reduce the gap between real and desired economic functioning that causes women to seek work. The economic factor can force or attract women to menial, boring dead-end jobs.

Finally, sex-typing of occupations seems to be an integral part of our economic system, though it violates one of capitalism's basic premises, obtaining the best person for the particular job. Sex-typing, as alluded to earlier, acts to limit or channel women's choice of jobs. Sex-typing links occupational roles with gender roles and tends to designate female occupations as those involving nurturing, helping, and empathizing, like nursing, teaching, and social work. Conversely, occupations requiring rationality, detachment, leadership, and outspokenness, like medicine and politics, are designated as masculine.

Sex-typing is generally universal throughout the professions. However, historically some jobs have changed their distribution by sex, such as typing, clerical, and secretarial work. The argument for sex-typing based on its "naturalness" is false. Within the professions, sex-typing also takes place at another level, intra-professionally. Should a women enter a male profession, there will be subspecialities considered appropriate for women. Such subspecialities are invariably rated lower by members of the profession in terms of status and prestige. Feminine subspecialities provide low pay.

Legal and Political Factors

The legal and political factors which influence women's decision to work and the type of work chosen include laws, rulings of judges, commissions and bureaus, and direct political action at the grassroots to national level. The Equal Pay Act was passed in 1963 and is the first federal legislation that addresses the issue of equal pay between men and women. It allows for differences in pay based on a nondiscriminatory seniority system, a merit based system, or "piece work" basis. Most states now prohibit pay differentials between the sexes for equal work.

Probably the most important legal prohibition against occupational segregation and discrimination is Title VII of the 1964 Civil Rights Act. The provisions of this bill are enforced by the Equal Employment Opportunity Commission whose powers of enforcement were strengthened in 1972. The two provisions which are important for women in the work force are

1. To fail or refuse to hire or to discharge any individual, or otherwise discriminate against any individual with respect to his compensation, terms, conditions, or privileges of employment, because of such individual's race, color, religion, sex or national origin; or
2. To limit, segregate, or classify his employees in any way which would deprive or tend to deprive any individual of employment opportunities or otherwise adversely affect his status as an employee, because of such individual's race, color, religion, sex or national origin. (Civil Rights Act of 1964)

The major problem with this law is the Bona Fide Occupational Qualification (BFOQ) which allows exceptions to the law when "reasonably necessary to the operation of that particular business or enterprise" (Section E, Civil Rights Act of 1964). This acts as a vehicle for channeling women away from certain jobs.

So-called protective legislation has also functioned to channel women from certain kinds of jobs. Although the intent of such legislation was to protect women, it often functioned to bar them from work at the employer's discretion. These various bills restricted the weight that could be lifted, or specified minimum weights which must be lifted. Much of this type of legislation has been disappearing because of conflict with the Civil Rights Act of 1964.

Starting in the 1970s, there was a change in the legal approach from barring discrimination to supporting Affirmative Action. Here the thrust is to give preferential treatment to women (and others) who are underrepresented in a job category or occupation, even if males "appear" to be better qualified. Affirmative Action has been a major response to issues of discrimination and wage inequality with programs, committees, and bureaus proliferating. Of course, cries of reverse discrimination have been heard throughout the land. The argument that unqualified women are getting jobs and they need to be better prepared for jobs has questionable validity. However, the impression of reverse discrimination haunts the Affirmative Action strategy.

The judicial thrust has been generally the same as the legislative, by emphasizing that employers cannot discriminate on the basis of sex, if the woman meets the necessary qualifications. The judiciary can be seen as the policers of legal imperatives. Since the 1960s, there have been thousands of sex discrimination cases taken to court. Several important cases will be presented as representative of the issues raised and decisions rendered.

The 1971 unanimous Supreme Court decision in Reed versus Reed ruled an Idaho law giving males preference over females in selecting administrators of an estate was in violation of the 14th Amendment. This was the first time the Court ruled an arbitrary discrimination law against women to be unconstitutional (U.S. Department of Labor, 1975:359).

Gates (1976:74) points out that courts can institute hiring quotas for employers found to be discriminating, as the following summarizes.

> Occupational segregation has often been reinforced by, but seldom created by, the law . . . legislators and jurists have created powerful legal remedies for workers who attempt to break gender-related barriers in the work force.

The impact of Affirmative Action programs is somewhat mixed. A consensus that affirmative action has not benefitted all groups of women equally or at least has not solved the wage inequality issue is beginning to emerge. Rosenbaum (1985) and Blum (1987) summarize these arguments by showing that Affirmative Action has had more positive effect for women entering professions (although not for women already there), management, and the trades. However, with the decline in skilled trade jobs and the limited number of women in these other categories, the idea that job integration policy has benefitted most women is clearly false. Bianchi and Spain (1983) point out that the 30% rise in managerial positions for women in the past decade only accounts for 7% of women in the labor force. Greer (1986) would agree that the 23% increase in high level professional occupations women have achieved also affects a small proportion of all female workers.

The effect of Affirmative Action has been limited for the bulk of women who work in lower level jobs. Furthermore, the emphasis on individual action precludes the possibility of whole groups of women benefitting from change. Thus, Affirmative Action has been unsuccessful in redressing most long-term discrimination by changing the wage inequalities that still exist a quarter of a century after the critical legislative efforts of 1963 and 1964.

Consequently, a new strategy has emerged and is attempting to gain legitimacy through legislation and the judicial process. This approach is called comparable worth or pay equity. Blum (1987:382) explains comparable worth as follows.

> Comparable worth aims to upgrade the wage scales for jobs that employ large numbers of women and therefore has the potential to provide benefits on a far broader scale than affirmative action. . . . While affirmative action challenged the allocation of jobs on the basis of stereotypical gender traits, comparable worth challenges the allocation of rewards on the basis of such traits.

However, the work equity strategy requires that an objective mechanism be developed to determine which job titles are equal. This creates a problem which must be resolved before significant change can be expected. The empirical work to date suggests that it is acceptable to use generalized indicators like amount of education required, number of persons supervised, or amount of job experience. However, Rosenbaum's (1985:138) caveat about job evaluation is also pertinent.

> The mechanisms underlying job evaluation need to be scrutinized to discover whether these inequalities are inequitable, and, if so, how job evaluation could be done in other ways to lead to more equitable results . . . evaluation programs may be a serious obstacle to advancing women's earning parity . . . they also suggest caution in relying on 'unreformed' job evaluation plans in comparable worth strategies.

The political and legal factors have functioned to remove barriers which unfairly limit or circumscribe women's potential choices, rather than focusing on the decision making process which has been viewed as the personal province of a woman and her family. However, the atmosphere has changed considerably over the years and should be expected to continue changing. The advocacy of the 1970s has given way to the entrenchment of the 1980s. Many women view the current political and legal arena as less supportive than a decade ago.

Other Cultural and Social Effects: Norms, Values and Attitudes

The importance of cultural considerations like values, attitudes, and norms cannot be overstated when considering why women work or not, as well as the types of jobs they select. It would be naive to state that there is one set of values, beliefs, or norms to which all Americans adhere. Rainwater et al. (1959) shows that working class women have values which differ from women of other classes. They did not necessarily hope for upwardly mobile children; however, traditional values regarding woman's place in the home and the importance of raising a family were very similar to the general value system previously discussed. Seifer (1973:38) finds working class women desire jobs less than their middle class counterparts when there is no pressing financial need. They also derive substantial satisfaction from housekeeping which middle class women tend to define as demanding and confining.

However, other studies suggest an altering of these trends. Epstein and Bronzaft (1972) find that values are changing among young, working class women. Some blue-collar female workers tended to express positive job satisfaction because they receive higher pay and define working in a nontraditional setting challenging (Walshok, 1981). Conversely, Rosen (1982) finds that most blue-collar female workers would prefer to not work at all. Clearly, blue-collar female workers' attitudes toward work are not uniform.

Fox and Hesse-Biber (1984) summarize the situation from the most occupationally sex-segregated group in America—clerical workers. Fully 35% of all employed women are concentrated in this category which has unique problems not experienced elsewhere, not the least of which is that a secretary should run personal errands for the boss, make coffee, and provide a shoulder to cry on, while being treated as a nonperson in most other respects (Fox and Hesse-Biber, 1984:125-26).

It seems that there is a rather permeable and shifting set of factors which influence women, and this influence flows from the woman's family, as well as from many other cultural sources. Perhaps it is the flexibility in the system of cultural values which women draw upon when making the critical decisions regarding work. Epstein (1971:49) addresses this issue directly when she suggests three strategies for women given the current cultural constraints.

> First, values are usually posed so generally that they can be redefined and reinterpreted to provide a rationale for many disparate types of behaviors. . . . Second, under certain circumstances individuals can more easily depart from norms. . . . Third, as institutions—and thus roles—change, the value system and normative structure change; transition periods cause ambivalence but also mean that new values are formed.

Thus, the impact of general cultural factors are probably second in importance to the family in terms of women and work decisions. However, there is one important aspect of cultural phenomenan which has been left out of this discussion because it is covered elsewhere. That is the concept of ideology. Ideas such as sexism, equality, patriarchy, and feminism are important considerations which at least indirectly influence all women and men today. Parts of our current ideology also feed into the dilemmas for women previously discussed, like issues of equality and patriarchal or male dominance.

In summary, cultural attitudes, values and norms seem to have most impact on women's decision regarding work, especially as they are brought to bear within the family setting. Since family members may not adhere to the total generalized pattern, individual women experience differential cultural influences. Other factors—education, political, legal, and economic—also function to expand or constrain decisions and choices, though it is difficult to separate them in terms of overall impact.

WOMEN'S EMPLOYMENT: THE EFFECTS ON SOCIETY

The task of this section is to briefly elucidate the social consequences which flow from women entering the employment arena. Trends suggest that women in younger age groups (20-34), more married women with children, and better educated women will enter the labor force in greater numbers. Some traditional women's occupations are expected to show low growth or declines (elementary and secondary teachers), while traditionally male occupations are increasing (technical and professional jobs). Growth in traditional female service jobs and clerical jobs is also expected.

If these trends continue, one of the most pressing needs women face is child care options. It is imperative that adequate child care arrangements be available to women who must work or want to work. The situation is especially acute for dual career families and single-parent families, whether male-headed or female-headed.

Until recently, young children were left with relatives (especially grandmothers) or inexpensive care was provided by neighbors or friends. Since many of these women are working or seeking employment, they are not available to provide free or low cost child care. The most obvious solution to this problem is organizing efficient, well run child care centers. This proposal meets great opposition and has yet to receive political support. The norm that women should raise their children until they are at least school age is still prevalent, in spite of the evidence which suggests that staying home with infants may not be as idyllic a situation as pictured (See Radke-Yarrow et al., 1962; Rossi, 1972). Child care centers are still grossly inadequate to meet current needs. Traditionally, women have sought and found individual solutions to this problem, but it seems that the magnitude of the problem will require a social solution.

Another major area of impact is that of unemployment. As previously noted, women have greatly increased their participation in the labor force vis-a-vis men. At the same time their unemployment rate has worsened. In 1947, women constituted 28% of the civilian labor force and 27% of the unemployed. By 1985, women constituted 44% of the labor force and 46% of the unemployed. Figure 9-4 presents the recent unemployment picture for men and women. Some female unemployment is accounted for by women leaving jobs because of marriage, family concerns, or moving. However, the bottom line is that high female unemployment does not allow society to fully use its labor resources.

The last general social effect to be discussed is that of worker productivity. This issue is very difficult to come to terms with. One reason (excuse) cited for pay differentials between men and women often boils down to a discussion of

Figure 9-4. Recent Male and Female Unemployment Rates

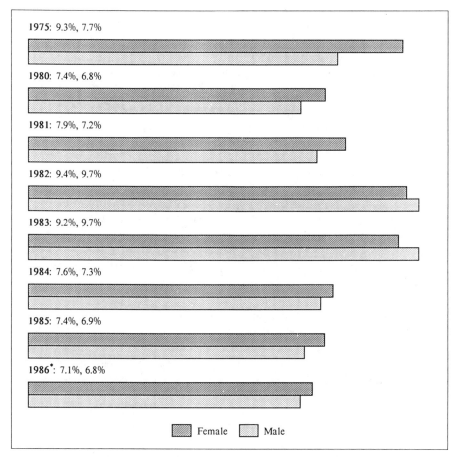

1975: 9.3%, 7.7%

1980: 7.4%, 6.8%

1981: 7.9%, 7.2%

1982: 9.4%, 9.7%

1983: 9.2%, 9.7%

1984: 7.6%, 7.3%

1985: 7.4%, 6.9%

1986*: 7.1%, 6.8%

Female   Male

* Calculation includes January-November, 1986 data.
Source: U.S. Department of Labor, 1987a.

differential productivity. Arguments can be legitimately made that women miss more work than men because of child care, illness, and other family responsibilities, although this indicator has been moving toward convergence between male and female rates. Technical problems also arise because, historically, jobs have been organized around male characteristics, jobs and job settings have been organized to make men, not women, more productive. Thus, women with equal production capacity with men may not be able to actualize their potential. Jobs and work settings can be reorganized to allow efficiency for all workers, regardless of sex.

Consumer preference and attitudes also are difficult to factor in or out of these considerations. Evaluations must address the issue of measuring quality of production rather than quantity, and actual rather than perceived quality. The feedback effects of undervaluing women's work on productivity must also be considered.

Thus, the issue of under-productivity of women cannot be definitively supported or summarily dismissed. Madden (1985:80) summarizes the current situation:

> There can be no question with respect to comparisons of individuals that (1) there remains substantial variation in productivity across individuals with equivalent education, work experience, and work hours; and (2) this variation is due in part to unmeasured factors such as innate ability, motivation, personality, and so forth. . . . When aggregated into groups with equivalent characteristics, individual variations are averaged out. Unless there is some reason to presume that women as a group have inferior innate ability, motivation, or personality relative to men *with the same objective characteristics* . . . these unmeasured factors cannot explain the sex differential.

EFFECTS OF WOMEN WORKING ON THEIR FAMILIES

Clearly a working wife and mother affects her family. Tensions, strains, and conflicts arise. How they are handled, especially the changes in family structure and interaction that occur, are particularly important for both the woman and her family. Female heads-of-households and dual career families may feel these strains most strongly because the woman tends to be employed on a full-time permanent basis.

There is also concern about the losses husbands will suffer. Husbands may fear concessions will have to be made in terms of their power, status, prestige, or household commitments. Many of these fears are baseless. Juster (1984) finds that men are working three hours per week more at home in 1982 than 1976 and women are working one hour less. The type of husband who will suffer real losses if his wife works is the "corporation man." There is little evidence that husbands are willing to take on this role for their "corporate woman" wives.

The effect of working women on their children is equivocal. It is still referred to as maternal deprivation in some writing. As the proportion of women in the labor force has grown the empirical evidence of extreme negative effects on children has decreased. There is little support for previously held ideas that working women produce more juvenile delinquents or mentally ill children. As the needs of society have changed in the direction of encouraging female labor force participation, so has the empirical evidence of research findings. This may suggest that social researchers are biased, but it may also be that some normative change mediates the effects of working or that asking questions differently results in new evidence.

Regardless, since most women are engaged in gainful productivity, as they have been throughout history, it will become more necessary to deal with the really pressing problem of adequate child care. The legal, political, moral, and cultural ramifications of not addressing this crisis is unquestionably the one major effect on a working woman's family that is completely unresolved.

In sum, over half of all women work outside the home in modern America. This is a long term trend which is expected to continue, with male and female labor force participation continuing to converge. The trend has not developed without problems arising for many of our social institutions. Perhaps the most surprising finding is that there have been substantially fewer changes in the past 25 years than most Americans expect. Wage discrimination continues unabated. The bulk of women are still located in low paying, boring jobs with no future for growth. Even professional women have not found doors for advancement opening at the rate that social, legal, and political action had hoped to attain. There is a great deal of waste in the labor force distribution of women. New strategies are being developed to help more women. However, there are real problems which must be overcome for these strategies to work.

Women as a group do not receive equal pay for equal work. Various rationales are offered to explain the wage gap. The recognition that discrimination and prejudice play an important role in understanding this phenomenon has emerged. Other important explanatory factors include gender role expectations and socialization, education and the changing tapestry of legal and political moods in the country. Virginia Wolfe (1929) summarized the overall need to get on with solutions as follows:

> All of this pitting of sex against sex, of quality against quality; all this claiming of superiority and imputing of inferiority, belongs to the private school stage of human existence where there are sides and it is necessary for one side to best the other side, and of the utmost importance to walk up to a platform and receive from the Headmaster himself a highly ornamental pot.

10

The Impact
of Education

"Genius is for them a useless and dangerous gift." (Madame de Genlis, *Adele et Theodore*, I, 39 [Paris, 1782])

Compared to society's other institutions, education is probably the most equitable. As children face the educational odyssey with eager anticipation, parents approach it with the conviction that the success of their children will be directly tied to how well they do in school. Increasingly, we are becoming a credential-oriented society and formal schooling provides us with those pieces of paper which allow access to the most prestigious and financially rewarding positions. Faced with the prospect of at least twelve years of education for their children, parents are likely to be concerned with the quality of teaching and extent of curricular offerings. For them, the issue of equity may focus on the amount of federal and state monies reserved for their district. Certainly they want the best education possible for their children. Many of these concerned parents would be indeed shocked if they discovered that their sons are experiencing a very different educational process than their daughters. In the most equitable of our institutions, the gender of the child becomes a key determinant of his or her educational experience.

A BRIEF LESSON IN HISTORY

The history of Western civilization demonstrates that education in general, and literacy in particular, was reserved for the elite of society, with the vast majority of the population excluded from even the rudiments of formal learning. It must be recognized that until the eighteenth century, both men and women remained unschooled. There is some evidence that during the Greek and Roman eras, certain upper class women were educated in the arts, with a focus on poetry and music, in order to entertain household guests (Stock, 1978). This tradition continued into the Middle Ages and served to reinforce the image of women as sources of diversion from a tedious world.

As already documented, it was during the Middle Ages that Christianity enveloped Europe and established a stronghold on most institutions. Convent schools arose to meet the need for some women to learn reading and writing, although even here it was essentially for religious purposes, especially as preparation for entering the convent to become nuns. The few other select women who attended these institutions became part of a system where schooling was designed to "preserve sexual purity and produce proper behavior in society" (Stock, 1978:26). Functionalism would view even the mediocre education during this era as paralleling family and broader societal values, with the religious institution dominating the entire system. Overall, then, in spite of the rise of universities in the twelfth and thirteenth centuries and the tremendous impact of the Renaissance, education was aimed at the sons of nobility and the emerging bourgeoisie, who would enter scholarly professions, law, medicine, or become clerics.

The first real rumblings of equality of education for both sexes and all classes came with the Enlightenment. It was during this period when Jean Rousseau published *Emile* (1762), a book that was destined to become one of the most influential works in the history of education. In describing a man, Emile, and a woman, Sophie, who would be Emile's wife, Rousseau provides educational principles consistent with his broader philosophy of naturalism. Whereas a man would be schooled or trained according to his natural talents and encouraged to cultivate his mind and spirit without restraint or coercion, a woman should be passive, weak, and humbly submissive, especially in terms of accepting a man's judgment in all matters (Kolesnik, 1969:56). Rousseau would not deny literacy to women, but even this should be "practically" oriented, since intellectual pursuits could wreak havoc on her naturally weak temperament.

Considered a radical by many of his contemporaries, Rousseau's discourses on boys' education laid the foundation for the twentieth century movement known as Progressive Education. Certainly his views on women caused little room for debate as they reflected accepted thought on her "nature" anyway. The so-called leveling effects of the Enlightenment were directed mainly at glaring class differences, with little thought given to equalizing educational opportunities for women. Given the roles men and women were expected to play, men's education was regarded as definitely unsuitable for women.

Dissonant voices were heard during the Eighteenth Century, although they had little impact in comparison to Rousseau and other major scholars of the time.[1] The Marquis de Condorcet declared that society should not only be responsible for education in general, but that it had a duty to instruct both sexes in common. Equality and justice demanded it. Madame de Lambert advised women to study Latin, philosophy, and science to bolster their resources in a world where the usual roads to success were closed to women (Stock 1978:110). She bitterly lamented that women have but "coquetry and the miserable function of pleasing" as their wealth (Greard, 1893). In essence, the true spirit of the Enlightenment emerged in the late nineteenth century in both Europe and the United States as policies advocating free and compulsory education for all children were adopted. These principles were strengthened during the civil rights turmoil of the 1960s when the issue of equality of opportunity, especially in education, was seriously debated.

Today most Americans wholeheartedly subscribe to the belief that education is the key to success and is the vehicle for upward mobility. Children may begin their formal education as early as three years of age, with preschool, and spend the next twelve to twenty years of their lives in educational institutions. As mentioned above, equality of education is assumed during these years. Yet when the female kindergarten teacher first removes Dick's mittens and helps Jane off with her coat, by virtue of their gender alone, their long educational journey will contain essential differences.

THE PROCESS OF EDUCATION

Kindergarten

Though many children have already been introduced to educational expectations through preschool experiences, their formal learning process begins with kindergarten. The trepidation that is often associated with this new environment is tempered with the excitement of being with others of the same age and realizing that the kindergarten classroom is to some degree an extension of familiar household surroundings. Kindergarten allows for the gradual structuring of the child's day so that ample time is set aside for play activities. Both boys and girls eagerly anticipate the time reserved for playing with the myriad of toys and games evident in most kindergarten classrooms, toys which they have probably already played with at home.

When play period begins, the girls rush off to the minikitchen reserved for them. Here they can pretend to cook, set the table, and clean with miniature household artifacts that are specially constructed for their small hands. This miniature house comes complete with dolls on which Jane can practice her domestic

[1]In following Rousseau's ideas, the renowned German philosopher Immanuel Kant wrote that woman's aesthetic mind and her weak and passive nature could potentially rule man, even though his mind was suited to abstraction and profound understanding. Therefore, education of women should be discouraged (Stock, 1978:108).

artistry. Barry (1975:119) notes that she enters the doll corner as a doll-like creature dressed in a manner that restricts her to the type of activities appropriate for the minihouse.

At times she will be allowed to wear "boy clothes" to run with the other children and play on the schoolyard equipment unencumbered by clothing that inhibits such activities. Lest she be labeled a tomboy, however, both teacher and parents reinforce these kinds of play activities to only a limited extent. The logic is simple. Her adult roles will not be substantially in line with this kind of behavior; thus socialization within the school should reflect this idea.

Throughout the kindergarten year Jane gains approval from her peers, parents, and teacher for her quiet demeanor as she pours tea for her dolls and her studiousness as she intently pages through her first schoolbooks. She may secretly envy the boys as they display both power and freedom in their play. But that admiration is also seen in light of the teacher's obvious disapproval of their boisterous behavior in the classroom. Jane rarely plays with the boys anymore and would prefer to play house with her best friend.

Meanwhile, Dick enters kindergarten more psychologically unprepared for the experience than Jane. His higher level of physical activity is incompatible with the sedate atmosphere of even the kindergarten classroom. He begins to realize that his teacher approves of the girls but is more stern with him. Rather than gaining her attention through emulating the girls and being threatened with the devastating label of sissy, he is prone to fast movements and large, noisy toys (Barry, 1975). Dick discovers that the teacher pays attention to him, listens to him, and even scolds him for his disruptive behavior, but he may also believe it is better to be reprimanded than ignored (Sadker and Sadker, 1974).

Dick and his friends regard trucks and building blocks as acceptable alternatives in toys. Occasionally a girl may wander over and attempt to join in the louder and seemingly more interesting activities of the boys. She is likely to be discouraged from long-term participation, however, by their rough-and-tumble play behavior and the very vibrancy by which she was originally attracted. Such activities are merely extensions of preschool environments which reward boys for being independent, active, and assertive, in sharp contrast to school norms, which call for docility and passivity, a realm where girls feel more at ease (Kagan, 1964). As Smith (1972:31) states, "the socially responsive girls are a joy; the aggressive overacting boys are often less than enchanting."

It is understandable then, that boys find their first school experience disconcerting, coping with a system of what they see as incongruous rewards and punishments. And, more importantly, these patterns established in kindergarten set the stage for the next crucial socialization level, the elementary years.

Elementary School

For girls, elementary school provides a vehicle for achievement. They exceed boys in most areas of verbal ability, reading, and mathematics, which is reflected in the higher grades they receive (Maccoby, 1966). Their teachers also put a premium on being good and being tidy, which may account for the more sparing use of negative comments given them (Dweck et al., 1978; Haber, 1983). Elementary school creates what can be referred to as a "feminine environment" to the extent that *both* boys and girls see teacher favoritism to girls. The children believe this shows up in areas such as allowing girls more chances for reading (McNeil, 1964). Are the children correct in this assessment? Davis and Slobodian (1967), in observing these teachers, found that in fact, they were impartial in not only rewarding opportunities for reading, but also in terms of overall criticism of boys versus girls. In assessing this finding, Smith (1972:33) points out that even if the teachers were impartial and the children saw it differently, the teachers still believed boys were less motivated and ready to read than girls.

It would appear that high achievement coupled with low criticism would provide an ideal environment for girls and that positive socialization experiences would result. Yet simultaneous processes are occurring which send different messages and which can have damaging consequences. The message that is communicated to girls very early in their elementary school lives is that they are less important than boys. They are virtually invisible or, at best, play insignificant roles in those curricula materials upon which most time in elementary school is spent.

Studies of textbooks which teach reading, social studies, and even mathematics consistently strengthen this idea that less importance is attached to females. An older study by Child et al. (1960) examining readers since 1930 found only 27% of the stories depict female characters. And even these few characters can be described as timid, uncreative, unambitious and inactive. Females are rarely mentioned as making any meaningful contributions to history, science or government. Girls help their mothers. Women do not work outside the home. Boys do interesting and exciting things. Girls do not (DeCrow, 1972; Weitzman and Rizzo, 1974). A similar study by Saario et al. (1973) finds that by the third grade the already limited number of female characters sharply decreases, with a concomitant increase in stereotyped portrayals for both males and females.

Probably the most revealing study of this pattern of female invisibility was conducted by Lenore Weitzman and her associates (1972) with their thorough examination of children's picture books. How are gender roles treated in those books which are considered the very best that are offered to children during these formative years? Weitzman defines "the best" as books chosen for the coveted Caldecott Medal given by the Children's Service Committee of the American Library Association for excellence in books geared to school-age children, mainly in the third through sixth grades. Finally, she examines best-sellers among the popular "Little Golden Book" series. The results are in line with other research on the subject.

> We found that females were underrepresented in the titles, central roles, pictures, and stories of every sample of books we examined. Most children's books are about boys, men, and male animals, and deal exclusively with male adventures. Most pictures show men singly or in groups. Even when women can be found in the books, they often play insignificant roles, remaining both inconspicuous and nameless. (Weitzman et al., 1972:1128)

The few female characters who can be described as independent or adventurous are successful only through their unobtrusiveness or ability to toil quietly behind the scenes. And since not one of the women in the Caldecott sample had a job or profession outside the home, it is realistic to assess socialization in these books as training girls for service activities and passive, dependent roles. What is perhaps more revealing is that the Caldecott sample is in fact less stereotyped in portrayals than the other book series she examined, and are not indicative of the "most blatant examples of sexism" (Weitzman et al., 1972:1127).

Considering the fact that Weitzman's study is now almost two decades old and that the consciousness of a nation has been raised regarding the extent of gender role stereotyping in education, it would be expected that instructional materials are today more reflective of the expanded roles of many women and some men. In replicating and extending the Weitzman study, Williams et al. (1987) does not find this to be true. The books children read today continue to present characters in line with traditional gender roles. Women and girls are portrayed as being dependent, cooperative, passive, submissive, and nurturing, whereas men and boys are seen as independent, creative, explorative, aggressive, and active.

Schau and Scott's (1984) review of research on the impact of sex-typed curricula materials concludes that gender role attitudes of students at all grade levels, from elementary school through college, are compromised. Instructional materials which perpetuate gender role stereotyping in turn reinforce sex-typed beliefs, with children in the younger grades being the most susceptible. On the other hand, it is clearly demonstrated that when textbooks in particular portray girls and boys and women and men in nontraditional roles and in situations where gender equity rather than gender stratification is evident, less sex-typed attitudes result. However, materials reflecting equity are still the exception rather than the rule. In educational institutions in general and in curricula materials in particular, Sadker et al. (1986) have determined it is boys who are the central figures, while girls are assigned a second class status.

The following illustrates the kind of sexism to which these studies are referring. The poem is taken from the Hallmark book, *What Girls Can Be* (Walley, n.d., a)

A girl can be:
a nurse, with white uniforms to wear, or
a stewardess, who flies everywhere.
a ballerina, who dances and twirls around, or
a candy shop owner, the best in town.
a model, who wears lots of pretty clothes or
a big star in the movies and on special TV shows.
a secretary who'll type without mistakes, or
an artist, painting trees and clouds and lakes.
a teacher in nursery school some day, or
a singer and makes records people play.
a designer of dresses in the very latest style, or
a bride, who comes walking down the aisle.
a housewife, someday when I am grown, and
a mother, with some children of my own.

Jane soon learns that her intellectual achievement is going to be less important than her physical attractiveness, and that options outside motherhood are seen as less desirable. As we shall see, this becomes more crystallized in high school.

Boys, on the other hand, are experiencing elementary school quite differently. We saw that they do not easily adjust to a classroom environment which emphasizes quietness and lack of physical activities. Teachers reprimand them more and give them lower grades. Lipmen-Blumen (1984) reports that even though boys possess the same intellectual capabilities as girls they receive lower grades on report cards. This demonstrates how classroom behavior may influence a teacher's perception of a student which then is translated to lower grades. Yet these same teachers will talk to them more about the subject matter, listen more to their complaints and questions, and praise them most for their intellectual competence (Dweck et al., 1978; Sadker and Sadker, 1974, 1985).[2]

The textbooks boys read in elementary school are replete with male characters doing interesting and exciting things, both in occupational and recreational activities, such as sports. They see active and resourceful adult males who are job holders and boys their own age who build, create and discover, as well as protect their younger sisters (Howe, 1975; Sadker and Sadker, 1974; Weitzman and Rizzo, 1974; Weitzman, 1984). It is true that males are also cast into father roles, but in contrast to mothers, they have a separate life and identity outside the home. Both boys and girls come to regard "daddies" as less restrictive than "mommies" in part because "they know you're brave enough to do lots of things that mommies think are much too hard for you" (Weitzman, 1972:1143).

Although Dick may find some aspects of elementary school frustrating and confusing, curricula materials confirm his masculine role and serve to strengthen his male identity. His primary role in life will be as a wage earner and, as the following volume of the Hallmark book, *What Boys Can Be* (Walley, n.d., b) illustrates, Dick can aspire to heights not available to Jane.

> A boy can be:
> a fireman who squirts water on the flames, and
> a baseball player who wins lots of games.
> a bus driver who helps people travel far, and
> a policeman with a siren in his car,
> a cowboy who goes on cattle drives, and
> a doctor who helps to save people's lives.
> a sailor on a ship that takes you everywhere, and
> a pilot who goes flying through the air.
> a clown with silly tricks to do, and
> a pet tiger owner who runs the zoo.
> a farmer who drives a big red tractor, and
> on a TV show if I become an actor.
> an astronaut who lives in a space station, and
> someday grow up to be President of the nation.

---

[2]Girls are praised less for the intellectual aspects of their work and more for qualities such as neatness, completeness, and turning in assignments on time (Dweck, et al., 1978).

High School

Based on Jane's intellectual achievement and superior grades in elementary school, it would appear that academic success in high school could be easily predicted. But, ironically, the process begins to reverse. Maccoby (1966) finds that scholastic accomplishment begins to decline for girls in areas such as reading and writing, but especially in mathematics, where boys are beginning to excel.

This finding has been seized as demonstrating that girls have lower analytic ability than boys. How accurate is this assertion? Milton (1958), as discussed in Weitzman (1984) finds that, indeed, male scores on tests involving mathematical reasoning exceed scores for females. However, when the content was changed to include "feminine" subjects such as cooking and sewing, but while retaining the same logical reasoning process, female scores increase. Ernest (1976) points out that there is disagreement about what constitutes mathematical ability, which indicates that such definitional problems make comparisons difficult. Sherman (1967) suggests that it is deceptive to label spatial perception, or the capacity to see things out of context, which is lower in girls, as comprising analytic ability. Verbal perception, in which girls score higher, should also be included. In a later study, Fennema and Sherman (1977) note that when the number of courses in mathematics is controlled, there are no differences between boys and girls in spatial perception capabilities. As Weitzman (1984:84) poignantly states, "one might speculate that if women had higher scores on spatial perception and men had higher scores on verbal perception, the latter would have been called analytic ability, for what the researchers have done is to seize upon one of the few traits in which men score higher and label it analytic ability." Since the evidence is contradictory and the definitions are not uniform, it would be better to suggest that if differences in mathematical ability exist, they cannot be very strong (Weitzman, 1979:68).

Perhaps the best explanation for the downturn of girls' academic performance can be answered from a gender role viewpoint: Many girls equate scholastic success with a loss of femininity. Popularity with boys is the key to fulfillment in high school; so girls choose to hide their intellectual abilities to not appear competitive to the boys they would like to attract. The peer pressure of high school may force some bright young women to view themselves as inadequate or unfeminine if they succeed academically or are interested in supposedly masculine subjects, like mathematics (Keniston and Keniston, 1964; Kaminski, 1985). It is understandable, then, that not only do grades decline, but upon graduation many girls do not have the prerequisites for majoring in science, engineering, or other subjects where a strong math-based competency is required (Sells, 1978).

High school girls are more often tracked into academic courses like English and vocational courses like typing and home economics, where they can succeed and, at the same time, pose no threat to boys. Contrary to popular opinion, more girls graduate from high school than boys and more girls are enrolled in vocational education courses than boys (Trecker, 1974; Stockard and Johnson, 1980). Girls are likely to need proof of competency for even rudimentary clerical work and this proof usually comes in the form of a high school diploma. Also, the higher female enrollment in vocational education courses reflects the fact that more men intend to pursue college. Women are taking courses where they can be employed immediately upon graduation (Saario et al., 1973; Trecker, 1974). This trend for higher female enrollment in high school vocational courses may reverse in the near future since women now attend college in slightly higher numbers than men (U.S. Bureau of the Census, 1987). Yet the fact remains that the overwhelming majority of students in courses geared to sales, secretarial, and other office occupations are female. Yet most vocational programs for girls are still dominated by the teaching of household skills, which mirrors the cultural assumption that working outside the home is optional for women (Trecker, 1974). Overall, high school vocational education for girls is geared to the non-college bound who either marry or wind up in low-paying, dead-end jobs.

Whereas more and more middle class girls are going to college, working class girls may not see this as a realistic option. This means that marriage looms as the proper alternative and the senior year in high school is the last chance to find a husband (Weitzman, 1979:47) as well as to obtain a marketable vocational skill until they do.

For Dick, the confusion of elementary school begins to dissipate as his independence is now rewarded more often. His grades have improved considerably and he is able to demonstrate his talents in courses specifically designed for boys. Although intent on pursuing a college education, he also finds industrial and graphic arts and woodworking and metallurgy open to him. For his friends who are not going to college, high school vocational education courses will help prepare them for jobs in printing, carpentry, engineering technology, and computer science. Unlike courses for girls, vocational education for boys will have potentially higher economic returns after high school graduation.

Although more girls are starting to enroll in what have been traditionally labeled as "male" courses, boys are less likely to take courses associated with "feminine" activities. When course titles are not as reflective of feminine content, boys will enroll more freely. For instance, Bachelor Living and Home Mechanics will allow boys to gain at least basic household skills without the stigma of taking a "girl's" course. Changing the title of a course to entice males to enroll may appear to be pandering and, again, it serves to devalue courses that females have taken all along. But it at least provides a mechanism to expose boys to needed content and helps to increase their skills in very practical domestic tasks.

Differential vocational education tracking is reinforced by other school mechanisms which help perpetuate the system. Both sexes are exposed to the same history and social studies courses. As with elementary school, these courses demonstrate that "boys do" and "girls don't." Trecker's (1975) study of high school United States history books finds not only few women portrayed, but those who are, conform to a definite stereotypical image of what women are supposed to be. Controversial men are portrayed. Potentially controversial women are omitted.

Even the standardized achievement and career interest tests taken by high school students represent a consistent male bias, from the content to the pronouns used (Saario et al., 1973). These tests are then administered by counselors who, themselves, may not be objective in helping with vocational and college planning. Research concludes that gender bias in counseling is a problem that can affect students' attitudes to career selection, choice of major, or even willingness to pursue a college education (Tiedt, 1972; Pringle, 1973; Donahue and Costar, 1977). Recognizing the insidious nature of this trend, there is now a call for developing intervention strategies that will help raise the gender role consciousness of counselors and also help them understand how their own cultural beliefs influence their work with students (Goldberg, 1972; Maslin and Davis, 1975; Wirtenberg and Nakamura, 1976; Donahue and Costar, 1977).

High school provides another instance of staffing patterns which demonstrate to students and the community alike that males are the leaders. The male high school principal reports to the male school superintendent who regularly meets with primarily male school board members. The community bestows laurels on the coaches who steer their basketball and football teams to victorious heights. Male achievement on the playing fields of high schools across America is invariably associated with community and school pride and respectability. How does this affect the boys who strive to become members of the coveted team?

Whereas popularity with boys is linked to prestige for girls, athletic success provides the same function for boys. At early ages, boys are told that athletic accomplishments will aid in success in life. They also realize that their prestige with both sexes rests on it (Coleman, 1961). Since Coleman completed this study 30 years ago, the situation has not changed. In fact, it may have accelerated as the public becomes more aware of the millions of dollars spent on professional sports and sees the personal glory of the athletes themselves. Their image is not tarnished, but made more lustrous by the injuries, fights, and general mayhem that occur in football and hockey games.

Team sports demonstrate the importance of competition and allow for participants to gain in confidence, concentration and courage, traits associated with successful American males (Fiske, 1972; Best, 1983; Blotnick, 1986). If boys cannot withstand the physical or emotional strains of athletics, they may feel inadequate and unpopular. If a boy gauges himself by his athletic prowess or physical deeds, and by his estimation cannot measure up to his peers, his self-esteem will suffer. By his values academic achievement is no real substitute for athletic rewards. In more extreme cases, he may begin to doubt his masculinity and harbor resentment toward women. Monagan (1983) asserts that a sufficient male gender identity can be formed and polished by sports. More importantly, this identity could be tarnished if a boy engages in coeducational sports, especially if a girl can outperform a boy in the same athletic competition. This kind of argument not only discourages coed teams, but again provides ammunition which implicitly deprecates those activities where girls can succeed at an equal or better level than boys.

The importance attached to high school athletics can be measured by the financial and organizational support given to male as opposed to female sports. Boys' teams have better equipment and facilities and higher paid coaches than comparable girls' teams, if the latter are represented in team sports at all (Weitzman, 1984). With these kinds of statistics, it is understandable that athletics is still viewed as a road to success for high school males. This is a gilded road for those boys who intend to pursue college through an athletic scholarship.

Higher Education

If high school tracking mechanisms have been successful, the best and the brightest students will pursue a college education. Since World War II, there has been a steady increase of both men and women attending college; women now exceed men and these women are increasingly older (over 35), part-time students. These trends are more meaningful since women are less likely to receive fellowships and get less financial aid from their parents (Roby, 1972:123). This pattern is likely to accelerate in the next decade as women who have not previously worked outside the home, especially on a full-time basis, realize they are no longer limited to household roles. Others see education as enhancing career choices later in life. Ideally, college should be the one educational institution which objectively evaluates students on criteria related to academic achievement and the potential for success. But the lessons of elementary school and high school are not easily forgotten. Even in coeducational colleges where men and women share the same classrooms, teachers, and take many of the same courses, their educational experiences differ significantly (Association of American Colleges, 1982).

Although many barriers have fallen as doors in higher education increasingly open to women, the classroom climate still offers subtle, as well as not so subtle, cues for women. Sandler (1987:115) reports that even overt discriminatory comments are frequently heard in the college classroom, as the following research examples illustrate.

> In ... classes they hear women described as fat housewives, dumb blondes, as physically dirty, as broads, chicks or dames, depending upon the age of the speaker. Class time is taken up by some professors with dirty jokes which ... often happen to be derogatory to women (i.e., referring to a woman by a part of her anatomy, portraying women in jokes as simple-minded or teases, showing women as part of the "decoration" on a slide).

Women discover early in their college years that they will receive less faculty encouragement for their work, which in turn promotes expectations of lower achievement levels (Almquist and Angrist, 1971; Jaffe, 1973; Fox, 1984). Women shun aggressiveness throughout their lives and the intellectual battles in the college classroom require difficult adjustment. Even highly motivated women will likely experience a moderate degree of anxiety as such values collide. Self-esteem drops for women and increases for men during college (Katz, 1980). Traditional values intrude again as the inevitable confrontation resurfaces for the college woman. There is pressure to find a partner and simultaneously work toward career goals. If the future is uncertain because of role conflicts, the present becomes more anxiety-ridden.

In studying achievement-related conflicts in women, Horner (1969, 1972) suggests that success in college may be seen as unfeminine. It is not that failure is the desirable outcome, but the anxiety is produced by success. A "fear of success" concept has been proposed to explain the anxiety women feel when they see their femininity threatened and may explain women's drop in grades in high school and lowered self-esteem in college. However, research on the fear of success concept has been criticized on both methodological and theoretical grounds in part because of inconsistent research results, (Sadd et al., 1978; Paludi, 1984) and has called into question Horner's notion that it is a consistent personality trait connected with certain expectations for behavior. Basow (1986:170) points out that a more satisfactory explanation is to consider fear of success as a *situational variable* where women can realistically evaluate the negative results from success in a given situation. To say that socialization into the female role motivates girls and women to avoid success is simply not empirically verifiable and does not do justice to the immense change that has taken place since Horner's original work.

Without a doubt, an academic environment that does not reinforce the invisibility of women would be beneficial. Invisibility may be a minor problem if one considers the impact of remarks made by the powerful and well-respected bastions of the academic community. In lamenting the impact of the draft on graduate applications, former president of Harvard, Nathan Pusey commented that "we shall be left with the blind, the lame and the women" (Harris, 1970:283). Today such overtly sexist comments are less likely to be heard, but, as already documented, the attitudes from which they stem are still pervasive.

Clear-visioned college women may choose the well-traveled road of majoring in the arts and humanities and continue to reserve science and mathematics for men. When coupled with the psychological barriers women face in college, for those who opt for graduate education, the routes on the academic map are already indelibly marked. By 1980 women were awarded one-half of all undergraduate degrees. In the same year, they received 28% of the doctorates, with the majority of those in literature, language, biology, and certain of the social sciences. Fox (1984:244) observes that not only were most of these found in the "traditional" female areas, but also in those disciplines already glutted with Ph.D.s. The expanding, more lucrative areas of business, engineering, and the physical and computer sciences are still dominated by men. It is conceivable that a Ph.D. in literature does not provoke the feelings of "unfemininity" that a female pursuing a chemical engineering doctorate might feel.

Psychological roadblocks are accentuated in graduate and professional education for both sexes as competition for grades and grants also increases. Besides dealing with pressures involving career, marriage, having children, and unfemininity, women must also cope with restrictive admission policies and the subtle discrimination existing in many, if not most, graduate departments. As Tobias (1972:85) notes,

> There is an incredible amount of second-guessing in faculty recommendations for female applicants to graduate school, we discovered. Reading some of them discreetly, we found phrases like "this woman is very unlikely to finish her degree because she is so pretty." And others like, "this woman is very unlikely to finish her degree. She is very insecure because she is not very pretty."

Legal barriers notwithstanding, more subtle modes exist which maintain differential admission standards for women applying to graduate school.

After acceptance into graduate school, the path to career success for those who choose academia rests with faculty support and references. Academic careers blossom through a protégé system which matches a talented graduate student with a recognized, established faculty member. Women graduate students spend less time with faculty, are less relaxed when they do, and find they are not suitable as protégés. Although not overtly discriminated against, these pervasive patterns keep both faculty and graduate student males in control of the powerful subculture of graduate school. Fox (1984:246) demonstrates how this operates on the professional level by quoting a Berkeley student.

> Have I been overtly discriminated against? Probably no. Have I been encouraged, congratulated, received recognition, gotten a friendly hello, a solicitous "can I help you out?" The answer is no. Being a woman here just makes you tougher, work harder, and hope that if you get a 4.0 GPA someone will say "You're good." (Quoted in Association of American Colleges, 1982:1)

Female faculty are important for undergraduate and graduate women as both role models and mentors. Where does the academic path lead for women Ph.D.s? Most are in two and four year state colleges, usually satellite campuses, with heavy teaching loads and administrative responsibilities. They are clustered in less prestigious schools and the less powerful fields. They are likely to be instructors and assistant professors, with only one-tenth at the full professor level (Fox, 1984:247). The pattern repeats itself throughout academia—the higher the rank, the fewer the women.

When tenure decisions are made, the years of subtle discrimination become manifest. Women are denied often because they have fewer publications in lesser known journals. Besides the inequity of such a system, it is a sad comment on college education in general that good teaching, where women excel, is not usually rewarded with tenure. Jane may then be caught with the agonizing decision of uprooting her life to seek employment elsewhere or finding part-time work at other local colleges. The latter course will be her likely choice, especially if she has children and an employed spouse. She will remain in academia but in a marginal position with little hope of advancement, influence or tenure.

Although both well-qualified women and men are likely to be admitted to college, it is less difficult for Dick (Walster et al., 1972; Stockard and Johnson, 1980). Once admitted, men find that American academic life exemplifies a male mode of performance (Riesman, 1972). Dick, too, is caught in the pressure to perform at a high scholastic level and still be socially adept. The "college man" is expected to date, drink, and "be cool" (Richardson, 1988:68). Yet the classroom atmosphere is probably easier for males to handle, with rewards coming for vigorous discussion and an emphasis on active learning and independence. This model of learning sets the stage for graduate school. In a study of six Pennsylvania colleges, Simpson (1972) finds that when all variables other than the sex of the candidate are equal, males are typically chosen over females for admission.

Compared to women, men appear to be confronted with fewer roadblocks in higher education and graduate school. College men are not immune to the gender role changes which are occurring on campuses, which means some are now caught in a double bind. Komarovsky (1987) states that many men are now coming to value originality and intelligence in their female classmates and associates; yet they have been unable to relinquish the cherished belief and internalized norm that men should be superior. Some typical attitudes that are expressed include

> I am looking for an intelligent girl who has opinions on politics, social problems—someone I could talk to about things guys talk about.
> If I were I woman I would want a career. It must be boring sitting around the house doing the same thing day in and day out.
> I would not want to marry a woman whose only goal is a housewife. (Komarovsky, 1987:124,127)

Such remarks indicate several things. First, men may be more sympathetic to women who are in housewife roles. Second, they demonstrate the continued negative values associated with being a housewife. Finally, tantalizing egalitarian ideals are held out to the college men who want to accept them. But as Komarovsky (1987:129) points out, they represent both "the lure and the threat" of the articulate, educated woman. A lifetime of socialization into gender roles is difficult to negate.

Men dominate the most influential fields where graduate work is required, such as medicine and law. They also remain concentrated at the top of the prestige hierarchy within such fields. Men are overrepresented as surgeons and women are overrepresented as pediatricians. Although pharmacy colleges now enroll 50% women, men are more likely to be retail store owners, chain store managers, and directors of hospital pharmacies. Women hold positions in pharmacy of considerably less power and prestige (Lindsey, 1984). The attorneys who represent international corporations are most often men. Women attorneys practice family law and work for the Legal Aid Society. In private firms, men are law partners; women are associates. The culmination of college or graduate school, whether as a holder of B.A., M.D. or Ph.D., is also the culmination of a lifetime of socialization into attitudes and behavior regarding gender roles.

The Lessons of Title IX

The educational patterns described here should become obsolete if sex discrimination in education becomes legally banned. At least, this was the intent behind the passage of Title IX of the Educational Amendment Act of 1972.[3] This act prohibited sex discrimination in any school receiving federal assistance, which meant that the majority of educational institutions fell under its mandate. At the overt and formal level it can be said that sex discrimination *has* decreased, especially in the areas of college admissions, athletics, and scholarships.

[3]See Chapter 13 for a detailed discussion of this.

We have seen, however, that at all educational levels noticeable discriminatory policies and practices still exist. As overviewed in a recent article (McMillen, 1985:27), women academics still say they "suffer extensively from stereotypes and sexist attitudes." They are still being called girls by male colleagues and are often ignored when serving on committees. Sympathetic women who can serve as role models for aspiring female faculty and administrators are cited as a key to help change such attitudes. Title IX has done little to alter gender segregation of academic fields, at either the student or faculty level. This pattern continues to show up throughout all levels of educational institutions. Girls take home economics in junior high school. Boys major in mathematics in college. Women Ph.D.s teach French. Even the more liberal world of the university remains essentially gender role oriented and separated.

It may be possible to reduce, even eliminate, blatant sex discrimination through legal means. And this assumes the existence of a favorable political climate that actively initiates and enforces such change. Certainly this is not a priority in these fiscally harsh times. Title IX can serve as a catalyst of change only if it is coupled with a major modification in those socialization practices that restrict the educational opportunities for boys and girls, women and men. Sex discrimination may disappear by the time Jane reaches college. Yet it is conceivable that her children and grandchildren will be influenced by lingering prejudices throughout their own school years.

Religion
and Patriarchy

I thank Thee, Lord, that Thou has not created me a woman. (Orthodox Jewish Prayer)

It is ironic that in the one institution which theoretically offers the most freedom of expression through liberating spirituality, religion still finds itself encumbered by interpretations and practices that are undeniably sexist in orientation. As with the other institutions, it is difficult to separate religion from the cultural framework within which it operates; hence religious principles and experiences are interpreted accordingly. As will be demonstrated, in some religions, especially ancient ones, women exercised a great deal of influence, although much of this was lost with the institutionalization of contemporary religious systems. Historical evidence suggests that as civilizations progress and societies become technologically advanced, people are likely to gain in terms of overall equality. Yet in most postindustrial societies, religion has lagged behind in regard to women and the amount of authority they have in relation to men.

THE GODDESS HERITAGE

Accustomed as we are to thinking about religion in terms of the major faiths in the contemporary world, religious heritage is certainly more ancient and diverse. The belief systems of so-called primitive peoples, buried for centuries and at times dismissed by scholars as incidental in relation to the span of human history, are being resurrected and examined. What is emerging is a heritage where women played a central role, where female deities were often worshipped and where religious life was essentially a partnership between men and women, much more so than modern institutionalized religions would have us believe. The intent here is to provide a brief chronicle of some images of women as they appear in the mythology and religious heritage of people in the ancient world. Such an account is important for grasping the significance of attitudes toward women in modern religion, which is the focus of the latter part of the chapter.

Probably the most thorough record of archaeological and anthropological evidence for the goddess heritage can be found in *The First Sex* (Davis, 1971) which sets out to document woman's dominance of prehistoric civilization. There is massive evidence of the matriarchal origins of human society, Davis contends, such that the "further back one traces *man's* history, the larger loomed the figure of woman" (Davis, 1971:16, italics mine). Though scholars might dispute certain of Davis's conclusions, there is strong evidence that women played a powerful role in the ancient world, especially as they related to religion or its mythological precursor. For example, what are seen as the oldest villages in the history of civilization have been uncovered in central Anatolia, which is now modern Turkey, with artifacts that indicate not only that the cult of the goddess was dominant but that the supreme deity was female (Alkim, 1968). Gynocracy[1] continued throughout the Neolithic period into the Bronze Age because the goddess remained the supreme deity (Alkim, 1968).

The goddess image is carried through to the idea of the creator when examining the ancient accounts of Greek, Assyrian, and Babylonian mythology. The earliest record of the creation of the universe is found in the Babylonian epic legend, the "Enuma Elish," which portrays the Creator of All as Tiamet, the mother of gods (Muss-Arnolt, 1901). In Greek mythology Metis, loosely translated as the creative principle of female intelligence, brings the world into being without a male partner (Davis, 1971:33). The goddess as the first creator can be found in mythology and religious principles in all corners of the world. It is only in later myth where she is replaced by a god, though even when the gender changes the female name often remains the same. This is demonstrated by Siva in India, Atea in Polynesia, and Ea in Syria. Or the process might be a gradual transformation of female to male as when the creative principle of Metis became the male Phanes in Greek mythology (Davis, 1971:33).

Moving to other parts of the world, the goddess theme continues to appear in antiquity. Anthropologists recognize Africa as the continent that has the oldest record of human habitation, and it is here where perhaps the best examples of the goddess as the Mother of All is found. On a continent with an incredible diversity of peoples, customs, and religious symbolism, the images of the goddess vary as well, from Mawu, creator of the world among the Dahomey, Goddess as the Moon to several Zimbabwe tribes, to the goddess as She Who Sends Rain among the Zulu of Natal and the Woyo of Zaire (Stone, 1979:131-133). Even given such diversity,

[1]Davis (1971:39) maintains that in all myth the goddess is synonymous with Gynocracy which means that where the goddess reigned, woman ruled.

the symbolism that emerges most consistently involves the concerns for honesty, courage, sympathy and humanitarianism which the goddess, and the peoples who worshiped them, revered. The ancient texts of China also speak clearly to the goddess image. The Chuang Tzu, written in the third century B.C. describes the Era of the Great Purity where life was characterized by harmony, innocence and spontaneity, and where people knew their mothers but not their fathers. This period ended when the laws of nature were defied. As human discord arose, the Great Cosmic Struggle ensued and the goddess era waned (Stone, 1979:23-24).

Beyond the goddess images that dominated many ancient practices and beliefs, some religious systems also incorporated principles of balance where, theoretically at least, neither sex was superior. Most notable among these is the ancient Chinese concept of Yin and Yang. Although Western interpretation often misrepresents the female principle of Yin as being completely passive and dominated by the more active and aggressive male principle of Yang, this is a distortion of the ancient belief, which emphasized equilibrium and complementarity. The Yin-Yang ideal of harmonious balance is yet part of the Chinese value system. However, much of the original intent was lost with the advent of the patriarchy that influenced all cultural elements, including religion. Tantric Buddhism in medieval India and Tibet was amenable to both male and female siddhas, or accomplished ones, whose sex was considered irrelevant to the goal of enlightenment. In support of this was the Tantric insistence that men and women have essentially the same potential for enlightenment (Ray, 1980:228-29). Even among some American Indian cultures, complementarity of men and women may be discovered, with each gender sharing in the religious practices of the tribe. The matrilineal Iroquois tribes of eastern North America participated in religious ceremonies where both the male and female dimensions were considered necessary, such as rites to encourage the male activity of hunting or the female activity of agriculture (Shimony, 1980).

Though such religious systems incorporated aspects of male and female complementarity and equilibrium, this is not to suggest that this kind of balance inevitably carried over into other realms. If Tantric Buddhism was a path open to both sexes, the Indian and Tibetan cultures made it very difficult for women to pursue such a path, given their restrictions in other institutional settings. Even among the Iroquois, women, who were influential due to their involvement with religious ceremonies, were prohibited from speaking at other public gatherings by virtue of their gender alone (Falk and Gross, 1980:226).

Regardless of the inequality that doubtlessly existed in other parts of the society, these accounts of goddess images and male-female complementarity in religious systems provide us with an alternative view of the heritage of religion. Such a perspective should help offset the more accepted interpretations offered by contemporary organized religions. Though the world is dominated by a relatively small number of "principle" religions, over two and a half billion people can be said to at least minimally subscribe to their beliefs. The vast majority of these numbers are made up of Christian, Jewish, Muslim, and Hindu adherents. Unlike many ancient beliefs, with these religions misogynous interpretations are the rule rather than the exception.

PURDAH: SEXUAL APARTHEID

As the mists of time veiled the ancient goddess images, the emergence of organized religion produced another veil for millions of women who adhere to the Islam and Hindu faiths. Although Muslim women are more likely to fall under the shroud of purdah, numerous Hindu women also observe this practice. *Purdah*, a Persian word loosely translated to mean "curtain," has come to refer to the separate world of males and females along with the virtual concealment of most women in the Islamic cultures as well as many Hindu women. The specific practices of purdah may vary considerably, but the fact remains that in these cultures, there is an overall separation of the sexes that is continually reinforced by daily activities in virtually all of their social institutions. Jeffrey (1979) labels such customs as "sexual apartheid" not only because of the physical separation of men and women but also due to the complexity of arrangements that sustain social distance.

Certainly the most recognized form of concealment of women is found in their distinctive clothing which symbolizes their separation. Whether the clothing takes the form of the *burqa*, consisting of a skull cap attached to mounds of material that drop around the face and all the way to the ground, or a *chaddar*, an immense shawl used to hide their faces and bodily features, women are, in essence, made invisible. As Jeffrey (1979:4) poignantly notes

> The effect of all these garments is the same, though, for the woman is rendered anonymous, a non-person, unapproachable, just a silent being skulking along, looking neither to the right nor left. To those who do not know her personally, she is nameless and faceless.

It is perhaps ironic that purdah is seen by many as primarily a characteristic of Islam as a religion rather than as resulting from broader, non-Islamic sociocultural forces. It is also extremely difficult and maybe impractical, to disentangle religion from other elements of the culture, and even scholars disagree as to the chain of causation (Saleh, 1972; Smith, 1980). In principle, however, Islam affirms the potential equality between the sexes. Mernissi (1987) points out that women's inferiority is the result of institutions developed to subordinate her legally and socially to the male in the family structure. Islamic law is nurtured by a code of ethics which sees woman's role as providing legitimate male heirs. This role may be compromised if women are not restricted in their activities, especially during childbearing years. Mohammad himself was awed by woman's power and what he saw as a mysterious, unlimited sexual drive that, if left unfettered, could wreak social havoc by casting doubt on the legitimacy of the husband's heirs. From a functionalist perspective, the practices involving purdah arose as a response to these attitudes. Therefore, Islam assumes that woman is both potentially powerful and dangerous. Among other institutions, the custom of purdah may be viewed as a strategy for restraining her passion and potential power. Though Islam recognizes the "democratic glorification of the individual," Muslim ideology socializes men and women to perceive each other as enemies, keeps them as separate as possible, and creates institutions which are repressive to women (Mernissi, 1987).

For Hindu women the customs and clothing surrounding purdah are extremely varied, with some regions exhibiting more exclusionary and separatist tactics than others. It is also difficult to assess and generalize about Hindu doctrine as it affects women since Hinduism is as incredibly diverse as the Indian subcontinent on which it is primarily practiced. As Islam is to Arab cultures, Hinduism is ancient and incorporated into the cultural milieu in so many ways that it is impossible to visualize what India would be like without it.

According to Radhakrishnan (1947), the Hindu ideal is that male and female are meant to be complementary, with man as the creator and woman as the lover, and with women's sexual tendencies being no less variational than man's. However, he laments, some women do not recognize this complementarity and are of the "masculine" type, full of energy and ambition, who may even forsake the most important roles they can assume, those of wife and mother. Such women

> take pride in proving that they never developed a talent for domesticity . . . (and) society will have to allow for them. Such "masculine" women do not reach the highest of which womanhood is capable. (Radhakrishnan, 1947:142)

Such beliefs are fostered by interpretations of the *Ramayana* and *Mahabharata* epics which describe many Hindu ideals, especially in terms of marriage and family roles, and which are powerful determinants of gender role socialization.

Despite this diversity of both Hinduism and India, it is safe to conclude that Hindu women practice rituals and ceremonies that are congruent with their roles as mothers, wives and homemakers. These customs exemplify the domestic sphere of life, the only one known to most Hindu women. For example, childbirth practices in some central Indian villages involve an elaborate series of rituals lasting from pregnancy until the child is introduced to a life outside of the home (Jacobson, 1980). Again, from a functionalist interpretation, these customs help increase cohesiveness among women who are required to live and work together in an extended family structure reigned over by their husbands or fathers. Many North Indian Hindu women also practice rituals which express their concerns for family and household. Observed only by women, these particular ceremonies do not require the services of male priests. Although these are not shared with men, they reflect a strong patriarchal society. Some practices involve the direct worship of husbands and brothers, for the purpose of obtaining their protection while others offer prayers and supplications for the happy marriages of daughters and for the joys of being blessed with male offspring. The extent of regard for males may be demonstrated through a letter written by an Indian judge to a friend in England which told of the death of his small daughter. His own grief is somewhat abated by the thought that it "would have been more disastrous had it been the death of a son" (Nehra, 1934).

It seems appropriate to end this section on Hindu women with a look at the ritual that has gained the most attention and infamy throughout Indian history, that of *suttee*, or widow-burning. It is evident that the practice originated during the ancient Vedic period where the widow performed a symbolic self-immolation upon her husband's death, although in later centuries, the symbol became the reality.

Suttee, literally translated to mean "virtuous woman," was mainly confined to the aristocracy and courts. There are instances, however, of it occurring on a massive scale such as among widows of soldiers who were spared the humiliation of surrendering to the victors (Thapar, 1966). In principle, this was a voluntary rite on the part of the widow. As indicated before, her husband was often given deity status and here was her chance to rejoin him through the purification of the flames on his funeral pyre. In practice, her grief was often used by relatives who desired the honor associated with a suttee ceremony. Brought up in a culture where widow remarriages were discouraged, where women were considered primarily in terms of their husbands, and where widows were even more likely to be dependent, subservient, and perhaps sexually exploited and abandoned, the grief stricken woman, if she could think rationally at this point in time, might consider that becoming a suttee would be the only feasible alternative. The British attempted to abolish the practice as early as 1829 but were not completely successful, in part because they were reluctant to disturb personal law and its intimate connection to the Hindu social order (Rudolph and Rudolph, 1967).

The modernization of India is becoming more evident, though many villages remain virtually untouched by this trend. It speaks to the extraordinary power of socialization that suttee is still much associated with the image of virtuosity for numerous Hindu women. In 1803 over 275 women immolated themselves around Calcutta alone and as late as 1980 there were still six. A recent column appearing in an Indian publication noted that there is continuing, perhaps resurgent, enthusiasm for the practice of suttee since it stems from society's conviction that the woman is the property of man to dispose of at his discretion. No longer do dying husbands extract oaths for suttee from grieving wives. But, as noted by this same columnist,

> In a village of Rajasthan, the seventh of a series of recent suttees burnt herself to death on the funeral pyre of her husband. Astrologers had predicted nine, so the village is breathlessly waiting for the remaining two. (*India Today*, 1981:92)

THE JUDEO-CHRISTIAN HERITAGE

From a Western viewpoint the practices of purdah and suttee are likely to seem esoteric, exotic, and mysterious, as well as far removed from one's own religious heritage. It is the Bible where both Jews and Christians turn to discover their origins and the basis of their beliefs and laws. Religious socialization of the young is apt to proceed from the teaching of Bible stories replete with colorful pictures of David confronting Goliath or Moses parting the sea. These childhood images are nurtured and strengthened by interpretations that perpetuate gender role stereotypes. Religion lends to socialization a pervasive credibility that is rarely questioned. The Bible is often evoked as the final authority in settling disputes in many areas but in particular those involving the sexes. This results in a divinely sanctioned patriarchy that is again bolstered.

Since the Bible expresses the basic attitudes of the patriarchal cultures in which it was written it is logical that its most popular texts would be representative of those cultures. Alternative images do exist but those which are congruent with prevailing sentiments are favored. Hence, Biblical interpretations may illustrate what Bem and Bem (1970) refer to as "non-conscious ideology" which result in a lack of awareness concerning alternative beliefs about women. The following examples, which are oft repeated from the pulpit, demonstrate how androcentric ideology permeates the Bible. It is appropriate to begin with the version of the creation story that is most accepted as representing the traditional view of the church.

> And the rib which the Lord God had taken from man, made he woman and brought her unto the man.
> And Adam said, This is now bone of my bones, and flesh of my flesh; she shall be called Woman, because she was taken out of Man. (Genesis 2:20-23)

Because woman is made from man which is, incidentally, contrary to all subsequent natural law, her status as helpmate and server to man (read males) is confirmed. In supporting this perspective St. Paul has the dubious honor of formulating views that continue to serve as bulwarks for contemporary religious views on women.

> But I want you to understand that the head of every man is Christ, the head of every woman is her husband, and the head of Christ is God. (I Corinthians 11:3)
> For a man ought not to cover his head since he is the image and glory of God; but woman is the glory of man. For man was not made from woman, but woman from man. Neither was man created for woman but woman for man. (I Corinthians 11:7-11)
> Let a woman learn in silence with all submissiveness. I permit no woman to teach or have authority over men; she is to keep silent. (I Timothy 2:11-12)
> Wives be subject to your husbands, as to the Lord. For the husband is the head of the wife as Christ is the head of the Church. As the Church is subject to Christ, so let wives also be subject in everything to their husbands. (Ephesians 5:22-24, from the New Oxford Annotated Bible, 1978)

Taken a step further, women are repeatedly viewed in terms of their status as possessions of men. The Ten Commandments lists a neighbor's wife, along with his house, fields, manservant, ox, and ass as property not to be coveted (Exodus 20:17). Lot offers his daughters to the male guests in his house.

> Behold, I have two daughters who have not known man. Let me bring them out to you and do to them as you please. (Genesis 19:8)

Pervasive views such as these continue today through compilations of stories about biblical women. On the surface it would seem that works like Edith Deen's *Wisdom from Women in the Bible* (1978) are focusing on women's accomplishments at a period in history where a liberating consciousness-raising in terms of religious interpretation is simultaneously occurring. Yet Deen presents narratives of women which provide ammunition for reinforcing stereotypes about women. For example, Jochebed, the mother of Moses, is praised for her role, as are modern mothers who recognize exceptional promise in their children. Selfish and posses-sive women, like the wife of Potiphar, who was responsible for the unfair impris-onment of Joseph, are admonished for their wickedness and deceit. Though Deen asserts that women are different than, but not inferior to men, the images that emerge from this book are consistently in line with women's traditional or "acceptable" roles. Those women who either refuse or challenge such roles are chastised, negatively portrayed or cast into historical oblivion (Lindsey, 1979:793).

Overall, these views explicitly support the notions that women should be admired for their unselfish, nurturing roles as wives and mothers and scorned, or at best dismissed as insignificant, for all else. Sometimes referred to as the Eve-Mary duality, it allows no room for deviation (Hole and Levine, 1971). It is Eve's fault that paradise is lost. As the temptress, Adam apparently succumbs to her feminine wiles and loses responsibility for his actions. On the other hand, Mary as the mother of Christ, is the idealized image of the perfect woman. It is obvious that with such women as powerful symbols, contemporary views are likely to be congruent. The fact that they are contradictory is deemed unimportant.

Language is a potent force in socialization and nowhere is this more apparent than in the language of religion. That God and God-language has taken on masculine traits is due to linguistic accident (Stendahl, 1974). But we evoke male imagery when conceptualizing God and in turn such images are used to support the subordination of women. The supposed equality of the sexes cannot easily be dismissed when the spiritual nature of human beings is related in male terms with sexuality viewed in female constructs. Miller and Swift (1976) suggest that women are portrayed as distracting men from godliness, as Eve did with her temptation of Adam. The language is clear in this regard; we have "Sons of God" but "Daughters of Eve" (Miller and Swift, 1976:74). Sociologists, linguists and even theologians would not argue with the notion that the use of the generic "man" impedes the understanding of God's view of the sexes. Yet when congregations begin the arduous task of altering liturgy, hymns, and prayers to conform to nonsexist language standards, resistance runs very high. The argument reappears that one is not only tampering with tradition but, more importantly, the "language of God."

Biblical alternatives to traditional viewpoints do exist but are for the most part overlooked. Many have been resurrected by reformists eager to demonstrate that the Bible is replete with stories, images and metaphors that offer interpretive options as far as women's role. Even St. Paul presents a forceful alternative with the statement that

> There is neither Jew nor Greek, there is neither slave nor free, there is neither male nor female, for you are all one in Jesus Christ. (Galatians 3:28)[2]

Such a passage directly relates to the idea that the equality of the sexes under God is yet possible.

---

[2]The rationale behind Paul's statement has been long debated by scholars and theologians, since it appears to contradict his other beliefs about the sexes. For a fuller discussion of this, see Chapter 6 of Schussler-Fiorenza (1983). Jewett (1979) argues that Paul acknowledges the idea of equality but insists on the "divinely given quality of sexual differences."

On the heels of the equality issue is the rediscovery of the non-traditional roles women played in biblical times. Mary Magdalene and the women who went to Jesus's tomb may be said to hold the credibility of Christianity since Jesus first appeared to them and were instructed to gather the disciples. Deborah, in the book of Judges, is seen as an arbitrator, queen, and commander of the army that she led in the defeat of the Canaanites. In Exodus it is the women who first disobeyed Pharoah, with his own daughter adopting Moses as her child. Women are seen as wives and mothers as well as leaders, prophetesses, teachers, and tillers of the soil. The stories often remain hidden or have been purposely ignored in favor of those representing traditional patriarchal viewpoints. Bennett (1974) calls for a rereading of the Gospels and, in particular, an examination of the life and teachings of Jesus. Nowhere, she contends, does Jesus distinguish between men and women as children of God and, in fact, his actions show he believed in the equality of the sexes. Given the patriarchal Jewish culture where Jesus lived, this in itself is revolutionary (Bennett, 1974:30).

THE CLERGY ISSUE

Alternative explanations in terms of the Bible become more important for how they have been applied to women seeking equal footing with men as leaders of the contemporary church. To date, three major Christian faiths have not ordained women, Missouri Synod Lutheran, Eastern Orthodox, and Roman Catholic. In Judaism it is primarily in the Reform branch where female rabbis have been recognized through ordination. After a long and bitter struggle which culminated in a controversial ceremony in Philadelphia in 1974 where 11 women were ordained Episcopal priests, the *legal* right for female priesthood was finally given in 1976.[3] It is now possible for women to join the ranks of their brothers as Episcopal priests. Although women are gradually assuming new roles within the religious hierarchy, the battle is far from won. Some parishes still refuse to accept female ministers, rabbis, or priests, whether legally ordained or not, which propels many of these women to seek leadership roles in more peripheral positions. It is probably that such women would be found on university campuses as heads of religious coalitions or leaders of campus churches or temples. The crux of the clergy issue can be traced back to doctrinal matters involving Biblical interpretations or Talmudic Law.

It is in this case where the male image of God is taken as a justification for women being unable to represent this image (Richardson, 1981). God chose to send a son who in turn selected male disciples. But as Stendahl (1974:120) succinctly states,

> Jesus Christ was a male but that may be no more significant to his being that the fact that his eyes were presumably brown. Incarnation is a great thing. But it strikes me as odd to argue that when the Word became flesh, it was to reinforce male superiority.

[3]The dramatic events leading up to the Philadelphia ceremony are recounted by Carter Heyward (1976) through her letters and diary. A moving, often bitter story, the depths of the Anglican church's view on women are demonstrated.

Jewish and Lutheran women have at least the option of shifting synods or branches without changing their religion per se, but for those Catholic women who seek the priesthood, their choices are limited. They can assume leadership roles as lay members of the church or they can become nuns. In either case, they remain excluded from the position that allows the greatest authority on both doctrinal and parish matters, that of priest. Novak (1974) believes that the issue is not political but symbolic, with male and female evoking differential symbols. But the issue is spiritual as well. The call of the spirit is what qualifies a person for the priesthood, and this occurs for both males and females (Novak, 1974:221).

The Second Vatican Council (1963-1965) brought monumental changes within the Catholic Church, but when the question of women's ordination was nominally debated, it was obvious that the church was unwilling to take this additional step. Expanded roles for lay people, including women, have been forthcoming but ordination was not to be one of them. Since Vatican II, there has been a swing back to more conservative stances and Vatican opposition was reiterated with the 1976 Declaration on the Question of the Admission of the Women to the Ministerial Priesthood. Although there is some recognition that ordained women would be able to alleviate the serious shortage of priests in many parts of the world (O'Connell, 1984), it appears that the ordination question will not be given serious consideration by the church hierarchy again soon.

American Protestantism has fared better in terms of women in positions of authority, with many women preachers emerging as early as the Colonial Era from the ranks of Quakers. America's first successful religious commune, the Shakers, was founded by Ann Lee who preached that God is both male and female. Although the Shakers had no formal ordination process, all adherents, regardless of gender, were permitted complete freedom in teaching and preaching. This is also generally true of other religious sects and churches where women are credited as founders or proved to be the dominant influence in their establishment (McBeth, 1979). Included here would be the Seventh Day Adventists, the Spiritualist Church, and the Christian Science Church.[4] By the middle of the twentieth century most of the mainstream Protestant denominations like the Methodist and Presbyterian Churches, the United Church of Christ, and the merged Evangelical Lutheran Church in America (ELCA) granted full ordination rights to women. Again, this must be tempered with the fact that ordination does not mean that the call to a church is readily forthcoming. For example, although the General Assembly of the Presbyterian Church officially ordained women in 1956, by 1975 there were only 190 women out of a total of 13,000 ordained ministers. And most of those 190 served as associate pastors, educational directors or in some other institutional capacity (Verdesi, 1973).

The issue of women assuming more viable roles within their respective religions, especially as clergy, becomes all the more significant when put in context

---

[4]Mary Baker Eddy founded the Christian Science Church in the nineteenth century; Ellen Harmon White founded the Seventh Day Adventists in the 1880s and Maggie and Katie Fox, who were sisters, provided the impetus for the founding of the Spiritualist Church in 1848.

of sociological research which demonstrates that women have a greater degree of religious orientation than men (Wilson, 1971). This orientation is suggested by higher rates for women in the areas of church attendance, expression of the need for a religious dimension in their daily lives, and involvement in church social activities. Given these data, it is not surprising that when women do assume leadership positions they usually fall within social and domestic realms with men dominating major administrative functions, such as overseeing the legal and financial matters of the church.

Church and family roles are also consistent. Women are more likely to be held responsible for the religious socialization of the children, with the patriarchal family structure carrying over to a similar one existing in the church. Finally, from a conflict theory viewpoint, as exemplified by a Marxian perspective, women are more apt to accept an "other worldly" ideology. Women would share this orientation with other oppressed minorities. Biblical interpretation that adopts such a model is referred to as "liberation theology" and issues a challenge to the supposed objectivity of academic theology. It recognizes that all theologies are ultimately engaged for or against the oppressed (Schussler-Fiorenza, 1983:6). Overall, then, with women having limited access to the leadership structure, the church may be viewed as an institution controlled by men for the purpose of serving women and children.

TOWARD RELIGIOUS REFORM

From this account of misogyny as it exists in Western religion, it might seem that feminism and the patriarchal vision of the church cannot be reconciled. Granted that harmony on both fronts may be exceedingly difficult, many feminists are unwilling to equate religion with oppression. They believe it is not real liberation to sever ties with an important element of their heritage and belief system. Instead they choose to work at reform in a number of areas, with a focus on providing an historical account of women's roles in ancient religions as well, such as reevaluating scripture, whether it be in the Koran, Talmud, Vedas, or Bible. Carmody (1979) argues that even if religious experience is filtered through misogynous cultural traditions, religion can transcend gender and be based on the willingness of the individual person to participate in what she refers to as the "Mystery." Only when women become aware of the root causes of their contemporary status and the sociopolitical nature of religious doctrine can they truly experience their religion. Historical reanalysis of world religions provides a consciousness-raising means for women coming to grips with their religious identity.

Doctrinal reinterpretation of scripture is also viewed as a mode of reform, especially if coupled with changes in linguistic reference. By pointing out alternative translations of key words, introducing nonsexist, inclusive language that minimizes the powerful aspects of male imagery, and discovering lesser known biblical texts and other significant religious works that demonstrate both the complementarity of the sexes and nontraditional images of women, a gradual shift in awareness of gender roles and relationships will occur. Pagels (1979) recounts the story of the archaeological discovery in Upper Egypt of what are now referred to as the Gnostic Gospels, which offer astonishing evidence that the early Christians viewed women in very different terms than those implied by the practices of the contemporary church. It is mainly with the esoteric and mystical schools of Christian Gnosticism, Islamic Sufism, and the Kabbalah movement of Judaism that women emerge as equal partners with men. The texts on which these views are based are critical for providing alternative perspectives concerning women.

Even St. Paul's writings can be reassessed with these standards of reform in mind. Reread Ephesians 5:22-24 and take out the verb "be subject." Richardson (1981:109-110) notes that the words "be subject" are actually not part of the original Biblical text and that a literal translation of the verse shows the absence of the verb. According to Gundry (1979) the accurate verse would read "Subjecting yourselves to one another, wives to your own husbands . . .," which suggests that Paul is calling for mutual submission of the sexes within marriage and *not* the superiority of the husband. It is really a matter of how key words are translated and where the verse actually begins or ends. The life of Jesus is also being scrutinized by reformists intent on altering misconceptions about his teachings as they relate to women. New Testament statements by Jesus do not reflect the antifeminism of the times. In fact, Daly (1975:79) asserts that because Jesus related to women as *persons*, which was in such contrast to the prevailing customs, many were astonished by his actions.

The question of inclusive language has already had an impact on liturgy by suggesting significant changes which incorporate a more neutral position. This is proceeding in congruence with the ecumenical trends some religions are emphasizing. *The Lutheran Book of Worship*, issued in 1978, contains substantial changes from the 1958 *Service Book and Hymnal* and has allowed for more inclusive imagery. In use by the ELCA, hymns, prayers, and elements of the service shifted to a less sexist posture in language. Reprinted here is a portion of the Nicene Creed which demonstrates that a one word change suggests a meaningful difference in imagery.

Who for us men, and for our salvation, came down from heaven. . . . (1958 version)
For us and for our salvation he came down from heaven. . . . (1978 version)

Though it is inappropriate to remove the word "he" from the second version since it refers directly to Jesus, the word "men" is now deleted. And an Easter hymn was titled "Good Christian *Men*, Rejoice and Sing" in the older hymnal; the newer version is "Good Christian *Friends*, Rejoice and Sing." Seemingly subtle changes can have a profound impact on views regarding men and women. It is expected that the gradual introduction of inclusive language will be followed by shifts in imagery that, at a minimum, will be less male-oriented.

However, even among feminists, there are critics of this kind of approach to reform in the church. Stortz (1984) acknowledges the power of church patriarchy to the extent that she suspects this very patriarchy of actually *creating* feminist theology. The rationale would be to direct feminist energy into areas viewed by the church as "safe," such as on matters involving suggestions for inclusive language (words), rather than deeds. The church, then protects itself from meaningful change. According to this logic

> Only a patriarchy would suggest that feminist theology exists, hire women to teach it and segregate it from other classical theological disciplines, so that it might not tarnish the patriarchal grandeur of the disciplines of Bible, systematic theology, and church history. (Stortz, 1984:21)

Although Stortz presents a plausible argument, it is likely that through processes such as scriptural reinterpretation and the elimination of sexist language, attitude shift will ultimately result in behavior change. This view is in congruence with the sociological perspective that words do influence deeds. The power of language and the imagery inevitably suggested by it should become evident by the prayer that is printed below. Written to evoke different images, a neutral language is purposely *not* used. Finally, consider the prayer in light of 2,000 years of religious heritage that reinforces the picture of God-the-Father.

> The Lord is my Mother,
> I want for nothing.
> She lays me down at night.
> She takes my hand by day
> as we stroll by the sea.
> She makes me feel good about myself.
> She guides me in the right direction
> for her Name's sake.
> Sometimes I must walk through lonely alleys,
> but you're with me, Mom.
> Your wit and Your compassion,
> they encourage me.
> You prepare me a strengthening meal
> in front of those who would make fun of me.
> You bathe me in Your perfumed oil.
> Your love spills over me.
> I expect good and even great things
> to happen to me.
> And I will be at home
> in the Lord's house forever.
> (Carroll, 1984)

12

The Media

The mass media impact on our daily lives in a variety of ways, often without our conscious awareness. We are bombarded by visual and auditory stimuli from the media throughout the day. We hear music, news and advertising at our office desks, in elevators, while jogging or driving to and from school or work. Advertisements on billboards and in buses and subways shout out the newest, best, modern, and most efficient products and services available. Cinema and television offerings allow for almost every conceivable programming taste. With the advent of video recorders and cable television, we can choose our entertainment specialties without ever leaving home.

As documented in Chapter 3, the process of socialization into gender roles occurs on multiple fronts. Although parents provide the earliest source, television soon becomes a potent socializer as well, even in the preschool years. Degree of television viewing is associated with conceptions of gender stereotypes. Heavy television viewing (25 hours per week or more) among children has been related to holding more traditional gender stereotypes (Fruch and McGhee, 1975). Viewing intensity also affects beliefs about gender in preschoolers (Gross and Jeffries-Fox, 1978). This study suggests that a "seduction of the innocent" occurs because young children are more vulnerable in believing that the images they encounter on television represent reality and truth. Eisenstock (1984) finds that this relationship also holds for young adults.

Television is strengthened by advertisements, books, magazines, and other media items which present the sexes in stereotyped ways. It is easy to see why, even at an early age, we form relatively rigid beliefs about what is considered "appropriate" behavior for boys and girls, women and men. Though media representatives may argue that what is presented merely reflects reality, the question of reinforcing an already sexist society cannot be dismissed as easily. After reviewing the media's record on how the sexes are portrayed, we will return to this question.

MAGAZINES

With the publication of *Feminine Mystique* in 1963, Betty Friedan challenged the notion that the American woman was completely content in her traditional homebound role. Freidan was one of the first to look at the role of the print media, in this case popular women's magazines, in the formation of attitudes about women. Concentrating on fiction, she traced the images of women from the emancipated views in the 1930s and 1940s to the "happy housewife" and glorified mother of the 1950s and early 1960s, whose aspirations went only as far as her own front door. From this beginning, there has been a great deal of research documenting gender role stereotypes in magazines and popular fiction (Ehrenreich, 1983; Ferguson, 1983; Radway, 1984).

As a further test of Friedan's research, examining women's magazine fiction from 1957 to 1967, Lefkowitz (1972) concludes that the happy housewife was even happier. By 1967 female characters were in less romantic upheaval and had more children, but also had increased psychological problems related to their roles of wives and mothers. Women who worked outside the home were considered to be unfeminine and posing threats to otherwise happy marriages.

Franzwa's (1974b, 1975) research on magazine fiction from 1940 to 1970 finds essentially the same patterns. The home oriented mother represents the ideal of magazine womanhood. As the baby boom accelerated in the 1950s, the birth rate also climbed into magazines. Having a baby was a good bet for saving a floundering marriage. Married women who remained childless and spinsters who remained childless and husbandless are pitied for their wasteful, unhappy lives. Fiction of this period cheered heroines, who, through virtue and passivity, won husbands for themselves. Even widows and divorcees were portrayed as unable to cope without a man.

By the late 1960s, changes were occurring for women in a number of realms. The birthrate was leveling off, thousands of women moved into the paid labor force and the feminist movement made headlines nationwide. Magazines focusing on the challenges of working outside the home emerged, some with editorial policies explicitly feminist oriented (Mather, 1973). Periodicals such as *MS.* continue to uphold nonsexist standards and favor articles geared to economic productivity, social awareness, and political engagement (Phillips, 1978). Even the older, more traditional magazines, like *Ladies Home Journal* and *McCall's*, began to reflect some changes. Articles on educational opportunities, employment options, and women's rights appeared with greater frequency (Matkov, 1972). A new type of magazine geared to single women or women who combine employment with marriage has also appeared, like *Savvy*, *New Woman*, and *Working Woman*. These magazines offer advice and tactics to women who are coping with expanded role responsibilities.

Nonetheless, considering the social upheaval which has occurred, magazines have been minimally affected. Magazine fiction continues to reward self-sacrificing wives and mothers whose identity revolves around the home (Lugenbeel, 1974) and who are encouraged in self-expression as long as it is confined to traditional roles (Silver, 1976). With emphases on beauty, hairstyles, and fashion, often showing before-after makeovers, nonfiction articles teach women to transform themselves from Cinderellas to princesses (Kidd, 1975). The bottom line is that physical appearance is viewed as necessary to attract and ultimately snare a man. Magazines for women persevere in this message.

ADVERTISING

The images of women in magazines are reinforced through advertisements testifying to the glories of shining kitchen floors, soft toilet tissue, and antiseptic children. Whether we view ads on television or through the print media, they are likely to present the sexes in stereotyped modes. Extensive research has documented the fact that even with some improvement over time, advertising images of women are on the basis of traditional gender role norms (Courtney and Whipple, 1983).

One of the first major studies on gender stereotyping in advertising was done by analyzing magazines in terms of the number and sexes of adults, the occupations and activities in which they were presented, and the kinds of products being promoted (Courtney and Lockeretz, 1971). The data show that women's place is in the home, they do not make important decisions, and are dependent on men, who in turn regard women as sex objects. Women are only interested in buying cosmetics and cleaning aids. Given the fact that by the early 1970s over 30% of women were in the work force and represented a critical portion of consumer buying, these ads clearly did not portray reality.

A number of studies quickly followed. A replication of Courtney and Lockeretz (1971) two years later shows that ads were beginning to depict women in more occupational roles, but the vast majority of women were still pictured exclusively in the home (Wagner and Banos, 1973). In viewing ads which span twenty years, Venkatesan and Losco (1975) find that there was a decline in the "most obnoxious" ads, but advertisers continue to be insensitive to the real world. Again, women are viewed as sex objects, interested in physical beauty, and dependent on men. A woman is concerned with appearance and domestic life, rather than with complex decision-making (Culley and Bennett, 1976). Advertisements rarely show them in nontraditional situations, even in magazines oriented to a wider audience such as *Newsweek*, *Look*, and *Sports Illustrated* (Sexton and Haberman, 1974).

To be effective, advertising must be aware of trends affecting products and services. The moment an "improvement" is made on a particular product, campaigns begin to sell the public on its virtues. The old is forgotten as the new appears on the scene. To sell means to change. Yet advertising is stubbornly persistent in the manner in which this job is done. Overall, magazine ads since the turn of the century show women in domestic roles, interested primarily in courtship and marriage, beauty, and clothing (Dispenza, 1975).

We know that ads are doing more than selling products. Opinions about men and women are being shaped as well. For example, drug advertising carries messages about women which are powerful and potentially harmful. Medical journals are a major source of information on drug products for physicians. These ads promote the idea that women do not have the psychological strength to solve their problems so they turn to the physician who is ready and willing to prescribe psychotropic drugs. Ads showing women receiving psychotropics outnumber men by 15 to 1 (Stimson, 1975). The answer to the problems of the housewife who cannot cope with the responsibilities of husband and children is to give an antidepressant.

In these ads, women are the sicker gender and especially prone to emotional trauma. They are stereotyped as chronic complainers who require sedatives or mood modifiers to deal with tedious household tasks (Prather and Fidell, 1975; Larned, 1975). They are shown in patronizing ways which endorse both psychological and sexual insecurity (Frankfort, 1972). Drugs, rather than a change of life style, are encouraged to solve problems (Seidenberg, 1971). Most important, these ads reinforce the physician's expectation that female patients presenting symptoms which cannot be readily correlated with a specific physical illness are in need of psychotropics. The deluge of new psychoactive drugs occurred in the late 1960s when research on the biochemical processes in mental illness was at its peak. Physicians who graduated from medical school prior to 1960 are especially vulnerable to such ads.

It is relatively easy to analyze ads according to general themes and images. But in order to assess the overall impact, we must recognize that ads also sell products and reinforce attitudes in ways that often go unrecognized by the casual reader. Goffman (1979) concentrates on the subtleties of posture, relative size and positioning of hands, eyes, knees and other parts of the body in ads. A man is pictured taller than a woman unless he is socially inferior to her. Men and boys are shown instructing women and girls. A woman's eye is averted to the man in the picture with her, but a man's eye is averted only to a superior. Womens' hands caress or barely touch. They are rarely shown grasping, manipulating, or creatively shaping. Women have faraway looks in their eyes, especially in the presence of men. Women act like children, and are often depicted with children (Gornick, 1979).

What is remarkable about all these findings is that women themselves are very critical of the images (Witkowski, 1975; Lundstrom and Sciglimpaglia, 1977).

Feminists and even antifeminists do not disagree about the way women are portrayed in advertising (Duker and Tucker, 1977). If the people to whom the ads are directed find them distasteful and irritating, how can a double standard continue? Pearson (1985:100) quotes the president of a large-circulation women's magazine, who suggests that an influential minority of advertisers dominate the industry. These few people would continue to sanction the idea that some products are beyond the comprehension of women and should not be advertised to them at all. From a pure business viewpoint, this type of sexism is disadvantageous in that the true market potential for products is not realized. It also hampers the broader changes which are occurring in other societal institutions.

Eventually, the newer status of women must be recognized by advertisers if they are to succeed with their sales pitches (Belkaoui and Belkaoui, 1976). Although minimal, some changes have occurred, primarily with regard to depicting women in more diverse occupational roles. Depicting women in working roles outside the home has increased along with portraying them in more responsible positions (Wagner and Banos, 1973; Levere, 1974). Brawlowe (1982) asserts that a new kind of woman is emerging. She is active, involved in an array of projects, and enjoys her home but is not monopolized by it. Some advertisers are only beginning to recognize that women are diverse and can successfully balance home and career (Pearson, 1985).

Advertising carries over the images initiated by the print media into television. But the images are even more powerful and affect a larger audience. Whereas Goffman (1979) highlights the nonverbals in print ads, their use in this medium is fairly limited compared to their prevalence in commercials appearing on television. Television can use hundreds of techniques to create a particular view of a product. Lighting, camera angle, tone of voice, body movement, animation, and color, to name a few, can be infinitely manipulated to provide the "ideal" sales mix.

Thousands of commercials have been studied to determine the gender roles in television advertising. The results are similar to print advertisements. The single largest occupation for a female is housewife. She is usually shown in the home testifying to the merits of bathroom and kitchen products. Though she is selling products to other women, a man's voice in the background tells her what to do (Dominick and Rauch, 1972; Hennessee and Nicholson, 1972; O'Donnell and O'Donnell, 1978). And particularly in prime time commercials, women are shown as more foolish, less mature, and less successful than male characters (Schneider, 1979). Consider the portrayal of the Mr. Whipple contingent at the toilet tissue shelf in the supermarket as an example of this.

Advertisements geared to children are even more gender-role oriented. Girls are shown in more passive activities and dependent upon another person or a doll for entertainment (Verna, 1975). They learn how to help their mothers, assist in household tasks, serve men and boys—especially where food is concerned—and see how to become beautiful (Cattin and Jain, 1979; Courtney and Whipple, 1983). Commercials do not teach independence or autonomy for young girls. A lifetime of viewing these commercials may actually inhibit achievement aspirations for women (Geis et al., 1984).

Assessments of change in patterns of how women are portrayed in commercials are not encouraging. They still need men to tell them what to do or buy, even for products like window cleaner, deodorant, or hair color. When a voice is heard in the background but no person is shown, that voice is from a male. Since the 1970s, male voice-overs increased to 92% of daytime commercials and 90% of prime-time commercials (Pesch et al., 1981). Gender stereotypes in children's commercials have actually increased (Doolittle and Pepper, 1975). Even though women are now seen with greater frequency in nondomestic roles, male images are not broadening (Scheibe, 1979).

FILM

Unlike the other media, women have played a more central position in the film industry. Although director and producer remain the province of men, women have succeeded as screenwriters, editors, costume designers, critics, and actors (Haskel!, 1974a:8). In the early days of film when the studio system was at its height, women dominated the star spotlight. This was reflected in popularity polls and the billings female leads received. Although the contract system allowed studios to virtually own actors, women had influence in determining their careers and the parts they received. It has only been since the 1940s that female stars have been overshadowed by male ones. With a few exceptions, this decline has continued to the present. In contrast to the reality of women's diverse contemporary roles, current film portrayals are sorely lacking in depth and authenticity.

The Second World War encouraged the independence and initiative of women, which were reflected in screen images. Women were shown as efficient homemakers who could make the transition from kitchen to war industry smoothly, without severely disrupting family life. Or they were shown as nurses serving overseas and even as combatants at times who, like men, could die for their country. Movies were a critical part of the war effort and emphasized the need for self-sacrifice if victory was to be won. Women on the home front were necessary components for this effort. The double-duty woman who worked in a defense plant was symbolized by Rosie the Riveter, who became the heroine of the home front.

Although women on the World War II screen had self-confidence and strength, a certain ambiguity was also evident. Baker (1980) suggests that these ambitious and capable women were thrown into unique circumstances by war, which upset the "natural balance." Both men and women left home to engage in the unlikely occupations of soldier and defense worker. They were fighting to save the American home, and films reassured audiences that after the war women would be as eager as men to return to the natural balance of things (Baker, 1980:5). True to this message, by the 1950s films reaffirmed the domestic subservience of women (Mellen, 1973).

Whereas the war years presented women as multifaceted, after the war they were portrayed as unidimensional, as either good or bad. The "good" woman embodied the feminine mystique. She was virtuous throughout her courtship. She might have a successful career, but Mr. Right would change her opinion of success. After marriage she became the perfect wife and mother. Doris Day and Debbie Reynolds represented this image. The "bad" woman, on the other hand, was the sexpot, who could entice a man away from his faithful wife and loving family. Marilyn Monroe and Ava Gardner symbolized the view of sexuality which hinted broadly of immorality in the innocent fifties.

Although the films of the fifties appear to display a concern for domestic righteousness, French (1978) asserts that they reflect a period which also shows women struggling with narrowly defined roles. A number of movies combined progressive and reactionary elements with women involved in the transition between domestic roles and newer alternatives.

> The transitional woman is often torn between her desire for a conventional, secure lifestyle and her longing for an unconventional, adventurous, largely uncharted course of action. (French, 1978:xxiii)

The conflicts and contradictions of the transitional women helped set the stage for the changes of the next two decades.

If the early days of film romanticized women and put them on a pedestal, the 60s and 70s compensated by adding a more blatant sexual dimension. The new women of this era were loosened from the constraints of family life, but with the breaking of the bonds, an attitude of "they deserve what they get" arose. Women who ventured outside the home were negatively portrayed and eventually punished (Mellen, 1973). The favorable images of the war years disintegrated and women were accorded fewer roles than ever before. Male speaking roles outdistanced female by 12 to 1 (Klemesrud, 1974). If a strong female model was portrayed at all, the film was likely to be set in the past (Farber, 1974). Haskell (1974a:323) calls this period the "most disheartening in screen history." She believes that as the women's liberation movement gained momentum and women were asserting themselves in new realms, a backlash occurred in commercial film.

Film romance was replaced by sexuality and violence, and this continues to the present. Romantic couples of the Fred Astaire-Ginger Rogers variety are gone, with prostitutes and girlfriends of questionable morals filling the void (Klemesrud, 1974). Females are victims in movies of horror, murder, and especially rape, in which film directors seem to have a macabre interest. Between 1971 and 1973, twenty rape movies appeared (Harmetz, 1973). As we move into a new decade, this trend shows little sign of slowing down. With the decline of the three dimensional woman, films depict females as birdbrains and ballbreakers (Reed, 1975), sexual mannequins (Mellen, 1974), and ineffectual bodies to be raped and flogged (Haskell, 1974b).

By the 70s sex and sexual violence became explicit enough to create a rating system which determined the degree of suitability for audiences below a certain age. This system emphasizes sex more than violence so that love scenes are more apt to get the film a restricted rating than rape scenes. The rating system also helps perpetuate the ideas that rape is inconsequential and that rapists are heroic. The James Bond films, which are immensely popular with teens, depict women enjoying rape, especially since Bond is the "good guy" and the supposed fantasy of every woman. Once raped they are then ignored by the male star. Rapes and murders are likely alternatives to women in token roles. A "now you see them, now you don't" pattern occurs.

And, as Bond ages, his "girls" do not. They are as sleek and young as ever, picture after picture. Unlike men, women must have youth to be seriously considered for romantic leads, which means their careers suffer in terms of longevity. Cary Grant became more distinguished as he aged. Katherine Hepburn becomes old. After a certain age, women are consigned to play shrews and jealous housewives as their movie husbands are turned by pretty faces and slim figures. New, younger female faces are sought to replace the "aging" forty year old star. Haskell (1977) argues that this creates a shortage of women in films, but that children are becoming replacements for women. These nymphets are targeted for movies which may even be classified as "child porn."

The film industry offers a number of excuses for not focusing on female stars or for portraying women in limited, stereotyped roles. They maintain that the public does not like "macho" women and that television offers a diverse range of female roles for free (Rosen, 1974). Another explanation is that men dominate the industry and are in the position of determining the image of women in it (Mellen, 1973). The image may be created out of male fantasies or the fear of dealing with women in positions of power. Farber (1974) states that men must learn to deal with assertiveness in women and the struggles facing contemporary women, but directors are afraid to confront the issues. So movies retreat into an unrealistic stereotyped world.

There are a few positive signs which suggest a return of women to movies offering greater role latitude and chances to display a wider range of talent. Two important and critically acclaimed films which did not rest on a male lead and which highlighted sensitive issues relating to friendship and loyalty between women were *Julia* and *Turning Point*. Haskell (1983) points to a postfeminist trend in films which suggests that the era when Barbra Streisand was the only bankable female is over. Actors like Meryl Streep, Jessica Lange, Diane Keaton, Jane Fonda, and Sally Field provide evidence for this.

Haskell (1983) cautions, however, that even these stars have less leverage and smaller paychecks than comparable males. Whereas Burt Reynolds receives $5 million per picture, co-star Sally Field gets half as much (Shearer, 1986). There is also less tolerance for films which are box office bombs starring women. Burt Reynolds and Paul Newman may emerge relatively unscathed from bad reviews and bad movies, which incidentally are not always identical. But studios are reluctant to offer parts to women who have fallen victim to the critic's ax.

The dilemma faced by that part of the film industry concerned with the image of women is how to successfully combine the elements of fantasy and realism which is what attracts the public to the movies in the first place. Should women be portrayed as victims of a patriarchal society, or as "vanquishers of mighty odds"? (Haskell, 1983). Will romance be forever crushed by realism? Haskell (1983) maintains that the movies can still have the requisite fantasy and magic without accepting a narrow range of behavior from female actors. Movies are creations of male fantasies. Women need to invent their own fantasies and portray these as well.

POPULAR SONGS

The media are change oriented, geared to an often fickle public which demands new sights and sounds to satisfy an unending thirst for entertainment variety. Nowhere is this more apparent than in the world of popular music. Whether it is country or rock, love songs or "heavy metal," the quest for notoriety, evidenced by the volume of album and tape sales, continues unabated. Although the music industry is diverse, it recognizes that a significant portion of the record market is in essence controlled by teens and young adults. With the advent of the rock video, the competition for the "teen dollar" becomes even stronger. Considering the money and time spent on records, especially by teens, contemporary music is an important source of socialization.

Experiments in musical patterns are responsible for trends being set and altered so rapidly. Music is always at the vanguard of change. Protest movements are fired by songs which unify members against a common foe. Rock musicians take conventional morality to the limits. Such music challenges the traditional and creates the conditions for further change. Since contemporary music in particular challenges social norms, it would appear to be the one medium where traditional gender roles are minimized. But the evidence counters this reasonable assumption.

Popular music of the last three decades sings to the beauty and sex appeal of women, who use them to control men. Through passivity and submissiveness a woman can manipulate even a possessive man so that she is in control of him and the relationship (Talkington, 1976; Wilkinson, 1976). Control, however, may be difficult to determine since she remains dependent on him. Country music stereotypes women in two categories. They are temptresses to men as well as wives who wait patiently for their two-timing husbands to return. (Sims, 1974). No matter what the consequences, "stand by your man" is the appropriate response for even the long-suffering woman.

Since the 1950s, views of women in rock songs have changed, but they are still in keeping with stereotyped notions. The virginal girl-next-door, teen-angel and California girl have been replaced by whores, bitches, and fantasy figures on whom violence is perpetrated. As Chmaj (1972) points out, rock lyrics present an image of a woman who makes her bed and then lies in it. She is a domesticated sex object. The misogyny in "cock rock" lyrics is unconcealed, with little attempt to be subtle. Women are nags, tramps, and brainless housewives. With violence as an increasing theme in rock music, such women are seen as legitimate targets for rape and murder.

These images are expanded by album covers depicting women being brutalized by men and animals. The love-hate dichotomy is featured on covers where men are kissing and killing women at the same time. Although more stylized in form, rock videos present similar views. Boycotts of records showing violent themes against women on their covers have generally failed. But as rock lyrics have become more sexually explicit, some record companies have agreed to put a "warning label" on their album covers indicating that the words may be unsuitable for audiences below a certain age. It is a significant comment on our society that sexual themes per se are considered more offensive than violence against women.

In the 1960s Janis Joplin broke into the rock culture and emerged as a unique, controversial, and often contradictory symbol for young women caught in the middle of a confusing period of history. She was viewed as a floozy as well as one who sang of the pains of womanhood. Rodnitzky (1976) states that she was a "victim of sexism within a sexual revolution she fueled," but she was also a feminist symbol who paved the way for other women destined to enter the sacred realm of the male rock kingdom.

A number of rock bands either led by women or with female and male lead singers and musicians, have emerged in the 80s, drawing large crowds at concerts. The names of Pat Benatar, Cindy Lauper, Madonna, Blondie, and Heart are recognizable as leading women in the rock charts. It cannot be said, however, that their songs are feminist in orientation. They, too, sing of love and pain, but with an abundance of masochistic reflections. With gyrating cleavages and tight costumes, songs of vulnerable women being abandoned by men are chanted. Revenge for a woman is to taunt the man she loves. He may respond with violence, yet it would be her own fault. Female rock artists do not produce many popular songs which show other women in a sympathetic light. Indeed, few can act as role models and challenge rock's misogynous lyrics. Janis Joplin opened up a range of alternatives for the images of women in rock. With possible exceptions of people such as Tina Turner, who recently reemerged in rock and has been catapulted to the superstar category, alternative views of women, demonstrated by female artists themselves, are rarer today than in the 60s.

TELEVISION

Though magazines, songs and films are important mass media socializers, television is by far the most pervasive. Statistics indicate that 98% of American households have at least one television, and 40% have two or more, which are turned on an average of six and one-half hours per day (Spencer, 1985). Unlike films, we see the same television characters come directly into our home, week after week, year after year. We learn about their joys and sorrows, how they raise their children, what their children like, and how they relate to one another as parents, spouses, siblings, employees, employers, and in the infinite variety of other roles that emerge from television series.

Television takes on a certain reality in the minds of many viewers, with some even finding it difficult to separate an actor from the character the actor is playing. Actors portraying TV doctors and lawyers receive mail from viewers asking for medical and legal advice. Soap opera actors are berated or praised for how they conduct their television lives. Viewers distinguish certain characters as personally meaningful for them. Lull (1980) finds that women are more likely to identify with less-than-perfect or demeaning rather than glamorous images. "Wonder Woman" is less of a role model than is Carol Burnett. Because television exerts such a powerful influence on how we view and understand our culture, fact and fiction become entangled. When women and men are shown in stereotyped roles, whether in a "factual" documentary or a fictional situation comedy, these images come together as being correct, appropriate and realistic. More disturbing is the research which reveals that television may actually encourage behavior that would be defined as antisocial. Reinhold (1983) reports on the National Institute of Mental Health study which concludes that by the age 15, a child has witnessed over 13,000 television killings (Julian, 1983:205).

Much of this violence is directed toward females. Television has a penchant for showing women as victims. Women are raped and murdered throughout prime-time TV. In order to find the murderer, women police officers dress up as prostitutes and put themselves in vulnerable situations, or they use their sex appeal to gain information. As the heroines of the series, and against all advice, they attempt to take the killers on their own. Of course they become emotionally involved in the justice of it all, find themselves surrounded by the bad guys, and need their male companions to rescue them. The message of this standard plot is clear. Women are vulnerable, cannot fend for themselves, and rely on men to be saved from adversity.

Television producers argue that to deviate from such images would risk popularity in the ratings. But there was a prime time police series which not only deviated but did so successfully for many years. The "Cagney and Lacey" series was the primary one which featured women in lead roles as crime fighters, bringing them together as partners. The show was an anomaly as well because the vast majority of prime-time television portrays women as younger, more attractive, and single (Stabiner, 1985), or on constant surveillance for a man. The series dealt with issues rarely seen on police shows, such as breast cancer, abortion, and child neglect. Female characters were shown sympathetically and realistically. Although the requisite drug busts and robberies were included, the show did not completely revolve around these. CBS has given its blessing to this format and stands behind the drive to insert more social issues into entertainment focused drama. Stabiner (1985) asserts that Cagney and Lacey are "good soldiers in the war against prime-time stereotypes."

Unfortunately, most of television does not acknowledge that this war ever exists, which may be closer to reality. The few changes in prime time TV must be weighed against all other programming, including reruns which date back as much as 25 years. Cagney and Lacey, Joyce Davenport, the assertive, compassionate attorney in "Hill Street Blues," and the cunning writer-sleuth Jessica Fletcher of "Murder She Wrote," must compete with "Charlie's Angels" (whose angels are they?) and "Police Woman" (who is frequently called out of the shower about a police emergency) in determining gender role stereotypes. Add to these the incredible competitiveness found in "The Brady Bunch" and the antics of

Chrissy, the naive blonde in "Three's Company." Regardless of any intent to make programming more gender role realistic, reruns may counter these efforts.

Television prime time revolves around men, with male characters outnumbering female 3 to 1 (Signorielli, 1982). Females are associated with stereotyped traits, such as emotionality and passivity. They play family and marital roles, and if seen occupationally, they are subordinate to men in their position (Estep, 1982). The male chef tyrannizes the waitresses and even the female manager in "It's A Living." Archie Bunker rules his household and Archie's wife Edith, who is scatter-brained but still portrayed for her wisdom, must accommodate to Archie's whims. And consider the implications of the title "Who's The Boss" where the male domestic help really determines how the household functions. In the shows which have the highest ratings, female characters are simply bystanders, who may add sex appeal. Consider "Dallas," "Dukes of Hazzard," and "Magnum P.I." as examples (Doyle, 1985). Powerful women are ruthless and will use any means to retain their position, like Alexis Carrington on "Dynasty" and Angela Channing on "Falcon Crest." Unlike a man, a woman cannot "have it all"—beauty, power, position, loving family—and still be favorably viewed on television.

Directed at a female audience, soap operas have about a 50-50 split in terms of male and female characters. The soaps are ludicrous in their distortion of reality but are popular because of it. Soaps provide the daytime opportunity for women to escape into a fantasy world of romance and adventure. Soap opera women come to one another for advice on family and sexual matters (Fine, 1981). They are schemers, victims, and starry-eyed romantics. Womanhood and motherhood are equated (Peck, 1974). The sanctity of the family is valued, as is creativity in the kitchen (Lopate, 1976). More than in prime-time TV, however, women are portrayed as intelligent, self-reliant, and articulate beings who may not fear getting old and can do so gracefully (Downing, 1974).

But problems related to sex often intrude on the soap opera family and become a dominant concern of the women. The family suffers because sexual partners are not married and usually affairs are revealed. The forgiving wife holds the family together until her errant husband returns and temporarily makes amends. Afternoon TV is replete with sexual content which bolsters this storyline. Explicit petting and references made to sex and sexual activities are in abundance (Greenberg et al., 1981). The most popular soap opera, "General Hospital," has the largest teen audience and the highest rate of sexual acts per hour (Lowry et al., 1981). The double standard in terms of gender role is alive and well on daytime television.

Children's programs parallel adult shows in the ratio of female to male characters. In cartoons, females are rarely seen, even as animals or make-believe characters, and those who are shown are often rescued by males (Streicher, 1974). The Star Wars movies have helped create a number of cartoon shows where a female princess who has been ousted from her planet by a villainous robot-like (male) creature needs help to restore her to her rightful place. She is kidnapped and rescued by her stalwart, heroic, male companions, who usually kill, at least in the cartoon sense, the villains. Notice the similarities in plot to some of the shows mentioned above.

An analysis of the most popular television shows for children reveals that the overwhelming majority of characters are males, who are portrayed as aggressive and rewarded for their behavior. Females are deferential and, if shown in high activity levels, are either ignored or punished (Sternglanz and Serbin, 1974). Those parents who scrupulously guard the television habits of their children may find much programming directed at children unsuitable. They applaud public television's efforts to both educate and entertain. "Sesame Street" has been recognized for its excellence in content which does exactly that. Moreover, this program has made every effort to minimize stereotypes. Its record on the portrayal of the sexes is not so distinguished. As with other children's programs, male characters outnumber female characters. Some of the most popular characters, like Big Bird, Bert, Ernie, Oscar the Grouch and the Cookie Monster are all male. In an important study done twenty years ago, Gardner (1970) finds that gender roles on "Sesame Street" are biased, and this includes the puppet characters. Even with the introduction of more females, "Sesame Street" can still be regarded as gender role stereotyped. This show has been on two decades, is aired in certain cities two or three times a day, and represents a major source of preschool television. It is a program of unquestionably superior educational value, especially in terms of preparation for reading and writing, but the gender role implications leave much to be desired.

Compared to overall television programming, women appear to be making the greatest strides in the news and documentary areas, at least gaining more on-screen visibility. Barbara Walters and Diane Sawyer, for example, demonstrate the professionalism and integrity of women broadcasters. Only several years ago, the few women who were seen during news programs were billed as "weather-girls" and held third rate positions on the news teams. Today many female meteorologists are responsible for preparing and broadcasting the weather. Metropolitan areas have male-female news teams which vie with one another for ratings. Gradually, inroads have been made by women in the news and weather departments, but the sports anchor is invariably a man.

But does increased visibility in news and information programs mean that barriers are finally eroding? The answer is both yes and no, and a look at early morning television helps explain why. Each of the three networks have produced two-hour shows which can be described as combining news with entertainment. Currently, each of these shows is hosted by a male and female team, with commercial ratings indicating that this kind of format is necessary for success. No longer can a man or completely male news team expect to carry the show. Yet the networks insist that the audience favors the male over the female, which justifies more money, more air time, and better stories being given to the male. Joan Lunden, co-host of "Good Morning America" with Charles Gibson, receives substantially less than his salary. Jane Pauley of the "Today" show lost in her battle to gain equal status with relative newcomer Bryant Gumbel, a former sportscaster (Bachrach, 1985).

Joan Lunden suggests that audience research and the political climate combine to hurt the advances gained by women in the news department. She adds that male network executives are the ones who can really put you under their thumbs. It's a boy's club, and if you're a male on the show you belong to the club. If you're a woman on the show, men barely say hello to you in the morning. (Bachrach, 1985:48)

This sentiment is shared by Christine Craft, former Kansas City anchor, who gained national attention in her sex discrimination suit against Metromedia, which she initially won but which was later overturned on appeal. She was told that people of Kansas City did not like her.

I was too old, too unattractive, and didn't defer to men. . . . The people who make the hiring decisions (for the networks) are aging, white males. . . . They're the ones who say, "Adios, senorita," after they see the first crow's foot on a woman anchor. And the thing is, the terrible thing is, that decision creates a model for the rest of society. (Bachrach, 1985:48)

WOMEN IN MASS MEDIA INDUSTRIES

All the media discussed have produced images of women which are based on stereotypes. By considering the lack of women in creative and decision-making positions in media industries, this pattern may be at least partly explained. Except as secretarial staff, women are numerically underrepresented in all phases of advertising. Scott (1976) shows that when men work with women on an equal basis, more positive attitudes are held than when the women are subordinates. Since advertising is the medium with the most pervasive and consistent stereotyping, an influx of women into managerial positions may provide the industry with more realistic images of women.

The same can be said for television. About 30% of the employees at network headquarters and network-owned stations are women, but only 10% are at the managerial level (Ceulemans and Fauconnier, 1979; UNESCO, 1980). Although women participate as actors in commercials, soap operas, and prime-time television, their representation in production, management and news is limited. The major qualifications for entry into these positions are educational background and experience. Although women have very similar educational profiles, their experience is less favorable when compared to male counterparts (Ceulemans and Fauconnier, 1979). Most women managers in television have entered the industry within the last decade. Until they move up the hierarchy, hopefully creating opportunities for those women who follow, occupational segregation of the sexes in the television industry will be the norm.

In film, the golden days of Hollywood occurred before and during the Depression. Ironically, this period was also the golden age for women in the industry. Women participated in every phase of production except camera operation (Ceulemans and Fauconnier, 1979). The position of director is considered the apex of the film industry. In the silent screen and prewar era, there were over twenty female directors (UNESCO, 1980). Today there are only a handful. Ida Lupino is one of these few, and she established herself even before the Second World War.

The Director's Guild lists 3,000 members, of which a mere 23 are women (UNESCO, 1980). These figures are similar for Britain and Australia, but continental Europe has produced a number of internationally renowned women film directors.

Whereas the position of director remains a male bastion, the number of women producers, editors, and screenwriters is increasing. Although less likely to be established with major studios which produce box office blockbusters, they are responding to opportunities which offer creative work in newer cinematic forms and techniques (Smith, 1975). Art, documentary, educational, experimental, and the emerging "alternative" cinema are areas where women are demonstrating their talents. Because women film critics do hold influential positions in the industry, efforts outside of so-called mainstream filmmaking are not ignored. This has helped the field of feminist film theory to emerge. In addition, prominent women critics have reviewed films in terms of newer perspectives, such as an evaluation of how women are portrayed, the quality of the roles women are being offered, and the degree to which films reflect social reality.

These achievements are impressive but, for the most part, they account for films outside the mainstream of well-known studios. These are the studios producing the movies for which people will line up outside on a cold Saturday night to see. Significant monetary reward and public recognition of one's creative work are reserved for commercially successful films. Although alternative cinema may provide creative, though not lucrative, outlets for women filmmakers, a male monopoly in the established film industry makes the switch from one system to the other difficult.

We have seen that the media are prime socializers and that women hold a minimum of influential positions within the industry. It would seem logical to assume that as women gain positions of power and prestige, stereotyped images will be altered. But the media are entrenched in a broader social system which supports the notion of female subordination. As Gallagher (1981:79) aptly notes,

> For images of women are constructed, and women find their identity, outside of media too: it is the marginality of women in cultural and social life generally which contributes to and reflects their subordination. This subordination is, moreover, constituted not simply through a particular configuration of media images, but also through basic political and economic structures.

Thus, when advertisers are singled out for their blatant sexist portrayals, they defend themselves by saying they are trend-followers, not trend setters (Scott, 1976). Although this ignores the impact of reinforcing stereotypes, it is a defensible argument in that other social institutions engage in similar, but perhaps more subtle, practices. For women in media industries to make truly significant impact, social change must also continue in other institutions as well.

MALE IMAGES IN THE MEDIA

When considering their multidimensional roles in the real world, women have not fared well in the media. Men star more in television series, sell more records, make more movies, and get greater financial rewards. But the price of this popularity is that men, too, must succumb to images which are less than realistic. From the media's standpoint, a man is a breadwinner who cheats on his wife, has no idea how to use a vacuum cleaner or an oven, is manipulated by his children, and uses brute force to solve problems. How have the media contributed to these images?

Advertisers believe products can be divided according to their emotional appeal; hence some are seen as masculine and some as feminine. Cars, life insurance, and beer are masculine; so men do the selling to other men (Stuteville, 1971). Men also sell women's products, such as cosmetics and pantyhose. In fact, men do most of the selling on television, as evidenced by the increased use of male voiceovers in both daytime and prime-time television (Pesch et al., 1981). Advertising puts men in positions where they direct what women buy, which subtly states to both sexes that men are in control and are literally the voice of authority.

Beer commercials, shown on television especially during sports events, are almost exclusively male-oriented. Themes surrounding these commercials are camping, cowboys, competition, and camaraderie. The "good old boys" who drink beer are adventuresome, play hard at sports, and have a country spirit. More than any other type of advertising geared to men, beer commercials instill the importance of a macho type image.

Overall, men are positively portrayed in TV commercials, especially on prime time. When compared to women, men are viewed as more mature, less foolish, and more successful, particularly since men are primarily shown in prestigious, higher income positions (Belkaoui and Belkaoui, 1976; Schneider, 1979). Although women have increased their activities outside the home, advertising has assumed men have not taken on additional family roles. They are still inept in the kitchen and cannot fathom the habits of a newborn infant. There is a trend toward showing more males in other than wage-earning positions, but rather than put them in the home, advertisers prefer to associate them with entertainment and sports (Wohleter and Lammers, 1978). The ironic result of this is that, like women, men are increasingly filling a sex-object role in advertising (Sharits and Lammers, 1982).

Whereas films also contribute to men being viewed as sex objects, they are at least shown as more multifaceted than women. The hard living, tough guy portrayals of actors like John Wayne, Clint Eastwood, and Charles Bronson are contrasted with "antiheroes and soulful ethnics" like Al Pacino, Dustin Hoffman, and Robert DeNiro (Haskell, 1983). Popular, too, are the "buddy" movies where two males are linked together in one or a series of films. The plot invariably calls for them to be competitive on the surface and then gradually move toward genuine, if begrudging, respect and camaraderie. They learn to admire one another for traits they see lacking in their own personalities. This formula has been successful in movies pairing Robert Redford and Paul Newman (*The Sting* and *Butch Cassidy and the Sundance Kid*), the unlikely combination of Dustin Hoffman and Steve McQueen (*Papillion*), and Dan Aykroyd and the late John Belushi (*Blues Brothers, Neighbors,* and *1941*) (Haskell, 1983).

These films may be the contemporary extensions of the comedian buddy teams of the past. Laurel and Hardy, Abbot and Costello, the Marx Brothers, Martin and Lewis, and even the Three Stooges starred in numerous movies combining adventure and comedy. If romance entered in, it was short-lived. Women may be necessary diversions, not permanent enough to keep the men from coming back together and continuing their carefree escapades. Through movies like these, men learn that family ties are tenuous, not particularly desirable, and keep them from adventuresome good times with their buddies.

War, crime, and western movies are other types where men excel. Recently two other genres have emerged, possibly reemerged, which speak to men about characteristics they should admire. Pure fantasy exists in adventure movies where the hero escapes unscathed from the very jaws of death. The twist for some of these movies is that the hero starts out insisting he is not brave, but really cowardly at heart. Circumstances prove otherwise as he rescues the maiden, finds the gold, or saves the world, all in reckless abandon, not seeming to care for his own life. The *Star Wars* epics and *Indiana Jones* follow this pattern. Second, we have those films which seem to be released solely for the sake of violence. Both heroes and villains are violent, and more violence is needed to end the violence. The kill and maim plots of films like *Death Wish*, *Halloween*, or *Friday the Thirteenth* attest to the belief that revenge and violence in a "good" cause are acceptable. Males who do not agree with this formula are viewed as unfit and are often labeled as wimps or nerds.

Violence is a recurrent theme in popular songs as well. Successful male rock bands combine sexual imagery with violent overtones. Men are to use women for their own needs and then cast them aside. The lyrics to the song "Squealer" by a group called AC/DC provide an example.

> she'd never been, never been balled before
> 'n I don't think she'll ever ball no more (fixed 'er good).
> . . . made her understand
> . . . made it hard to stop

"Squealer" affirms the notion that women cannot resist certain men. The song is in praise of sexual exploitation and implicitly condones sexual acts regardless of the woman's intent.

Rather than think that this is the exception, the 80s have given us the band Judas Priest and the following lyrics from a song titled "Love Bites."

> Into your room, where in deep sleep
> There you lie still, to you I creep
> Then I descend, close to your lips
> Now you are mine, in my control

These lyrics are less subtle and more threatening toward women. But the result is the same. She is compliant to his sexual conquest and in the end enjoys it. In essence this is the myth associated with rape and one which popular songs bolster. Other examples abound. Bands like Krokus, Twisted Sister, and The Scorpions sell millions of records to teens who learn that rape, violence, sexual victories, and crime are male prerogatives.

The argument that these groups are not representative of the recording industry is somewhat valid, but popular music geared to a mainstream audience provides similar, though less blatant, impressions. Kenny Rogers, who successfully combines country and "Top 40" music, has produced a string of hit records portraying men as violent or potentially violent in their thoughts or behavior. The violence is seen as acceptable and usually involves a woman. In "Ruby, Don't Take Your Love to Town," the singer is a man who is paralyzed from war and whose wife is seeing another man. He loves her dearly, but if he could move "he'd get a gun and put her in the ground." His own wretched condition and her apparent lack of sympathy justifies it. In "Coward of the County," we learn of a man who is told "you don't have to fight to be a man." He continually turns the other cheek until his wife, Becky, is violated by a gang. He avenges Becky's honor, actually his own, by fighting it out. These songs support a sexual double standard and legitimize physical force in the way men handle problems. They *do* have to fight to be men.

Finally, we turn to television, which generally portrays men as being in control of most situations. They also recognize that power may bring adversity as well as rewards (Downs and Gowan, 1980) but are willing to accept whatever the consequences. Men are active, less tied to relationships (Downing, 1974) and can solve their own problems (Downs, 1981). Television equates male strength with lack of emotion and self-reliance as well as the ability to fight out of a difficult spot.

The major exception to this image is the situation comedy where men exhibit what Brenton (1966) calls the "Dagwood Bumstead Syndrome." Brenton refers to the multitude of television images of a father who is outwitted by his wife, children, and the family dog. He has good intentions but bungles when it comes to his household or family relationships. His world is outside of the home; so this kind of behavior is expected. The 80s have given us comedy shows like "Family Ties" where dad is an equal household participant and not negatively portrayed as a result, but the inept father image is much more the rule. Ostensibly in charge of his family, his authority is forever questioned and often ridiculed. Unless decisions must be made involving discipline of the children, or perhaps his wife, and linking the family to the outside world, usually through financial matters, "father knows best" is not backed up as far as the contemporary television family is concerned.

The media allow men to display a greater range of roles than women, but stereotypes still account for the majority of this imagery. Like the women the media have created, men cannot be all that they are meant to be, or all that they are. Until we see men consistently portrayed as loving fathers, compassionate husbands, and household experts, our attitudes about masculinity will not be significantly altered.

MEDIA AND SOCIAL CHANGE

We have seen that the media present views of women and men which are not in line with reality. Although men are portrayed as more multidimensional than women, the additional characteristics are stereotyped as well. Media producers, especially advertisers, argue that categorical images are what the public wants to see and that even if somewhat inaccurate, these portrayals generally reflect society. If a sexist society exists, the media reinforce it. From their viewpoint, to do otherwise would risk public acceptance and monetary returns. The question of moral responsibility is rarely an issue in deliberations over media images of the sexes.

To some extent, the media are powerful because of their ability to take the mundane and create fantasy and excitement. Is it possible to retain fantasy and public acceptance while simultaneously providing alternative, more realistic images of the sexes? Since it has been demonstrated that many people are uncomfortable with what they see and that financial success can occur when media formulas do change, the answer to this question is affirmative. One of the ironies of the media is that they thrive on change, yet seem unwilling to deviate from rigid, traditional patterns. When convinced that success can be packaged differently, media change will likely excel.

Finally, there is the question of moral responsibility, which usually becomes an issue when sexual and violent content of the media are examined. Publicity is directed at effects of programming on children, with little explicit concern for gender role portrayals. Yet this does provide a latent function. Since gender roles are inextricably bound to this content anyway, change in one will affect change in the other.

The media are formidable socializers and provide images which both reflect and reinforce gender roles. They have this responsibility whether they acknowledge it or not. The media also have the power to alter stereotypes, which they do whenever more genuine views of the sexes are presented. As the public demands entertainment, news, and advertising that is more indicative of social reality, the media will respond with more realistic images.

13

Power, Politics, and the Law

Power is a basic element of the fabric of society and is possessed in varying degrees by different social actors in different social categories. Max Weber (1946) defined power in terms of the likelihood a person may achieve personal ends despite possible resistance from others. Since this definition views power as potentially coercive, Weber also considered ways in which power can be achieved through justice. Authority, he contended, is power which people determine to be legitimate rather than coercive. When power becomes encoded into law, it is legitimized and translated into the formal structure of society. In Weberian terms, this is known as rational-legal authority. As will be demonstrated, women as a group are at a distinct disadvantage when both power and authority are considered.

We have already seen how this holds true economically through a hierarchy of occupations in which women are rewarded less than men in terms of money and prestige. Interpersonal power is also compromised, even in the family where women are assumed to carry more weight in terms of decision-making. To this list can be added the limited political and legal power which women wield. Social stratification is based on differential power which in turn underlies all inequality. Thus, inequality between the sexes persists because the power base women possess is more circumscribed than that of men. Restrictions in terms of political power and legal authority are at the core of inequality.

THE LAW

According to Richardson (1988:104) certain assumptions about the sexes permeate the law and these provide the bases for how the law is then differentially applied.

1. Women are incompetent, childlike, and in need of protection.
2. Men are the protectors and financial caretakers of women.
3. Husband and wife are treated as "one" under the law. The "one" is the husband.
4. Males and females are biologically different which gives them differing capabilities and differing standards on which to judge their actions. Richardson calls this a double standard of morality based on biological deterministic thought.

Because these are assumptions, they are "taken-for-granted beliefs" and are rarely questioned. When formally developed into law, they become sacrosanct.

Throughout this text, reference has been made to legislation which has served to perpetuate yet also alter traditional gender roles. At all governmental levels laws have been enacted which may be viewed as giving one sex certain advantages or disadvantages. There is considerable variation on how laws are interpreted and how they are enforced. This means that even federal legislation is inconsistently applied depending on the specifics of the situation. What will become clear is that, regardless of the notions of equality and justice which are supposedly inherent in the legal process, the law cannot realistically be defined as gender-neutral, much less gender-equal. Although efforts to remedy this continue, the following discussion will demonstrate the difficulty of the task ahead.

Employment

One of the most important pieces of legislation to prohibit discrimination in employment based on sex is the 1964 Civil Rights Act. The story of how this act was eventually passed at all is both instructive in regard to our legal process and ironic as well. The original bill called for the elimination of job discrimination based on race, color, religion or national origin. Ultra-conservative Howard W. Smith (D., Va.), chair of the House Rules Committee at the time, introduced the word "sex" to these provisions because he did not want to see the bill passed at all. He felt that even liberals would consider the elimination of job discrimination based on sex as too radical a step. His strategy backfired and the bill was passed with the word "sex" included in the amendment. The obvious irony is that someone who would have otherwise taken an extremely conservative position by the standards of the day was responsible for a major advance of a "liberal" cause. Title VII of the 1964 Civil Rights Act makes it explicit that it is unlawful for an employer to refuse to hire an applicant, to discharge an employee, or to discriminate against any individual with respect to "compensation, terms, conditions, or privileges of employment, because of such individual's race, color, religion, sex, or national origin."

The only way that Title VII can be legally circumvented is through the "bona fide occupational qualification" (BFOQ) which allows for hiring an employee on the basis of sex, thereby "discriminating" against the other sex, if it is deemed as critical for carrying out the job. For example, a woman can be hired over a man as an actor for a specific part in a movie to establish "authenticity or genuineness" of the role. Also, if characteristics of one sex are necessary for the job, a person of that sex is hired, such as for the job of wet-nurse. With such few exceptions, the BFOQ rule is very narrowly interpreted by the courts and is seldom used as a defense for charges of sex discrimination (Thorkelson, 1985:480).

Another accomplishment of Title VII has been the elimination of many policies used by employers which may appear to be neutral but can have a "disparate impact" on women. When an employer states that all employees have to be within certain height or weight limits, it often means that a large proportion of one sex or the other is excluded from that particular job option. Women have been systematically denied employment opportunities in areas such as law enforcement, security, paramedical fields, and mining and construction through setting such limits. In defending these qualifications, the employer must now demonstrate that the policy is a "business necessity" without which the job could not be safely or efficiently carried out. Height and weight designations are often used to assess strength levels. But Thorkelson (1985:481) suggests that since strength can be measured directly, a direct strength test would be more instrumental in serving the purposes designated by the company and would do so with less disparate impact on women, as well as some men.

If Title VII mandates the elimination of sex as a basis for hiring, the corollary should be an end to wage discrimination on the same basis. In 1963 the Equal Pay Act (EPA) which requires that females and males receive the same pay for the same job became federal law. However, the U.S. Bureau of the Census estimated that in 1985 a woman earned about 64 cents for every dollar earned by a man, and that figure has remained fairly steady since. How can this obvious disparity in pay continue with the definite provision of the EPA? The answer is found in the fact that women and men typically hold different jobs, and women's jobs remain undervalued and, hence, underpaid, in comparison to those held by men. Occupations are gender segregated and become gender stratified. The question then becomes how to assess jobs on the basis of skill level, effort, and responsibility. By this argument, equal pay should be judged in terms of "equal worth."

The issue of "comparable worth" has surfaced and has been interpreted through the provisions of Title VII. In a suit against the state of Washington, Helen Castelli charged that as a hospital secretary she was being paid much less than men employed by the state even though her job was "worth" much more. The same case brought evidence showing that laundry workers who are mostly female earned $150 less per month than truck drivers who are mostly male. In 1983, a federal court ordered the state of Washington to raise the wages of 15,500 employees in predominantly female occupations, which amounted to almost $1 billion in back pay (Macionis, 1987:311). Two years later a higher court overturned the decision with the argument that market forces created the inequity and the government has no responsibility to correct them.

Thus, even if objective measurements for comparable worth can be established, new interpretations suggest that the government should not interfere if the assumption is that "supply and demand" in a free-market economy determines wages. In this context, comparable worth is seen as a radical departure from traditional economic beliefs. Feldberg (1984) states that the notion of comparable worth issues a challenge to reevaluate all the work that women do, and it can ultimately call into question the gender-based hierarchy in American society, particularly as it systematically denies earnings to women compared to men. To date the courts have been inconsistent in decisions regarding comparable worth (Remick, 1984). Title VII and EPA notwithstanding, it is obvious the courts are at present reluctant to seriously confront comparable worth if it means "interfering" in economic principles which allow private employers to determine salary structures.

The viability of a law is demonstrated by how earnestly it is enforced. Although the Equal Employment Opportunity Commission (EEOC) was created to ensure that Title VII mandates are carried out, enforcement is primarily aimed at protecting minorities, particularly black men, rather than women. Freeman (1984:394) points out that EEOC essentially ignores the sex provision since there is fear it would dilute enforcement efforts for minorities. Fortunately, as Freeman notes, the National Organization for Women was formed in part to protect women's rights and directed its initial efforts at changing EEOC guidelines. But these efforts have since been seriously hampered during the Reagan years. Kennelly (1984) shows that cases of sex discrimination filed by the EEOC between 1981 and 1983 dropped by over 70%.

Education

As mentioned in Chapter 10, Title IX of the Educational Amendments Act of 1972 was enacted to prohibit sex discrimination in any school receiving federal assistance. Specifically, the key provision of Title IX states that

> No person in the United States, shall, on the basis of sex, be excluded from participation in, be denied the benefits of, or be subjected to discrimination under any educational program or activity receiving federal financial assistance.

Overall, this law is very comprehensive and has helped to at least alter, and in some instances eliminate, blatant discriminatory practices involving the sexes in relation to admissions, promotion and tenure of faculty, health care, dress codes, counseling, housing, formerly sex-segregated programs, financial aid, and organizational membership. In each of these cases, policies must be made in regard to equitable treatment of both sexes.

The courts have allowed for a number of exceptions to the law. Fraternities and sororities may still be sex-segregated, as can sex education classes. Housing and living arrangements can also be restricted by gender as long as comparable facilities are available for both men and women. However, the most notable exception concerns the number of educational institutions which remain exempt from Title IX provisions—those which do not receive federal funds as well as those public institutions which historically have always been sex-segregated. When considering *all* schools, those which fall under the Title IX mandate include previously integrated public schools and universities and most vocational, professional, and graduate schools (Thorkelson, 1985:485). A number of private, religious, and military institutions remain excluded.

Beyond the elimination of flagrant sex discrimination policies in schools, Title IX has impacted a great deal on athletic programs. Traditionally, budget allocations to female athletic activities have been minimal in comparison to monies provided for male sports. Before Title IX, few colleges offered female athletes adequate facilities or training, and no institution of higher education offered females athletic scholarships (Basow, 1986:135). In 1974, 60 colleges had athletic scholarships for women but by 1981, this had increased to 500 (Fox, 1984:251). Budgetary allotments for female athletics in schools have steadily increased as well, which may account for the incredible 600% increase in the number of girls in interscholastic athletics in secondary schools between 1971 and 1978 (Basow, 1986:134). Among Division I colleges, the average women's athletic budget was $7,000 in 1973. In 1981, it was $338,000. This is an impressive gain, but the figures must be tempered with Division I men's athletic programs which in 1981 was almost ten times that of women's programs, an astounding $3.2 million on the average (Basow, 1986:135).

The power behind Title IX lies in the potential to cut off federal funding to schools not in compliance with its dictates. But beyond voluntary efforts to reduce gender inequity in the schools, efforts at enforcement of Title IX have been severely curtailed. Title IX requires that any institution receiving federal monies over $50,000 must undergo a self-evaluation on how it measures up to gender equality. If found to be discriminatory, a formal plan must be submitted to rectify the problem. Richardson (1988:110) reports that as late as 1977, at the university level, approximately two-thirds had not submitted either the required compliance forms or the assurance statements indicating that a plan to tackle issues of sex discrimination was in progress.

The conservative political climate of the Reagan years and inconsistent court rulings have also hampered Title IX enforcement. A major setback occurred with a Supreme Court ruling which stated that if an educational institution was proven to be in violation of Title IX, only the specific program involved would have federal funding eliminated, and not the institution as a whole. Many programs which practice some form of sex discrimination, intentional or not, are allowed to continue in schools although they may directly violate the intent of Title IX. This is particularly true of athletic programs which can exist independent of school budgets since they are often supported by revenue from sports events and contributions from parents of team members and alumni.

Admittedly, Title IX is a major effort in dealing with gender inequity in education. Yet it is a formal, legal approach which must be assessed in light of the informal biases in education, particularly higher education. Men and women are segregated into different areas of study. High school females are discouraged from taking science and math courses which are required for certain majors in college, such as engineering or medicine. If discouraged from pursuing athletics in high school, even the limited scholarship opportunity for college athletics is unavailable. There are far fewer women than men in the higher ranks in academic institutions. As such, they have limited exposure and influence in serving as role models for aspiring students or for impacting social change. As Fox (1984:251) points out, "the presence and availability of female faculty members would broaden women's aspirations, increase their opportunities for interaction with faculty, and most critically, reduce the male dominance of educational practices and processes." Informal processes which operate to continue sex discrimination are powerful. Any legal approach needs to take into account the sources of bias emanating from informal sources as well.

Domestic Relations

Perhaps more than any other area, it is in domestic law where gender inequality is the most evident. We have already documented the impact of divorce on women and the failure of the law to do much about collecting child support or alimony when it is awarded. The fact that women gain custody of children who are minimally or not supported by their fathers helps to propel many divorced women into poverty. Between 1969 and 1981, the number of families in poverty increased by over five million. The increase is largely due to the number of female-headed poverty families. The female-headed family is the fastest growing family type in the United States (Shortridge, 1984:497).

Property division at the dissolution of the marriage has been partly responsible for this as well. Although the trend is to have individual attorneys work out the details of the divorce, these details must be considered in the light of overriding state laws. For example, only eight states[1] have community property laws. In a community property state, all property which is acquired during the marriage is jointly owned by the spouses; so in the event of divorce, each partner is entitled to half of the said property. Community property at least implicitly recognizes the value of the housewife role. Residing in a community property state, however, is not a panacea. Weitzman (1985) states that equal division of property, which originally was intended to help women, can actually hurt them. A woman is forced to sell her home, often the couple's only "real" property, and she and her children find themselves in less than desirable rental property, often in a new location. She and her children are dislocated from home, friends, schools, and other primary relationships at the very time they are most needed psychologically.

The other states are referred to as "common law" states with property belonging to the spouse in whose name it is held. Any property acquired during the marriage belongs to each spouse individually. Unless a house or car is also in the wife's name, the husband can lay claim to it in a divorce. Since the common law system has severely restricted and penalized women economically, most states (all but three of the 42 which do not have community property laws) have also passed "equitable distribution" laws. Rather than viewing property solely on the

---

[1] Arizona, California, Idaho, Louisiana, Nevada, New Mexico, Texas, and Washington.

basis of whose name it is in, courts are now considering a number of factors, such as length of the marriage, the contributions of both parties to child care and domestic functions, earning ability, age, health, and other resources (Thorkelson, 1985:489). Most important, this kind of arrangement takes into account the fact that marriage is an economic partnership where both wage earning and homemaking should be considered as contributions, even though the latter is unpaid (Freeman, 1984:383). This is at least an attempt to redress past abuses where the legal system puts women at a major disadvantage in divorce. But this must be tempered with the fact that regardless of the newer equitable distribution laws, women still get much less than half of marital property in divorce, many divorced women who are also single parents were not covered by such laws when their divorces were finalized, and community property is the exception rather than the rule.

In regard to Social Security, the housewife role is an economic liability. Women are unpaid for this role and do not contribute to disability or retirement funds for ensuring their future. If a woman is married less than ten years prior to divorce from or the death or her husband, she is not eligible for his benefits. All the years she put into child rearing and domestic duties are ignored. In 1984, the Retirement Equity Act was passed to deal with some of these issues and to make pension benefits fairer to women (Basow, 1986:273). However, statistics are dismal in indicating how poverty has become "feminized," particularly for elderly and black women. Inequities related to Social Security can be seen as partly responsible for this trend. The legal premise of the marital relationship is that husbands and wives have reciprocal but not equal rights. A husband is required to support his wife and children and in return a wife must provide services as companion, housewife, and mother (Freeman, 1984:382). It is left up to the individual couple to determine how these requirements are actualized. In some families the wife controls all household expenses and decides on how one or both salaries are apportioned. In others, husbands provide their wives with allowances and "pin money" to take care of household or personal needs. She may file for divorce if there is evidence of gross financial neglect, or he may do so for unkempt children, a dirty house, or if she refuses to have intercourse (Kanowitz, 1969). To date, about half of the states maintain that a husband cannot be brought up on charges of raping his wife. Sexual intercourse is seen as her duty and his right. Certainly the doctrine of reciprocity is largely unenforceable and rarely used as grounds for divorce today. Yet the courts consider this implicit contract as "so fundamental to public policy that any contract before or during marriage altering the nature of these reciprocal duties is void" (Freeman, 1984:382).

Given this kind of implicit contract, it is understandable that the courts have been inconsistent in efforts to prosecute cases of wife abuse. It is ironic that perhaps the most disheartening evidence that the courts continue to be gender biased is in the area of "domestic relations" which is also the most life threatening. We have seen how Western history reflects the belief that wives are expected to be controlled by their husbands with the use of physical force as an often acceptable means of control. The women's liberation movement has been helpful in publicizing the issue of wife abuse to the extent that there is at least a growing awareness of its incidence. This awareness has led to police training programs in family violence and the establishment of hotlines to provide emergency help and counseling. Judges are now handling cases of wife abuse with greater frequency, with all indications suggesting this trend will continue. The problem is that while societal disapproval of wife abuse has grown, judges have not rejected the traditional viewpoint that wives are to be controlled by husbands. Crites (1987:41) maintains that while more judges are assuring that the rights of abused wives are enforced, a significant number remain unwilling to implement the newer legislation protecting battered women. They are less likely to view wife abuse as criminal behavior and tend to take the side of the husband in what they define simply as a "domestic dispute." Justifications for judicial response in this manner are tied to historical beliefs concerning women and the family as well as which laws are viewed as the more important ones to enforce. Crites (1987:46-51) proposes several reasons these beliefs endure. First, judges are reluctant to issue temporary orders of protection, such as temporarily barring a husband from his home, because of the notion that the due process rights of the husband may be violated. In this sense, a husband's right to due process is more important that his wife's right to be protected from assault. Second, judges are reluctant to hear cases of domestic violence because the family itself is seen as sacrosanct, and its privacy should not be invaded. A "family matter" is not seen as legitimate for the courtroom.

Third, some judges believe that criminal charges against the husband would cause the family to dissolve or work a financial hardship. The abusive husband is protected over the wishes of the victim. Obviously, these judges have not considered how it is the violence which will destroy the family unit. Finally, and most disquieting, is the belief that it is the wife's behavior which caused the battering anyway, the classic "blaming the victim" ideology. Crites (1987:50) cites the case of an Ohio judge's comments to a woman who appeared in court to testify against her husband regarding his attacks on her. He told her to study the Bible and "try harder to be a good wife." The law is gradually changing to allow for more protection of battered wives. But enforcement will be hampered as long as judges maintain a stereotyped, traditional image of the husband-wife relationship.

Reproductive Rights

Until 1973, legal abortions could be performed in most states only if the continued pregnancy would endanger the life of the mother. This changed on January 22, 1973, with two landmark decisions by the Supreme Court. In Roe v. Wade and Doe v. Bolton, the Supreme Court voted seven to two in support of the right to privacy of the women involved in the cases. The states in question, Texas and Georgia, had failed to establish "any compelling interest" which would restrict abortions to the first trimester of pregnancy. Abortion in this instance would be between a woman and her physician. In the second trimester, when an abortion is deemed more dangerous, the state could exert control to protect the health of the mother (Bishop, 1984:42). A broadening of the legal right to an abortion was thus established, but the courts still have refused to consider it an absolute right.

Thom (1984) reports that the majority of both women and men (60% to 65%) do not support a constitutional ban on abortion. Yet since the 1973 decisions to legalize abortion, persistent campaigns have been waged to limit or eliminate this reproductive right of women. Tactics range from providing antiabortion films, commercials and brochures to picketing or boycotting hospitals where abortions or performed, and in the extreme, bombing clinics where women go as outpatients for abortions. It is difficult to judge the success of these campaigns. Public opinion appears to be against any tactic which would promote violence to achieve a goal. Legally, the evidence is mixed.

In 1983 the Supreme Court reaffirmed the 1973 decisions by ruling that second trimester abortions may be performed in other sites than hospitals since data clearly showed that outpatient clinics and other surgical facilities provide safe conditions. Also, a city ordinance requiring a physician to inform the woman that "the unborn child is a human life from the moment of conception" was struck down because the Roe v. Wade decision held that a "state may not adopt one theory of when life begins to justify its regulation of abortion. (Bishop, 1984:44). The same ordinance was unacceptable as well because it intruded on the discretion of the woman's physician. The fact that such an ordinance was put on the books *after* the right to seek a legal abortion was granted, demonstrates the tenacity of organized attempts to work around the law.

While this can be seen as a victory for reproductive rights, a major setback occurred in 1977 with the enactment of the Hyde Amendment which restricts funding for abortions for women who also receive Medicaid (unless the pregnancy is considered life threatening). Because Medicaid is the health insurance program for the very poor which is paid out of public monies, some supporters of the Hyde Amendment argue that the government should not be in the business of funding abortions. In 1980, a federal judge in New York ruled that a denial of Medicaid funds for medically necessary abortions was unconstitutional. If funds for therapeutic abortions were denied, a woman's religious freedom and right to privacy were impinged upon (Bishop 1984:45). Although he ordered the state government to resume funding, two weeks later the Supreme Court overturned this ruling, thereby upholding the constitutionality of the Hyde Amendment.

According to Williams (1978), with the Supreme Court reducing the availability of legal abortions to poor women, it may ultimately have an effect on access to abortions in general. And for poor women, "the existence of the right to choose an abortion is divorced from the realization of that right" (Williams, 1978:240). The impact of the Hyde Amendment is stated in Justice Thurgood Marshall's dissenting opinion.

> The enactments challenged here brutally coerce poor women to bear children society will scorn for every day of their lives. . . . I am appalled at the ethical bankruptcy of those who preach a "right to life" that means under present social policies, a bare existence in utter misery for so many poor women and their children. . . . The effect will be to regulate millions of people to lives of poverty and despair. (Cited in Bishop, 1984:45)

POLITICS

The ability to change the law to reflect equality and justice regarding the sexes is linked to the presence of women in legislative bodies at all governmental levels. In addition, once the law is changed, interpretation and enforcement must be consistent with gender equality. This also assumes that the women who serve the nation in their political roles view issues related to gender differently than men. Thus, voting behavior should mirror such differences. As we shall see, this assumption has been substantiated. However, women represent only a small minority of the political elites who wield power in the United States.

   Women are increasingly being elected to public office but not in the numbers necessary for achieving numerical equality with men. Poole and Zeigler (1985:151) indicate that of the 7,438 seats in the 50 state legislatures, only 13% were held by women by 1984. According to the National Women's Political Caucus this increased to 14% by 1985. Whereas in 1971 only 1% of big city mayors (population over 30,000) were women, by 1984 women held almost 9% of those public offices. While the rate of increase is significant, most of it occurred between 1971 and 1977, with only 2% of it between 1977 and 1984, an era of more conservative politics. Poole and Zeigler (1985:152) estimate that at this rate, it will be well into the next century before women would make up half the mayors of big cities. And even given this possibility, it is more important for long-term impact that women increase their numbers in state legislatures. At the rate they have been doing so, Poole and Zeigler (1985) suggest that a 50% male-female ratio may occur by the year 2000. Considering how close we are to that date, this forecast appears overly optimistic. Except for a decline in the years 1961 through 1969, women have been slowly increasing their numbers in Congress, specifically with expansion in the House of Representatives. As Table 13-1 indicates, the number of women in the House has gradually increased, with those in the Senate holding at 2 since 1979. Although increases have occurred, no clear, consistent growth pattern is evident. Note, too, that some of these seats were filled by women who completed the unexpired terms of their late husbands. These figures show that approximately 3% of the Congressional seats are held by women. Because of the seniority system in Congress, it will be some time before this small group gains prominence on important committees and exerts the influence necessary to see goals realized.

   Women have been appointed to high administrative positions, but again the growth pattern is inconsistent and unclear, indicating both gains and losses. Reagan has been criticized for being the first president in a decade who has failed to appoint more women to high level federal posts than his immediate predecessor. Basow (1986:266) reveals that by 1984 Reagan had appointed only 86 women to positions requiring Senate confirmation compared to the 98 appointed by Carter in the same time period. Reagan can be credited with being the first president to appoint a woman, Sandra Day O'Connor, as a justice to the Supreme Court. But as Lynn (1984:419) notes, this appointment lagged far behind public opinion. A Gallup Poll showed that 86% of those surveyed approved of a woman serving on the Supreme Court. Justice O'Connor's appointment came long after the public was willing to

TABLE 13-1.   Female Members of Congress: 1947-1988

CONGRESS	YEAR	SENATE	HOUSE
80th	1947-1948	0	8
81st	1949-1950	1	9
82nd	1951-1952	1	10
83rd	1953-1954	2	11
84th	1955-1956	1	16
85th	1957-1958	1	15
86th	1959-1960	1	16
87th	1961-1962	2	17
88th	1963-1964	2	11
89th	1965-1966	2	10
90th	1967-1968	1	11
91st	1969-1970	1	10
92nd	1971-1972	1	12
93rd	1973-1974	0	16
94th	1975-1976	0	19
95th	1977-1978	0	18
96th	1979-1980	1	16
97th	1981-1982	2	19
98th	1983-1984	2	21
99th	1985-1986	2	21
100th	1987-1988	2	23

Source: Congressional Directory (1987).

accept a female in this position. For other judgeships, Reagan awarded less than 10% to women compared to Carter's 15%. When women do achieve these top level positions, many feel isolated from decision-making routes because of lack of entrance into the exclusive all male club (Lynn, 1984:419).

Barriers to the Female Candidate

Public opinion has changed to the extent that there is now a willingness to elect qualified women to public office at all levels. Female elected and appointed officials have proven themselves in their competence, decisiveness, and fairness as they confront the issues of the day. Although the loss to the Republican Reagan-Bush ticket was overwhelming, the choice of a woman, Geraldine Ferraro, as a vice presidential candidate for the Democratic Party was significant. The Mondale-Ferraro ticket made it clear that women would no longer be relegated to behind the scenes positions. It cannot be said that prejudice against female candidates has been eliminated (Sloane, 1983), but only that there is growing public support for them. Yet women still find themselves barred from entering the political arena in large numbers.

Women are scarce in public office in part because few actively seek it. Socialization into gender roles which precludes political participation for women can be said to underlie this fact. Evidence for this is cited in a now classic study by Jeane Kirkpatrick (1976:411). She states that regardless of party, age, or candidate group, women have lower levels of ambition for public office than men. If politics demands a self-serving style and a high degree of competitiveness to be effective, men have the advantage. Women in public office appear to be more public-spirited and oriented to principles rather than narrower issues. Lynn and Flora (1977) characterize such an approach as amateurish and less effective for the style of American politics which has emerged. It is ironic that to be successful in "masculine" politics, strategies are called for which are less likely to serve broader public interests. But Randall (1982:86) does question these findings by suggesting that other research shows women in politics to be especially earnest and conscientious, traits which are certainly not compatible with amateurism. And at the local level, a later study by Merritt (1982) indicates that women are no less politically ambitious than men.

Whether differential socialization patterns restrict the supply of female candidates remains debatable. Githens and Prestage (1977) state that women may succumb to the tension created by being caught between ascribed and achieved status, thereby maintaining a marginal role. Marginality is psychologically debilitating and instrumental in preventing women from becoming candidates. If political office is attained, women may still be conditioned by feeling marginal. Kelley and Boutilier (1978, cited in Randall, 1982:85) point out that the critical factor in political potency is a sense of control over one's life-space. The activist woman who gains this mastery will find that political success can be hers. What this points out, then, is that socialization into the female gender role may initially be an inhibiting factor for women entering politics, but one which can be adequately dealt with to achieve political success.

Beyond the impact of socialization a major situational barrier to women in politics is the constraint imposed by being a mother and a wife. Women must contend with the potential for social disapproval if the public believes their children and husbands are being neglected in the quest for public office. Male candidates can begin their ascent in politics sooner in their careers than women. Even activist women who have a high degree of political saliency must often wait until their children are grown to reduce the risk of being labeled a neglectful mother. By earnestly starting their political careers later in life, women as a group have a difficult time catching up to men and seeking the higher public offices. A woman must also be mindful of the relationship with her husband who may be unwilling or unprepared to deal with his wife's candidacy. Some husbands play vital, supportive roles in promoting their wives' campaigns, but cultural proscriptions are likely to prevent men from enthusiastically carrying out such activities (Lynn, 1984:412).

Structural barriers also limit women in their political pursuits. To be viewed as realistic and eligible candidates for public office, both women and men must fall within a range of acceptability in terms of educational and occupational background. There are certain professions such as private law practice, journalism, and university teaching which are compatible with a political career. Celebrities in the fields of sports and acting have been drawn into the political arena. Such occupations offer visibility, flexibility, opportunities for developing communication skills, and substantial financial rewards, thus serving as significant training grounds for future politicians. We have already witnessed the financial and social effects of occupational segregation on women. Politically, such segregation hampers women from being recruited as candidates. On the positive side, women have made great inroads into a major source of political eligibility, the legal profession, if only at the lower levels. It is likely that the next decade will witness a rise in women seeking public office who are drawn from these ranks.

The Gender Gap

When women gained the right to vote in 1920 it was widely believed that womens' opinions regarding social and political issues differed considerably from those held by men and that such differences would be evident in voting behavior. For over half a century this belief remained unfounded; women, like men, tended to vote along class, ethnic and regional lines. By the early 1980s, however, a new political trend emerged, first showing up in the shift in party identification of women. By May of 1982, 55% of women and 49% of men identified themselves as Democrats. Only 34% of women identified themselves as Republican compared to 37% of men (Lynn, 1984:404). Women have shifted to the Democratic side at a faster rate than men. The political "gender gap" was born.

The gender gap phenomenon was so named after the 1980 presidential election which demonstrated a higher percentage of males voting for Ronald Reagan than females. In this election, Reagan won with eight percentage points' less support from women than from men (Abzug and Kelber, 1984:1). Abzug and Kelber also point out that within two years of his election, the gap had widened. Women were increasingly more opposed to Reagan's policies regarding the economy, foreign relations, environmental protection, and the treatment of the sexes. A poll conducted by *Parade* magazine shows that both sexes agreed that the two most important issues for 1984 were controlling nuclear weapons and controlling inflation. But women felt more strongly about both of these than men (Michaels, 1984:4). Frankovic (1982) suggests that the issues of war, peace, and the environment are major concerns which divide the sexes. Overall, she contends that women view Reagan more negatively than do men, and that this gender difference is a significant one.

If women and men are viewed in terms of those issues which have a differential impact on women, the gap may be wider. Older women who are better off financially are more in the Reagan camp than younger women who are struggling with economic uncertainty (Perlez, 1984). Opinion poll results show that there is widespread dissatisfaction with Reagan economic policies. Abzug and Kelber (1984:119) cite opinion poll statistics which reveal that when compared to men, women are more likely to disapprove of Reagan's handling of the economy and his efforts to reduce unemployment and inflation. Perhaps a more important fact is that a 1983 survey shows that 61% of women, compared to 53% of men, believed their families were worse off than when Reagan took office (Abzug and Kelber, 1984:119).

Whether these figures indicate that women will vote as a block on any one issue is still debatable. A surprising finding in this regard is that the gender gap is apparently not widened by what can be referred to as specifically "women's issues." Lynn (1984:408) suggests that age may be a more important factor than gender in some areas. Although political analysts believe that concerns such as reproductive rights and the Equal Rights Amendment may be more salient for women, younger men and women are equally supportive of them. Women are much more likely to support social programs which can impact on them, such as funding for day care, and are sympathetic to programs involved with helping the poor and disadvantaged (Michaels, 1984:4). It may be argued that this support is related to the economically disadvantageous position in which women find themselves. Yet when it comes to a reduced role of the federal government in spending, the sexes close ranks. Both women and men are reluctant to support more federal funding for both social and defense related programs (Michaels, 1984; Poole and Zeigler, 1985). Age and socioeconomic status are factors which may explain these findings and are likely to hamper the widening of the gender gap.

It may be that the gender gap will play a less prominent role in the politics of the 1990s, but it will certainly not be ignored. The Reagan years clearly demonstrated that males, particularly white males, were drawn to the mystique of "toughness" which he exuded. In his successful 1984 presidential campaign against Walter Mondale, Reagan's political strategists capitalized on the "cowboy" image, with one aide stating that "Reagan is a healthy dose of macho, and Mondale is part of the Brie-and-Chablis crowd. The Mondale people need to toughen the boy up" (quoted in Dowd, 1984). Put squarely on the defensive, the Democrats countered with citing Mondale's enjoyment of "masculine" activities such as fishing, hunting, and sports. "He likes to sit around and have a drink in the evening with his shoes off and a cigar in his mouth with his friends" (quoted in Dowd, 1984). Thus, both parties believed it necessary to use male stereotypes to encourage votes. The George Bush presidential campaign used the same successful tactics. It apparently made little difference that while elevating what "men do," an implicit disdain for the supposed opposite, what "women do" was also made. While the Reagan "man's man" image allowed solid support among males, women feared this very aura of toughness. Half of the women and only 36% of the men in a 1983 poll expressed concern that Reagan policies would result in war (Friedman, 1983). Specifically, overwhelming opposition came from black and Jewish women who felt that "Mr. Reagan lacks compassion and would too easily use military force" (Perlez, 1984:76). In recognizing this opposition and the impossibility of gaining votes from women on issues of equal rights, the politically astute Reagan camp based its appeal to women on economic issues and, as one aide stated, "keeping women from being scared about war" (Perlez, 1984:76).

This 1984 example highlights the fact that both parties understand that women have the potential for voting as a bloc if the right mix of issues and circumstances are present. Women are not a homogeneous group, but mobilization around issues of gender may occur. The Reagan era ushered in the idea of a gender gap. Whether that gap is increased will depend on how party leaders respond to the political power women are beginning to demonstrate and even take for granted. They cannot afford to ignore existing gender differences and will attempt to use them to the realization of their political goals. As the new President, George Bush already appears to be distancing himself from Reagan in that he is keenly mindful of the chasm Reagan created between the Republican party and certain groups, such as blacks. It remains to be seen if he can bridge that chasm and then extend a hand to women and mend the gender gap.

THE EQUAL RIGHTS AMENDMENT

Although the Equal Rights Amendment (ERA) to the United States Constitution was first introduced in Congress in 1923, and proposed yearly after that, Congress did not pass it until almost half a century later. The House of Representatives passed it with a vote of 354 to 23; the Senate approved it with a vote of 84 to 8. After passage by the Senate on March 22, 1972, the Ninety-Second Congress submitted it to the state legislatures for the three-fourths votes needed for ratification. The original deadline for ratification was in 1979, but ERA proponents managed to muster the support to get this extended until 1982. Despite ratification by 38 states, three additional votes were needed by 1982 when the deadline ran out. Since then, the ERA has been reintroduced yearly into Congress and Congress has not passed it again. Whereas, in this regard, history seems to be repeating itself, ERA proponents remain optimistic. The battle for ratification has enhanced their political sophistication and provided a basis of understanding for dealing with the forces which challenge them.

The complexity of issues surrounding the ERA is shrouded by its deceptively simple language. The complete text of the ERA is as follows:

Section 1. Equality of rights under the law shall not be denied or abridged by the United States or by any State on account of sex.
Section 2. The Congress shall have the power to enforce, by appropriate legislation, the provisions of this article.
Section 3. This Amendment shall take effect two years after the date of ratification.

When again passed by Congress, the state legislatures will have another seven years to ratify it. Once ratified, it will become the Twenty-Seventh Amendment to the Constitution.

Support for the ERA is wide and its passage is favored by a majority of both sexes. It has been part of the platform of both political parties and supported by presidents as diverse as Eisenhower, Kennedy, Johnson and Nixon. Almost 500 major organizations (with well over 50 million members), representing men and women with different interests and philosophies and number support it. This broad base of support is seen with organizations which include the National Education Association, the International Union of Electrical Radio and Machine Workers, the American Public Health Association, and the United Presbyterian Church. Yet even with this kind of public affirmation, the ERA has yet to be ratified.

During the ten year ratification process, a number of factors combined to defeat the ERA. It is not simply a matter of saying who is in favor of equality and who is not. Few would argue against the principle of equality, but many are suspicious of how equality is to be implemented. According to Mansbridge (1986:4), the death of the ERA was related to other changes which were occurring in American political attitudes. One had to do with the increased "legislative skepticism" concerning the U.S. Supreme Court's authority to review legislation. States feared that the Supreme Court would be harsh in reviewing efforts at implementation and balked at what they assumed would be undue interference in state proceedings.

The second change had to do with the growing power and organization of the New Right. Where once national defense and communism were targeted issues of the "old" Radical Right, the ERA became a focus for new attacks. Mansbridge (1986:5) states that "for many conservative Americans, the personal became political for the first time when questions of family, children, sexual behavior and women's roles became subjects of political debate." Aligned with fundamentalist churches and interpretations which made traditional homemakers sympathetic to the anti-ERA cause and anxious to retrieve what they believed was a lost status, the New Right mounted a massive effort against ratification. As Crawford (1980) indicates, the most ardent "soldiers" of the New Right army were homemakers. With opponents like Phyllis Schlafly fueling "nonissues" like unisex bathrooms and an end to alimony, enough fear and innuendo were generated which minimized viable debate on substantive issues such as the increasing economic disparity between men and women.

The STOP-ERA movement used religious rhetoric, stereotyped biological beliefs, and images of ERA supporters as mutinous radicals to sway women, in particular, to their cause. Marshall (1984:570) contends that the anti-ERA literature also embodies an ideology of antifeminism with three arguments that were continually brought up during the debates over ERA. These include

> the reaffirmation of divinely ordained sex differences, support for the traditional family as a necessary basis for the continuation of society, and the alignment of antifeminism with unselfish patriotism. The women's rights issue is thus cast as a moral battle over the basic institutions and values of American society.

These views are exemplified by those known as representing the "Moral Majority," such as the Reverend Jerry Falwell, who believes that the ERA is a "Satanic attack upon the family and the Bible." Falwell contends that ERA is an assault on the social fabric and is not a political issue at all, but a moral one (Childs, 1982:4). Feminists are blamed for challenging the traditional female role, but antifeminists are against ERA in part because of their distrust of men. Klatch (1987:136) argues that the full-time homemaker may be convinced that the ERA will abolish the requirement that the husband supports the wife, and if he finds another woman, he will be free of all responsibility to his former spouse. As Phyllis Schlafly warns, the most tragic effect of ERA would thus fall on the woman who has been a good wife and homemaker for decades, and who can now be turned out to pasture with impunity because a new, militant breed of liberationist has come along. (Cited in Klatch, 1987:137)

Such scare tactics were not only used against ERA ratification, but also served to heighten and reinforce conventional suspicion between the sexes.

During the ratification process, much confusion was generated over what ERA would actually change, augment, or accomplish. Whereas anti-ERA groups capitalized on this lack of understanding to help sow the seeds for its defeat, even interpretations among its supporters of what ERA would do were somewhat inconsistent. Some help in this regard comes from the seventeen states which already have equal rights amendments in their own constitutions. Feinberg (1986:4) provides the following information from several states which illustrate what a fully enacted ERA could mean. For example, although both parents are required in Texas to provide child support, the services of a housewife are counted in kind. In this way Texas recognizes the value of a mother's services not just in terms of financial contributions. Pennsylvania has a similar specification under its own equal rights amendment which has been interpreted to mean that a divorced mother is not required to work outside the home because her value as a homemaker is recognized. When Medicaid money for abortion was curtailed, Massachusetts and Connecticut ordered funding on privacy and other grounds. In Washington, same-sex marriage is still prohibited under their equal rights amendment. And state equal rights amendments do not protect males for committing sex crimes. These examples give some indication of how equal rights have been carried out in the various states and can serve as a basis for considering the impact of a federal ERA. Organizations such as Common Cause, the National Organization for Women, and the American Civil Liberties Union have provided partial answers to the unsettling questions which many have raised regarding ERA. The summary outlined below is indicative of some probable interpretations of ERA.

1. Women will not be deprived of alimony, child custody, or child support. However, men will be eligible for alimony under the same conditions as women, as they are already in one-third of the states.
2. Individual circumstances and need will determine domestic relations and community property. ERA does not require both spouses to contribute equal financial support to the marriage. But the law will recognize the homemaker's contribution to the support of the family. Social custom and interpersonal relations in a marriage remain a matter of individual choice.
3. ERA will fit into existing constitutional structures regarding privacy. The sexes will continue to be segregated with regard to public restrooms, sleeping quarters at coeducational colleges, prison dormitories, and military barracks.
4. It will be illegal to enact "protective" labor regulations. Such laws have been shown to restrict employment opportunities by keeping women out of those jobs offering higher pay and advancement.

5. ERA will allow meaningful choices to women in terms of family, careers, or both, as well as any alternatives to these roles. Those who choose to be housewives will not be deprived in any way.

6. Since ERA applies to government practices only, it cannot have a direct effect on the private sector's credit practices. However, it will have a long-range effect on lessening discrimination; and it will abolish sex discrimination in government credit programs such as loans from the Federal Housing Administration and the Veteran's Administration.

7. ERA will nullify state laws which have greater penalties for one sex or the other when committing the same crime. But it will not invalidate laws which punish rape, since the Senate has already stated that such laws are designed to protect women in a way that they are uniformly distinct from men.

8. The ERA will require that all the benefits of publicly supported education be available to women and men on an equal basis. Enforcement of Title IX has been uneven. ERA will ensure against discrimination in admissions, curriculum, facilities, counseling, and placement.

9. Women will be subject to the draft, if there is one. However, Congress can provide exemptions applying equally to men and women, such as a parent with a dependent child. Exemptions based solely on sex would be prohibited. Women will be permitted to enlist in the active services if they meet the entrance requirements. Only those who meet the high physical demands of combat duty would be eligible for such assignments. At the height of the Viet Nam war, only 14% of all men in the military served in combat zones.[2]

It is this last issue of women in combat which generated the most controversy during ratification. Feinberg (1986:13) notes that the definition and rules relating to combat have changed over time and for the different services. There is no evidence that women are incapable of performing in combat, and under ERA women would be subject to combat according to qualifications and service requirements as men now are. ERA would eliminate the barriers to women's full participation in the armed services. This means that they will no longer be discriminated against in terms of assignment or promotion and would be entitled the same benefits as men, such as in education and health care, when they leave active duty.

The interpretation of women being subject to the draft and assuming combat roles varies with pro-ERA literature. Contrary to the position of Common Cause, Mansbridge (1986:83) suggests that most of the pamphlets in support of ERA state that it would *not* require Congress to send women into combat. But since this was never explained in legal terms, readers were unsure about the claims which were being made. ERA supporters also remained unaware of the amount of discretion the military has in assigning women. This information could have been used to a political advantage. But as Mansbridge (1986:84) notes,

> Instead, the speakers told their audiences of the infinitesimal chance that any individual woman could ever be drafted for combat, of the fact that Congress already had the power to send women into combat, of the possible consequences in a nuclear age of a military made up exclusively of men, and, most powerfully, that full citizenship required full responsibility.

[2]Adapted from a Common Cause pamphlet on questions and answers to the proposed ERA (n.d.)

On the issue of women in combat, the egalitarian position was favored over the deferential position, although there were merits and liabilities in both. Whether a clearer legal statement on women in the military would have helped ERA ratification remains debatable. It may be that a future Congress will insist on a constitutional exception to women in combat if they are to pass another ERA. Although unsure about how other feminists approach this issue, Mansbridge opposes such specific provisions that would permanently exempt the draft or combat from ERA coverage. As she explains,

> After 1976, when the practical costs of losing diminished, I would have been inclined to gamble on an egalitarian interpretation, on the grounds that if one is going to fight for a symbol, it is better to lose fighting for a good symbol than to win fighting for a bad one. (Mansbridge 1986:89)

FEMINISM IN THE 1990S

The New Right hailed the defeat of the ERA as a defeat for feminism in general and a harbinger of returning women to the pedestal. The inability to garner enough support in the last three states pointed out not only the power of the New Right but the internal problems which were seen as hampering the feminist movement. The movement of the 1960s and 1970s focused on the root causes of gender inequality; yet in doing so, issues surrounding motherhood and family were given less priority. Minority women in particular felt overlooked in the quest for economic parity with men and the inclusion of women in higher level positions. The movement itself was spawned by women who wanted to escape the shackles of the feminine mystique and gain a new sense of independence. To a great extent, this has been accomplished. The challenge ahead is to integrate this new found independence with continuing concerns related to marriage, motherhood and parenting.

The confrontational tactics which worked 20 years ago may be less effective today. Friedan (1981, 1983) now argues that the feminine mystique has been transcended and that the male model of equity has been taken as far as it can go. The model needed today must encompass female experience and values, which men can also share. Recognizing that the early movement was most vulnerable on the family issue, a postfeminist generation needs to address the fact that the family is the "new frontier" and that feminist issues of the second stage will be joined. The politics of accommodation are starkly different from the old politics of separatism, and Freidan's model has been criticized by some current leaders of the movement (Wickenden 1986:25). In the 1970s Chafe (1974:515) argued that a major obstacle faced by the women's movement is that of internal dissension that existed despite the advantages of a decentralized structure. This dissension mainly concerned visions of the family. Considering the criticisms leveled at Friedan's contemporary approach to feminism, Chafe's words may be seen as haunting the movement today.

On the positive side, however, the movement is reconciled to the fact that women do not have to be in full agreement with one another to work for feminist goals. Chavez (1987) notes that the basic questions which inspired the movement over 20 years ago have been resolved, but as has been documented throughout this book, this has resulted in women now being confronted with new issues surrounding home, children, mates, and careers. It has also produced an atmosphere where discrimination is subtler and less easy to document. The decentralized structure may provide the very catalyst for the feminist movement to work on the myriad of issues confronting women today. Local feminist groups can target specific concerns which they deem most critical, such as delivering the message to area corporations that maternity leave or adequate day care are necessities. They may lobby for safe homes for abused women or work with other organizations to deal with the problem of violence within families. The National Organization for Women will continue to work for broader political goals and will spearhead the next ERA campaign.

Although tactics like these are hallmarks of the earlier movement, they are approached today with a more sophisticated understanding of the political intricacies involved and greater knowledge and skill in how to deal with opponents. The 1980s witnessed a rise in antifeminism coupled with the advance of a New Right allied with the conservative politics of the nation. A backlash occurred which tried

> to make real problems of work and family go away by pushing us back to traditional solutions we know won't work. It attempts to redirect our energies away from equalizing and humanizing our world, by dismissing feminism's accomplishments and making our goals seem impossible. Its cruelest side is that it plays on things some women value most—their legitimate desire to have families. . . . It implies that for women there must be a choice between equality and humanity, between work and family. (Chodorow et al., 1984:102)

In confronting the backlash, the feminist movement is being reenergized. Feminism in the 1990s will be diverse in programs, tactics, and goals. With a heightened degree of political sophistication, that very diversity will contribute to the strength of the movement.

References

ABEL, GENE, JUDITH BECKER, and LINDA SKINNER. 1980. "Aggressive behavior and sex." *Psychiatric Clinics of North America* 3(2):133–51.

ABELSON, H. I., R. COHEN, D. SCHRAYER, and M. RAPPEPORT. 1973. *National Commission on Marijuana and Drug Abuse: Drug Use in America: Problems in Perspective*. Washington, D.C.: U.S. Government Printing Office.

ABZUG, BELLA, and MIM KELBER. 1984. *Gender Gap: Bella Abzug's Guide to Political Power for American Women*. Boston: Houghton-Mifflin.

ALDRIDGE, DELORES P. 1978. "Interracial marriages: Empirical and theoretical considerations." *Journal of Black Studies* 8(March):355–68.

ALKIM, V. BAHADIR. 1968. *Anatolia I*. Tr. James Hogarth. New York: World.

ALLOTT, SUSAN. 1985. "Soviet rural women: Employment and family life." In Barbara Holland (ed.), *Soviet Sisterhood*. Bloomington, IN: Indiana University.

ALMQUIST, ELIZABETH, and SHIRLEY ANGRIST. 1971. "Role model influences on college women's career aspirations." In Athena Theodore (ed.), *The Professional Woman*. Cambridge, MA: Schenkman.

ALSBROOK, LARRY. 1976. "Marital communication and sexism." *Social Casework* 57(October):517–22.

AMIR, NEBACHEM. 1971. *Patterns of Forcible Rape*. Chicago: University of Chicago.

ANDERSON, KAREN. 1981. *Wartime Women: Sex Roles, Family Relations and the Status of Women during World War II*. Westport, CT: Greenwood.

ANGRIST, SHIRLEY S., and ELIZABETH ALMQUIST. 1975. *Careers and Contingencies: How College Women Juggle with Gender*. New York: Dunellen.

ARAFAT, J., and G. YORBURG. 1973. "On living together without marriage." *Journal of Sex Research* 9(May):97–106.

ARIZPE, LOURDES. 1971. "Women in the informal labor sector: The case of Mexico City." In Wellesley Editorial Committee (eds.), *Women and National Development: The Complexities of Change*. Chicago: University of Chicago.

ARTHUR, MARILYN B. 1984. "Early Greece: The origins of the Western attitude toward women." In John Peradotto and J.P. Sullivan (eds.), *Women in the Ancient World: The Arethusa Papers*. Albany: SUNY.

Association of American Colleges. 1982. "The classroom climate: A chilly one for women?" Project on the Status and Education of Women. Washington, D.C.: Association of American Colleges.

ASTIN, A. W. 1984. "Freshman characteristics and attitudes." *Chronicle of Higher Education* 16(January):15–16.

ASTRACHAN, ANTHONY. 1986. *How Men Feel: Their Response to Women's Demands for Equality and Power*. Garden City: Doubleday (Anchor).

ATWATER, LYNN. 1982. *The Extramarital Connection: Sex, Intimacy, Identity*. New York: Irvington.

BACHRACH, JUDY. 1985. "What goes with scrambled eggs and toast? The professional problems of Pauley, Shriver and Lunden." *SAVVY* (November):46–50.

BACKETT, KATHRYN C. 1982. *Mothers and Fathers*. New York: St. Martin's.

BAKER, HUGH D.R. 1979. *Chinese Family and Kinship*. New York: Columbia University.

BAKER, M. JOYCE. 1980. *Images of Women in Film: The War Years, 1941–1945*. Ann Arbor: UMI Press and University Microfilms International.

BALSDON, JOHN. 1962. *Roman Women: Their History and Habits*. New York: Barnes and Noble.

BALSWICK, JACK, and CHARLES PEEK. 1971. "The inexpensive male: A tragedy of American Society." *The Family Coordinator* 20:363–68.

BANDURA, ALBERT. 1973. *Aggression: A Social Learning Analysis*. Englewood Cliffs: Prentice-Hall.

BANDURA, ALBERT, and RICHARD H. WALTERS. 1963. *Social Learning and Personality Development*. New York: Holt, Rinehart & Winston.

BANNER, LOIS W. 1984. *Women in Modern America: A Brief History*. San Diego: Harcourt Brace Jovanovich.

BARASH, DAVID P. 1982. *Sociobiology and Behavior*. New York: Elsevier.

BARCUS, F. EARLE. 1983. *Images of Life on Children's Television Sex Roles, Minorities and Families*. New York: Praeger.

BARRY, KATHLEEN. 1975. "A view from the doll corner." In Elizabeth Steiner Maccia (ed.), *Women and Education*. Springfield, IL: Charles C. Thomas.

BASHAM, A. L. 1959. *The Wonder that Was India*. New York: Grove.

BASOW, SUSAN A. 1984. "Ethnic group differences in educational achievement in Fiji." *Journal of Cross-Cultural Psychology* 15:435–51. 1986. *Gender Stereotypes: Traditions and Alternatives*. (2nd ed.) Belmont, CA: Wadsworth.

BECKETT, J. 1976. "Working wives: A racial comparison." *Social Work* 21(November): 463–71.

BEDDOE, DEIRDRE. 1983. *Discovering Women's History: A Practical Manual*. London: Pandora.

BEER, WILIAM R. 1983. *Househusbands: Men and Housework in American Families*. New York: Praeger.

BELKAOUI, AHMED, and JANICE M. BELKAOUI. 1976. "A comparative analysis of the roles portrayed by women in print advertisements: 1958, 1970, 1972." *Journal of Market Research* 13:168–72.

BELL, ALAN P., and MARTIN S. WEINBERG. 1978. *Homosexualities: A Study of Diversity Among Men and Women*. New York: Simon and Schuster.

BELLINGER, DAVID C., and JEAN BERKO GLEASON. 1982. "Sex differences in parental directives to young children." *Sex Roles* 8:1123–1139.

BELSKY, JAY, and BRENT C. MILLER. 1986. "Adolescent fatherhood in the context of the transition to parenthood." In Arthur B. Elster and Michael E. Lamb, (eds.), *Adolescent Fatherhood*. Hillsdale, NJ: Lawrence Erlbaum.

BEM, SANDRA L. 1974. "The measurement of psychological androgyny." *Journal of Consulting and Clinical Psychology* 42:155–62. 1975. "Sex role adaptability: One consequence of psychological androgyny." *Journal of Personality and Social Psychology* 31:634–43.

BEM, SANDRA L., and DARYL J. BEM. 1970. "Case study of a nonconscious ideology: Training the woman to know her place." In D. J. Bem (ed.), *Beliefs, Attitudes and Human Affairs*. Belmont, CA: Brooks and Cole.

BENNETT, ANNE McGREW. 1974. "Overcoming the Biblical and traditional subordination of women." *Radical Religion* 1(2):26–31.

BENSTON, MARGARET. 1971. "The political economy of women's liberation." In Edith Hashino Altbach (ed.), *From Feminism to Liberation*. Cambridge, MA: Schenkman.

BENTLER, P. M., and M. D. NEWCOMB. 1978. "Longitudinal study of marital success and failure." *Journal of Consulting and Clinical Psychology* 46:1053–70.

BERG, BARBARA J. 1987. "Good news for mothers who work." In Ollie Pocs and Robert H. Walsh (eds.), *Marriage and Family Annual Editions*. Guilford, CT: Duskin.

BERK, RICHARD A., and SARAH F. BERK. 1979. *Labor and Leisure at Home: Content and Organization of the Household Day*. Beverly Hills, CA: Sage.

BERNARD, JESSIE. 1971. *Women and the Public Interest*. Chicago: Aldine and Atherton. 1972. *The Future of Marriage*. New York: World. 1975. "The future of motherhood." *Penguinews* (August). 1981. The Female World. New York: The Free Press. 1982. "The two marriages." In Jeffrey P. Rosenfeld (ed.), *Relationships: The Marriage and Family Reader*. Glenview, IL: Scott, Foresman.

BERSCHEID, E., and E. WALSTER. 1974. "Physical attractiveness." In L. Berkowitz (ed.), *Advances in Experimental Social Psychology*. New York: Academic Press.

BEST, RAPHAELA. 1983. *We've Got all the Scars: What Boys and Girls Learn in Elementary School*. Bloomington: Indiana University.

BIANCHI, S., and D. SPAIN. 1983. "American women: Three decades of change." *Special Demographic Analysis* CD3–80–8 (August). Washington, D.C.: U.S. Bureau of the Census.

BILLINGSLEY, ANDREW. 1970. "Black families and white social science." *Journal of Social Issues* 26:132–33.

BIRD, CAROLINE. 1971. "The case against marriage." *New Woman* (September). 1975. "The case against marriage." In Kenneth C.W. Kammeyer, *Confronting the Issues, Sex Roles, Marriage and the Family*. Boston: Allyn and Bacon.

BIRD, GLORIA W., GERALD A. BIRD, and MARGUERITE SCUGGS. 1984. "Determinants of family task sharing: A study of husbands and wives." *Journal of Marriage and the Family* 46(May):345–55.

BIRKE, LYNDA. 1986. *Women, Feminism and Biology: The Feminist Challenge*. New York: Metheun.

BIRNBAUM, JUDITH ABELEW. 1975. "Life patterns and self-esteem in gifted family-oriented and career-committed women." In Martha T. Schuch Mednick, Sandra Schwartz Tangri, and Lois Wladis Hoffman (eds.), *Women and Achievement: Social and Motivational Analyses.* New York: Halstead.

BISHOP, NADEAN. 1984. "Abortion: The controversial choice." In Jo Freeman (ed.), *Women: A Feminist Perspective.* Palo Alto, CA: Mayfield.

BLACKWELL, JAMES E. 1985. *The Black Community.* New York: Harper and Row.

BLAU, FRANCENE. 1978. "The data on women workers, past, present and future." In Ann Stromberg and Shirley Harkness (eds.), *Women Working: Theories and Fact.* Palo Alto, CA: Mayfield.

BLAU, FRANCENE, and M. A. FERBER. 1985. "Women in the labor market: The last twenty years." In L. Larwood, A. Stromberg, and B. Gutek (eds.), *Women and Work: An Annual Review, Vol. I.* Beverly Hills, CA: Sage.

BLOCK, JEANNE H. 1979. "Another look at sex differentiation in the socialization behavior of mothers and fathers." In J. A. Sherman and F. L. Denmark (eds.), *The Psychology of Women: Future Directions in Research.* New York: Psychological Dimensions. 1984. *Sex Role Identity and Ego Development.* San Francisco: Jossey-Bass.

BLOOD, ROBERT O., JR., and DONALD M. WOLFE. 1960. *Husbands and Wives: The Dynamics of Married Living.* New York: The Free Press.

BLOTNICK, SRULLY. 1986. "Dangerous times for middle managers." *SAVVY* (May):33–37.

BLUM, L. 1987. "Possibilities and limits of the comparable worth movement." *Gender & Society* 1(4):380–99.

BONEPARTH, ELLEN. 1986. "In the land of the patriarchs: Public policy on women in Israel." In Lynn B. Iglitzen and Ruth Ross (eds.), *Women in the World, 1975–1985, The Women's Decade.* Santa Barbara, CA: ABC-Clio.

BOOTH, A. 1979. "Does wives' employment cause stress for husbands?" *Family Coordinator* 28: 445–49.

The Boston Women's Health Book Collective. 1984. *The New Our Bodies, Our Selves.* New York: Simon and Schuster.

BOWEN, GARY LEE, and DENNIS K. ORTHNER. 1983. "Sex role congruency and marital quality." *Journal of Marriage and the Family* 45(February):223–30.

BOWMAN, HENRY A., and GRAHAM B. SPANIER. 1978. *Modern Marriage.* New York: Mc-Graw-Hill.

BOZETT, FREDERICK W. 1985. "Gay men as fathers." In Shirley M. H. Hanson and Frederick W. Bozett (eds.), *Dimensions of Fatherhood.* Beverly Hills, CA: Sage.

BRANNON, ROBERT. 1976. "The male sex role: Our culture's blueprint of manhood and what it's done for us lately." In D. David and R. Brannon (eds.), *The 49% Majority.* Reading, MA: Addison-Wesley.

BRAWLOWE, MARY. 1982. "Advertising world's portrayal of women is starting to shift." *The Wall Street Journal,* October 28:33.

BRENTON, MYRON. 1966. *The American Male.* Greenwich, CT: Fawcett.

BRIERE, J., S. CORNE, M. RUNTA, and N. MALAMUTH. 1984. "The rape arousal inventory: Predicting actual and potential sexual aggression in a university population." Paper presented at the meeting of the American Psychological Association, Toronto, Canada (August).

BRINKERHOFF, DAVID B., and LYNN K. WHITE. 1988. *Sociology.* St. Paul, MN: West.

BRINN, JANET, KATHEY KRAEMER, and JOEL S. WARM. 1984. "Sex-role preferences in four age levels." *Sex Roles* 11:901–09.

BRONZAFT, ARLENE L. 1974. "College women want a career, marriage and children." *Psychological Reports* 35(December):1031–34.

BROPHY, JERE E. 1977. *Child Development and Socialization.* Chicago: Science Research.

BROVERMAN, I., D. M. BROVERMAN, F. E. CLARKSON, P. S. ROSENKRANTZ, and S. R. VOGEL. 1970. "Sex-role stereotypes and clinical judgements of mental health." *Journal of Consulting and Clinical Psychology* 34:1–7.

BROWN, P., and R. MANELA. 1978. "Changing family roles: Women and divorce." *Journal of Divorce* 1:315–28.

BROWNING, GENIA. 1985. "Soviet politics: Where are the women?" In Barbara Holland (ed.), *Soviet Sisterhood.* Bloomington: Indiana University.

BROZAN, NADINE. 1986. "Feminist says sexual equality in Israel is illusory." *New York Times,* February 21:A18.

BRYANT, ANITA. 1976. *Bless this House.* New York: Bantam.

BUMPASS, LARRY, and R. RINDFUSS. 1979. "Children's experience of marital disruption." *American Journal of Sociology* 85(July):49–65.

BUNCH, C. 1975. "Lesbians in revolt." In M. Myron and C. Bunch (eds.), *Lesbianism and the Women's Movement.* Oakland, CA: Diana Press.

BURKETT, ELINOR C. 1978. "Indian women and white society: The case of sixteenth century Peru." In *Latin American Women: Historical Perspectives.* Westport, CT: Greenwood.

BUSS, DAVID M. 1985. "Human mate selection." *American Scientist, Journal of Sigma Xi* 73:47–51.

BUSS, DAVID M., and MICHAEL BARNES. 1986. "Preferences in human mate selection." *Journal of Personality and Social Psychology* 50:559–70.

CAIN, G. G. 1984. "Women and work: Trends in time spent in housework." University of Wisconsin/Madison, Institute on Research on Poverty. Paper No. 747–84.

CALDWELL, M. A., and L. A. PEPLAU. 1984. "The balance of power in lesbian relationships." *Sex Roles* 10:587–99.

CAMPBELL, A., P. E. CONVERSE, and W. L. RODGERS. 1975. *The Quality of American Life.* Ann Arbor, MI: ISR Social Science Archive.

CAMPBELL, D'ANN. 1984. *Women at War with America: Private Lives in a Patriotic Era.* Cambridge, MA: Harvard University.

CANCIAN, FRANCESCA M. 1986. "The feminization of love." *Signs* 11:692–709.

CARLSON, NEIL R. 1977. *Physiology of Behavior.* Boston: Allyn and Bacon.

CARMODY, DENISE L. 1979. *Women and World Religions.* Nashville: Abingdon Press.

CARROLL, RAMONA C. 1984. "The Lord is my mother." *Lutheran Women* (February).

CARTER, H., and P. C. GLICK. 1976. *Marriage and Divorce: A Social and Economic Study.* (Rev. ed.) Cambridge: Harvard University.

CASEY, KATHLEEN. 1976. "The cheshire cat: Reconstructing the experience of medieval woman." In Bernice A. Carroll (ed.), *Liberating Women's History: Theoretical and Critical Essays.* Urbana: University of Illinois.

CASHION, BARBARA G. 1982. "Female-headed families: Effects on children and clinical implications." *Journal of Marital and Family Therapy* (April):77–85.

CATTIN, PHILIPPE, and SUBHASH C. JAIN. 1979. "Content analysis of children's commercials." In N. Beckwith, M. Houston, R. Mittelstaedt, K. B. Monroe, and S. Ward (eds.), *Educators' Conference Proceedings.* Chicago: American Marketing Association.

CAZENAVE, NOEL A. 1979. "Middle-income black father: An analysis of the provider role." *The Family Coordinator* 28(October):583–93. 1981. "Black men in America: The quest for 'Manhood'." In Harriet Pipes McAdoo (ed.), *Black Families*. Beverly Hills, CA: Sage. 1983. "Black male-black female relationships: The perceptions of 155 middle-class black men." *Family Relations* 32:341–50.

CEULEMANS, MIEKE, and G. FAUCONNIER. 1979. "Mass Media: The image, role and social conditions for women." Reports and Papers on Mass Communication #84, UNESCO, Paris.

CHAFE, WILLIAM. 1972. *The American Woman: Her Changing Social, Economic and Political Roles, 1920–1970*. New York: Oxford University. 1974. "Feminism in the 1970's." *Dissent* 21(Fall):508–17. 1977. *Women and Equality: Changing Patterns in American Culture*. New York: Oxford University.

CHANEY, ELSA M. 1979. *Supermadre: Women in Politics in Latin America*. Austin: University of Texas.

CHANG, P., and A. DEINARD. 1982. "Single father caretakers: Demographic characteristics and adjustment process." *American Journal of Orthopsychiatry* 52:236–43.

CHARLTON, SUE ELLEN M. 1984. *Women in Third World Development*. Boulder: Westview.

CHAVEZ, LYDIA. 1987. "Women's movement, its ideals accepted, faces subtler issues." *New York Times*, July 17:A10.

CHERLIN, ANDREW. 1981. *Marriage, Divorce and Remarriage*. Cambridge: Harvard University Press.

CHESLER, PHYLLIS. 1972. *Women and Madness*. Garden City, NY: Anchor Press/Doubleday.

CHILD, IRWIN, ELMER POTTER, and ESTELLE LEVINE. 1960. "Children's textbooks and personality development: An exploration in the social psychology of education." In Morris L. Haimowitz, and Natalie Reader Haimowitz (eds.), *Human Development: Selected Readings*. New York: Crowell.

CHILDS, MARJORIE. 1982. *Fabric of the ERA: Congressional Intent*. Smithtown, NY: Exposition.

CHIRIBOGA, D. A., and M. THURNHER. 1980. "Marital lifestyles and adjustments to separation." *Journal of Divorce* 3:379–90.

CHMAJ, BETTY E. 1972. "It ain't me babe! or is it? American women through the eyes of the counter-culture music, films." In *Image, Myth and Beyond (American Women and American Studies, 2)*. Pittsburgh: KNOW.

CHODOROW, NANCY. 1978. *The Reproduction of Mothering: Psychoanalysis and the Sociology of Gender*. Berkeley: University of California.

CHODOROW, NANCY, DEIDRE ENGLIS, ARLIE HOCHSCHILD, KAREN PAIGE, ANN SWIDLER, and NORMA WINKLER. 1984. "Feminism 1984: Taking stock of an uncertain future." *MS.* (January):102.

CIERNIA, JAMES R. 1985. "Myths about male midlife crises." *Psychological Reports* 56:1003–07.

CLAVAN, SYLVIA, and ETHEL VATTER. 1972. "The affiliated family: A continued analysis." *The Family Coordinator* 21(October):499.

COHEN, LUCY M. 1973. "Women's entry to the professions in Columbia: Selected characteristics." *Journal of Marriage and the Family* 35(May):322–30.

COKER, DANA ROSENBERT. 1984. "The relationships among gender concepts and cognitive maturity in preschool children." *Sex Roles* 10(January):19–31.

COLE, CHARLES LEE. 1977. "Cohabitation in social context." In Roger W. Libby and Robert N. Whitehurst (eds.), *Marriage and Alternatives: Exploring Intimate Relationships*. Glenview, IL: Scott Foresman.

COLEMAN, JAMES S. 1961. *The Adolescent Society: The Social Life of the Teenager and Its Impact on Education*. Glencoe, IL: The Free Press.

COLEMAN, MARILYN and LAWRENCE H. GANONG. 1985. "Love and sex role stereotypes: Do macho men and feminine women make better lovers." *Journal of Personality and Social Psychology* 49:170–76.

COLLARD, E. D. 1964. "Achievement motive in the four-year-old child and its relationship to achievement expectancies of the mother." *Ph. D Dissertations*: University of Michigan.

COLLINS, RANDALL. 1975. *Conflict Sociology*. New York: Academic Press. 1979. *The Credential Society: An Historical Sociology of Education and Stratification*. New York: Academic Press.

Congressional Directory. 1987. 100th Congress. Washington, D.C.: U.S. Government Printing Office.

COOK, ALICE. 1980. "Collective Bargaining as a strategy for achieving equal opportunity and equal day: Sweden and West Germany." In Ronnie S. Ratner (ed.), *Equal Employment Policy for Women*. Philadelphia: Temple University Press.

COSER, LEWIS A., and ROSE LAUB COSER. 1982. "The housewife and her greedy family." In Jeffrey P. Rosenfeld (ed.), *Relationships: The Marriage and Family Reader*. Glenview, IL: Scott Foresman.

COTT, NANCY, and ELIZABETH PLECK. 1979. *A Heritage of Her Own: Toward a New Social History of American Women*. New York: Simon and Schuster.

COURTNEY, ALICE E., and SARAH WERNICK LOCKERETZ. 1971. "A woman's place: An analysis of the roles portrayed by women in magazine advertisements." *Journal of Marketing Research* 8:92.

COURTNEY, ALICE E., and THOMAS W. WHIPPLE. 1983. *Sex Stereotyping in Advertising*. Lexington, MA: Lexington Books.

COVALT, PATRICIA. 1982. "If real men don't eat quiche, do real men go through menopause?" Paper for Sociology of Sex Roles, St. Louis College of Pharmacy. (November 22).

CRAWFORD, ALAN. 1980. *Thunder on the Right*. New York: Pantheon.

CRITES, LAURA L. 1987. "Wife abuse: The judicial record." In Laura L. Crites and Winifred L. Hepperle (eds.), *Women, the Courts and Equality*. Beverly Hills, CA: Sage.

CROLL, ELIZABETH. 1981. *The Politics of Marriage in Contemporary China*. Cambridge: Cambridge University. 1983. *Chinese Women since Mao*. Armonk, NY: M.E. Sharpe.

CROVITZ, ELAINE, and ANNE STEINMANN. 1980. "A decade later: Black-white attitudes toward women's familial role." *Psychology of Women Quarterly* 5:170–76.

CULLEY, JAMES D., and REX BENNETT. 1976. "Selling women, selling blacks." *Journal of Communication* 26:160–74.

DAHRENDORF, RALF. 1959. *Class and Class Conflict in Industrial Society*. Stanford, CA: Stanford University.

DALY, MARY. 1975. *The Church and the Second Sex*. New York: Harper and Row. 1978. *Gyn/Ecology: The Metaethics of Radical Feminism*. Boston: Beacon.

DARNTON, NINA. 1985. "Women and stress on job and at home." *New York Times* August 8:C1.

DAVIDSON, E. S., A. YASUNA, and A. TOWER. 1979. "The effects of television cartoons on sex-role stereotyping in young girls." *Child Development* 50: 597–600.

DAVIS, ELIZABETH GOULD. 1971. *The First Sex*. New York: Penguin.

DAVIS, KEITH E. 1985. "Near and dear: Friendship and love compared." *Psychology Today* 19(February):22–30.

DAVIS, O., and S. SLOBODIAN. 1967. "Teacher behavior toward girls and boys during first grade reading instruction." *American Educational Research Journal* 4:261–69.

DEAUX, KAY, and BRENDA MAJOR. 1987. "Putting gender into context: An interactive model of gender-related behavior." *Psychological Review* 94(3):369–89.

DEBEAUVIOR, SIMONE. 1953. *The Second Sex*. H. M. Parshey (tr.). New York: Knoft.

DECKARD, BARBARA SINCLAIR. 1983. *The Women's Movement: Political, Socioeconomic and Psychological Issues*. New York: Harper and Row.

DECROW, KAREN. 1972. "Look, Jane, look! See Dick run and jump! Admire him!" In Scarvia Anderson (ed.), *Sex Differences and Discrimination in Education*. Belmont, CA: Wadsworth.

DEEN, EDITH. 1978. *Wisdom from Women in the Bible*. San Francisco: Harper and Row.

DIAMOND, MILTON. 1982. "Sexual identity, monozygotic twins reared in discordant sex roles and a BBC follow-up." *Archives of Sexual Behavior* 11:181–86.

DINO, GERI A., MARK A. BARNETT, and JEFFREY A. HOWARD. 1984. "Children's expectations of sex differences in parent's responses to sons and daughters encountering interpersonal problems." *Sex Roles* 11:709–15.

DION, K. L., and K. K. DION. 1973. "Correlates of romantic love." *Journal of Consulting and Clinical Psychology* 41:41–56.

DISPENZA, JOSEPH E. 1975. *Advertising the American Women*. Dayton: Pflaum.

DOHRENWEND, BRUCE, and BARBARA DOHRENWEND. 1969. *Social Status and Psychological Disorder*. New York: John Wiley and Sons.

DOMINICK, JOSEPH R., and GAIL E. RAUCH. 1972. "The image of women in network TV commercials." *Journal of Broadcasting* 16:259–65.

DONAHUE, T., and J. COSTAR. 1977. "Counselor discrimination in career selection." *Journal of Counseling Psychology* 24:481–86.

DONOVAN, JOSEPHINE. 1985. *Feminist Theory: The Intellectual Traditions of American Feminism*. New York: Frederick Ungar.

DOOLITTLE, JOHN, and ROBERT PEPPER. 1975. "Children's TV ad content: 1974." *Journal of Broadcasting* (Spring):131–32.

DOUGLAS, EMILY TAFT. 1966. *Remember the Ladies: The Story of Great Women Who Helped Shape America*. New York: G. P. Putnam.

DOWD, MAUREEN. 1984. "Other side of gender gap: Reagan seen as man's man." *New York Times* September 17:A1,B13.

DOWNING, M. 1974. "Heroine of the daytime serial." *Journal of Communication* 24:130–37.

DOWNS, CHRIS A. 1981. "Sex-role stereotyping on prime-time television." *The Journal of Genetic Psychology* 138:253–58.

DOWNS, CHRIS A., and DARRYL C. GOWAN. 1980. "Sex differences in reinforcement and punishment on prime time television." *Sex Roles* 6:683–94.

DOYLE, JAMES A. 1983. *The Male Experience*. Dubuque, IA: Wm. C. Brown. 1985. *Sex and Gender: The Human Experience*. Dubuque, IA: Wm. C. Brown.

DRUCKER, ALISON R. 1984. "The influence of western women on the anti-footbinding movement in 1840–1911." In Karen T. Wei (ed.), *Women in China: A Selected and Annotated Bibliography*. Westport, CT: Greenwood.

D'SOUZA, NEILA, and RAMINI NATARAJAN. 1986. "Women in India: The reality." In Lynn B. Iglitzin and Ruth Ross (eds.), *Women in the World, 1975–1985: The Women's Decade*. Santa Barbara, CA: ABC-Clio.

DUBBERT, JOE L. 1979. *A Man's Place: Masculinity in Transition*. Englewood Cliffs: Prentice Hall.

DUBERMAN, LUCILLE. 1975. *Gender and Sex in Society*. New York: Praeger.

DUKER, JACOB M., and LEWIS R. TUCKER. 1977. "Women libbers' versus independent women: A study of preferences for women's roles in advertisements." *Journal of Marketing Research* 14: 469–75.

DULEY, MARGOT I. 1986. "Women in India." In Margot I. Duley and Mary I. Edwards (eds.), *The Cross-Cultural Study of Women: A Comprehensive Guide*. New York: Feminist.

DUNN, ANGELA. 1986. "Why women are the superior sex." An Interview with Ashley Montague. *St. Louis Post-Dispatch*, January 12:C1,C13.

DWECK, C. S., W. DAVIDSON, S. NELSON, and B. ENNA. 1978. "Sex differences in learned helplessness. II. The contingencies of evaluative feedback in the classroom. III. An experimental analysis." *Developmental Psychology* 14:268–76.

DWORKIN, ANDREA. 1974. *Women Hating*. New York: E. P. Dutton.

DYER, E. 1963. "Parenthood as crises: A restudy." *Marriage and Family Living* 25:196–201.

EAKINS, BARBARA WESTBROOK, and R. GENE EAKINS. 1978. *Sex Differences in Human Communication*. Boston: Houghton Mifflin.

EATON, BEV. 1979. "A decade of healthy feminism: The Boston Women's Health Book Collective." *New Roots* (September-October):38–41.

ECKARDT, KENNETH. 1968. "Deviance, visibility and legal action: The duty to support." *Social Problems* 15:470–77.

EDWARDS, D. A. 1968. "Mice: Fighting by neonatally androgenized females." *Science* 161:1027–28.

EHRENREICH, BARBARA. 1983. *The Hearts of Men: American Dreams and the Flight from Commitment*. Garden City, NY: Anchor Press/Doubleday.

EISENSTOCK, B. 1984. "Sex role differences in children's identification with counterstereotypical televised portrayals." *Sex Roles* 10:417–30.

EL SAADAWI, NAWAL. 1980. *The Hidden Faces of Eve: Women in the Arab World*. London: Zed.

EMIHOVICH, CATHERINE A., EUGENE L. GAIER, and NOREEN C. CRONIN. 1984. "Sex-role expectations changes by fathers for their sons." *Sex Roles* 11:861–67.

ENGELS, FRIEDRICH. 1942 (original 1884). *The Origin of the Family, Private Property, and the State*. New York: International.

EPOSITO, JOHN L. 1982. *Women in Muslim Family Law*. Syracuse: Syracuse University.

EPSTEIN, CYNTHIA. 1971. *Woman's Place*. Los Angeles: University of California.

EPSTEIN, GILDA, and A. L. BRONZAFT. 1972. "Female freshmen view their roles as women." *Journal of Marriage and Family* 34(4):671–72.

ERIKSON, ERIK. 1964. "Inner and outer space: Reflections on womanhood." *Daedalus* 93(2):282–606.

ERNEST, JOHN. 1976. "Mathematics and sex." *American Mathematical Monthly* 83:595–614.

ESHLEMAN, J. ROSS. 1988. *The Family: An Introduction*. (5th ed.) Boston: Allyn and Bacon.

ESTEP, RHODA. 1982. "Women's roles in crimes as depicted by television and newspapers." *Journal of Popular Culture* 16(Winter):151–56.

ETAUGH, C. 1980. "Effects of nonmaterial care on children." *American Psychologist* 35:309–19.

EXLINE, R. V., S. ELLYSON, and B. LONG. 1974. "Visual behavior as an aspect of power role relationships." In P. Pliner, L. Kramer, and T. Alloway (eds.), *Nonverbal Communication in Aggression*. New York: Plenum.

FAGOT, BEVERLY I. 1978. "The influence of sex of child on parental reactions to toddler children." *Child Development* 49:459–65. 1984. "The child's expectancies of differences in adult male and female interactions." *Sex Roles* 11:593–600.

FAGOT, BEVERLY I., and G. R. PATTERSON. 1969. "An in vivo analysis of reinforcing contingencies for sex-role behaviors in the preschool child." *Developmental Psychology* 1:563–68.

FALK, NANCY AUER, and RITA GROSS (eds.). 1980. *Unspoken Words: Women's Religious Lives in Nonwestern Cultures.* New York: Harper and Row.

FARAGHER, JOHNNY, and CHRISTINE STANSELL. 1980. "Women and their families on the Overland Trail, 1842–1867." In Esther Katz and Anita Rapone (eds.) *Women's Experience in America: An Historical Anthology.* New Brunswick, NJ: Transaction.

FARBER, STEPHAN. 1974. "The Vanishing Heroine." *Hudson Review* 27:570–76.

FARRELL, WARREN T. 1974. *The Liberated Man.* New York: Random House. 1975. "Beyond masculinity: Liberating men and their relationships with women." In Lucile Duberman (ed.), *Gender and Sex in Society.* New York: Praeger.

FASTEAU, M. F. 1974. *The Male Machine.* New York: McGraw Hill.

FAULK, M. 1974. "Men who assault their wives." *Medicine, Science and Law* 14:180–83.

FAUSTO-STERLING, ANNE. 1987. "Myths of gender." *The New Republic* (February 3):37–39.

FEIN, G., D. JOHNSON, N. KOSSON, S. STARK, and L. WASSERMAN. 1975. "Sex stereotypes and preference in the toy choices of 20-month-old boys and girls." *Developmental Psychology* 11:527–28.

FEINBERG, RENEE. 1986. *The Equal Rights Amendment: An Annotated Bibliography of the Issues, 1976–1985.* Westport, CT: Greenwood.

FELDBERG, R. L. 1984. "Comparable worth: Toward theory and practice in the United States." *Signs* 10:311–28.

FELDMAN, S. SHIRLEY, and SHARON CHURRIN NASH. 1984. "The transition from expectancy to parenthood: Impact of the firstborn child on men and women." *Sex Roles* 11:61–69

FENGLER, ALFRED P. 1974. "Romantic love in courtship: Divergent paths of male and female students." *Journal of Comparative Family Studies* 5:134–39.

FENNEMA, ELIZABETH, and JULIA SHERMAN. 1977. "Sex related differences in mathematics achievement: Spatial visualization and affective factors." *American Educational Research Journal* 14:51–71.

FERGUSON, M. 1983. *Forever Feminine: Women's Magazines and the Cult of Femininity.* Exeter, N.H.: Heinemann Educational Books.

FEŞHBACH, S., and N. MALAMUTH. 1978. "Sex and aggression: Proving the link." *Psychology Today* 12(6):110.

FINE, MARLENE G. 1981. "Soap opera conversations: The talk that binds." *Journal of Communication* 31(Spring):97–107.

FIRESTONE, SHULAMITH. 1970. *The Dialectic of Sex: The Case for Feminist Revolution.* New York: Bantam.

FISHER, B., and J. BERDIE. 1978. "Adolescent abuse and neglect: Issues of incidence, intervention and service delivery." *Child Abuse and Neglect* 8:173–92.

FISKE, SHIRLEY. 1972. "Pigskin review: An American initiation." In Marie Hart (ed.), *Sport in the Sociocultural Process.* Dubuque, IA: Wm. C. Brown.

FLEENER, MARILYN G. 1977. "The lesbian lifestyle." Paper presented to the Western Social Science Association. (April).

FLEMING, ANNE TAYLOR. 1986. "The American wife." *The New York Times Magazine* (October 26):29–39.

FOX, GREER LITTON. 1977. "'Nice Girl': Social control of women through a value construct." *Signs* 2:805–17.

FOX, MARY F. 1984. "Women and higher education: Sex differentials in the status of students/scholars." In Jo Freeman (ed.), *Women: A Feminist Perspective.* Palo Alto, CA: Mayfield.

FOX, MARY F., and SHARLENE HESSE-BIBER. 1984. *Women at Work.* Palo Alto, CA: Mayfield.

FRANKFORT, ELLEN. 1972. "Drugs and consumer rights, the media." *Vaginal Politics.* New York: Quadrangle Books.

FRANKOVIC, KATHLEEN A. 1982. "Sex and politics: New alignments, old issues." *Political Sciences* Vol. 15.

FRANZWA, HELEN H. 1974a. "Pronatalism in women's magazine fiction." In Ellen Peck and Judith Senderowitz (eds.), *Pronatalism: The Myth of Mom and Apple Pie.* New York: T. Y. Crowell. 1974b. "Working women in fact and fiction." *Journal of Communication* 24(2):104–09. 1975. "Female roles in women's magazine fiction, 1940–1970." In Rhoda Unger and Florence Denmark (eds.), *Women: Dependent or Independent Variable.* New York: Psychological Dimensions.

FREEMAN, JO. 1984. "Women, law and public policy." In Jo Freeman (ed.), *Women: A Feminist Perspective.* Palo Alto, CA: Mayfield. 1984. "The women's liberation movement: Its origins, structure, activities and ideas." In Jo Freeman (ed.), *Women: A Feminist Perspective.* Palo Alto, CA: Mayfield.

FRENCH, BRANDON. 1978. *On the Verge of Revolt: Women in American Film of the Fifties.* New York: Frederick Ungar.

FREUD, SIGMUND. 1962. *Three Contributions to the Theory of Sex.* Tr. A. A. Brill. New York: E. P. Dutton.

FREUDIGER, PATRICIA. 1983. "Life satisfaction among three categories of married women." *Journal of Marriage and the Family* 45(February):213–19.

FREY, SYLVIA R., and MARION J. MORTON. 1986. *New World, New Roles: A Documentary History of Women in Pre-Industrial America.* Westport, CT: Greenwood.

FRIEDAN, BETTY. 1963. *The Feminine Mystique.* New York: W. W. Norton. 1970. "Our revolution is unique." In Mary Lou Thomspon (ed.), *Voices of the New Feminism.* Boston: Beacon. 1981. *The Second Stage.* New York: Summit Books. 1983. "Twenty years after the Feminine Mystique." *New York Times Magazine* (February 27):35–36,42,54–57.

FRIEDMAN, S. 1983. "Polls: White males—Reagan's biggest supporters." *The Easton Express* December 23:A10.

FRUCH, T., and P. MCGHEE. 1975. "Traditional sex role development and the amount of time watching television." *Developmental Psychology.* 11:109.

GALBRAITH, KENNETH. 1983. "The economics of housework." *MS.* April:125–28.

GALLAGHER, MARGARET. 1981. *Unequal Opportunities: The Case of Women and the Media.* Paris: UNESCO.

GALLUP, GEORGE. 1980. "Most women want marriage and babies." *St. Louis Post-Dispatch* June 15:3F.

GALSTON, ARTHUR. 1975. *Daily Life in People's China.* New York: Washington Square.

GARDNER, J. 1970. "Sesame Street and the sex role stereotypes." *Women* 1(3):42.

GARFINKEL, PERRY. 1985. *In a Man's World: Father, Son, Brother, Friend and Other Roles Men Play.* New York: New American Library.

GATES, MARGARET. 1976. "Occupational segregation and the law." *Signs* 1(3):61–74.

GEERKIN, MICHAEL, and WALTER GOVE. 1983. *At Home and at Work: The Family's Allocation of Labor.* Beverly Hills, CA: Sage.

GEIS, F. L., VIRGINIA BROWN, J. JENNINGS, and N. PORTER. 1984. "TV commercials as achievement scripts for women." *Sex Roles* 10(7–8):513–25.

GELLER, S. E., M. I. GELLER, and C. J. SCHEIRER. 1979. "The development in sex attitudes and selective attention to same-sex models in young children." Paper presented at the Eastern Psychological Association Convention, Philadelphia (April).

GELLES, RICHARD J., and MURRAY A. STRAUS. 1979. "Determinants of violence in the family: Toward a theoretical integration." In Wesley R. Burr. Reuben Hill, F. Ivan Nye and Ira L. Reiss (eds.) *Contemporary Theories about the Family*. Vol. 1. New York: The Free Press.

GELMAN, D., N. GREENBERG, V. COPPOLA, B. BURGOWER, S. DOHERTY, M. ANDERSON, E. WILLIAMS. 1985. "The single parent: Family albums." *Newsweek* (July 15):44–50.

GERSON, MARY JOAN. 1980. "The lure of motherhood." *Psychology of Women Quarterly* 5:207–18. 1984. "Feminism and the wish for a child." *Sex Roles* 11(5–6):389–97.

GERSTEL, NAOMI, and HARRIET GROSS. 1984. *Commuter Marriage: A Study of Work and Family*. New York: The Guilford Press.

GERZON, MARK. 1982. *A Choice of Heroes: The Changing Faces of American Manhood*. Boston: Houghton Mifflin.

GILDER, GEORGE. 1974. "In defense of monogamy." *Commentary* 58 (November):31–36.

GINGOLD, JUDITH. 1976. "One of these days—Pow! Right in the kisser." *MS*. 5(August):51–52.

GITHENS, MARIANNE, and JEWEL L. PRESTAGE (eds.). 1977. *A Portrait of Marginality: The Political Behavior of the American Woman*. New York: Longman.

GLENN, NORVAL D. 1975. "Psychological well-being in the postparental stage: Some evidence from national surveys." *Journal of Marriage and the Family* 37 (February):105–10.

GLICK, PAUL C. 1975. "A demographer looks at American families." *Journal of Marriage and the Family* 37 (February):18. 1981. "A demographic picture of black families." In Harritte Pipes McAddo (ed.), *Black Families*. Beverly Hills, CA: Sage.

GLICK, PAUL C., and ARTHUR J. NORTON. 1977. "Marrying, divorcing and living together in the U.S. today." *Population Bulletin*. Washington D.C.: Population Reference Bureau.

GOFFMAN, ERVING. 1959. *The Presentation of Self in Everyday Life*. Garden City, NY: Doubleday (Anchor). 1963. *Behavior in Public Places*. New York: The Free Press. 1971. *Relations in Public*. New York: Basic Books. 1979. *Gender Advertisements*. New York: Harper and Row.

GOLDBERG, P. A. 1972. "Prejudice toward women: Some personality correlates." Paper presented at the American Psychological Association Meeting, Honolulu, Hawaii (September).

GOODE, WILLIAM J. 1960. "A theory of role strain." *American Sociological Review* 25 (3):483–96. 1982. *The Family*. (2nd ed.). Englewood Cliffs: Prentice Hall.

GORDON, ANN D., and MARI JO BUHLE. 1976. "Sex and class in colonial and nineteenth century America." In Berenice A. Carroll (ed.), *Liberating Women's History: Theoretical and Critical Essays*. Urbana: University of Illinois.

GORDON, ANN D., MARI JO BUHLE, and NANCY E. SCHROM. 1973. "Women in American society: An historical contribution." *Radical America* 5(4):1–69. Warner Modular Publication Reprint.

GORN, GERALD J., and MARVIN E. GOLDBERG. 1977. "The impact of television advertising on children from low income families." *Journal of Consumer Research*. 4(2):86–88.

GORNICK, VIVIAN. 1979. "Introduction." In Erving Goffman *Gender Advertisements*. New York: Harper and Row, pp. vii–ix.

GOVE, WALTER R. 1972. "Relationships between sex roles, marital status and mental illness." *Social Forces* 51(1):34–44. 1973. "Sex, marital status and mortality." *American Journal of Sociology* 79:45–67.

GOVE, WALTER R., and JEANETTE F. TUDOR. 1973. "Adult sex roles and mental illness." *American Journal of Sociology* 78(4).

GRAVES, ROBERT. 1955. *The Greek Myths*. (Volume I.) Baltimore, MD: Penguin.

GREARD, OCTAVIA. 1893. *L'Education des Femmes par les Femmes*. Paris: Librairie Hachette.

GREENBERG, BRADLEY S., ROBERT ABELMAN, and KIMBERLY NEUENDORF. 1981. "Sex on the soap operas: Afternoon delight." *Journal of Communication* 31(Spring):83–89.

GREENBERG, M., and N. MORRIS. 1974. "Engrossment: The newborn's impact upon the father." *American Journal of Orthopsychiatry*. 44:520–31.

GREENE, RICHARD. 1978. "Study on children reared by lesbian mothers." *The Advocate* May 31.

GREENWALD, MAURINE W. 1980. *Women, War, and Work: The Impact of World War I on Women Workers in the United States*. Westport, CT: Greenwood.

GREER, W. 1986. "Women gain a majority in jobs." *New York Times*, March 19:C1.

GREIF, GEOFFREY L. 1985a. "Children and housework in the single father family." *Family Relations* 34:353–57. 1985b. *Single Fathers*. Lexington, MA: D.C. Heath and Co.

GROSS, HARRIET. 1980. "Dual career couples who live apart: Two types." *Journal of Marriage and the Family* 42(August):567–76.

GROSS, L., and S. JEFFRIES-FOX. 1978. "What do you want to be when you grow up, little girl?" In G. Tuchman, A. Daniels, and J. Benet (eds.), *Hearth and Home*. New York: Oxford University.

GROSSMAN, TRACY BARR. 1986. *Mothers and Children Facing Divorce*. Ann Arbor, MI: UMI Research.

GUNDRY, PATRICIA. 1979. *Woman Be Free*. Grand Rapids, MI: Zondervan.

HAAS, LINDA. 1980. "Role sharing couples: A study of egalitarian marriages." *Family Relations* 29:289–96.

HABER, BARBARA. 1983. *The Women's Annual*. Boston: G. K. Hall.

HACKER, HELEN MAYER. 1951. "Women as a minority group." *Social Forces* 30 (October):60–69.

HAGEN, RICHARD. 1979. *The Bio-Sexual Factor*. Garden City, NY: Doubleday.

HALL, EDWARD T. 1966. *The Hidden Dimension*. Garden City, NY: Doubleday.

HALLBERG, EDMOND C. 1980. "Anxiety, alcoholism, affairs: They're often evidence of men's middle-aged metapause." *People* (August 25):43–47.

HALLETT, JUDITH P. 1984. "The role of women in Roman elegy: Counter-cultural feminism." In John Peradotto and J. P. Sullivan (eds.), *Women in the Ancient World: The Arethusa Papers*. Albany: SUNY.

HAMILL, PETE. 1986. "Great expectations: The American imperative for perfection meets a new generation." *MS.* 15(3):34–7.

HANSON, SHIRLEY M. H. 1985. "Single custodial fathers." In Shirley M.H. Hanson and Frederick W. Bozett (eds.), *Dimensions of Fatherhood*. Beverly Hills, CA: Sage.

HANSSON, ROBERT O., MARIETA F. KNOFT, ANNA E. DOWNS, PAULA R. MONROE, SUSAN E. STEGMAN, and DONNA S. WADLEY. 1984. "Femininity, masculinity and adjustment of divorce among women." *Psychology of Women Quarterly* 8(3):248–49.

HARE-MUSTIN, RACHEL T., and PATRICIA C. BRODERICK. 1979. "The myth of motherhood: A study of attitudes toward motherhood." *Psychology of Women Quarterly* 4:114–28.

HARE-MUSTIN, RACHEL T., SHEILA KISHLER BENNETT, and PATRICIA C. BRODERICK. 1983. "Attitude toward motherhood: Gender, generational and religious comparisons." *Sex Roles* 9(5):643–61.

HARMETZ, ALJEAN. 1973. "Rape—an ugly movie trend." *The New York Times* September 30:D1.

HARRAGAN, BETTY LEHAN. 1977. *Games Mother Never Taught You*. New York: Rawson.

HARRIMAN, LYNDA COOPER. 1986. "Marital adjustment as related to personal and marital changes accompanying parenthood." *Family Relations* 34:233–39.

HARRIS, ANN SUTHERLAND. 1970. "The second sex in academe." *American Association of University Professors Bulletin.* 56:283–95.

HARRY, JOSEPH. 1984. *Gay Couples.* New York: Praeger.

HARTMANN, SUSAN M. 1982. *The Home Front and Beyond: American Women in the 1940's.* Boston: Twayne.

HASKELL, MOLLY. 1974a. *From Reverence to Rape: The Treatment of Women in the Movies.* New York: Holt, Rinehart and Winston. 1974b. "Women in films: A decade of going nowhere." *Human Behavior* 3(3):64–69. 1977. "What's Hollywood trying to tell us?" *MS.* 5(10):49–51. 1983. "Women in the movies grow up." *Psychology Today* 17(January):18–27.

HEER, DAVID. 1974. "The prevalence of black-white marriage in the United States: 1960–1970." *Journal of Marriage and the Family* 36:246–58.

HENLEY, NANCY M. 1975. "Power, sex and nonverbal communication." In Barrie Thorne and Nancy Henley (eds.), *Language and Sex: Difference and Dominance.* Rowley, MA: Newbury. 1977. *Body Politics: Power, Sex and Nonverbal Communication.* Englewood Cliffs: Prentice Hall.

HENNESSEE, JUDITH ADLER, and JOAN NICHOLSON. 1972. "NOW says: Commercials insult women." *New York Times Magazine* (May 28):12.

HENZE, LURA F., and JOHN W. HUDSON. 1974. "Personal and family characteristics of cohabitating and noncohabitating college students." *Journal of Marriage and the Family* 36(November):722–27.

HEREK, GREGORY M. 1986. "On heterosexual masculinity." *American Behavioral Scientist* 29(5):563–77.

HERMAN, JUDITH. 1981. *Father-Daughter Incest.* Cambridge: Harvard University.

HESS, BETH B., ELIZABETH W. MARKSON, and PETER J. STEIN. 1988. *Sociology.* New York: Macmillan.

HETHERINGTON, E. M. 1979. "Divorce: A child's perspective." *American Psychologist* 34:851–58.

HEWLETT, SYLVIA ANN. 1986. "How our laws hurt working mothers and their families." *Family Circle* (October 21):20–59. 1987. "When a husband walks out." *Parade* (June 7):4–5.

HEYWARD, CARTER. 1976. *A Priest Forever: The Formation of a Woman and a Priest.* New York: Harper and Row.

HOFFMAN, CHARLES D., and EDWARD C. TEYBER. 1985. "Naturalistic observations of sex differences in adult involvement with girls and boys of different ages." *Merrill-Palmer Quarterly* 31(1):93–97.

HOFFMAN, CHARLES D., SANDRA EIKO TSUNEYOSHI, MARILYN EBINA, and HEATHER FITE. 1984. "A comparison of adult males' and females' interactions with girls and boys." *Sex Roles* 11(9–10):799–811.

HOFFMAN, D. M., and L. A. FIDELL. 1979. "Characteristics of androgynous, undifferentiated masculine and feminine middle-class women." *Sex Roles* 5:765–81.

HOFFMAN, L. W. 1977. "Changes in family roles, socialization, and sex differences." *American Psychologist* 32:644–57.

HOFFNUNG, MICHELE. 1984. "Motherhood: Contemporary conflict for women." In Jo Freeman (ed.), *Woman: A Feminist Perspective.* Palo Alto, CA: Mayfield.

HOLE, JUDITH, and ELLEN LEVINE. 1971. *The Rebirth of Feminism.* New York: Quadrangle. 1984. "The first feminists." In Jo Freeman (ed.), *Woman: A Feminist Perspective.* Palo Alto, CA: Mayfield.

HOLT, ALIX. 1985. "The first Soviet feminists." In Barbara Holland (ed.), *Soviet Sisterhood.* Bloomington, IN: Indiana University Press.

HORNER, MARTINA S. 1969. "Fail: Bright women." *Psychology Today* 3(6):36–38. 1972. "Toward an understanding of achievement related conflicts in women." *Journal of Social Issues* 28:157–76.

HOSKEN, FRAN P. (ed.). 1980. *Female Sexual Mutilations: The Facts and Proposals for Action.* Lexington, MA: Women's International Network News.

HOWE, FLORENCE. 1975. "Sexual stereotypes start early." In Elizabeth Steiner Maccia (ed.), *Women and Education.* Springfield, IL: Charles C. Thomas.

HOWELL, MARY C. 1979. "Pediatricians and mothers." In J. Ehrenreich (ed.), *The Cultural Crises of Modern Medicine.* New York: Monthly Review.

HUMPHRIES, MARTIN. 1985. "Gay machismo." In Andy Metcalf and Martin Humphries (eds.), *The Sexuality of Men.* London: Pluto.

HUNT, M. 1974. *Sexual Behavior in the 1970's.* Chicago: Playboy.

HYDE, JANET SHIBLEY. 1985. *Half the Human Experience: The Psychology of Women.* (3rd Edition.) Lexington, MA: D.C. Heath.

India Today. 1981. "Ladies are for burning." *India Today* (February 1–15):92.

INTONS-PETERSON, MARGARET JEAN. 1985. "Fathers' expectations and aspirations for their children." *Sex Roles* 12(7–8):877–95.

ISR. 1982. "Women's well-being at midlife." *Institute for Social Research Newsletter* (Winter):5–6.

JACKLIN, CAROL N., JANET A. DIPIERTRO, and ELEANOR E. MACCOBY. 1984. "Sex-typing behavior and sex-typing pressure in child-parent interaction." *Archives of Sexual Behavior* 13(5):413–15.

JACOBSON, DORANNE. 1980. "Golden handprints and the red-painted feet: Hindu childbirth rituals in central India." In Nancy Auer Falk and Rita Gross (eds.), *Unspoken Worlds: Women's Religious Lives in Nonwestern Cultures.* New York: Harper and Row.

JACQUETTE, JANE. 1980. "Female political participation in Latin America." In June Nash and Helen Icker Safa (eds.), *Sex and Class in Latin America.* Brooklyn, NY: J. F. Bergin. 1986. "Female political participation in Latin America: Raising feminist issues." In Lynn B. Iglitzin and Ruth Ross (eds.), *Women in the World, 1975–1985: The Women's Decade.* Santa Barbara, CA: ABC-Clio.

JAFFE, LORNA. 1973. "Women's place in academe." *Midwest Quarterly* 15(1):16–29.

JEFFERY, PATRICIA. 1979. *Frogs in a Well: India Women in Purdah.* London: Zed.

JELIN, ELISABETH. 1977. "Migration and labor force participation of Latin American women: The domestic servants in cities." In Wellesley Editorial Committee (eds.), Women and National Development. Chicago: University of Chicago.

JENCKS, CHRISTOPHER. 1982. "Divorced mothers, unite!" *Psychology Today* 16(November)73–75.

JEWETT, R. 1979. "The sexual liberation of the Apostle Paul." *JAAR Supplements* 47(1):55–87.

JOHNSON, KAY. 1986. "Women's rights, family reform, and population control in the People's Republic of China." In Lynn B. Iglitzin and Ruth Ross (eds.), *Women in the World, 1975–1985: The Women's Decade.* Santa Barbara, CA: ABC-Clio.

JOHNSON, WARREN R. 1968. *Human Sexual Behavior and Sex Education.* Philadelphia: Lea and Febiger.

JOSLYN, W. O. 1973. "Androgen-induced social dominance in infant female Rhesus monkeys." *Journal of Child Psychology and Psychiatry* 14:137–45.

JOY, S. S., and P. S. WISE. 1983. "Maternal employment, anxiety, and sex differences in college students' self descriptions." *Sex Roles* 9:519–25.

JULIAN, JOSEPH. 1983. *Social Problems.* (4th ed.) Englewood Cliffs: Prentice Hall.

JUSTER, F. T. 1984. "A note on recent changes in time use." In L. Larwood, A. Stromberg, and B. Gutek (eds.), *Women and Work: An Annual Review*, Vol. 1. Beverly Hills, CA: Sage.

KAGAN, JEROME. 1964. "The acquisition and significance of sex-typing." In M. Hoffman (ed.), *Review of Child Research*. New York: Russell Sage.

KAMINSKI, DONNA M. 1985. "Where are the female Einsteins: The gender stratification of math and science." In Jeanne Ballentine (ed.), *Schools and Society: A Reader in Education and Society*. Palo Alto, CA: Mayfield.

KAMM, HENRY. 1988. "Afghan refugee women suffering under Islamic custom." *New York Times International* March 27:8.

KANIN, E. J., K. R. DAVIDSON, and S. R. SCHECK. 1970. "A research note on male-female differentials in the experience of heterosexual love." *Journal of Sex Research* 6:64–72.

KANOWITZ, LEO. 1969. *Women and the Law: The Unfinished Revolution*. Albuquerque: The University of New Mexico.

KANTER, ROSABETH. 1976. "The impact of hierarchical structures on the work behavior of women and men." *Social Problems* 23(4):415–30.

KAPLAN, A., and J. P. BEAN. 1976. "From sex stereotypes to androgyny: Considerations of societal and individual change." In A. Kaplan and J. P. Bean (eds.), *Beyond Sex Role Stereotypes*. Boston: Little, Brown.

KATZ, ESTHER, and ANITA RAPONE (eds.). 1980. *Women's Experience in America: An Historical Anthology*. New Brunswick, NJ: Transaction.

KATZ, J. 1980. "The new and old lives of men and women undergraduates." In a Report of the Brown Project, *Men and Women Learning Together: A Study of College Students in the Late 70's*. Providence, RI: Brown University.

KAY, HERMA HILL, and CAROL AMYX. 1982. "Marvin vs. Marvin: Preserving the options." In Jeffrey P. Rosenfeld (ed.), *Relationships: The Marriage and Family Reader*. Glenview, IL: Scott Foresman.

KELLEY, R. M., and M. BOUTILIER. 1978. *The Making of Political Women: A Study of Socialization and Role Conflict*. Chicago: Nelson Hall.

KELLY, J. 1983. "Sex role stereotypes and mental health: Conceptual models in the 1970's and issues for the 1980's." In V. Franks and E. Rothblum (eds.), *The Stereotyping of Women*. New York: Springer.

KEMPER, SUSAN. 1984. "When to speak like a lady." *Sex Roles* 10(5–6):435–43.

KEMPER, THEODORE D. 1983. "Predicting the divorce rate: Down?" *Journal of Family Issues* 4:507–24.

KENISTON, KENNETH, and ELLEN KENISTON. 1964. "An American anachronism: The image of women and work." *The American Scholar* 33(3):355–75.

KENNELLY, E. 1984. "Republicans in fear of a gender gap, feature women at convention." *National NOW Times* (September-October):3.

KESSLER, R., and J. MCRAE, JR. 1982. "The effects of wives' employment on men and women." *American Sociological Review* 47:216–26.

KESSLER, SUZANNE J., and WENDY MCKENNA. 1978. *Gender: An Ethnomethodological Approach*. New York: John Wiley and Sons.

KIDD, VIRGINIA. 1975. "Happily ever after and other relationship styles: Advice on interpersonal relationships in popular magazines, 1951–1973." *Quarterly Journal of Speech* 61:31–39.

KINSEY, A. E., W. B. POMEROY, and C. E. MARTIN. 1948. *Sexual Behavior in the Human Male*. Philadelphia: Saunders.

KINSEY, A. E., W. B. POMEROY, C. E. MARTIN, and H. GEPHARD. 1953. *Sexual Behavior in the Human Female*. Philadelphia: Saunders.

KINZER, NORA SCOTT. 1973. "Women professionals in Buenos Aires." In Ann Pescatello (ed.), *Female and Male in Latin America*. Pittsburgh: Pittsburgh University. 1977. "Sociocultural factors mitigating role conflicts of Buenos Aires professional women." In Ruby Rohrlich-Leavitt (ed.), *Women Cross-Culturally: Change and Challenge*. The Hague: Mouton.

KIRKPATRICK, JEANE J. 1976. *The New Presidential Elite*. New York: Russell Sage.

KLATCH, REBECCA E. 1987. *Women of the New Right*. Philadelphia: Temple University Press.

KLEIN, V. 1984. "The historical background." In Jo Freeman (ed.), *Women: A Feminist Perspective*. Palo Alto, CA: Mayfield.

KLEMESRUD, JUDY. 1974. "Feminist goal: Better image at the movies." *The New York Times* October 13:L–82.

KNAUB, PATRICIA KAIN. 1986. "Growing up in a dual-career family: The children's perceptions." *Family Relations* 35:431–37.

KNAUB, PATRICIA KAIN, DEANNA BAXTER EVERSOLL, and JAQUELINE VOSS. 1983. "Is parenthood a desirable adult role? An assessment of attitudes held by contemporary women." *Sex Roles* 9(3):355–62.

KNOX, D., and M. SPORAKOWSKI. 1968. "Attitudes of college students toward love." *Journal of Marriage and the Family*. 30:638–42.

KNUDSEN, D. 1969. "The declining status of women: Popular myths and the failure of functionalist thought." *Social Forces* 48(4):183–95.

KOHLBERG, LAWRENCE. 1966. "A cognitive-developmental analysis of children's sex role concepts and attitudes." In Eleanor Maccoby (ed.), *The Development of Sex Differences*. Stanford: Stanford University.

KOLESNIK, WALTER B. 1969. *Co-education: Sex Differences in the Schools*. New York: Vantage.

KOLTAK, C. 1974. *Cultural Anthropology*. New York: Random House.

KOMAROVSKY, MIRRA. 1946. "Cultural contradictions and sex roles." *American Journal of Sociology* 52(6):182–89. 1973. "Cultural contradictions and sex roles: The masculine case." *American Journal of Sociology* 78(4):873–84. 1976. *Dilemmas of Masculinity*. New York: W. W. Norton. 1987. "College men: Gender roles in transition." In Carol Lasser (ed.), *Educating Men and Women Together: Coeducation in a Changing World*. Englewood Cliffs: Prentice Hall.

KONOPKA, GISELA. 1976. *Young Girls: A Portrait of Adolescence*. Englewood Cliffs: Prentice Hall.

KOTKIN, MARK. 1983. "Sex roles among married and unmarried couples." *Sex Roles* 9(9): 975–85.

KREUTZ, L., and R. ROSE. 1972. "Assessment of aggressive behavior and plasma testosterone in a young criminal population." *Psychosomatic Medicine* 34:321–32.

KUHN, D., S. C. NASH, and L. BRUCKEN. 1978. "Sex role concepts of two- and three-year olds." *Child Development* 49:445–51.

KUHN, MANFRED. 1955. "How mates are sorted." In Howard Becker and Reuben Hill (eds.), *Family, Marriage and Parenthood*. Boston: D.C. Heath.

LADNER, J. A. 1972. *Tomorrow's Tomorrow: The Black Woman*. Garden City: Doubleday (Anchor).

LAKOFF, ROBIN. 1975. *Language and Woman's Place*. New York: Colsphon.

LAMB, MICHAEL F. 1979. "Paternal influences and the father's role." *American Psychologist* 32:938–43.

LAMBERT, WALLACE E. 1981. "Social influences of the child's development of an identity." In Robert C. Gardner and Rudolph Kalin (eds.), *A Canadian Social Psychology of Ethnic Relations*. Toronto: Methuen.

LAMM, M. 1980. *The Jewish Way in Love and Marriage*. San Francisco: Harper and Row.

LARNED, DEBORAH. 1975. "The selling of valium." *MS.* 4(5):32–33.

LAWS, JUDITH LONG. 1979. *The Second X: Sex Role and Social Role*. New York: Elsevier North Holland.

LAWS, JUDITH LONG, and PEPPER SCHWARTZ. 1977. *Sexual Scripts: The Social Construction of Female Sexuality*. Hinsdale, IL: The Dryden Press.

LAZARUS, ARNOLD. 1987. "The five most dangerous myths about marriage." In O. Pocs and R. H. Walsh (eds.), *Marriage and Family Annual Editions*. Guilford, CT: Dushkin.

LEAHY, ROBERT L., and STEPHEN R. SHIRK. 1984. "The development of classificatory skills and sex-trait stereotypes in children." *Sex Roles* 10(3–4):281–92.

LEBRA, TAKIE SUGIYAMA. 1984. *Japanese Women: Constraint and Fulfillment*. Honolulu: University of Hawaii.

LEFKOWITZ, MARGARET B. 1972. "The women's magazine short story heroine in 1957 and 1967." In Constantine Safilios-Rothschild (ed.), *Toward a Sociology of Women*. Lexington, MA: XEROX.

LEIFER, M. 1977. "Psychological changes accompanying pregnancy and motherhood." *Genetic Psychology Monographs* 95:55–96.

LEMASTERS, E. 1957. "Parenthood as Crisis." *Marriage and Family Living* 19:352–55.

LESTER, DAVID. 1984. "Suicide." In Cathy S. Widom (ed.), *Sex Roles and Psychopathology*. New York: Plenum.

LESTER, DAVID, NANCY BRAZILL, CONSTANCE ELLIS, and THOMAS GUERIN. 1984. "Correlates of romantic attitudes toward love: Androgyny and self disclose." *Psychological Reports* 54(April):554.

LEVER, J., and PEPPER SCHWARTZ. 1971. *Women at Yale*. Indianapolis: Bobbs-Merrill.

LEVERE, JANE. 1974. "Portrayal of women in ads defended by top ad women." *Editor and Publisher* (June 8):11.

LEVIN, JACK, and ARNOLD ARLUKE. 1985. "An exploratory analysis of sex differences in gossip." *Sex Roles* 12(3–4):281–86.

LEWIS, SASHA GREGORY. 1979. *Sunday's Women: A Report on Lesbian Life Today*. Boston: Beacon.

LIDDY, GORDON G. 1980. *Will*. New York: Dell.

LINDSEY, LINDA L. 1979. "Book review of *Wisdom from Women in the Bible* by Edith Deen." *Review for Religious* 38(5):792–93. 1982. "Pharmacy and health care in India." *American Pharmacy* NS22(9):474–77. 1983. "Health care in India: An analysis of existing models." In John H. Morgan (ed.), *Third World Medicine and Social Change*. Lanham, MD: University Press of America. 1984. "Career paths in pharmacy: An exploration of male and female differences." Paper presented at the Midwest Sociological Society Meetings, Chicago. 1985. "Health care and counter-modernization in India." Paper presented at the North Central Sociological Association Meeting, Louisville, KY (April). 1988a. "The health status of women in Pakistan: The impact of Islamization." Paper presented at the Midwest Sociological Society meeting, Minneapolis, MN (March). 1988b. "The health status of Afghan refugees: Focus on women." Paper presented at the National Council for International Health Meeting, Washington, D.C. (May).

LIPMEN-BLUMEN, JEAN. 1984. *Gender Roles and Power*. Englewood Cliffs: Prentice Hall.

LITTLE, E. 1848–1849. "What are the rights of women?" *Ladies Wreath*, E2:133.

LOCKSLEY, A. 1980. "On the effect of wives' employment on marital adjustment and companionship." *Journal of Marriage and the Family* 42:337–46.

LOCKSLEY, A. and M. E. COLTEN. 1979. "Psychological androgyny: A case of mistaken identity?" *Journal of Personality and Social Psychology* 39:821–31.

LOPATA, HELEN. 1971. *Occupation: Housewife.* New York: Oxford University.

LOPATE, CAROL. 1976. "Daytime television: You'll never want to leave home." *Feminist Studies* 3(314):69–82.

LORBER, JUDITH. 1986. "Dismantling Noah's Ark." *Sex Roles* 14(11–12):567–79.

LOVE, MARSHA. 1978. "Health hazards of office work." *Women and Health* 3(3):18–22.

LOWRY, DENNIS T., GAIL LOVE, and MALCOLM KIRBY. 1981. "Sex on the soap operas: Patterns of intimacy." *Journal of Communication* 31(Spring):90–96.

LUCAS, ANGELA M. 1983. *Women in the Middle Ages: Religion, Marriage and Letters.* New York: St. Martin's.

LUEPTOW, LLOYD B. 1985. "Conceptions of femininity and masculinity: 1974–1983." *Psychological Reports* 57:859–62.

LUGENBEEL, BARBARA DERRICK. 1974. "A content analysis of Good Housekeeping's Short Fiction from November 1972-October 1973." M.A. Thesis, University of South Carolina.

LULL, JAMES. 1980. "Girls' favorite TV females." *Journalism Quarterly Review* 57:146–50.

LUNDSTROM, W. J., and D. SCIGLIMPAGLIA. 1977. "Sex role portrayals in the media." *Journal of Marketing* 41:72–79.

The Lutheran Book of Worship. 1978. Minneapolis, MN: Augsburg.

LUTWIN, DAVID R., and GARY N. SIPERSTEIN. 1985. "Househusband fathers." In Shirley M. H. Hanson and Frederick W. Bozett (eds.), *Dimensions of Fatherhood.* Beverly Hills, CA: Sage.

LYLE, J., and H. R. HOFFMAN. 1972. "Explorations in patterns of television viewing by pre-school-age children." In E. A. Rubinstein, G. A. Comstock, and J. P. Murray (eds.), *Television and Social Behavior Vol. 4, Television in Day-to-Day Life: Patterns of Use.* Washington, D.C.: U.S. Government Printing Office.

LYNESS, JUDITH, L. MILTON, E. LIPETZ, and KEITH E. DAVIS. 1972. "Living together: An alternative to marriage." *Journal of Marriage and the Family* 34 (May):305–11.

LYNN, DAVID B. 1959. "A note on sex differences in the development of masculine and feminine identification." *Psychological Review* 66:126–35. 1969. *Parental and Sex Role Identification: A Theoretical Formulation.* Berkeley: McCutchan. 1979. *Daughters and Parents: Past, Present and Future.* Monterey, CA: Brooks-Cole.

LYNN, NAOMI B. 1984. "Women and politics: The real majority." In Jo Freeman (ed.), *Women: A Feminist Perspective.* Palo Alto, Ca: Mayfield.

LYNN, NAOMI, and CORNELIA BUTLER FLORA. 1977. "Societal punishment and aspects of female political participation: 1972 National Convention delegates." In Marianne Githens and Jewel L. Prestage (eds.), *A Portrait of Marginality: The Political Behavior of the American Woman.* New York: Longman.

MACCOBY, ELEANOR EMMONS. 1966. "Sex differences in intellectual functioning." In E. E. Maccoby (ed.), *The Development of Sex Differences.* Stanford: Stanford University.

MACCOBY, ELEANOR EMMONS, and CAROL NAGY JACKLIN. 1974. *The Psychology of Sex Differences.* Stanford: Stanford University.

MACE, DAVID R. 1975. "What I have learned about family life." In Kenneth C. W. Kammeyer (ed.), *Confronting the Issues: Sex Roles, Marriage and the Family.* Boston: Allyn and Bacon.

MACIONIS, JOHN J. 1989. *Sociology.* Englewood Cliffs: Prentice Hall.

MACKIE, MARLENE. 1983. *Exploring Gender Relations: A Canadian Perspective.* Scarborough, Ontario: Butterworth.

MACKINNON, CATHERINE A. 1982. "Feminism, marxism, method and the state: An agenda for theory." *Signs* 7(3):515–44.

MACKLIN, ELEANOR D. 1983. "Nonmarital heterosexual cohabitation: An overview." In Eleanor D. Macklin, & Roger H. Rubin (eds.), *Contemporary Families and Alternative Lifestyles*. Beverly Hills, CA: Sage.

MACLEAN, IAN. 1980. *The Renaissance Notion of Woman: A Study in the Fortunes of Scholasticism and Medical Science in European Intellectual Life*. Cambridge, England: Cambridge University.

MADDEN, J. R. 1985. "The persistence of pay differentials: The economics of sex discrimination." In L. Larwood, A. Stromber, and B. Gutek (eds.), *Women and Work: An Annual Review*, Vol. 1. Beverly Hills, CA: Sage.

MAGEE, JONI. 1975. "The pelvic examination: A view from the other end of the table." *Annals of Internal Medicine* 83(4):28–29.

MALSON, MICHELENE RIDLEY. 1983. "Black women's sex roles: The social context for a new ideology." *Journal of School Issues* 39(3):101–13.

MAMONOVA, TATYANA (ed.). 1984. *Women and Russia: Feminist Writings from the Soviet Union*. Boston: Beacon.

MANDEL, WILLIAM M. 1975. *Soviet Women*. Garden City: Doubleday (Anchor).

MANDLE, JOAN D. 1979. *Women & Social Change in America*. Princeton: Princeton Book Company.

MANSBRIDGE, JANE J. 1986. *Why We Lost the ERA*. Chicago: University of Chicago.

MARET, ELIZABETH, and BARBARA FINLAY. 1984. "The distribution of household labor among women in dual-earner families." *Journal of Marriage and the Family* (May):357.

MARGOLIS, MAXINE E. 1984. *Mothers and Such: View of American Women and Why They Changed*. Berkeley: University of California.

MARKEY, JUDITH. 1986. "When he gets custody." In Ollie Pocs and Robert H. Walsh (eds.), *Marriage and Family Annual Editions*. Guilford, CT: Dushkin.

MARKLE, GERALD E., and CHARLES B. NAM. 1973. "The impact of sex predetermination on fertility." Presented at the annual meetings of the Population Association of America (April).

MARSHALL, SUSAN E. 1984. "Keep us on the pedestal: Women against feminism in Twentieth-Century America." In Jo Freeman (ed.), *Women: A Feminist Perspective*. Palo Alto, CA: Mayfield.

MARTIN, DEL. 1976. *Battered Wives*. San Francisco: Glide.

MARTIN, DOROTHY H. 1985. "Fathers and adolescents." In Shirley M. H. Hanson and Frederick W. Bozett (eds.), *Dimensions of Fatherhood*. Beverly Hills, CA: Sage.

MARWELL, GERALD. 1975. "Why ascription? Parts of a more-or-less formal theory of the functions and dysfunctions of sex roles." *American Sociological Review* 40:445–55.

MARX, KARL. 1964 (original, 1848). T. B. Bottomore and Maxilien Rubel (eds.), *Selected Writings in Sociology and Social Philosophy*. Baltimore, MD: Penguin. 1967 (original, 1867–95). *Das Capital*. New York: International.

MASLIN, A., and L. DAVIS. 1975. "Sex-role stereotyping as a factor in mental health standards among counselors-in-training." *Journal of Counseling Psychology* 2:87–91.

MASNICK, GEORGE, and MARY JO BANE. 1980. *The Nation's Families: 1960–1990*. Boston: Auborn House.

MASTERS, WILLIAM H. 1983. Lecture on Human Sexuality. St. Louis University Medical School, September 19.

MASTERS, WILLIAM H., and VIRGINIA JOHNSON. 1966. *Human Sexual Response*. Boston: Little, Brown. 1970. *Human Sexual Inadequacy*. Boston: Little, Brown.

MATHER, ANNE D. 1973. "A history of analysis of feminist periodicals." MA Thesis: University of Georgia.

MATKOV, REBECCA ROPER. 1972. "Ladies' Home Journal and McCall's in 1960 and 1970: A content analysis." M. A. Thesis: University of North Carolina.

MATRIA, C., and PATRICIA MULLEN. 1978. "Reclaiming menstruation: A study of alienation and repossession." *Women and Health* 3(May-June):23–30.

MCBETH, LEON. 1979. *Women in Baptist Life*. Nashville: Broadman.

MCBRIDE, ANGELA BARRON. 1973. *The Growth and Development of Mothers*. New York: Harper and Row.

MCCRAY, CARRIE ALLEN. 1980. "The black woman and family roles." In La Frances Rodgers-Rose (ed.), *The Black Women*. Beverly Hills, CA: Sage.

MCLANAHAN, SARA S. 1983. "Family structures and stress: A longitudinal comparison of two parent and female headed families." *Journal of Marriage and the Family* 45(May):347–57.

MCLAUGHLIN, E. 1974. "Equality of souls, inequality of sexes: Women in medieval theology." In R. Ruether (ed.), *Religion and Sexism*. New York: Simon and Schuster.

MCMILLEN, LIZ. 1985. "Despite new laws and college policies, women say sexism lingers on campuses." *Chronicle of Higher Education* 29(February 6):27–28.

MCNEIL, JOHN. 1964. "Programmed instruction versus visual classroom procedures in teaching boys to read." *American Educational Research Journal* 1:113–20.

MEAD, GEORGE HERBERT. 1934. *Mind, Self and Society*. Chicago: University of Chicago.

MEAD, M. 1935. *Sex and Temperament*. New York: William Morrow.

MELLEN, JOAN. 1973. "Bergman and women: Cries and whispers." *Film Quarterly* 27(1):2–11. 1974. *Women and Their Sexuality in the New Film*. New York: Horizons.

MELTON, WILLIE, and LINDA L. LINDSEY. 1987. "Instrumental and expressive values in mate selection among college students revisited: Feminism, love and economic necessity." Paper presented at the Annual Meeting of the Midwest Sociological Society, Chicago (April).

MELTON, WILLIE, and DARWIN L. THOMAS. 1976. "Instrumental and expressive values in mate selection of black and white college students." *Journal of Marriage and Family* (August):509–17.

MEREDITH, DENNIS. 1985. "Mom, dad and the kids." *Psychology Today (June):62–67.*

MERNISSI, FATIMA. 1987. *Beyond the Veil: Male-Female Dynamics in Modern Muslim Society*. Bloomington: Indiana University.

MERRITT, SHARYNE. 1982. "Sex roles and political ambition." *Sex Roles* 8:1025–36.

MICHAELS, MARGUERITE. 1984. "The myth of the gender gap." *Parade* (March 4):4.

MILLER, BARBARA D. 1981. *The Endangered Sex: Neglect of Female Children in North India*. Ithaca: Cornell University.

MILLER, BRIAN. 1979. "Unpromised paternity: Life-styles of gay fathers." In Martin P. Levene (ed.), *Gay Men: The Sociology of Male Homosexuality*. New York: Harper and Row.

MILLER, CASEY, and KATE SWIFT. 1976. *Words and Women: New Language in New Times*. Garden City: Doubleday (Anchor).

MILLER, M. M., and B. REEVES. 1976. "Dramatic TV content and children's sex-role stereotypes." *Journal of Broadcasting* 20(1):35–50.

MILTON, G. A. 1958. "Five studies of the relations between sex role identification and achievement in problem solving." *Technical Report, No. 3*. New Haven, CT: Yale University.

MINCES, JULIETTE. 1982. *The House of Obedience: Women in Arab Society*. London: Zed.

MINTZ, WARREN. 1975. "Book review of *Open Marriage: A New Life Style for Couples*." In Kenneth C. W. Kammeyer (ed.), *Confronting the Issues: Sex Roles, Marriage and the Family*. Boston: Allyn and Bacon.

MISCHEL, W. A. 1966. "A social learning view of sex differences in behavior." In E. E. Maccoby (ed.), *The Development of Sex Differences*. Stanford: Stanford University.

MITCHELL, JULIET. 1971. *Women's Estate*. Baltimore: Penguin. 1974. *Psychoanalysis and Feminism*. New York: Pantheon.

MONAGAN, D. 1983. "The failure of coed sports." *Psychology Today (March):58–63.*

MONEY, JOHN, and ANKE A. EHRHARDT. 1972. *Man and Woman, Boy and Girl*. Baltimore: Johns Hopkins University.

MONTAGU, ASHLEY. 1974. *The Natural Superiority of Women*. London: Collier MacMillan.

MOONEY, ELIZABETH C. 1985. *Men and Marriage: The Changing Roles of Husbands*. New York: Franklin Watts.

MOORE, R., and G. MCDONALD. 1976. "The relationship between sex role stereotypes, attitudes toward women and male homosexuality in a non-clinical sample of homosexual men." Paper presented at Canadian Psychology Association, Toronto.

MORGAN, KATHRYN P. 1982a. "Androgyny: A conceptual critique." *Social Theory and Practice* 8(3):245–83.

MORGAN, MARABEL. 1973. *The Total Woman*. New York: Pocket Books.

MORGAN, ROBIN. 1982b. *The Anatomy of Freedom: Feminism, Physics and Global Politics*. Garden City: Doubleday (Anchor).

MOSES, JOEL C. 1986. "The Soviet Union in the women's decade." In Lynn B. Iglitzin and Ruth Ross (eds.), *Women in the World: 1975–1985, The Women's Decade*. Santa Barbara, CA: ABC-Clio.

MOSS, HOWARD A. 1967. "Sex, age and state as determinants of mother-infant interaction." *Merrill-Palmer Quarterly* 13(1):19–36.

MOYNIHAN, DANIEL P. 1965. "The Negro Family: The case for national action." Office of Policy Planning and Research, U.S. Department of Labor, Washington D.C.

MULLAN, BOB. 1984. *The Mating Trade*. London: Routledge & Kegan Paul.

MURSTEIN, BERNARD I. 1980. "Mate selection in the 1970's." *Journal of Marriage and the Family* (November):777–92. 1986. *Paths to Marriage*. Beverly Hills, CA: Sage.

MUSS-ARNOLT, WILLIAM. 1901. "The Enuma Elish." In *Assyrian and Babylonian Literature, Selected Translations*. New York: Appleton.

NADELMAN, L. 1974. "Sex identity in American children: Memory, knowledge and preference tests." *Developmental Psychology* 10:413–17.

NAHAS, REBECCA, and MYRA TURLEY. 1980. *The New Couple: Women and Gay Men*. New York: Seaview.

NASH, JUNE. 1986. "A decade of research on women in Latin America." In June Nash and Helen I. Safa (eds.), *Women and Change in Latin America*. South Hadley, MA: Bergin and Garvey.

NASHAT, GUITY. 1983. "Women in the ideology of the Islamic Republic." In Guity Nashat (ed.), *Women and the Revolution in Iran*. Boulder: Westview.

NATHANSON, CONSTANCE A. 1975. "Illness and feminine roles: A theoretical review." *Social Science and Medicine* 9(2): 57–62.

NAZZARI, MURIEL. 1986. "Women in Latin America." In Margot I. Duley and Mary I. Edwards (eds.), *The Cross-Cultural Study of Women*. New York: The Feminist Press.

NEHRA, ARVIND. 1934. *Letters of an Indian Judge to an English Gentlewoman*. London: Peter Davies.

NELTON, SHARON, and KAREN BERNEY. 1987. "Women: The second wave." *National Business* (May):18–27.

NEMY, ENID. 1980. "The new roles can cause stress in women." *St. Louis Post-Dispatch* September 8:3D.

New Oxford Annotated Bible. 1978. May, H. A. and B. M. Metzger (eds.). Oxford: Oxford University Press.

NEWCOMB, PAUL C. 1982. "Cohabiting in America: An assessment of consequences." In Jeffrey P. Rosenfeld (ed.), *Relationships: The Marriage and Family Reader*. Glenview, IL: Scott, Foresman.

NILSON, LINDA BURZOTTA. 1978. "The social standing of a housewife." *Journal of Marriage and the Family* (August):541–48.

NOCK, STEPHEN L. 1987. *Sociology of the Family*. Englewood Cliffs: Prentice Hall.

NOLAN, J. D., J. D. GALST, and M. A. WHITE. 1977. "Sex bias on children's television programs." *Journal of Psychology* 96:197–204.

NOLEN, WILLIAM A. 1980. "What you should know about male menopause." *McCall's* (June):84,153.

NOVAK, MICHAEL. 1974. "Should women be priests?" *Commonweal* 101(8):206,221–22.

OAKLEY, ANN. 1974a. *The Sociology of Housework*. New York: Pantheon. 1974b. *Women's Work: The Housewife, Past and Present*. New York: Vintage Books.

O'CONNELL, MARY. 1984. "Why don't Catholics have women priests?" *U.S. Catholic* (January):6–12.

O'DONNELL, WILLIAM J., and KAREN J. O'DONNELL. 1978. "Update: Sex-role messages in TV commercials." *Journal of Communication* 28 (Winter):156–58.

OMVEDT, GAIL. 1980. *We Will Smash this Prison*. London: Zed.

O'NEILL, JUNE. 1985. "The trend in the male-female wage gap in the United States." *Journal of Labor Economics* 3(1):91–116.

O'NEILL, NENA. 1977. *The Marriage Premise*. New York: M. Evans.

O'NEILL, NENA, and GEORGE O'NEILL. 1972. *Open Marriage: A New Life Style for Couples*. New York: M. Evans.

ORTHNER, DENNIS K., TERRY BROWN, and DENNIS FERGUSON. 1976. "Single parent fatherhood: An emergency lifestyle." *The Family Coordinator* 25(October):429–37.

PAGELS, ELAINE. 1979. *The Gnostic Gospels*. New York: Random House.

PALUDI, M. A. 1984. "Psychometric properties and underlying assumptions of four objective measures of fear and success." *Sex Roles* 10:765–81.

PARISH, WILLIAM L., and MARTIN K. WHYTE. 1978. *Village and Family in Contemporary China*. Chicago: University of Chicago.

PARKE, ROSS D., and S. E. O'LEARY. 1976. "Father-mother-infant interaction in the newborn period." In K. Riegel and J. Meacham (eds.), *The Developing Individual in a Changing World, Vol. 2*. The Hague: Mouton.

PARKE, ROSS D., and B. R. TINSLEY. 1981. "The father's role in infancy: Determinants of involvement in caregiving and play." In Michael F. Lamb (ed.), *The Role of the Father in Child Development*. (2nd ed.) New York: John Wiley and Sons.

PARLEE, MARY B. 1973. "The premenstrual syndrome." *Psychological Bulletin* 80:454–65. 1978. "The rhythms in men's lives." *Psychology Today* 11(April):82–91.

PARRY, H. L., M. BALTER, G. MELLINGER, I. H. CISIN, and D. I. MANHEIMER. 1973. "National patterns of therapeutic drug use." *Archives of General Psychiatry* 28:769–83.

PARSONS, TALCOTT. 1942. "Age and sex in social structure of the United States." *American Sociological Review* 7:604–16. 1955. "Family structure and the socialization of the child." In Talcott Parsons and Robert Bales (eds.), *Family Socialization and Interaction Process*. Glencoe, IL: The Free Press. 1964. *Social Structure and Personality*. Glencoe, IL: The Free Press.

PARSONS, TALCOTT, and ROBERT F. BALES (eds.). *Family Socialization and Interaction Process*. Glencoe, IL: The Free Press.

PASTNER, CARROLL. 1980. "Access to property and the status of women in Islam." In Jane I. Smith (ed.), *Women in Contemporary Muslim Societies*. Lewisburg, PA: Bucknell University.

PAVALKA, RONALD. 1971. *Sociology of Occupations and Professions*. Itasca, IL: F. E. Peacock.

PEARSON, JUDY CORNELIA. 1985. *Gender and Communication*. Dubuque, IA: Wm. C. Brown.

PECK, ELLEN. 1974. "Television's romance with reproduction." In Ellen Peck and Judith Senderowitz (eds.), *Pronatalism, the Myth of Mom and Apple Pie*. New York: T. Y. Crowell.

PEDERSON, F. A., B. ANDERSON, and R. CAIN. 1980. "Parent-infant and husband-wife interactions observed at age 5 months." In F. A. Pederson (ed.), *The Father-Infant Relationship: Observational Studies in a Family Setting*. New York: Praeger.

PEERS, JO. 1985. "Workers by hand and womb: Soviet women and the demographic crisis." In Barbara Holland (ed.), *Soviet Sisterhood*. Bloomington, IN: Indiana University.

PEEVERS, BARBARA HOLLANDS. 1979. "Androgyny on the TV screen? An analysis of sex-role portrayal." *Sex Roles* 5(6):797–809.

PERADOTTO, JOHN, and J. P. SULLIVAN (eds.). 1984. *Women in the Ancient World: The Arethusa Papers*. Albany: SUNY.

PERLEZ, JANE. 1984. "Women, power and politics." *New York Times Magazine* (June 24):23–31,72,76.

PERUTZ, KATHRIN. 1972. *Marriage is Hell*. New York: William Morrow. 1975. "The anachronism of marriage." In Kenneth C. W. Kammeyer (ed.), *Confronting the Issues: Sex Roles, Marriage and the Family*. Boston: Allyn and Bacon.

PESCH, MARINA, et al. 1981. "Sex role stereotypes on the airwaves of the eighties." Paper delivered an the Annual Convention of the Eastern Communication Association, Pittsburgh (April 23–25).

PETERSON, ROLF A. 1983a. "Attitudes toward the childless spouse." *Sex Roles* 9(3):321–31.

PETERSON, TIMM. 1983b. "The unemployment blues and masculinity." *M.* (Spring): 7,35.

PHARR, SUSAN. 1977. "Japan: Historical and contemporary perspectives." In Janet Zollinger Giole and Audrey Chapman Smock (eds.), *Women: Role and Status in Eight Countries*. New York: John Wiley.

PHILLIPS, E. BARBARA. 1978. "Magazines' heroines: Is Ms. just another member of the Family Circle?" In Gaye Tuchman (ed.), *Hearth and Home: Images of Women in the Mass Media*. New York: Oxford University.

PHILLIPS, ROGER D., and FAITH D. GILROY. 1985. "Sex-role stereotypes and clinical judgements of mental health: The Brovermans' findings reexamined." *Sex Roles* 12(1–2):179–93.

PIAGET, JEAN. 1950. *The Psychology of Intelligence*. London: Routledge & Kegan Paul. 1954. *The Construction of Reality in the Child*. New York: Basic Books.

PIERCY, MARGE. 1982. *The Moon is Always Female*. New York: Alfred A. Knopf.

PIETROPINTO, ANTHONY, and JACQUELINE SIMENAUER. 1979. *Husbands and Wives*. New York: New York Times Books.

PLECK, JOSEPH H. 1975. "Masculinity-femininity: Current and alternative paradigms." *Sex Roles* 1:161–78. 1979. "Men's family work: Three perspectives and some new data." *The Family Coordinator* 28(October):481–88. 1983. "Husbands' paid work and family roles: Current research issues." In H. Lopata (ed.), *Research in the Interweave of Social Roles, Jobs and Families*. 1985. *Working Wives, Working Husbands*. Beverly Hills, CA: Sage.

POLOMA, MARGARET M., and T. NEAL GARLAND. 1971. "The married professional woman: A study in the tolerance of domestication." *Journal of Marriage and the Family* 33(3):531–39.

POLOMA, MARGARET, BRIAN F. PENDLETON, and T. NEAL GARLAND. 1982. "Reconsidering the dual-career marriage: A longitudinal approach." In Joan Aldous (ed.), *Two Paychecks: Life in Dual-Earner Families*. Beverly Hills, CA: Sage.

POMEROY, SARAH B. 1975. *Goddesses, Whores, Wives and Slaves: Women in Classical Antiquity*. New York: Schocken.

POOLE, KEITH T., and L. HARMON ZEIGLER. 1985. *Women, Public Opinion and Politics: The Changing Political Attitudes of American Women*. New York: Longman.

PRATHER, JANE, and LINDA S. FIDELL. 1975. "Sex differences in the content and style of medical advertisements." *Social Science and Medicine* 9:23–26.

PRINGLE, M. B. 1973. "The responses of counselors to behaviors associated with independence and achievement in male and female clients." Doctoral Dissertation. Ann Arbor, MI: University of Michigan.

PROPPER, ALICE MARCELLA. 1972. "The relationship of maternal employment to adolescent roles. activities and parental relationships." *Journal of Marriage and the Family* (August):417–21.

PRUETT, KYLE D. 1987. *The Nurturing Father: Journey Toward the Complete Man*. New York: Warner.

RADHAKRISHNAN, SARVEPALLI. 1947. *Religion and Society*. London: Allen and Unwin.

RADKE-YARROW, MARIAN, PHYLLIS SCOTT, LOUISE DE LEEVIEV, and CHRISTINE HEINIG. 1962. "Child-rearing in families of working and nonworking women." *Sociometry* 25(2):122–40.

RADWAY, J. R. 1984. *Reading and Romance: Women Patriarchy and Popular Literature*. Chapel Hill, NC: University of North Carolina Press.

RAINWATER, L., R. COLEMAN, and G. HANDEL. 1959. *Workingman's Wife*. New York: Oceana.

RAMEY, JAMES. 1978. "Experimental family forms: The family of the future." *Marriage and Family Review* 1:1–9.

RANDALL, VICKY. 1982. *Women and Politics*. New York: St. Martin's Press.

RAO, V. V. PRAKASA, and V. NANDINI RAO. 1980. "Instrumental and expressive values in mate selection among black students." *The Western Journal of Black Studies* 4(Spring):50–56.

RAPOPORT, RHONA, and ROBERT RAPOPORT. 1971. *Dual Career Families*. New York: Viking.

RAY, REGINALD A. 1980. "Accomplished women in tantric Buddhism of medieval India and Tibet." In Nancy Auer Falk and Rita Gross (eds.), *Unspoken Worlds: Women's Religious Lives in Non-Western Cultures*. New York: Harper and Row.

REED, REX. 1975. "Movies: Give them back to the women." *Vogue* 165(March):130–31.

REINHOLD, R. 1983. "An overwhelming violence—TV tie." *The New York Times* May 6 :C27.

REISS, IRA L. 1972. "Premarital sexuality: Past, present and future." In Ira L. Reiss (ed.), *Readings on the Family System*. New York: Holt, Rinehart and Winston.

REMICK, HELEN (ed.). 1984. *Comparable Worth and Wage Discrimination*. Philadelphia: Temple University.

RENDELY, JUDITH G., ROBERT M. HOLMSTROM, and STEPHAN A. KARP. 1984. "The relationship of sex-role identity life style, and mental health in suburban American homemakers: 1. Sex role, employment and adjustment." *Sex Roles* 11(9–10):839–48.

RENNE, KAREN S. 1976. "Childlessness, health and marital satisfaction." *Social Biology* 23(Fall):183–97.

RESICK, P. A. 1983. "Sex role stereotypes and violence against women." In V. Franks and E. Rothblum (eds.), *The Stereotyping of Women: Its Effects on Mental Health*. New York: Springer.

RESKIN, BARBARA F. 1988. "Bringing the man back in: Sex differentiation and the devaluation of woman's work." *Gender and Society* 2(1):58–81.

RHEINGOLD, H., and K. COOK. 1975. "The content of boys' and girls' rooms as an index of parent behavior." *Child Development* 46:459–63.

RICHARDSON, LAUREL WALUM. 1981. *The Dynamics of Sex and Gender: A Sociological Perspective.* Boston: Houghton Mifflin. 1986. "Another world." *Psychology Today* (February):23–27. 1988. *The Dynamics of Sex and Gender: A Sociological Perspective.* New York: Harper and Row.

RIESMAN, DAVID. 1972. "Some dilemmas of women's education." In Scarvia Anderson (ed.), *Sex Differences and Discrimination in Education.* Belmont, CA: Wadsworth.

RISMAN, BARBARA J. 1987. "Intimate relationships from a microstructural perspective: Men who mother." *Gender and Society* 1(1):6–32.

ROBERTSON, IAN. 1987. *Sociology.* New York: Worth.

ROBERTSON, THOMAS S., and JOHN R. ROSSITER. 1977. "Children's responsiveness to commercials." *Journal of Communication* 27(1):101–06.

ROBY, PAMELA. 1972. "Structural and internalized barriers to women in higher education." In Constantina Safilios-Rothschild (ed.), *Toward A Sociology of Women.* Lexington, MA: Xerox.

RODNITZKY, JEROME L. 1976. "The southwest unbound: Janis Joplin and the new feminism." *Feminist Art Journal* 5(4):22–25.

Roper Organization. 1980. *The 1980 Virginia Slims American Women's Opinion Poll: A Survey of Contemporary Attitudes.* Storrs: Roper Center, University of Connecticut.

ROSE, MARY BETH (ed.). 1986. *Women in the Middle Ages and the Renaissance: Literary/Historical Perspectives.* Syracuse: Syracuse University.

ROSE, R. M., T. P. GORDON, and J. S. BERNSTEIN. 1972. "Plasma testosterone levels in the male rhesus: Influences of sexual and social stimuli." *Science* 178:643–45.

ROSEN, E. 1982. "The changing jobs of American women factory workers." Paper presented at the Conference on the Changing Jobs of American Women Workers. Washington, D.C.: George Washington University.

ROSEN, MARJORIE. 1974. "Isn't it about time to bring on the girls?" *The New York Times* December 15:D19.

ROSENBAUM, J. E. 1985. "Persistence and change in pay inequalities: Implications for job evaluation and comparable worth." In L. Larwood, A. Stromberg and B. Gutek (eds.), *Women and Work: An Annual Review, Vol. 1.* Beverly Hills, CA: Sage.

ROSENTHAL, DOREEN A., and DIANNE C. CHAPMAN. 1982. "The lady spaceman: Children's perceptions of sex-stereotyped occupations." *Sex Roles* 8(9):959–65.

ROSENWASSER, SHIRLEY M., M. HOPE GONZALES, and VIKKI ADAMS. 1985. "Perceptions of a housespouse: The effects of sex, economic productivity and subject background variables." *Psychology of Women Quarterly* 9:258–64.

ROSSI, ALICE. 1968. "Transition to parenthood." *Journal of Marriage and the Family* 30:26–39. 1972. "Family development in a changing world." *American Journal of Psychiatry* 128:1957–65. 1984. "Gender and parenthood: An evolutionary perspective." *American Sociological Review* 49(February):1–19.

ROTENBERG, KEN J. "Sex differences in children's trust in peers." *Sex Roles* 11(9–10):953–57.

ROY, MARIA. 1977. "A current survey of 150 cases." In I. M. Roy (ed.), *Battered Women.* New York: Van Nostrand.

RUBBO, ANNA, and MICHAEL TAUSSIG. 1977. "Up off their knees: Servanthood in southwest Columbia." *Michigan Discussions of Anthropology* 3(Fall).

RUBENSTEIN, CARIN. 1983. "The modern art of courtly love." *Psychology Today* 19:40–49. 1986. "About love." In Carol Travis (ed.), *Everywoman's Emotional Well-Being.* Garden City: Doubleday.

RUBENSTEIN, CARIN, and P. SHAVER. 1982. *In Search of Intimacy.* New York: Delacorte.

RUBIN, JEFFREY Z., FRANK J. PROVENZANO, and ZELLA LURIA. 1974. "The eye of the beholder: Parent's views on sex of newborns." *American Journal of Orthopsychiatry.* 44(4):512–19.

RUBIN, ZICK. 1973. *Liking and Loving: An Invitation to Social Psychology.* New York: Holt, Rinehart and Winston. 1983. "Are working wives hazardous to their husband's mental health?" *Psychology Today* 17:70–72.

RUDOLPH, LLOYD, and SUSANN HOEBER RUDOLPH. 1967. *The Modernity of Transition: Political Development in India.* Chicago: University of Chicago.

RUPP, LEILA. 1978. *Mobilizing Women for War: German and American Propaganda, 1939–1945.* Princeton: Princeton University.

RUSSEL, D. and N. VANDE VEN. 1976. "International crimes against women." *Proceedings les Femmes:* Conference Publication.

RUSSELL, C. 1975. "Transition to parenthood: Problems and gratifications." *Journal of Marriage and the Family* 36:294–301.

RUSSO, NANCY FELIPE. 1975. "Eye contact, interpersonal distance and the equilibrium theory." *Journal of Personality and Social Psychology* 31(March):497–502. 1979. "Overview: Sex roles, fertility and the motherhood mandate." *Psychology of Women Quarterly* 4:7–15.

RUSSO, VITO. 1986. "Whoopi Goldberg: Steven Spielberg chose the Broadway phenom to help him paint the color purple." *Moviegoer* 5(1).

RYAN, S. 1975. "Gynecological considerations." *Journal of Health, Physical Education, and Recreation.* (January):4044.

SAARIO, T. N., C. N. JACKLIN, and C. K. TITTLE. 1973. "Sex role stereotypes in the public schools." *Harvard Educational Review* 43(3):386–416.

SADD, S., M. LENAUER, P. SHAVER, and N. DUNIVANT. 1978. "Objective measurement of fear of success and fear of failure." *Journal of Consulting and Clinical Psychology* 46:405–16.

SADD, S., F. O. MILLER, and B. ZEITZ. 1979. "Sex roles and achievement conflicts." *Personality and Social Psychology Bulletin* 5:(552–55).

SADKER, MYRA, and DAVID SADKER. 1974. "Sexism in schools: An issue for the 70's." *Educational Digest* (April):58–61. 1985. "Sexism in the schoolroom of the 80's." *Psychology Today* 19(3):54–56.

SADKER, MYRA, DAVID SADKER, and SUSAN S. KLEIN. 1986. "Abolishing misconceptions about sex equity in education." *Theory into Practice* 25(Autumn):219–26.

SAKOL, JEANNIE, and LUCIANNE GOLDBERG. 1975. "Married is better." In Kenneth C. W. Kammeyer (ed.), *Confronting the Issues: Sex Roles, Marriage and the Family.* Boston: Allyn and Bacon.

SALEH, SANEYA. 1972. "Women in Islam: Their status in religious and traditional culture." *International Journal of the Family* (March):35–42.

SANASARIAN, ELIZ. 1982. *The Women's Rights Movement in Iran: Mutiny, Appeasement and Repression from 1900 to Khomeni.* New York: Praeger. 1986. "Political activism and Islamic identity in Iran." In Lynn B. Iglitzin and Ruth Ross (eds.), *Women in the World, 1975–1985: The Women's Decade.* Santa Barbara, CA: ABC-Clio.

SANDERSON, LILIAN PASSMORE. 1981. *Against the Mutilation of Women.* London: Ithaca.

SANDLER, BERNICE R. 1987. "The classroom climate: A chilly one for women." In Carol Lasser (ed.), *Educating Men and Women Together: Coeducation in a Changing World.* Chicago: University of Illinois.

SAPIRO, VIRGINIA. 1986. *Women in American Society.* Palo Alto, CA: Mayfield.

SCANZONI, LETHA, D., and JOHN SCANZONI. 1988. *Men, Women and Change: A Sociology of Marriage and Family.* New York: McGraw-Hill.

SCARR, S. 1984. *Mother Care/Other Care.* New York: Basic.

SCHAU, C. G., and K. P. SCOTT. 1984. "Impact of gender characteristics of instructional materials: An integration of research literature." *Journal of Advertising Research* 19:23–27.

SCHEIBE, CYNDY. 1979. "Sex roles in television commercials." *Journal of Advertising Research* 19:23–27.

SCHLAFLY, PHYLLIS. 1981. *Testimony: Sex Discrimination in the Workplace.* Washington, D.C.: U.S. Government Printing Office.

SCHNEIDER, KENNETH C. 1979. "Sex roles in television commercials: New dimensions for comparison." *Akron Business and Economic Review* (Fall):20–24.

SCHORR, ALVIN, and PHYLLIS MOEN. 1982. "The single parent and public policy." In Jeffrey P. Rosenfeld (ed.), *Relationships: The Marriage and Family Reader.* Glenview, IL: Scott, Foresman.

SCHREIBER, C. T. 1979. *Changing Places.* Boston: MIT Press.

SCHUSSLER-FIORENZA, ELIZABETH. 1983. *In Memory of Her: A Feminist Theological Reconstruction of Christian Origins.* New York: Crossroads.

SCHWARTZ, A. 1979. "Androgyny and the art of loving." *Psychotherapy: Theory, Research and Practice.* 16:405–8.

SCHWARTZ, PEPPER. 1973. "Social Games and Social Roles: Effects of a College Dating System." Ph.D. Dissertation, Yale University.

SCOTT, R. 1976. *The Female Consumer.* London: Associated Business Programs.

SCOTT, RONALD L. 1982. "Analysis of the need systems of twenty male rapists." *Psychological Reports* 51:1119–25.

SCOTT, W. J., and C. S. MORGAN. 1983. "An analysis of factors affecting traditional family expectations and perceptions of ideal fertility." *Sex Roles* 9:901–14.

SCULLY, DIANA, and P. BART. 1973. "A funny thing happened on the way to the orifice: Women in gynecology textbooks." *American Journal of Sociology* 78:1045–50.

SCULLY, DIANA, and JOSEPH MAROLLA. 1984. "Convicted rapists' vocabulary of motive: Excuses and justifications." *Social Problems* 31(5):530–44. 1985. "'Riding the bull at Gilley's': Convicted rapists describe the rewards of rape." *Social Problems* 32(3):251–63.

SEARS, R., E. MACCOBY, and H. LEVIN. 1957. *Patterns of Child Rearing.* Evanston, IL: Rew and Peterson.

SEIDENBERG, ROBERT. 1971. "Drug advertising and perception of mental illness." *Mental Hygiene* 55:21–30.

SEIFER, NANCY. 1973. *Absent From the Majority: Working Class Women in America.* New York: National Project on Ethnic America.

SELLS, LUCY. 1978. "Mathematics: A critical filter." *The Science Teacher* (February):28–29.

SELNOW, GARY W. 1985. "Sex differences in uses and perceptions of profanity." *Sex Roles* 12(3–4):303–12.

Service Book and Hymnal. 1958. Lutheran Church in America. Minneapolis: Augsburg.

SEXTON, DONALD E., and PHYLLIS HABERMAN. 1974. "Women in magazine advertisements." *Journal of Advertising Research* 14:41–46.

SHAPIRO, JERROLD LEE. 1987. "The expectant father." *Psychology Today* 21(January):36–39.

SHARITS, DEAN, and H. BRUCE LAMMERS. 1982. "Men fill more TV sex roles." *Market Roles* (September 3).

SHARMA, RAM SHARAN. 1983. *Material Culture and Social Formations in Ancient India.* New Delhi: Macmillan.

SHARMA, URSULA. 1980. *Women, Work and Property in Northwest India.* London: Tavistock.

SHEARER, LLOYD. 1986. "Money, money, money." *Parade* (January 12):18–19.

SHEEHY, G. 1976. *Passages: Predictable Crises of Adult Life.* New York: Bantam.

SHEHAN, CONSTANCE L., MARY ANN BURG, and CYNTHIA A. REXROAT. 1986. "Depression and the social dimensions of the full-time housewife role." *The Sociological Quarterly* 27(1):403–21.

SHERIF, CAROLYN W. 1982. "Needed concepts in the study of gender identity." *Psychology of Women Quarterly* 6:375–98.

SHERMAN, JULIA. 1967. "Problems of sex differences in space perception and aspects of intellectual functioning." *Psychological Review* 74:290–99.

SHIMONY, ANNE MARIE. 1980. "Women of influence and prestige among the native American Iroquois." In Nancy Auer Falk and Rita Gross (eds.), *Unspoken Worlds: Women's Religious Lives in Nonwestern Cultures.* New York: Harper and Row.

SHIRAZI, MANNY. 1985. "Work-Soviet Union." In Debbie Taylor, Anita Desu, et. al. (eds.), *Women: A World Report.* New York: Oxford University.

SHORTRIDGE, KATHLEEN. 1984. "Poverty is a woman's problem." In Jo Freeman (ed.), *Women: A Feminist Perspective.* Palo Alto, CA: Mayfield.

SHOWALTER, ELAINE. 1986. *The Female Malady: Women, Madness and English Culture: 1830–1980.* New York: Pantheon.

SIDOROWICZ, LAURA S., and G. SPARKS LUNNEY. 1980. "Baby X revisited." *Sex Roles* 6:67–73.

SIGNORIELLI, NANCY. 1982. "Marital status in television drama: A case of reduced options." *Job* 24(2)(Spring).

SILBERT, M. H., and A. M. PINES. 1984. "Pornography and sexual abuse of women." *Sex Roles* 10:857–68.

SILKA, L., and S. KIESLER. 1977. "Couples who choose to remain childless." *Family Planning Perspective* 9:16–25.

SILVER, SHEILA J. 1976. "Then and now: Women's roles in *McCall's Magazine* in 1964 and 1974." Paper presented at the Annual Meeting of the Association for Education in Journalism.

SILVERBLATT, IRENE. 1980. "Andean women under Spanish rule." In Mona Etienne and Eleanor Leacock (eds.), *Women and Colonization: Anthropological Perspectives.* New York: Praeger.

SILVERN, L. E. 1977. "Children's sex-role preferences: Stronger among girls than boys." *Sex Roles* 3:159–71.

SIMS, BARBARA, B. 1974. "She's got to be a saint, lord knows, I ain't: Feminine Masochism in American Country Music." *Journal of Country Music* 5:24–30

SIMMONS, A., A. FREEDMAN, M. DUNKLE, and F. BLAU. 1975. *Exploitation from 9 to 5.* Lexington, MA: Lexington.

SIMPSON, LAWRENCE A. 1972. "A myth is better than a Miss: Men get the edge in academic employment." In Scarvia Anderson (ed.), *Sex Differences and Discrimination in Education.* Belmont, CA: Wadsworth.

SLOAN, ETHEL. 1985. *Biology of Women.* (2nd Edition.) New York: John Creiley.

SLOANE, B. K. 1983. "In brief." *National NOW Times* (November):16.

SMELSER, NEIL J. 1981. *Sociology.* Englewood Cliffs: Prentice Hall.

SMITH, M. L. 1980. "Sex bias in counseling and psychotherapy." *Psychological Bulletin* 87:392–407.

SMITH, MARGO. 1973. "Domestic service as a channel of upward mobility for the lower-class women: The Lima case." In Ann Pescatello, (ed.), *Female and Male in Latin America.* Pittsburgh: University of Pittsburgh.

SMITH, MARSHALL P. 1972. "He only does it to annoy." In Scarvia Anderson (ed.), *Sex Differences and Discrimination in Education.* Belmont, CA: Wadsworth.

SMITH, SHARON. 1975. *Women Who Make Movies.* New York: Hopkinson and Blake.

Soo, CHONG. 1969. "The monetary value of a housewife." *American Journal of Economics and Sociology*. 28(3):271–84.

SPANIER, GRAHAM, and PAUL C. GLICK. 1980. "Mate selection differentials between whites and blacks in the United States." *Social Forces* 53(3):707–25.

SPENCER, META. 1985. *Foundations of Modern Sociology*. Englewood Cliffs: Prentice Hall.

SPITZE, GLENNA. 1986. "The division of task responsibility in U.S. households: Longitudinal adjustments to change." *Social Forces* 64(March):689–701.

STABINER, KAREN. 1985. "Cagney and Lacey! Lacey's pregnancy is a natural for TV social comment." *St. Louis Post-Dispatch* September 29:3F–10F.

STAFFORD, REBECCA, ELAINE BARKMAN, and PAMELA DIBONA. 1977. "The division of labor among cohabiting and married couples." *Journal of Marriage and the Family*. 39(February):43–57.

STANLEY, JULIA P. 1972. "Paradigmatic woman: The Prostitute." Paper presented at South Atlantic Modern Language Association, Jacksonville, FL. (November).

STAPLES, ROBERT. 1970. "The Myth of Black matriarchy." *The Black Scholar* 1(January-February):8–16. 1973. *The Black Woman in America*. Chicago: Nelson-Hall.

STAYTON, WILLIAM R. 1984. "Lifestyle Spectrum 1984." (Sex Information and Educational Council of the U.S.) *SIECUS Reports* 12(3):1–4.

STEIL, J. 1984. "Marital relationships and mental health: The psychic costs of inequality." In Jo Freeman (ed.), *Women: A Feminist Perspective*. Palo Alto, CA: Mayfield.

STEIN, A., and M. BAILEY. 1973. "The socialization of achievement orientation in females." *Psychological Bulletin* 80(5):345–66.

STEIN, HARRY. 1987. "The case for staying home." In Ollie Pocs and Robert H. Walsh (eds.), *Marriage and Family: Annual Editions*. Guilford, CT: Dushkin.

STENDAHL, KRISTEN. 1974. "Enrichment or threat: When the Eves come marching in." In Alice L. Hageman (ed.), *Sexist Religion and Women in the Church*. New York: Association Press.

STEPHAN, COOKIE WHITE, and JUDY CORDER. 1985. "The effects of dual-career families on adolescent's sex roles, attitudes, work and family plans, and choices of important others." *Journal of Marriage and the Family* (November):921.

STERN, GERALDINE. 1979. *Israeli Women Speak Out*. Philadelphia: J. B. Lippincott.

STERNGLANZ, SARAH H., and LISA A. SERBIN. 1974. "Sex role stereotyping in children's television programs." *Development Psychology* 10(5):710–15.

STEVENS, EVELYN P. 1973. "Marianismo: The other face of machismo in Latin America." In Ann Pesscatello (ed.), *Female and Male in Latin America*. Pittsburgh: Pittsburgh University.

STIMSON, GERRY V. 1975. "The message of psychotropic drug ads." *Journal of Communication* 25(3):153–60.

ST. JOHN-PARSONS, D. 1978. "Continuous dual-career families: A case study." In J. B. Bryson and R. Bryson (eds.), *Dual-Career Couples*. New York: Human Sciences.

STOCK, PHYLLIS. 1978. *Better than Rubies*. New York: G. P. Putnam's Sons.

STOCKARD, J., and M. M. JOHNSON. 1980. *Sex Roles: Sex Inequality and Sex Role Development*. Englewood Cliffs: Prentice Hall.

STONE, E. 1979. "Mothers and daughters: Taking a new look at Mom." *The New York Times Magazine* (May 13):14–15,17,62,79,90–92.

STORTZ, MARTHA E. 1984. "The mother, the son and the bullrushes." *Dialog: A Journal of Theology* 23(1):21–26.

STRATHAM, ANNE, SUZANNE VAUGHN, and SHARON K. HOUSEKNECHT. 1987. "The professional involvement of higher educated women: The impact of the family." *Sociological Quarterly* 28(1):119–33.

STRATTON, JO ANNA L. 1981. *Pioneer Women: Voices from the Kansas Frontier*. New York: Simon and Schuster.

STRAUS, M. 1980. "A sociological perspective on the causes of family violence." In M. Green (ed.), *Violence in the Family*. Boulder: Westview.

STREICHER, HELEN WHITE. 1974. "The girls in the cartoons." *Journal of Communication* 24(Spring):125–29.

STRONG, BRYAN, and CHRISTINE DEVAULT. 1988. *Understanding our Sexuality*. St. Paul: West.

STUTEVILLE, JOHN R. 1971. "Sexually polarized products and advertising strategy." *Journal of Retailing* 47(Summer):3–13.

SUGISAKA, KAZUKO. 1986. "From the moon to the sun: Women's liberation in Japan." In Lynn B. Iglitzin and Ruth Ross (eds.), *Women in the World: 1975–1985, The Women's Decade*. Santa Barbara, CA: ABC-Clio.

SUTKER, PATRICIA B. 1982. "Drug dependent women." *Grassroots: Special Populations* (May-June):19–29.

SUTTON-SMITH, BRIAN. 1979. "The play of girls." In Claire B. Kopp (ed.), *Becoming Female*. New York: Plenum.

SWACKER, MARJORIE. 1975. "The sex of the speaker as a sociolinguistic variable." In Barrie Thorne and Nancy Henley (eds.), *Language and Sex: Difference and Dominance*. Rowley, MA: Newbury House.

SYMONS, DONALD. 1979. *The Evolution of Human Sexuality*. New York: Oxford University Press.

TABARI, AZAR. 1982. "Islam and the struggle for emancipation of Iranian women." In Azar Tabari and Nahid Yeganeh (eds.), *The Shadow of Islam: The Women's Movement in Iran*. London: Zed.

TALKINGTON, TRACY F. 1976. "An analysis of sex role stereotypes in popular songs, 1955–1976." Unpublished master's thesis, University of Oregon.

TAMIR, LOIS M. 1982. "Men at middle age: Developmental transitions." *Annals, AAPSS* 464(November):47–64.

TANNAHILL, REAY. 1980. *Sex in History*. New York: Stein and Day.

THAPAR, ROMILA. 1966. *A History of India*, Volume I. New York: Penguin.

THEODORE, ATHENA (ed.). 1971. *The Professional Woman*. Cambridge, MA: Schenkmann.

THOM, M. 1984. "The all-time definitive map of the gender gap." *MS.* (July):55–60.

THOMAS, WILLIAM I. 1966 (original, 1931). "The relation of research to the social process." In Morris Janowitz (ed.), *W.I. Thomas on Social Organization and Social Personality*. Chicago: University of Chicago.

THOMPSON, EDWARD H., CHRISTOPHER GRISSANTI, and JOSEPH H. PLECK. 1985. "Attitudes toward the male role and their correlates." *Sex Roles* 13(7–8):413–27.

THORKELSON, ANNE E. 1985. "Women under the law: Has equity been achieved?" In Alice G. Sargent (ed.), *Beyond Sex Roles*. St. Paul: West.

THORNTON, ARLAND, and DEBORAH FREEDMAN. 1986. "Changing attitudes toward marriage and single life." In Ollie Pocs and Robert H. Walsh (eds.), *Marriage and Family Annual Editions*. Guilford, CT: Dushkin.

TIEDT, I. M. 1972. "Realistic counseling for high school girls." *The School Counselor* (May):354–56.

TIEFER, LENORE. 1986. "In pursuit of the perfect penis." *American Behavioral Scientist* 29(5):579–99.

TIGER, LIONEL. 1969. *Men in Groups*. New York: Random House.

TIGER, LIONEL, and ROBIN FOX. 1971. *The Imperial Animal*. New York: Dell.

TIGER, LIONEL, and JOSEPH SHEPHER. 1975. *Women in the Kibbutz*. New York: Harcourt Brace Jovanovich.

TOBIAS, SHEILA. 1972. "How co-education fails women." In Scarvia Anderson (ed.), *Sex Differences and Discrimination in Education*. Belmont, CA: Wadsworth.

TOLSON, ANDREW. 1977. *The Limits of Masculinity: Male Identity and Women's Liberation*. New York: Harper and Row.

TREBILCOT, JOYCE. 1977. "Two Forms of Androgynism." *Journal of Social Philosophy* 8(1).

TRECKER, JANICE. 1974. "Room at the bottom: Girls' access to vocational training." *Social Education* 38(October):533–37. 1975. "Women in U.S. history high school textbooks." In Elizabeth Steiner Maccia (ed.), *Women and Education*. Springfield, IL: Charles C. Thomas.

UNESCO. 1980. *Women in the Media*. Paris: UNESCO.

United Nations. 1985. *The State of the World's Women, 1985*. World Conference to Review and Appraise the Achievements of the United Nations Decade for Women: Equality, Development and Peace. Nairobi, Kenya (July 15–26). Oxford, UK: New Internationalist Publications.

United Nations High Commissioner for Refugees. 1987. "Geography of Exile." *Refugees* 48(December).

U.S. Bureau of the Census. 1975. *Statistical Abstract of the United States*. U.S. Department of Commerce. Washington, D.C.: U.S. Government Printing Office. 1985. *Statistical Abstract of the United States*. U.S. Department of Commerce. Washington, D.C.: U.S. Government Printing Office. 1987. *Statistical Abstract of the United States*. U.S. Department of Commerce. Washington, D.C.: U.S. Government Printing Office.

U.S. Department of Health and Human Services. 1987. *Health: United States*. Washington, D.C.: U.S. Government Printing Office.

U. S. Department of Labor. 1969. *Handbook on Women Workers*. Bulletin No. 294. Women's Bureau. Washington, D.C.: U.S. Government Printing Office. 1975. *Handbook on Women Workers*. Bulletin No. 297. Women's Bureau. Washington, D.C.: U.S. Government Printing Office. 1977. *U.S. Working Women: A Databook*. Bureau of Labor Statistics. Washington, D.C.: U.S. Government Printing Office. 1982. *Employment and Earnings* (March). Bureau of Labor Statistics. Washington, D.C.: U.S. Government Printing Office. 1983. *Monthly Labor Review: Research Summaries*. 108 (1):55–59. Bureau of Labor Statistics. Washington, D.C.: U.S. Government Printing Office. 1985. *Civilian Labor Force*. Table 18: 1975–1984 & Projections to 1995. Bureau of Labor Statistics. Washington, D.C.: U.S. Government Printing Office. 1986a. *Median Full-Time Wage and Salary Workers: Annual Average, 1984*. Table 7. Bureau of Labor Statistics. Washington, D.C.: U.S. Government Printing Office. 1986b. *Employment and Earnings*. Table 1–2: Employment Status, 1947–1981. Bureau of Labor Statistics. Washington, D.C.: U.S. Government Printing Office. 1986c. *Employment and Earnings*. Table A–2: Employment Status, 1948–1983. Bureau of Labor Statistics. Washington, D.C.: U.S. Government Printing Office. 1987a. *Employment and Earnings*. Table A–2: Household Data (Historical), 1975–1986. Bureau of Labor Statistics. Washington, D.C.: U.S. Government Printing Office. 1987b. *Employment and Earnings*. Table 1: Employment Status, 1950–1983. Bureau of Labor Statistics. Washington, D.C.: U.S. Government Printing Office.

U. S. Public Health Service. 1985. *Women's Health: Report of the Public Health Service Task Force on Women's Health Issues*. (Volume I). 100(1):73–106.

VANEK, JOANN. 1974. "Time spent in housework." *Scientific American* (November):116–20.

VEBLEN, THORSTEN. 1953 (original, 1899). *The Theory of the Leisure Class*. New York: Mentor Books.

VEEVERS, J. E. 1972. "The violation of fertility mores: Voluntary childlessness as deviant behavior." In C. Boydell (ed.), *Deviant Behavior and Societal Reaction*. Toronto: Holt, Rinehart and Winston.

VENKATESAN, M., and JEAN LOSCO. 1975. "Women in magazine ads: 1959–71." *Journal of Advertising Research* 15(October):49–54.

VERBRUGGE, LOIS M. 1976. "Females and illness: Recent trends in sex differences in the United States." *Journal of Health and Social Behavior* 17:387–403. 1984. "Physical health of clerical workers in the U.S., Framingham and Detroit." *Women and Health* 9(1):17–41.

VERDESI, ELIZABETH HOWELL. 1973. *In But Still Out: Women in the Church.* Philadelphia: Westminster.

VERNA, MARY ELLEN. 1975. "The female image in children's TV commercials." *Journal of Broadcasting* (Summer):301–09.

VINOVSKIS, MARIS A. 1986. "Young fathers and their children: Some historical and policy perspectives." In Arthur B. Elster and Michael E. Lamb (eds.), *Adolescent Fatherhood.* Hillsdale, NJ: Lawrence Erlbaum.

WAGNER, LOUIS C., and JANIS D. BANOS. 1973. "A woman's place: A follow-up analysis of the roles portrayed by women in magazine advertisements." *Journal of Marketing Research* (May):213–14.

WALDROP, M. F., and C. F. HALVERSON, JR. 1975. "Intensive and extensive peer behavior: Longitudinal and cross sectional analysis." *Child Development* 46:19–26.

WALKER, K. E., and W. H. GAUGER. 1973. "Time and its dollar value in household work." *Family Economic Review* 7:8–13.

WALKER, KATHRYN, and MARGARET WOODS. 1976. "Time use: A measure of household production of family goods and services." Washington, D.C.: American Home Economics.

WALLERSTEIN, J. 1984. "Children of divorce: Preliminary report of a ten-year follow-up of young children." *American Journal of Orthopsychiatry* 54:444–58.

WALLEY, D. (n.d.)a. "What girls can be." Kansas City: Hallmark.

WALLEY, D. (n.d.)b. "What boys can be." Kansas City: Hallmark.

WALSHOK, M. L. 1981. *Blue-Collar Women: Pioneers on the Male Frontier.* Garden City, New York: Anchor.

WALSTER, ELAINE, T. ANNE CLEARY, and MARGARET N. CLIFFORD. 1972. "The effects of race and sex on college admission." In Scarvia Anderson (ed.), *Sex Differences and Discrimination in Education.* Belmont, CA: Wadsworth.

WATSON, ROY E. L. 1986. "Premarital cohabitation vs. traditional courtship: Their effects on subsequent marital adjustment." In Ollie Pocs and Robert H. Walsh, *Annual Editions Marriage and Family, 86–87.* Guilford, CT: Dushkin.

WEAVER, CHARLES N., and SANDRA L. HOLMES. 1975. "A comparative study of the work satisfaction of females with full-time employment and full-time housekeeping." *Journal of Applied Psychology.* 60(1):117–18.

WEBER, MAX. 1946. *From Max Weber: Essays in Sociology.* H.H. Gerth and C. W. Mills (eds. & trs.). New York: Oxford University Press.

WEINGARTEN, K. 1978. "The employment pattern of professional couples and their distribution of involvement in the family." In J. B. Bryson and R. Bryson (eds.), *Dual-Career Couples.* New York: Human Sciences.

WEISS, ROBERT. 1979. *Going it Alone: The Family Life and Social Situation of the Single Parent.* New York: Basic Books.

WEITZ, SHIRLEY. 1977. *Sex Roles: Biological, Psychological and Social Foundations.* New York: Oxford University Press.

WEITZMAN, LENORE J. 1979. *Sex Role Socialization: A Focus on Women.* Palo Alto, CA: Mayfield. 1984. "Sex-role socialization: A focus on women." In Jo Freeman (ed.), *Women: A Feminist Perspective.* (3rd Edition.) Palo Alto, CA: Mayfield.

WEITZMAN, LENORE J., DEBORAH EIFLER, ELIZABETH HOKADA, and CATHERINE ROSS. 1972. "Sex-role socialization in picture books for preschool children." *American Journal of*

Sociology 77(May):1125–50. 1985. *The Divorce Revolution: The Unexpected Social and Economic Consequences for Women and Children in America.* New York: The Free Press.

WEITZMAN, LENORE, and DIANA RIZZO. 1974. *Images of Males and Females in Elementary School Textbooks.* New York: NOW Legal Defense and Education Fund.

WELTER, BARBARA. 1980. "The cult of true womanhood: 1820–1860." In Esther Katz and Anita Rapone (eds.), *Women's Experiences in America: An Historical Anthology.* New Brunswick, NJ: Transaction.

WENDER, DOROTHEA. 1984. "Plato: Misogynist, Phaedophile, and Feminist." In John Peradotta and J.P. Sullivan (eds.), *Women in the Ancient World: The Arethusa Papers.* Albany: SUNY.

WERTHEIMER, BARBARA M. 1984. "Union is power: Sketches from women's labor history." In Jo Freeman (ed.), *Women: A Feminist Perspective.* Palo Alto, CA: Mayfield.

WHITE, ELIZABETH H. 1978. "Legal reform as an indicator of women's status in Muslim nations." In Lois Beck and Nikki Keddie (eds.), *Women in the Muslim World.* Cambridge: Harvard University.

WHITE, STEPHEN. 1979. *Political Culture and Soviet Politics.* London: Macmillan.

WICKENDEN, DOROTHY. 1986. "The women's movement looks beyond equality: What now?" *New Republic* (May 5):19–25.

WILBOURN, B. L. 1978. "The myth of the perfect mother." In L. Harmon, J. Bert, L. Fitzgerald, and M. F. Tanney (eds.), *Counseling Women.* Monterey, CA: Brooks and Cole.

WILKINSON, MELVIN. 1976. "Romantic love: The great equalizer? Sexism in popular music." *The Family Coordinator* 25:161–66.

WILL, JERRIE, PATRICIA SELF, and NANCY DATAN. 1974. Unpublished paper presented at 82nd Annual Meeting of the American Psychological Association, 1974, as cited in Carol Tavris and Carole Offir, *The Longest War: Sex Differences in Perspective.* New York: Harcourt Brace Jovanovich, 1977.

WILLIAMS, J. ALLEN, JOETTA VERNON, MARTHA WILLIAMS, and KAREN MALECHA. 1987. "Sex role socialization in picture books: An update." *Social Science Quarterly.* 68(1):148–56.

WILLIAMS, JUANITA H. 1987. *Psychology of Women: Behavior in a Biosocial Context.* New York: W.W. Norton.

WILLIAMS, WENDY. 1978. *Sex Discrimination and the Law: Causes/Remedies.* (1978 Supplement). Boston: Little, Brown.

WILLIAMSON, N. E. 1976. *Sons or Daughters: A Cross-Cultural Survey of Parental Preferences.* Beverly Hills, CA: Sage.

WILSON, EDWARD O. 1975. *Sociobiology: The New Synthesis.* Princeton: Princeton University. 1978. *On Human Nature.* Cambridge: Harvard University.

WILSON, EVERETT K. 1971. *Sociology: Rules, Roles and Relationships.* Homewood, IL: Dorsey.

WIRTENBERG, T., and C. NAKAMURA. 1976. "Education: Barrier or boon to changing occupational roles of women?" *Journal of Social Issues* 32:165–79.

WITKOWSKI, TERRENCE H. 1975. "An experimental comparison of women's self and advertising image." In R. C. Carham (ed.), *New Marketing for Social and Economic Progress.* Chicago: American Marketing Association.

WOHLETTER, MARALINDA, and BRUCE H. LAMMERS. 1978. "An analysis of roles in print advertisements over a 20-year span: 1958–1978." In J. C. Olsen (ed.), *Advances in Consumer Research.* Ann Arbor: Association for Consumer Research.

WOLDOW, NORMAN. 1987. "Explaining male/female biological differences: Social science, culture and sociobiology." Unpublished manuscript from Biology Department, Maryville College, St. Louis.

WOLF, DEBORAH G. 1979. *The Lesbian Community.* Berkeley: University of California.

WOLF, MARGARET. 1975. "Women and suicide in China." In Margaret Wolf and Roxanne Wilke (eds.), *Women in Chinese Society*. Stanford: Stanford University.

WOLFE, B., and G. E. HAVERMAN. 1983. "Time allocation, market work, and changes in female health." *American Economic Review* 73(2):134–39.

WOLFE, VIRGINIA. 1928. *A Room of One's Own*. London: Hogarth.

WOLLSTONECRAFT, M. A. 1975 (original, 1792). *A Vindication of the Rights of Women*. New York: Norton.

YANKELOVICH, DANIEL. 1981. *New Rules*. New York: Bantam.

YOGEV, SARA, and ANDREA VIERRA. 1983. "The state of motherhood among professional women." *Sex Roles*. 9(3):391–96.

ZIMMERMAN, DON H., and CANDACE WEST. 1975. "Sex roles, interruptions and silences in conversation." In Barrie Thorne and Nancy Henley (eds.), *Language and Sex: Difference and Dominance*. Rowley, MA: Newbury House.

ZUCKERMAN, DIANA M., and DONALD H. SAYRE. 1982. "Cultural sex-role expectations and children's sex-role concepts." *Sex Roles* 8(August):853–62.

NAME INDEX

Fox, Robin, 31
Frankfort, Ellen, 235
Frankovic, Kathleen A., 263
Franzwa, Helen H., 233
Freedman, Deborah, 130
Freeman, Jo, 80, 81, 254, 257
French, Brandon, 238
Freud, Sigmund, 28–30
Frey, Sylvia R., 64, 65
Friedan, Betty, 11, 79, 80,
   195, 233, 269
Friedman, S., 264
Fruch, T., 232

Galbraith, Kenneth, 185
Gallagher, Margaret, 246
Gallup, George, 113, 121, 260
Galston, Arthur, 89
Gandhi, Indira, 91
Gandhi, Mahatma, 91, 93
Ganong, Lawrence H., 111
Gardner, J., 244
Garfinkel, Perry, 167, 171
Garland, T. Neal, 125
Gates, Margaret, 197
Gauger, W. H., 124
Geerkin, Michael, 124
Geis, F. L., 236
Geller, S. E., 41
Gelles, Richard J., 175
Gelman, D., 155
Genlis, Madame de, 204
Gerson, Mary Joan, 138
Gerstel, Naomi, 128
Gerth, H. H., 10
Gerzon, Mark, 168, 177, 178
Gibson, Charles, 244
Gilder, George, 130
Gingold, Judith, 174
Githens, Marianne, 262
Gleason, Jean Berko, 49
Glenn, Norval D., 121
Glick, Paul C., 111, 116, 131,
   145, 149
Goffman, Erving, 8, 235, 236
Goldberg, Lucianne, 118
Goldberg, Marvin E., 53
Goldberg, P. A., 213
Goldberg, Whoopi, 47
Goode, William J., 108, 124,
   125, 136, 181
Gordon, Ann D., 65, 68
Gorn, Gerald J., 53

Gornick, Vivian, 235
Gottfried, Adele, 143
Gottfried, Allen, 143
Gove, Walter R., 25, 26, 124,
   130
Gowan, Darryl C., 249
Graves, Robert, 56
Greard, Octavia, 206
Greenberg, Bradley S., 243
Greenberg, M., 139
Greene, Richard, 153
Greenwald, Maurine W., 183
Greer, W., 198
Greif, Geoffrey L., 156, 157,
   167
Gross, Harriet, 128
Gross, L., 232
Gross, Rita, 221
Grossman, Tracy Barr, 147
Gumbel, Bryant, 244
Gundry, Patricia, 230

Haas, Linda, 129
Haber, Barbara, 208
Haberman, Phyllis, 235
Hacker, Helen Mayer, 9
Hagen, Richard, 31
Hall, Edward T., 51
Hallberg, Edmond C., 170
Hallett, Judith P., 60
Halverson, C. F., Jr., 46
Hamill, Pete, 168
Hanson, Shirley M. H., 156
Hansson, Robert O., 147
Hare-Mustin, Rachel T., 138
Harmetz, Aljean, 238
Harragan, Betty Lehan, 46
Harriman, Lynda Cooper,
   138, 139
Harris, Ann Sutherland, 215
Harry, Joseph, 152
Hartmann, Susan M., 71, 72,
   73, 74
Haskell, Molly, 237, 238,
   239, 247
Hatfield, Elaine, 108
Haverman, G. E., 23
Heer, David, 111
Henley, Nancy M., 49, 50
Hennessee, Judith Adler, 236
Henze, Lura F., 131
Herek, Gregory M., 165
Herman, Judith, 140

Hess, Beth B., 4
Hesse-Biber, Sharlene, 183,
   199
Hetherington, E. M., 155
Hewlett, Sylvia Ann, 148
Heyward, Carter, 227
Hoffman, Charles D., 45, 49
Hoffman, D. M., 147
Hoffman, H. R., 52
Hoffman, L. W., 43
Hoffnung, Michele, 137
Hole, Judith, 71, 78, 79, 226
Holmes, Sandra L., 125
Holt, Alix, 86
Horner, Martina S., 181, 214,
   215
Hosken, Fran P., 103, 104
Howe, Florence, 210
Howe, Julia, 78
Howell, Mary C., 27
Hudson, John W., 131
Humphries, Martin, 167
Hunt, M., 32, 33
Hyde, Janet Shibley, 24, 34, 61

**Intons-Peterson, Margaret
   Jean, 169**

**Jacklin, Carol N., 18, 40, 41,
   45, 141, 152**
Jacobson, Doranne, 223
Jacquette, Jane, 97, 98
Jaffe, Lorna, 214
Jain, Subhash C., 236
Jeffery, Patricia, 222
Jeffries-Fox S., 232
Jelin, Elizabeth, 97
Jencks, Christopher, 149
Jesus Christ, 60, 227, 230
Jewett, R., 226
Johnson, Kay, 87
Johnson, M. M., 211, 216
Johnson, Virginia, 32, 33
Johnson, Warren R., 34
Joplin, Janis, 241
Joslyn, W. O., 18
Joy, S. S., 143
Julian, Joseph, 242
Juster, F. T., 202

Kagan, Jerome, 207
Kaminski, Donna M., 211
Kamm, Henry, 105

Rosen, E., 199
Rosen, Marjorie, 239
Rosenbaum, J. E., 197, 198
Rosenthal, Doreen A., 47
Rosenwasser, Shirley M., 151
Rossi, Alice, 35, 136, 200
Rossiter, John R., 53
Rotenberg, Ken J., 46
Rousseau, Jean, 205, 206
Roy, Maria, 175
Rubbo, Anna, 97
Rubenstein, Carin, 108, 110, 111, 123
Rubin, Jeffrey Z., 43
Rubin, Zick, 109, 125, 126
Rudolph, Lloyd, 224
Rudolph, Susann Hoeber, 224
Rupp, Leila, 74
Russel, D., 172
Russell, C., 297
Russo, Nancy Felipe, 49, 136
Russo, Vito, 47
Ryan, S., 64

Saario, T. N., 208, 212
Sadd, S., 147, 215
Sadker, David, 207, 210
Sadker, Myra, 207, 209, 210
Saint John-Parsons, D., 143
Sakol, Jeannie, 118, 119
Saleh, Saneya, 222
Salk, Lee, 142
Sanasarian, Elizabeth, 101, 102
Sanderson, Lilian Passmore, 104
Sandler, Bernice R., 214
Sapiro, Virginia, 12
Sayre, Donald H., 41
Scanzoni, John, 33
Scanzoni, Letha D., 33
Scarr, S., 143
Schau, C. G., 209
Scheibe, Cyndy, 237
Schlafly, Phyllis, 27, 118, 152, 266
Schneider, Kenneth C., 236, 247
Schorr, Alvin, 155
Schussler-Florenza, Elizabeth, 226, 229
Schwartz, A., 111
Schwartz, Pepper, 8
Sciglimpaglia, D., 235

Scott, K. P., 209
Scott, R., 245, 246
Scott, Ronald, 173
Scott, W. J., 138
Scully, Diana, 27, 173
Sears, R., 191
Seidenberg, Robert, 235
Seifer, Nancy, 199
Sells, Lucy, 211
Selnow, Gary W., 49
Serbin, Lisa A., 244
Sexton, Donald E., 235
Shah of Iran, 101, 102
Shapiro, Jerrold Lee, 169
Sharits, Dean, 247
Sharma, Ram Sharan, 90
Sharma, Ursula, 91
Shaver, P., 123
Shearer, Lloyd, 239
Sheehy G., 170
Shehan, Constance L., 123
Shepher, Joseph, 100
Sherif, Carolyn W., 3
Sherman, Julia, 211
Shimony, Anne Marie, 221
Shirazi, Manny, 86
Shirk, Stephen R., 41
Shortridge, Kathleen, 155, 256
Showalter, Elaine, 26
Signorielli, Nancy, 243
Silbert, M. H., 173
Silka, L., 138
Silver, Sheila J., 234
Silverblatt, Irene, 96
Silvern, L. E., 40
Simenauer, Jacqueline, 129
Simmons, A., 186, 190
Simpson, Lawrence A., 216
Sims, Barbara B., 240
Siperstein, Gary N., 150
Slater, Samuel, 183
Sloan, Ethel, 22, 23, 25
Sloane, B. K., 261
Slobodian, S., 208
Smelser, Neil J., 4, 6
Smith, Howard W., 252
Smith, M. L., 222
Smith, Margo, 91
Smith, Marshall P., 207, 208
Smith, Sharon, 246
Soo, Chong, 185
Spain, D., 198
Spanier, Graham, 33, 116

Spencer, Meta, 241
Spitze, Glenna, 122
Sporakowski, M., 110
Stabiner, Karen, 242
Stafford, Rebecca, 132
Stanley, Julia P., 48
Stansell, Christine, 66
Stanton, Elizabeth Cady, 76, 77, 78
Staples, Robert, 144, 145
Stayton, William R., 132
Steil, J., 25
Stein, A., 192
Stein, Harry, 141, 142
Steinmann, Anne, 146
Stendahl, Kristen, 226, 227
Stephan, Cookie White, 143
Stern, Geraldine, 99, 100
Sternglanz, Sarah H., 244
Stevens, Evelyn P., 96
Stimson, Gerry V., 235
Stock, Phyllis, 205, 206
Stockard, J., 211, 216
Stone, E., 220, 221
Stone, Lucy, 77, 78
Stortz, Martha E., 230, 231
Stratton, Jo Anna L., 67
Straus, Murray A., 174, 175
Streicher, Helen White, 243
Strong, Bryan, 3
Stuteville, John R., 247
Sugisaka, Kazuko, 94, 96
Sullivan, J. P., 56
Sutker, Patricia B., 24
Sutton-Smith, Brian, 44, 46
Swacker, Marjorie, 49
Swift, Kate, 48, 226
Symons, Donald, 31

Tabari, Azar, 101
Talkington, Tracy F., 240
Tamir, Lois M., 171
Tannahill, Reay, 57, 58, 60, 61
Taussig, Michael, 97
Teyber, Edward C., 45
Thapar, Romila, 224
Theodore, Athena, 188
Thom, M., 259
Thomas, Darwin L., 112
Thomas, William I., 7
Thompson, Edward H., 162, 163

Thorkelson, Anne E., 253, 255, 257
Thornton, Arland, 130
Thurnher, M., 147
Tiedt, I. M., 213
Tiefer, Lenore, 165
Tiger, Lionel, 31, 100, 166, 167
Tinsley, B. R., 139, 140
Tobias, Sheila, 215
Tolson, Andrew, 165
Trebilcot, Joyce, 13
Trecker, Janice, 211, 212
Tsuneyoshi, Sandra Eiko, 212
Tucker, Lewis R., 236
Tudor, Jeannette F., 26
Turley, Myra, 153
Turner, Tina, 241

VandeVen, N., 172
Vanek, Joann, 122, 124
Vatter, Ethel, 154
Veblen, Thorsten, 195
Veevers, J. E., 138
Venkatesan, M., 234
Verbrugge, Lois M., 22
Verdesi, Elizabeth Howell, 228
Verna, Mary Ellen, 236
Vierra, Andrea, 138
Vinovskis, Maris A., 139

Wagner, Louis C., 234, 236
Waldrop, M. F.. 46
Walker, Kathryn, 124
Wallerstein, J., 147
Walley, D., 209, 210
Walshok, M. L., 199
Walster, Elaine, 112, 216
Walters, Richard H., 39
Watson, Roy E. L., 131
Weaver, Charles N., 125
Weber, Max, 10, 251
Weinberg, Martin S., 152, 153
Weingarten, K., 143
Weiss, Robert, 155
Weitz, Shirley, 18, 41
Weitzman, Lenore J., 38, 39, 40, 45, 147, 148, 149, 208, 209, 210, 211, 212, 213, 256
Welter, Barbara, 65, 66
Wender, Dorothea, 57
Wertheimer, Barbara M., 68, 69, 70
West, Candace, 48, 49
Whipple, Thomas W., 234, 236
White, Ellen Harmon, 228
White, Elizabeth H., 101
White, Lynn K., 2, 3
White, Stephen, 84
Whyte, Martin K., 89

Wickenden, Dorothy, 269
Wilbourn, B. L., 137
Wilkinson, Melvin, 240
Williams, J. Allen, 209
Williams, Juanita H., 18, 30, 145
Williams, Wendy, 259
Williamson, N. E., 43
Wilson, Edward O., 30
Wilson, Everett K., 229
Wirtenberg, T., 213
Wise, P. S., 143
Witkowski, Terrence H., 235
Wohletter, Maralinda, 247
Woldow, Norman, 16
Wolf, Deborah G., 152
Wolf, Margaret, 88
Wolfe B., 23
Wolfe, Donald M., 123
Wollstonecraft, M. A., 75, 76
Woods, Margaret, 124
Woolf, Virginia, 203

Yankelovich, Daniel, 129
Yogev, Sara, 138
Yorburg, G., 132

Zeigler, L. Harmon, 260, 264
Zimmerman, Don H., 48, 49
Zuckerman, Diana M., 41

SUBJECT INDEX

Abortion, 258–59
Abuse, 174–75, 257–58
AC/DC, 248
Achievement syndrome, 192
Adele et Theodore
    (de Genlis), 204
Adversity, frontier, 67
Advertising, 234–37, 245,
    247
Affairs, 132–34
Affiliated families, 154
Affirmative Action, 197–98
Afghan refugees, 105
AFL. *See* American
    Federation of Labor
Africa, 220
Age:
    employment and,125, 187,
        193, 194
    gender gap and, 263, 264
    mate selection and, 113–114
    sexuality and, 34
Aggression, 17–18, 164–65
Alcohol, 24, 175
Alimony, 148, 267
Alternatives to Living in
    Violent Environments
    (ALIVE), 174
Amazons, 56
American Federation of
    Labor (AFL), 69
American Indians, 221
American Woman Suffrage
    Association (AWSA),
    78
Anatolia, 220
Andrenogenital syndrome, 16
Androgens, 18
Androgen sensitivity
    syndrome, 16
Androgyny, 13, 54, 110–11,
    141
Anxiety, 25
Apartheid, sexual, 222
Arab cultures, 100–104,
    222

Arapesh, 15
Association of American
    Colleges, 214, 216
Athens, 57
Athletics, 213–14, 160,
    255
Attitudes, 198–200
Attractiveness, 112
Authority, 251
AWSA. *See* American
    Woman Suffrage
    Association

Bad woman, 238
Bars, 8
Battered wives, 174–75,
    257–58
Beer commercials, 247
Bem Sex Role Inventory, 26,
    54
Berkeley Men's Center
    Manifesto, 176–77
BFOQ. *See* Bona Fide
    Occupational
    Qualification
Bible, 224–27
Big Wheel, 162, 163–64
Biology, 14–35
    environment and, 34–35
    health in, 19–28
    hormones in, 16–19
    sexuality in, 32–34
    theories of, 28–32
Birth experience, 18, 169
Blacks, 116, 144–46
Blaming the victim, 258
Bona Fide Occupational
    Qualification (BFOQ),
    197, 252–53
Bonding, 31, 166–67
Books, 208, 209, 210
Boston Women's Health
    Book Collective, 27
Breadwinner, 139, 144
Buddhism, 221
Business, 59, 189

"Cagney and Lacy," 242
Caldecott Medal, 208, 209
Career, 124–25, 137–38, 184
Castration anxiety, 29
CCP. *See* Chinese Communist
    Party
Chaddar, 222
Change, 7, 181, 250
Chattels, 57
Childbirth, 18, 169
Child care, 31, 129, 193, 200, 20?
    dual earners and, 141–43
    fathers and, 139, 151, 156
    Soviet, 86
    World War II, 72–73
Childlessness, 138
Child pornography, 239
Children, 191
    advertising and, 236
    Chinese, 89, 90
    cohabitation and, 131
    divorce and, 147, 148
    dual earners and, 141–44
    homosexual parents and,
        152–53
    Israeli, 99
    television and, 243–44
China, 43, 87–90, 221
Chinese Communist Party
    (CCP), 87
Christianity, 205, 224–27
    medieval, 60–61
    Renaissance, 62–63
Chromosomes, 16
Chuang Tzu, 221
Circumcision, female, 103–4
Civil Rights Act of 1964,
    196, 197, 252–53, 254
Class, 6
Classical history, 56–60
Clergy, 227–29
Clerical workers, 22, 199
Climateric, male, 170–71
Clitoris, 33
Cognitive development
    theory, 40–42